THE
MANUFACTURE
OF MADNESS

THE MANUFACTURE OF MADNESS

*A Comparative Study of the Inquisition
and the Mental Health Movement*

Thomas S. Szasz, M.D.

HARPER TORCHBOOKS
Harper & Row, Publishers
New York, Cambridge, Philadelphia, San Francisco
London, Mexico City, São Paulo, Sydney

First HARPER COLOPHON edition published 1977

ISBN 0–06–131984–8

84 85 86   10 9 8 7 6

The purpose of this essay is . . . an attempt to understand the times in which we live. One might think that a period which, in a space of fifty years, uproots, enslaves, or kills seventy million human beings should be condemned out of hand. But its culpability must still be understood. In more ingenuous times, when the tyrant razed cities for his own greater glory, when the slave chained to the conqueror's chariot was dragged through the rejoicing streets, when enemies were thrown to the wild beasts in front of the assembled people, the mind did not reel before such unabashed crimes, and judgment remained unclouded. But slave camps under the flag of freedom, massacres justified by philanthropy or by the taste for the superhuman, in one sense cripple judgment. On the day when crime dons the apparel of innocence—through a curious transposition peculiar to our times—it is innocence that is called upon to justify itself.

—Albert Camus

To my daughter, Suzy

CONTENTS

x   *Contents*

ACKNOWLEDGMENTS

I am deeply grateful to a number of people for their generous help with this book.

I owe a very special debt to my brother, Dr. George Szasz, who shared with me his extensive knowledge of cultural history, directed me to important sources, supplied materials from European newspapers and periodicals, and critically read various drafts of the entire manuscript.

I wish to thank also Dr. Bruce deMonterice, for reading successive drafts of the manuscript and offering many valuable suggestions; Dr. Shirley Rubert, for calling attention to and supplying important bibliographic sources; Professor George J. Alexander, Associate Dean of the Syracuse University College of Law, for reading Chapter 13 and for clarifying discussions of law and psychiatry; Mr. Norbert Slepyan and Mrs. Ann Harris, my editors at Harper & Row, for excellent suggestions for improving and organizing the manuscript; Mrs. Arthur Ecker, for editorial assistance; the staff of the Library of the Syracuse University College of Law, and especially Miss Judith Smith, and the staff of the Library of the State University of New York, Upstate Medical Center, for untiring efforts to secure many of the references consulted in the preparation of this volume; and the secretarial staff of the Department of Psychiatry at the Upstate Medical Center—Mrs. Frances Rogers, Mrs. Betty Handley, Miss Lois Fay, and especially my secretary, Mrs. Margaret Bassett—for typing various drafts of the manuscript.

Grateful acknowledgment is made to the following publishers for permission to quote throughout this book:

Anti-Semite and Jew by Jean-Paul Sartre, translated by George J. Becker. Copyright © 1948 by Schocken Books, Inc. Reprinted by permission of Schocken Books, Inc.

The Anxiety Makers by Alex Comfort. Copyright © 1967 by Books and Broadcasts Ltd., Used by permission of the publishers, Delacorte Press, New York, and Thomas Nelson & Sons Ltd., London.

The Autobiography of Benjamin Rush, edited by George W. Corner. Copyright, 1948 by the American Philosophical Society. Reprinted by permission of the publisher, Princeton University Press.

Collected Papers of Sigmund Freud, edited by Ernest Jones, from Volume XII of the Standard Edition of *The Complete Psychological Works of Sigmund Freud,* 1959. Reprinted by permission of Basic Books, Inc., Sigmund Freud Copyrights Ltd., The Institute of Psycho-Analysis, and the Hogarth Press Ltd., London.

Corydon by André Gide. Reprinted by permission of the publisher, Farrar, Straus & Giroux, Inc. and Editions Gallinard (© 1924).

The Encyclopedia of Witchcraft and Demonology by Rossell Hope Robbins. © 1959 by Crown Publishers, Inc. Used by permission.

Epilegomena to the Study of Greek Religion and Themis by Jane Ellen Harrison. Reprinted by permission of University Books, Inc., New Hyde Park, N.Y., 1962.

The Golden Bough by James George Frazer. New York, Macmillan, 1942. Reprinted by permission of The Macmillan Company.

Handbook of Community Psychiatry and Community Mental Health by Leopold Bellak. New York, Grune & Stratton, 1964. Reprinted by permission of Grune & Stratton, Inc.

A History of Medical Psychology by Gregory Zilboorg, in collaboration with George W. Henry, M.D. Copyright, 1941 by W. W. Norton & Company, Inc. Reprinted by permission of the publisher.

A History of the Inquisition of Spain by H. C. Lea. New York, Macmillan, 1906–1907. Reprinted by permission of the University of Pennsylvania Press.

The Individual and Society in the Middle Ages by Walter Ullman. Baltimore, The Johns Hopkins Press, 1966. By permission of the publisher.

The Inquisition of the Middle Ages by H. C. Lea. New York, Citadel, 1961. Reprinted by permission of Citadel Press, Inc.

"The Kreutzer Sonata," from *The Death of Ivan Ilych and Other Stories* by Leo Tolstoy, translated by Aylmer Maude. Reprinted by permission of the publisher, Oxford University Press, London.

The Lost World of Thomas Jefferson by Daniel J. Boorstin. Copyright © 1948 by Daniel J. Boorstin. Reprinted by permission of Beacon Press.

Malleus Maleficarum by James Sprenger and Heinrich Krämer. Reprinted by permission of Marianne Rodker and the Hogarth Press Ltd., London.

"Masturbatory Insanity" by E. H. Hare. From *The Journal of Mental Science,* London, 108:1–25. Reprinted by permission of the *British Journal of Psychiatry,* London.

The Medical Man and the Witch During the Renaissance by Gregory

Zilboorg. Baltimore, The Johns Hopkins Press, 1935. Reprinted by permission of the publisher.

The Mentally Ill in America by Albert Deutsch. New York, Columbia University Press, 1952. Reprinted by permission of Columbia University Press.

Nineteen Eighty-Four by George Orwell. Copyright, 1949 by Harcourt, Brace & World, Inc. Reprinted by permission of Brandt & Brandt and A. M. Heath, London.

"No Neurotics in China" by Goffredo Parise, reprinted by permission of *Atlas Magazine* and Corriere Della Sera, Milan.

One Hundred Years of Psychiatry by Emil Kraepelin. Philosophical Library, 1962, New York. Reprinted by permission of Philosophical Library, Inc.

The Painted Bird by Jerzy Kosinski. Reprinted by permission of the Houghton Mifflin Company, Boston.

Perceval's Narrative by Gregory Bateson. Stanford University Press, 1961. Reprinted by permission of the publisher.

"Psychopathic Personality and Sexual Deviation" by Thomas R. Byrne, Jr., and Francis M. Mulligan. From *40 Temple Law Quarterly*. Copyright © 1967 by Temple University. Used with permission of the publisher.

"Rejection: A Possible Consequence of Seeking Help for Mental Disorders" by Derek L. Phillips. From *The American Sociological Review*, 28: 963–972, Dec., 1963. Reprinted by permission of The American Sociological Association.

Revolutionary Doctor: Benjamin Rush, 1746–1813 by Carl Binger, M.D. Copyright © 1966 by W. W. Norton & Company, Inc. Reprinted by permission of the publisher, W. W. Norton & Company, Inc.

Saint Genêt by Jean-Paul Sartre, translated by Bernard Frechtman. Reprinted by permission of George Braziller, Inc. and W. H. Allen & Co. Ltd.

Satanism and Witchcraft by Jules Michelet. New York, Citadel, 1965. Reprinted by permission of Citadel Press, Inc.

Three Hundred Years of Psychiatry by Richard Hunter and Ida Macalpine, published by the Oxford University Press. Used by permission.

The Waning of the Middle Ages by Johan Huizinga. Copyright, 1949 by St. Martin's Press. Garden City, N.Y.: Doubleday-Anchor, 1954. Reprinted by permission of the author, St. Martin's Press, and Edward Arnold (Publishers) Ltd., London.

Witchcraft in England by Christina Hole. Reprinted by permission of B. T. Batsford Ltd., London, and The Macmillan Company, New York.

PREFACE

. . . the writer's function is not without arduous duties. By definition, he cannot serve today those who make history; he must serve those who are subject to it.

Albert Camus[1]*

It is widely believed today that just as some people suffer from diseases of the liver or kidney, others suffer from diseases of the mind or personality; that persons afflicted with such "mental illnesses" are psychologically and socially inferior to those not so afflicted; and that "mental patients," because of their supposed incapacity to "know what is in their own best interests," must be cared for by their families or the state, even if that care requires interventions imposed on them against their will or incarceration in a mental hospital.

I consider this entire system of interlocking concepts, beliefs, and practices false and immoral. In an earlier work, *The Myth of Mental Illness*,[2] I tried to show how and why the concept of mental illness is erroneous and misleading. In the present work, I shall try to show how and why the ethical convictions and social arrangements based on this concept constitute an immoral ideology of intolerance. In particular, I shall compare the belief in witchcraft and the persecution of witches with the belief in mental illness and the persecution of mental patients.

The ideology of mental health and illness serves an obvious and pressing moral need. Since the physician's classic mandate is to

* Reference notes begin on page 323.

treat suffering patients with their consent and for their own benefit, it is necessary to explain and justify situations where individuals are "treated" without their consent and to their detriment. The concept of insanity or mental illness supplies this need. It enables the "sane" members of society to deal as they see fit with those of their fellows whom they can categorize as "insane." But having divested the madman of his right to judge what is in his own best interests, the people—and especially psychiatrists and judges, their medical and legal experts on madness—have divested themselves of the corrective restraints of dialogue. In vain does the alleged madman insist that he is not sick; his inability to "recognize" that he is, is regarded as a hallmark of his illness. In vain does he reject treatment and hospitalization as forms of torture and imprisonment; his refusal to submit to psychiatric authority is regarded as a further sign of his illness. In this medical rejection of the Other as a madman, we recognize, in up-to-date semantic and technical garb, but underneath it remarkably unchanged, his former religious rejection as a heretic.

Well-entrenched ideologies—such as messianic Christianity had been, and messianic Psychiatry now is—are, of course, not easily refuted. Once the basic premises of an ideology are accepted, new observations are perceived in its imagery and articulated in its vocabulary. The result is that while no fresh observation can undermine the belief system, new "facts" generated by the ideology constantly lend further support to it. This was true in the past for the belief in witchcraft and the corresponding prevalence of witches, and it is true today for the belief in mental disease and the corresponding prevalence of mental patients.

Unfortunately, it is easier to perceive the errors of our forebears than those of our contemporaries. We all know that there are no witches; however, only a few hundred years ago, the greatest and noblest minds were deeply convinced that there were. Is it possible, then, that our belief in mental illness is similarly ill conceived? And that our practices based on this concept are similarly destructive of personal dignity and political liberty?

These are not idle or unimportant questions. On our answers to them depends not only the fate of millions of Americans labeled mentally ill, but, indirectly, the fate of all of us. For, as we have been warned time and again, an injustice done to one—especially in a society that aspires to be free—is an injustice done to all. In my opinion, the "mental health"—in the sense of spiritual well-being—of Americans cannot be improved by slogans, drugs, community mental health centers, or even with billions of dollars expended on a "war on mental illness." The principal problem in psychiatry has always been, and still is, violence: the threatened and feared violence of the "madman," and the actual counter-violence of society and the psychiatrist against him. The result is the dehumanization, oppression, and persecution of the citizen branded "mentally ill." If this is so, we had better heed John Stuart Mill's warning that ". . . it is contrary to reason and ex-perience to suppose that there can be any real check to brutality, consistent with leaving the victim still in the power of the execu-tioner."[3] The best, indeed the only, hope for remedying the prob-lem of "mental illness" lies in weakening—not in strengthening—the power of Institutional Psychiatry.* Only when this peculiar institution is abolished will the moral powers of uncoerced psycho-therapy be released. Only then will the potentialities of Contractual Psychiatry† be able to unfold—as a creative human dialogue un-fettered by institutional loyalties and social taboos, pledged to serving the individual in his perpetual struggle to rise, not only above the constraints of instinct, but also above those of myth.[4]

In sum, this is a book on the history of Institutional Psychiatry—from its theoretical origins in Christian theology to its current practices couched in medical rhetoric and enforced by police power. The importance for man of understanding his history has perhaps never been greater than today. This is because history, as Collingwood reminds us, "is 'for' human self-knowledge. . . . Know-ing yourself means knowing what you can do; and since nobody knows what he can do until he tries, the only clue to what man

---

* By Institutional Psychiatry I refer generally to psychiatric interventions im-posed on persons by others. Such interventions are characterized by the complete loss of control by the client or "patient" over his participation in his relationship with the expert. The paradigm service of Institutional Psychiatry is involuntary mental hospitalization. For further discussion, see pp. xxii–xxvii.

† By Contractual Psychiatry I refer generally to psychiatric interventions as-sumed by persons prompted by their own personal difficulties or suffering. Such interventions are characterized by the retention of complete control by the client or "patient" over his participation in his relationship with the expert. The paradigm service of Contractual Psychiatry is autonomous psychotherapy. For further discussion, see pp. xxii–xxiii.

can do is what man has done. The value of history, then, is that it teaches us what man has done and thus what man is."[5] By showing what man has done, and continues to do, to his fellow man *in the name of help,* I hope to add to our understanding of what man is, where coercion, however well-justified by self-flattering rhetoric, leads him, and what might yet become of him were he to replace control of the Other with self-control.

This book presupposes no special competence or training in the reader—only open-mindedness. But it requires of him one more thing—that he seriously consider, with Samuel Johnson, that "hell is paved with good intentions," and that he conscientiously apply this caveat to the ideology, rhetoric, and rituals of the political organization characteristic of our age—the Therapeutic State.

Syracuse, New York   Thomas S. Szasz
December 1969

INTRODUCTION

> . . . was there ever any domination which did not
> appear natural to those who possessed it?
>
> —*John Stuart Mill*[1]

The concept of mental illness is analogous to that of witchcraft.
In the fifteenth century, men believed that some persons were
witches, and that some acts were due to witchcraft. In the twentieth
century, men believe that some people are insane, and that some
acts are due to mental illness. Nearly a decade ago, I tried to show
that the concept of mental illness has the same logical and empirical
status as the concept of witchcraft; in short, that witchcraft and
mental illness are imprecise and all-encompassing concepts, freely
adaptable to whatever uses the priest or physician (or lay "diagnostician") wishes to put them.[2] Now I propose to show that the
concept of mental illness serves the same social function in the
modern world as did the concept of witchcraft in the late Middle
Ages; in short, that the belief in mental illness and the social actions
to which it leads have the same moral implications and political
consequences as had the belief in witchcraft and the social actions
to which it led.

Henry Sigerist, dean of American medical historians, has written
that "In the changing attitude towards witchcraft, modern psychiatry was born as a medical discipline."[3] This view has been
interpreted to mean that people thought to be witches were actually mentally sick, and that instead of being persecuted for
heresy they should have been treated for insanity.

Although I agree with Sigerist and other medical historians that psychiatry developed as the persecution of witches declined and disappeared, my explanation differs radically from theirs. They say it happened because of the gradual realization that persons supposed to be heretics were actually mentally sick. I say it happened because of the transformation of a religious ideology into a scientific one: medicine replaced theology; the alienist, the inquisitor; and the insane, the witch. The result was the substitution of a medical mass-movement for a religious one, the persecution of mental patients replacing the persecution of heretics.

Men who believed in witchcraft created witches by ascribing this role to others, and sometimes even to themselves. In this way they literally manufactured witches whose existence as social objects then proved the reality of witchcraft. To claim that witchcraft and witches did not exist does not mean, of course, that the personal conduct exhibited by alleged witches or the social disturbances attributed to them did not exist. In the days of the witch-hunts, there were, indeed, people who disturbed or upset others—for example, men whose religious beliefs and practices differed from those of the majority, or women who, as midwives, assisted at the delivery of stillborn infants. Such men and women were often accused of witchcraft and persecuted as witches. The point is that *these* witches did not choose the role of witch; they were defined and treated as witches against their will; in short, the role was *ascribed* to them. As far as the accused witches were concerned—they would have elected, had they been given a choice, to be left alone by the holders of Church and State power.

To be sure, once the social role of witch had been established by the irresistible combination of authoritative opinion, widespread propaganda, and popular credulity, it happened occasionally that people claimed to be witches. They declared that they experienced the ideas and feelings characteristic of witches; and they openly proclaimed their deviant status to gain their particular ends (which might have been to impart meaning to their lives or to commit a kind of indirect suicide). *These* witches chose the role they were playing; they were defined and treated as witches voluntarily; in short, they *assumed* the role of witch.

In the past, men created witches; now they create mental patients. But, again, it is important to keep in mind that to claim that mental diseases and insane patients do not exist does not mean that the personal conduct exhibited by persons classified as mentally sick, or certain kinds of social disturbances attributed to them, do not exist. In our day, there are, indeed, individuals who break the law, or flout the conventions of morality and society—for example, men who use heroin, or women who neglect their newborn infants. Such men and women are often accused of mental illness (by being classified as "addicts" or "post-partum psychotics"), and persecuted as mental patients (by means of involuntary hospitalization and treatment).* The point is that *these* mental patients do not choose the role of mental patient; they are defined and treated as mental patients against their will; in short, the role is *ascribed* to them. As far as the accused mental patients are concerned— they would elect, were they given a choice, to be left alone by the holders of Medical and State power.

In other words, if our aim is to see things clearly, rather than to confirm popular beliefs and justify accepted practices, then we must sharply distinguish three related but distinct classes of phenomena: first, *events* and *behaviors,* such as the birth of a stillborn baby, or a mother's rejection of her healthy infant; second, their *explanations* by means of religious or medical concepts, such as witchcraft or mental illness; third, their *social control,* justified by the religious or medical explanations, utilizing theological or therapeutic interventions, such as burning witches at the stake or hospitalizing the insane against their will.

One may accept the reality of an event or a behavior, but reject its generally accepted explanation and methods of social control. Indeed, the most passionate disputes in both religion and science have centered not on whether or not particular events were real, but on whether or not their explanations were true and the actions used to suppress them good. The true believers in witchcraft thus maintained that human problems were caused by witches and that burning them at the stake was good; whereas those opposed to

---

* The mental patient, especially if so defined against his will, is perhaps best viewed as a "deviant," either of society as a whole, or of a smaller group, typically the family. The individual who differs from his peers, who disturbs or scandalizes his family or society, is often branded as insane; sometimes he need not even play a deviant role but is declared mad nevertheless. Such psychiatric derogation fulfills important needs for the "mentally healthy" members of the group.

this theory regarded the explanation as false and the measures justified by it as evil. The true believers in mental illness similarly maintain that human problems are caused by madmen and that incarcerating them in mental hospitals is good; whereas those opposed to this theory regard the explanation as false and the measures justified by it as evil.*

The social role of mental patient having been established by the still irresistible combination of authoritative opinion, widespread propaganda, and popular credulity, it happens occasionally that people claim to be mentally ill. They say that they experience the ideas and feelings characteristic of mentally ill persons; and they openly proclaim their deviant status to gain their particular ends (which might be to escape military service or some other obligation or to injure themselves and their families). Of course, individuals may also define themselves as mentally ill in order to secure the psychiatric assistance they need and want. As a rule, such persons know that they are not physically ill and that their illness is metaphoric. They assume the role of mental patient as the price they must pay to obtain the services of an expert whose clients are socially defined in this way. The concept of mental illness is, however, neither necessary nor useful for the practice of contractual psychotherapy.[4] Indeed, "psychotherapy patients" are often "treated" by nonmedical therapists, such as psychologists and social workers. *Most of what is written in this book does not pertain to these patients, their therapists, or to the relationship between them.*

Although individuals occasionally assumed the role of witch voluntarily, in historical studies of the witch-hunts it is rightly taken for granted that the witch was cast into her role involuntarily, and that the institution responsible for her situation was the Inquisition. I shall proceed similarly in the present study. Although individuals occasionally assume the role of mental patient voluntarily, I shall presume that the mental patient is cast into

* Since people abhor unexplained events and unsolved problems, they tend to embrace blindly—rather than examine critically and, if necessary, reject—global explanations, such as those of witchcraft and mental illness. No doubt this is why the belief in witchcraft and the remedial practices of the Theological State were not simply abandoned, but were replaced by the belief in madness and the remedial practices of the Therapeutic State. The mythology of mental illness and the repressive measures it justifies will perhaps also not be abandoned until they can be replaced by another belief system and a social institution based on it. Let us hope that the change, when it comes, will be an improvement.

his role involuntarily, and that the organization responsible for his situation is Institutional Psychiatry. To clearly distinguish between the voluntary and involuntary patient, I usually refer to the victim of the psychiatric relationship as the "involuntary patient," to his oppressor as the "institutional psychiatrist," and to the system authorizing and embodying their interaction as "Institutional Psychiatry."

The most important economic characteristic of Institutional Psychiatry is that the institutional psychiatrist is a bureaucratic employee, paid for his services by a private or public organization (not by the individual who is his ostensible client); its most important social characteristic is the use of force and fraud. In addition to the commitment procedure and the long-term incarceration of the "insane," the interventions of the institutional psychiatrist include such diverse measures as the examination of defendants to determine their sanity or fitness to stand trial, of employees to determine their fitness for a job, of applicants to college, medical school, or psychoanalytic institute to determine their suitability for admission to these institutions, of the histories of deceased persons to determine their "testamentary capacity," and so forth.[5] Psychiatrists employed by state mental hospitals, college health services, military organizations, courts, prisons, and others in similar positions are, according to this definition, institutional psychiatrists.

The most important economic characteristic of Contractual Psychiatry is that the contractual psychiatrist is a private entrepreneur, paid for his services by his client; its most important social characteristic is the avoidance of force and fraud (and the existence of legal penalties for their use). The relationship between contractual psychiatrist and patient is based on contract, freely entered into by both, and, in general, freely terminable by both (except where the therapist relinquishes some of his options in this regard). The contract consists of an exchange of psychiatric services for money.[6] In short, whereas the institutional psychiatrist imposes himself on his "patients," who do not pay him, do not want to be his patients, and are not free to reject his "help"—the contractual psychiatrist offers himself to his patients, who must pay him, must want to be his patients, and are free to reject his help.

Like the typical European witch in the fifteenth century, the typical American mental patient today is usually a poor person in trouble or accused of making trouble, who is declared mentally ill against his will. Such a person may accept the role or may try to repudiate it; the institutional psychiatrist confronted with him may try to keep him confined in his role, and perhaps in a hospital, for a long time, or may release him after a relatively brief period of incarceration. In any case, the psychiatric authorities are in full control of the relationship.

For an illustration of the way being poor and unwanted predisposes a person to being cast into the role of mental patient, the following example, culled at random from the newspapers, should suffice. "Attorneys representing welfare clients testified . . . before the State Board of Social Welfare that 'on six or seven occasions within the past two years, relief recipients who threatened trouble for [New York] city Department of Welfare caseworkers were sent to Bellevue psychiatric ward.'"[7]

For an illustration of the way being accused of troublemaking predisposes a person to being cast into the role of mental patient, consider these examples. In 1964, a total of 1,437 individuals "under complaint or indictment before the criminal courts of Massachusetts were committed . . . for pretrial observation of their mental status."[8] In plain English, 1,437 persons were treated—for a shorter or longer time—as if they were mentally sick, simply because they had been charged with an offense. This is about double the number so committed eight years earlier. Moreover, of the 1,437 persons committed for temporary observation (usually for two months), 224, or about one sixth, were recommitted for an indefinite period of incarceration. In 1964, in the Manhattan Criminal Court alone, 1,388 defendants were committed for pretrial psychiatric examinations; of these, one fourth were recommitted for an indefinite period of incarceration.[9]

I cite these reports *not* as examples of the unfortunate abuses of the mental hospital system in need of correction by an enlightened citizenry, but rather as characteristic examples of a pervasive psychiatric pattern of harassment, intimidation, and degradation, authenticating the right of certain social authorities to cast individuals, especially from the lower socioeconomic classes, into the role of mental patient. To maintain that a social institution suffers from certain "abuses" is to imply that it has certain other desirable or good uses. This, in my opinion, has been the fatal weakness of the countless exposés—old and recent, literary and professional—of private and public mental hospitals.[10] My thesis is quite different: Simply put, it is that there are, and can be, no abuses *of* Institutional Psychiatry, because Institutional Psychiatry *is*, itself, an abuse; similarly, there were, and could be, no abuses *of* the Inquisition, because the Inquisition *was*, itself, an abuse. Indeed, just as the Inquisition was the characteristic abuse of Christianity, so Institutional Psychiatry is the characteristic abuse of Medicine.

In other words, it is reasonable and useful to speak of the uses and abuses of such complex human enterprises as Religion and Medicine (or Science and Law). But it is unreasonable and misleading to speak of the uses and abuses of institutions (whether they be religious, medical, political, or still other) which, because of their characteristic and indispensable methods, we deem incompatible with our standards of human decency and morality. Clearly, what is compatible or incompatible with one's standard of human decency or morality varies from time to time and from person to person. While it flourished, the Inquisition did not offend the sensibilities of most people—though individually men did all they could to stay out of its clutches. In the same way, Institutional Psychiatry does not now offend the sensibilities of most people—though individually men do all they can to stay out of its clutches.

Resting squarely on the moral judgment that Institutional Psychiatry *is* an abuse of both the human personality and the healing relationship, I want it to be clearly understood that in describing its operations, I shall be illustrating its uses, not its abuses. I shall thus try to show that if Institutional Psychiatry is harmful to the so-called mental patient, this is not because it is liable to abuse, but rather because harming persons categorized as insane is its essential function: Institutional Psychiatry is, as it were, designed to protect and uplift the group (the family, the State), by persecuting and degrading the individual (as insane or ill).[11]

Although I have used the sociological approach to deviance in this study, I have, whenever possible, avoided calling witches and mental patients "deviants." Words have lives of their own. However much sociologists insist that the term "deviant" does not diminish the worth of the person or group so categorized, the implication of inferiority adheres to the word. Indeed, sociologists are not wholly exempt from blame: They describe addicts and homosexuals as deviants, but never Olympic champions or Nobel Prize winners. In fact, the term is rarely applied to people with admired characteristics, such as great wealth, superior skills, or fame —whereas it is often applied to those with despised characteristics, such as poverty, lack of marketable skills, or infamy.

For this reason, I repudiate the tacit assumption inherent in designating mental patients as deviants: that, because such persons differ, or are alleged to differ, from the majority, they are *ipso facto* sick, bad, stupid, or wrong, whereas the majority are healthy, good, wise, or right. The term "social deviants" for individuals incriminated as mentally ill is unsatisfactory for another reason: it does not make sufficiently explicit—as the terms "scapegoat" or "victim" do—that majorities usually categorize persons or groups as "deviant" in order to set them apart as inferior beings and to justify their social control, oppression, persecution, or even complete destruction.

Roles, it is well to remember, are social artifacts. Role-deviance, therefore, has meaning only in the context of specific social customs and laws. The criminal is deviant because he breaks the law; the homosexual because most people are heterosexuals; the atheist because most people believe, or say they believe, in God. Although departure from a statistical norm of behavior is an important criterion of social deviance, it is not the only criterion. A person may be considered deviant not only because his conduct differs from a socially observed norm, but also because it differs from a morally professed ideal. Thus, although a happy marriage is probably more the exception than the rule, the unmarried or unhappily married person is often considered psychologically abnormal and socially deviant. In earlier days, when masturbation was no doubt just as prevalent as it is at present, psychiatrists considered the practice both a symptom and a cause of insanity.

Social deviance is thus a term naming a vast category. Which kinds of social deviance are regarded as mental illnesses? The answer is, those that entail personal conduct not conforming to psychiatrically defined and enforced rules of mental health. If narcotics-avoidance is a rule of mental health, narcotics ingestion will be a sign of mental illness; if even-temperedness is a rule of mental health, depression and elation will be signs of mental illness; and so forth.

However obvious this may be, its implications for our understanding of mental illness and Institutional Psychiatry are vastly unappreciated. The fact is that every time psychiatrists formulate a new rule of mental health, they create a new class of mentally sick individuals—just as every time legislators enact a new restrictive law, they create a fresh category of criminals. For example, the proposition that prejudice against Jews is a manifestation of psychopathology,[12] existing side by side with the view that American servicemen who marry Vietnamese women[13] or whites who marry blacks[14] are mentally ill—a few of the countless instances in the contemporary inflation of the concept of mental illness—is simply a strategy for expanding the category of people who may be legitimately classified as mentally sick. Since the consequences of being labeled mentally ill include such penalties as personal degradation, loss of employment, loss of the right to drive a car, to vote, to make valid contracts, or to stand trial—and, last but not least, incarceration in a mental hospital, possibly for life—the expansion of the category of people who can be so designated is essential for increasing the scope and power of the Mental Health Movement and its psychiatric methods of social control. How these social controls—their underlying concepts, rhetorical forms, and precise legal applications—resemble those of the Inquisition, will be demonstrated in Part I. In Part II, we shall follow the development of modern methods for the manufacture of madness and will show that Institutional Psychiatry fulfills a basic human need—to validate the Self as good (normal), by invalidating the Other as evil (mentally ill).

PART I

THE INQUISITION AND INSTITUTIONAL PSYCHIATRY

In desperate situations man will always have recourse to desperate means . . . If reason has failed us, there remains always the *ultima ratio,* the power of the miraculous and mysterious.

–Ernst Cassirer[1]

[The Grand Inquisitor:] . . . we care for the weak too. They are sinful and rebellious, but in the end they too will become obedient. They will marvel at us and look on us as gods, because we are ready to endure the freedom which they have found so dreadful and to rule over them—so awful it will seem to them to be free. But we shall tell them that we are Thy servants and rule them in Thy name. We shall deceive them again . . . That deception will be our suffering, for we shall be forced to lie.

–Fyodor Dostoyevsky[2]

1

SOCIETY'S INTERNAL ENEMIES
AND PROTECTORS

> I cannot accept your canon that we are to judge
> Pope and King unlike other men, with a favourable
> presumption that they did no wrong. If there is any
> presumption it is the other way against holders of
> power, increasing as the power increases. Historic
> responsibility has to make up for the want of legal
> responsibility.
>
> –Lord Acton[1]

In the past, most people believed in sorcery, sympathetic magic, and witchcraft. Men have a powerful need to perceive the causes of natural disasters, epidemics, personal misfortunes, and death. Magic and witchcraft supply a primitive theory for explaining such occurrences, and appropriate methods for coping with them.

The behavior of persons whose conduct differs from that of their fellows—either by falling below the standards of the group or by surpassing them—constitutes a similar mystery and threat; the notions of demonic possession and madness supply a primitive theory for explaining such occurrences and appropriate methods for coping with them.

These universal beliefs and the practices connected with them are the materials out of which men build social movements and institutions. The beliefs that led to the witch-hunts existed long before the thirteenth century, but it was not until then that European society used them as a foundation for an organized movement. This movement—whose ostensible aim was to protect society from harm—became the Inquisition. The danger was the witch; the protector, the inquisitor. Similarly, although the concept of madness existed long before the seventeenth century, only then did European society begin to organize a movement based on it. This movement—whose ostensible aim was likewise to protect society from harm—was Institutional Psychiatry. The danger was the madman; the protector, the alienist. The persecution of witches lasted for more than four centuries. The persecution of mental patients has lasted for more than three centuries and its popularity is still increasing.

Immediately, two questions arise: If the concept of witchcraft was old and familiar, why, in the thirteenth century, did a persecutory mass-movement crystallize around it? Similarly, if the concept of madness was old and familiar, why, in the seventeenth century, did a persecutory mass-movement crystallize around it?

As a result of a number of historical developments—among them, contacts with alien cultures during the Crusades, the evolution of the "feudal contract," and the growth of mercantilism and a middle class—people bestirred themselves from their centuries-old stupor and began to seek fresh answers to life's problems. They challenged clerical authority and relied increasingly on observation and experimentation. Modern science was thus born, setting the stage for the protracted conflict between it and theology that was to follow.

Medieval European society was dominated by the Church. In a religious society, deviance is conceptualized in theological terms: the deviant is the witch, the agent of Satan. Thus the sorceress who healed, the heretic who thought for himself, the fornicator who lusted too much, and the Jew who, in the midst of a Christian society, stubbornly rejected the divinity of Jesus—however much they differed from one another—all were categorized as "heretics"; and thus was each, as an enemy of God, persecuted by the Inquisition. The medieval historian Walter Ullman puts it this way: "Publicly to hold opinions which ran counter to or attacked the faith determined and fixed by law was heresy, and the real reason for making heresy a crime was—as Gratian's *Decretum* had explained it—that the heretic showed intellectual arrogance by preferring his own opinions to those who were specially qualified to pronounce upon matters of faith. Consequently, heresy was high treason, committed against the divine majesty, committed through aberration from the faith as laid down by the papacy."[2]

From the medieval point of view, however, as Ullman reminds us, "this suppression of the individual's opinion was not by any means seen as a violation of his rights or of his dignity as a Christian, because a Christian attacking established faith forfeited his dignity. . . . Killing this individual did not violate his dignity, just as killing an animal did not affect anyone's dignity."[3]

In those days, the bond that held men together was not the secular law to which, as citizens, they had given their *consent;* instead, it was the divine law which, as Christians, they unquestioningly obeyed because they had *faith* in God and his vicars on earth. For a millennium, until the latter part of the Middle Ages, the ideal of social relations was not reciprocity but benevolent domination and dutiful submission. The subject's obligations were one-sided: he had no means of enforcing the ostensible duties which his superiors owed him. In the manner of classical Roman writers, the ruler was regarded as "the common father of all." Medieval tracts never tire of emphasizing the royal duty of the king to care for the "feebler members" of society. But this recognition, as Ullman remarks, "was a very long way from ascribing to the subjects . . . any indigenous, autonomous rights with which they could confront the king. If he did not fulfill this duty of his, no power existed on earth to make him do it. The frequency of these hortatory statements stood in inverse proportion to the practical as well as theoretical feasibility of translating them into reality."[4]

For millennia, the hierarchical model of social relations, regarded as the divine blueprint for life on earth as well as in heaven and hell, appeared to men as the only conceivable ordering of human affairs. For obvious psychological reasons, this model has perennial appeal to men. This ideal of a nonreciprocal social relationship began to be undermined, in the twelfth century, by the development of the feudal contract which established a reciprocity of obligations between lord and vassal. *Diffidatio,* or the repudiation of the feudal contract by the vassal if the lord did not fulfill his duties or went beyond the contractual bond, was not based on any sophisticated theories or doctrines, but grew out of feudal practice.[5] Ullman emphasizes that "feudal principles were not imposed upon society 'from above,' but developed gradually by slowly taking into account the actual social exigencies. . . . Historical scholarship has come to recognize that in the West, the turn of the twelfth and thirteenth centuries formed the period in which the seeds for the future constitutional development as well as for the standing of the individual in society were sown. . . . It is easy today to sit back and complacently take for granted the constitutionally fixed position of the individual as a citizen, but one forgets too easily that it was not always so and there was a time spanning the greater part of the Middle Ages, something approaching a millennium, when there was no such thing as a citizen. . . ."[6]

Social transformations of such magnitude do not occur, however, without terrible human sufferings. The rulers, afraid of losing power, redouble their domination; the ruled, afraid of losing protection, redouble their submission. In such an atmosphere of change and uncertainty, rulers and ruled unite in a desperate effort to solve their problems; they find a scapegoat, hold him responsible for all of society's ills, and proceed to cure society by killing the scapegoat.

In 1215, the year King John granted the Magna Carta, Pope Innocent III convened the Fourth Lateran Council. "The assembly was an impressive tribute to his universal power; more than fifteen hundred dignitaries came to Rome from all over the world, to consider the problem of disciplining heretics and Jews. . . ."[7] The Council denounced the Albigensian heresy and proclaimed a holy war against it; and it decreed that Jews must wear a yellow badge on their clothing to identify them as Jews.[8]

Beginning in the thirteenth century, all manner of misfortunes— from failing crops to epidemics—were blamed on witches and Jews; their massacre became accepted social practice.[9] "Though the centuries between 1200 and 1600 were four agonizing centuries for the Jews," writes Dimont, "they were equally agonizing centuries for the Christians. Because the charges against the Jews bore such labels as 'ritual murder' and 'Host desecration,' instead of 'witchcraft' and 'heresy,' this should in no way mislead us. The same psychology, the same thinking, the same type of trial, the same type of evidence, the same type of torture went into both. Even as Jews accused of ritual murder were hauled to the stake, Christians accused of witchcraft were burned in adjacent market places."[10]

For more than two centuries, the main brunt of the persecution was borne by the Jews. They were expelled from England and

France, converted or killed in vast numbers in the rest of Europe. In one six-month period alone, at the end of the thirteenth century, a hundred thousand Jews were massacred in Franconia, Bavaria, and Austria.[11] The persecution of witches, during this period, was haphazard and sporadic. Their turn came at the end of the fifteenth century.

As the Crusades for the reconquest of the Holy Land were launched by papal bulls, so was this crusade for the reconquest of the spiritual purity of Christian Europe. The decrees of the Fourth Lateran Council were reshaped and redirected by a bull issued by Pope Innocent VIII on December 9, 1484. It read, in part, as follows:

Desiring with the most heartfelt anxiety, even as Our Apostleship requires, that the Catholic Faith should especially in this Our day increase and flourish everywhere, and that all heretical depravity should be driven far from the frontiers and bournes of the Faithful, We very gladly proclaim and even restate those particular means and methods whereby Our pious desire may obtain its wished effect . . .

It has indeed lately come to Our ears, not without afflicting Us with bitter sorrow, that . . . many persons of both sexes, unmindful of their own salvation and straying from the Catholic Faith, have abandoned themselves to devils, incubi, and succubi. . . .

Wherefore We . . . decree and enjoin that the aforesaid Inquisitors be empowered to proceed to the just correction, imprisonment, and punishment of any persons, without let or hindrance, in every way as if the provinces, townships, dioceses, districts, territories, yes, even the persons and their crimes in this kind were named and particularly designated in Our letters . . .[12]

Two years later, in 1486, this papal bull was implemented by the publication of that famous manual for witch-hunters, the *Malleus Maleficarum (The Hammer of Witches)*.[13] There soon followed an epidemic of witchcraft: the incidence of witches increased, as the authorities charged with their suppression covertly demanded that it should; and a corresponding increase of interest in methods aimed at combating witchcraft developed. For centuries the Church struggled to maintain its dominant role in society. For centuries the witch played her appointed role as society's scapegoat.

From the beginning of its labors, the Inquisition recognized the problem of correctly identifying witches. The inquisitors and secular authorities were accordingly provided with criteria of witchcraft, and with specific guidelines for their work. The vast medieval literature on witchcraft is concerned primarily with one or both of these subjects. Among these works, the *Malleus Maleficarum* is recognized as the most important.

Sprenger and Krämer, the Dominican inquisitors who wrote the *Malleus,* begin by asserting that ". . . the belief that there are such beings as witches is so essential a part of the Catholic faith that obstinately to maintain the opposite opinion manifestly savours of heresy."[14] In other words, Satan and his witches are as much a part of the Christian religion as God and his saints; a true believer can no more entertain doubt about the former than about the latter. To question the existence of witches is thus itself a sign of being a heretic (witch).

More precise criteria of witchcraft were soon forthcoming. We are told, for example, that ". . . those who try to induce others to perform . . . evil wonders are called witches. And because infidelity in a person who has been baptized is technically called heresy, therefore such persons are plainly heretics."[15]

The authors of the *Malleus* further narrow the range of suspects when they observe that it is women who are "chiefly addicted to Evil Superstitions." Among women, they assert, "midwives . . . surpass all others in wickedness."[16] The reason why witches are usually women is that "All witchcraft comes from carnal lust, which is in women insatiable."[17] And the reason why men are protected from this heinous crime is that Jesus was a man: ". . . blessed be the Highest who has so far preserved the male sex from so great a crime: for since He was willing to be born and suffer for us, therefore He has granted to men this privilege."[18] In short, the *Malleus* is, among other things, a kind of religious-scientific theory of male superiority, justifying—indeed, demanding—the persecution of women as members of an inferior, sinful, and dangerous class of individuals.

Having thus defined witchcraft, the authors of the *Malleus* offer specific criteria for identifying witches. Several of these pertain to the characteristics of diseases. They hold, for example, that the sudden, dramatic onset of illness, or what looks like illness, is a typical sign that the disease is caused by witchcraft: ". . . evil may come so suddenly upon a man that it can only be ascribed to witchcraft";[19] and they cite case histories to substantiate this contention. Here is one:

A certain well-born citizen of Spires had a wife who was of such an obstinate disposition that, though he tried to please her in every way, yet she refused in nearly every way to comply with his wishes, and was always plaguing him with abusive taunts. It happened that, on going into his house one day, and his wife railing against him as usual with opprobrious words, he wished to go out of the house to escape from quarreling. But she quickly ran before him and locked the door by which he wished to go out; and loudly swore that, unless he beat her, there was no honesty or faithfulness in him. At these heavy words he stretched out his hand, not intending to hurt her, and struck her lightly with his open palm on the buttock; whereupon he suddenly fell to the ground and lost all his sense, and lay in bed for many weeks afflicted with a most grievous illness. Now it is obvious that this was not a natural illness, but was caused by some witchcraft of the woman. And very many similar cases have happened, and been made known to many.[20]

Next Sprenger and Krämer recommend physicians as expert diagnosticians—and as expert witnesses in witch trials—upon whose professional judgment inquisitors and laymen are asked to rely in distinguishing diseases due to natural causes from those due to witchcraft.

And if it is asked how it is possible to distinguish whether an illness is caused by witchcraft or by some natural physical defect, we answer that the first is by means of the judgment of doctors. . . . For example, doctors may perceive from the circumstances, such as the patient's age, healthy complexion, and the reaction of his eyes, that his disease does not result from any defect of the blood or the stomach, or any other infirmity; and they therefore judge that it is not due to any natural defect, but to some extrinsic cause. And since that extrinsic cause cannot be any poisonous infection, which would be accompanied by ill humours in the blood and stomach, they have sufficient reason to judge that it is due to witchcraft.[21]

A third method of distinguishing natural illness from illness caused by witchcraft consisted of interpreting the form assumed by molten lead poured into water. "There are some," say the authors of the *Malleus,* "who can distinguish such illnesses by means of a certain practice, which is as follows. They hold molten lead over the sick man, and pour it into a bowl of water. And if the lead condenses into some image, they judge that the sickness is due to witchcraft."*[22]

In the days of the witch-hunts, physicians and priests were thus much concerned with the problem of the "differential diagnosis" between natural illness and demonic illness. This distinction seems simple to us only because we disbelieve in supernatural illness; but to our forebears, who believed in it, making this differentiation was a difficult task.† Moreover, the doctors and inquisitors engaged in ferreting out witches carried out their work against the backdrop of a closely related problem that was very real indeed: they had to distinguish between persons allegedly guilty of injurious acts, especially poisoners or *veneficae*—and those innocent of any wrongdoing, that is, ordinary persons. By being considered simultaneously a malefactor (as bewitched), like the poisoner, and a victim (as mere instrument of demonic powers), like ordinary all-suffering mankind, the witch helped to obliterate the sharp distinction between poisoner and nonpoisoner, guilty and innocent person.

Significantly, the word *witch* comes from a Hebrew word that has been rendered *venefica* in Latin, and *witch* in English. Its original meaning was poisoner, dabbler in magical spells, or fortuneteller. The concept of witch combines occult powers with possibilities of benefaction or malefaction.[23] In Renaissance Europe, poisoning, mainly by means of arsenical compounds, was a common practice. Making and selling poisons became a large and profitable trade, often engaged in by women. "So rooted had [slow poisoning] become in France between the years 1670 and 1680," remarks Mackay, "that Madame de Sévigné, in one of her letters, expresses the fear that Frenchman and poisoner would become synonymous terms."[24]

* Since this was prescribed by the Inquisition and helped its cause, it was not considered magic or sorcery. When individuals employed similar methods in the pursuit of their own interests, they were declared heretics and were severely punished. See, for example, Charles Williams, *Witchcraft,* p. 85.

† The classification of diseases as either natural or demonic, and of patients as either sick requiring treatment or possessed requiring exorcism, was still popular toward the end of the eighteenth century, and has, indeed, survived to the present. In this connection, see Henri F. Ellenberger, "The Evolution of Depth Psychology," in Iago Galdston (Ed.), *Historic Derivations of Modern Psychiatry;* and also Jean Lhermitte, *True and False Possession.*

The problem of the correct diagnosis of witchcraft must be viewed against this background.

Johann Weyer (1515–1588), physician to Duke William of Cleves, was one of the few medical men of his age to speak out against the witch-hunts. Like his contemporaries, Weyer believed in witchcraft and witches;* he differed from them only in holding that witch-hunters made the diagnosis of witchcraft too often and too readily. He especially attacked "the uninformed and unskilled physicians [who] relegate all of the incurable diseases, or all of the diseases the remedy for which they overlook, to witchcraft"; and concluded that "they, the physicians themselves are thus the real malefactors."[25] In short, he did not oppose the witch-hunts themselves, but only their "abuses" or "excesses."

Significantly, the full title of Weyer's classic work is *De Praestigiis Daemonum, et Incantationibus ac Veneficiis*—that is, *On the Trickery of Demons and the Prayers of Poisoners*. Beginning with the title and throughout the book Weyer distinguishes between "witches" and "poisoners." He acknowledges that there are evil people who use a variety of poisons to harm and kill their enemies. They are criminals and should be punished. However, the majority of people accused of witchcraft are not of this type. Innocent of any wrongdoing, they are unfortunate, miserable, and perhaps "deluded" individuals. In a letter to his patron, Duke William, explaining the aims of *De Praestigiis* and dedicating it to him, Weyer writes that his "final object" in this work "is legal, in that I speak of punishment, *in another than the accustomed way,* of sorcerers and witches."[26] (Italics added.) And he concludes the letter with an uncompromising rejection of the inquisitorial process and a plea for respect for established judicial procedures. "To you, Prince [he writes], I dedicate the fruit of my thought. . . . You do not, like others, impose heavy penalties on perplexed, poor old women. You demand evidence, and only if they have *actually given poison,* bringing about the death of men or animals, do you allow *the law* to take its course."[27] (Italics added.)

Weyer thus insists that, from a legal point of view, it is necessary

* Weyer not only believed in the reality of witches, but claimed to know their exact number and organization. There were, he said, "seven million, four hundred nine thousand, one hundred and twenty-seven, and all of them were controlled by seventy-nine princes." (Quoted in Jerome M. Schneck, *A History of Psychiatry,* p. 41.)

to distinguish between two classes of persons: poisoners or persons guilty of criminal acts, and nonpoisoners or persons innocent of criminal acts. But this is precisely the point on which his opponents assail him: because the witches *are* criminals, they maintain, there is no such distinction to be made. Contemporary authorities are quite clear on this. Jean Bodin (1530–1596), a French jurist, leading defender of the Inquisition, and one of Weyer's most impassioned critics, asserts that Weyer is ". . . wrong . . . a witch and a poisoner are one and the same thing. Everything imputed to witches is true."[28] Another critic of Weyer's, a Marburg physician named Scribonius, writing in 1588, objects specifically to Weyer's attempt to prove "that witches only imagine their crimes but that in reality they have done nothing untoward!" To Scribonius, this means that "Weyer does nothing more than to remove the guilt from the shoulders of the witches to free them from the need of any punishment. . . . Yes, I shall say it openly: with Bodin, I believe that Weyer has consecrated himself to the witches, that he is their comrade and companion in crime, that he himself is a wizard and a mixer of poisons who has taken upon himself the defense of other wizards and poison-mixers."[29]

Mystification of the concept of witchcraft and its amalgamation with that of poisoning were useful for the Inquisition; hence, inquisitors opposed attempts to undo this process and punished, as enemies of the established theological order, those who persisted in such efforts. Weyer's critics, as we just saw, objected precisely to his attempts to de-mystify the harmfulness of alleged witches. Doing so was, as the *Malleus* had clearly laid down, a grave and sinful error: "And yet there are some who rashly opposing themselves to all authority publicly proclaim that witches do not exist, or at any rate that they can in no way afflict and hurt mankind. Wherefore, strictly speaking those who are convicted of such evil doctrine may . . . be excommunicated, since they are openly and unmistakably to be convicted of false doctrine."[30]

Because it is essential for a clear grasp of our subsequent discussion of witchcraft and its parallels with mental illness, I have tried to show in some detail that the emphasis of Weyer's argument is not where modern psychopathologists claim it is—that is, on a criticism of the concept of witchcraft and on a plea for its replacement by that of mental illness;* instead it is on the *procedures* employed by the inquisitors. These methods will be surveyed in the next chapter.

With the decline of the power of the Church and of the religious world view, in the seventeenth century, the inquisitor-witch complex disappeared and in its place there arose the alienist-madman complex.

In the new—secular and "scientific"—cultural climate, as in any other, there were still the disadvantaged, the disaffected, and the men who thought and criticized too much. Conformity was still demanded. The nonconformist, the objector, in short, all who denied or refused to affirm society's dominant values, were still the enemies of society. To be sure, the proper ordering of this new society was no longer conceptualized in terms of Divine Grace; instead, it was viewed in terms of Public Health. Its internal enemies were thus seen as mad; and Institutional Psychiatry came into being, as had the Inquisition earlier, to protect the group from this threat.

The origins of the mental hospital system bear out these generalizations. "The great confinement of the insane," as Michel Foucault aptly calls it, began in the seventeenth century: "A date can serve as a landmark: 1656, the decree that founded, in Paris, the *Hôpital Général*."[31] The decree founding this establishment, and others throughout France, was issued by the king, Louis XIII: "We choose to be guardian and protector of said *Hôpital Général* as being of royal founding . . . which is to be totally exempt from the direction, visitation, and jurisdiction of the officers of the General Reform . . . and from all others to whom we forbid all knowledge and jurisdiction in any fashion or manner whatsoever."[32]

The original, seventeenth-century, definition of madness—as the

---

* Indeed, since Weyer believed in witchcraft, and since the concept of witchcraft was inextricably intertwined with that of malefaction, he was unable to persuade his critics, or the public, that witches were harmless. Robbins cogently observes that "Weyer was activated by pity rather than by reason. Consequently, his attempted distinction between harmless witches and wicked wizards was easily demolished by his more logical opponents, like Bodin." (Rossell Hope Robbins, *The Encyclopedia of Witchcraft and Demonology*, p. 539.)

Today, the "moderate" critic of the overuse of involuntary psychiatric hospitalization finds himself in the same bind. Since he believes in mental illness, and since the concept of mental illness is inextricably intertwined with malefaction, he, like Weyer before him, is also unable to persuade his critics, or the public, that mental patients are not dangerous.

condition justifying confinement in the asylum—conformed to the requirements for which it was fashioned. To be considered mad, it was enough to be abandoned, destitute, poor, unwanted by parents or society. The regulations governing admission to the Bicêtre and the Salpêtrière—the two Parisian mental hospitals destined to become world famous—put into effect on April 20, 1680, provided that "children of artisans and other poor inhabitants of Paris up to the age of twenty-five, who used their parents badly or who refused to work through laziness, or, in the case of girls, who were debauched or in evident danger of being debauched, should be shut up, the boys in the Bicêtre, the girls in the Salpêtrière. This action was to be taken on the complaint of the parents, or, if these were dead, of near relatives, or the parish priest. The wayward children were to be kept as long as the directors deemed wise and were to be released only on written order by four directors."[33] In addition to these persons "prostitutes and women who ran bawdy houses" were to be incarcerated in a special section of the Salpêtrière.[34]

The consequences of these "medical" practices are described by a French observer after the Salpêtrière had been in operation for a century:

In 1778, the Salpêtrière is the largest hospital in Paris and possibly in Europe: this hospital is both a house for women and a prison. It receives pregnant women and girls, wet nurses and their nurselings; male children from the age of seven or eight months to four or five years of age; young girls of all ages; aged married men and women; raving lunatics, imbeciles, epileptics, paralytics, blind persons, cripples, people suffering from ringworm, incurables of all sorts, children afflicted with scrofula, and so on and so forth. At the center of this hospital is a house of detention for women, comprising four different prisons: *le commun,* for the most dissolute girls; *la correction,* for those who are not considered hopelessly depraved; *la prison,* reserved for persons held by order of the king; and *la grande force,* for women branded by order of the courts.[35]

Surveying this scene, George Rosen bluntly states that "the individual was committed not primarily to receive medical care but rather to protect society and to prevent the disintegration of its institutions."[36]

As recently as 1860, it was not necessary to be mentally ill to be incarcerated in an American mental institution; it was enough to be a married woman. When the celebrated Mrs. Packard was hospitalized in the Jacksonville State Insane Asylum for disagreeing with her minister-husband, the commitment laws of the state of Illinois explicitly proclaimed that "Married women . . . may be entered or detained in the hospital at the request of the husband of the woman or the guardian . . . without the evidence of insanity required in other cases."[37]

In short, it is only a relatively recent rationalization in the history of psychiatry that a person must "suffer" from a "mental disease"— like schizophrenia or senile psychosis—to justify his commitment. Being an unemployed young man, a prostitute, or a destitute old person used to suffice. "We must not forget," remarks Foucault, "that a few years after its foundation [in 1656], the *Hôpital Général* of Paris alone contained six thousand persons, or around one percent of the population."[38] As a means of social control and of the ritualized affirmation of the dominant social ethic, Institutional Psychiatry immediately showed itself to be a worthy successor to the Inquisition. Its subsequent record, as we shall see, has been equally distinguished.

The French *hôpital général*, the German *Irrenhaus*, and the English insane asylum thus become the abodes of persons called mad. Are they considered mad, and therefore confined in these institutions? Or are they confined because they are poor, physically ill, or dangerous, and therefore considered mad? For three hundred years, psychiatrists have labored to obscure rather than clarify this simple problem. Perhaps it could not have been otherwise. As happens also in other professions—especially in those pertaining to the regulation of social affairs—psychiatrists have been largely responsible for creating the problems they have ostensibly tried to solve. But then, like other men, psychiatrists cannot be expected to act systematically against their own economic and professional self-interests.

The decree of Louis XIII was not a solitary occurrence. It has been repeated time and again through the history of psychiatry. The German mental hospital system, for example, was inaugurated in 1805 with the following declaration by Prince Karl August von Hardenberg:

The state must concern itself with all institutions for those with damaged minds, both for the betterment of the unfortunates and for the advancement of science. In this important and difficult field of medicine only unrelenting efforts will enable us to carve out advances for the good of suffering mankind. Perfection can be achieved only in such institutions [state mental hospitals] . . .[39]

The patients upon whose behavior men like Kahlbaum and Kraepelin later erected their systems of psychiatric diagnosis were the inmates of these institutions. During the one hundred years following Prince Hardenberg's declaration, the diversity of mental diseases requiring "diagnosis" and "treatment" multiplied throughout Europe, and so did the number of mental patients requiring confinement.

In our own day—a half millennium after the bull of Innocent VIII, and 150 years after the German declaration of war on insanity—we are exhorted to combat mental illness by no less a personage than a President of the United States of America. On February 5, 1963, President Kennedy declared:

I propose a national mental health program to assist in the inauguration of a wholly new emphasis and approach to care for the mentally ill. . . . Government at every level—Federal, State, and local—private foundations and individual citizens must all face up to their responsibilities in this area. . . . We need . . . to return mental health care to the mainstream of American medicine.[40]

It is sobering to contemplate the similarities among these inspirational messages. The good intentions and sincerity of the speakers need not be doubted. Pope, Prince, President—each claims to be trying to help his suffering fellow man. What is chilling is that each ignores the possibility that the alleged sufferer, whether of witchcraft or of mental illness, might prefer to be let alone; that each refuses merely to offer his help and grant his beneficiary the right to accept it or reject it; and, finally, that each denies the painful truth that men upon whom the ministrations of the militant Church and the therapeutic State are imposed by force rightly regard themselves not as beneficiaries and patients but as victims and prisoners.

As we have seen, in the days of the witch-hunts, the methods for identifying a person as a poisoner and as a patient differed radically; the method for identifying him as a witch differed from both, constituting a special procedure. In our day, the methods for identifying a person as a criminal and as a medical patient differ similarly; and the method for identifying him as a mental patient differs from both, again constituting a special procedure. There are good reasons for these distinctions.

We are plagued by some of the same kinds of social problems which plagued people during the declining Middle Ages, and we try to solve them by similar methods. We use the same legal and moral categories: lawbreakers and law-abiding citizens, guilt and innocence; and we, too, use an intermediate category—the madman or mental patient—whom we try to fit into one class or the other. Formerly, the question was: In which class do witches belong? Now it is: In which class do mental patients belong? Institutional psychiatrists and men of enlightened popular opinion hold that, because they are "dangerous to themselves and others," madmen belong in the class of quasi-criminals; this justifies their involuntary incarceration and general mistreatment.

Moreover, to support their ideology and to justify their powers and privileges, institutional psychiatrists combine the notions of mental illness and criminality and resist efforts to separate them. They do this by claiming that mental illness and crime are one and the same thing and that mentally ill persons are dangerous in ways that mentally healthy persons are not. Philip Q. Roche, who received the American Psychiatric Association's Isaac Ray Award for helping to bring law and psychiatry closer together, articulates this view in a characteristic fashion when he asserts that "criminals differ from mentally ill people only in the manner we choose to deal with them. . . . All felons are mental cases . . . crime is a disturbance of communication, hence a form of mental illness."[41] This view—namely, that crime is a product and symptom of mental illness in the same way as, say, jaundice is of hepatitis—held today by most psychiatrists and many lawyers and jurists, is not as novel as its proponents would have us believe. For example, Sir Matthew Hale (1609–1678), Lord Chief Justice of England and, curiously, himself an ardent believer in witchcraft, declared that ". . . doubtless, most persons that are felons . . . are under a degree of partial insanity, when they commit these offenses."[42] We recognize in this view an early manifestation of the change from a religious to a scientific mode of thinking and talking about people and human relations. Instead of saying that "criminals are evil," the authorities say that they are "sick"; in either case, however, the suspects continue to be seen as dangerous to society and hence fit subjects for its sanctions.

It is consistent with this close mental and verbal association between crime and madness* that commitment laws are formulated in terms of the individual's supposed "dangerousness" (to himself and others), rather than in terms of his health and illness. Dangerousness, of course, is a characteristic the alleged mental patient shares with the criminal, rather than with the medically ill person.

Mystification of the concept of mental illness and its amalgamation with that of crime are now useful for Institutional Psychiatry, just as mystification of the concept of witchcraft and its amalgamation with poisoning had formerly been useful for the Inquisition. In Weyer's day, the effect of obfuscating the differences between witchcraft and poisoning—theological offense (heresy) and law-breaking (crime)—was the replacement of accusatorial with inquisitorial procedures. In our day, the effect of obfuscating the differences between madness and dangerousness—psychiatric offense (mental illness) and lawbreaking (crime)—is the replacement of the Bill of Rights with the Bill of Treatments. The upshot in each case is therapeutic tyranny, clerical in the first instance, clinical in the second. The Inquisition thus combined the arbitrariness of theological judgments with the punitiveness of then prevalent penal sanctions. Institutional Psychiatry similarly combines the arbitrariness of psychiatric judgments with the punitiveness of now prev-

---

* In actual practice, what does it mean, or can it mean, to assert that crime is a form of mental illness? It can only mean a blurring of the distinctions, which I shall discuss presently, between illness and law-breaking. Suffice it to note here that the judgment of whether a person is sick is made by a physician, typically on the basis of an examination of that person's (called the "patient") body, submitted to the physician voluntarily by the patient himself; regardless of the outcome of this diagnostic process, the decision of whether a therapeutic intervention should be undertaken rests ultimately with the patient. In contrast, the judgment of whether a person is a criminal is made (in Anglo-American law) by a lay jury, typically on the basis of an examination of information about that person's (called the "defendant") conduct, submitted to the jury, often over the objections of the accused, by the defendant's adversary (called the "prosecutor"); finally, if the outcome of this "diagnostic" process is a finding of guilt, the decision of whether a punitive intervention should be undertaken rests with the jury and the judge (whose choice of actions are, however, prescribed by law).

alent penal sanctions. Moreover, institutional psychiatrists now oppose attempts to undo the mystification inherent in the idea of mental illness, and punish, as enemies of the established therapeutic order, those who persist in such efforts*—just as formerly the inquisitors opposed attempts to undo the mystification inherent in the idea of witchcraft and persecuted those (like Weyer) who persisted in such efforts.

Nevertheless, we too shall persist in such efforts. Let us begin with the differences between crime and ordinary (bodily) illness. Crime threatens society, not the criminal. When a crime has been committed, the public interest requires the use of broad and vigorous police-diagnostic methods: to protect the public welfare, the criminal must be found and apprehended. Against this, there is a countervailing private interest to carefully limit and supervise such methods: to protect individual liberties, the innocent citizen must be safeguarded against false accusation and imprisonment. Procedures for detecting crime must thus be carefully balanced to satisfy both of these competing interests. These ideas are contained in the legal concept of "due process."[43]

Disease threatens the individual, not society.† Since there is no public interest pressing for a diagnosis of illness when an individual suffers pain (as there is for a diagnosis of criminality, when a crime has been committed), the patient is left free to use or avoid whatever medical-diagnostic methods he wishes. If he pursues the

* "The question will inevitably be raised," writes Frederick G. Glaser, "whether sanctions of some form ought to be taken against Dr. Szasz, not only because of the content of his views but because of the manner in which he presents them. He has not chosen to limit his discussion to professional circles, as his magazine article [in *Harper's*], not the first that he has written, testifies." (Frederick G. Glaser, The dichotomy game: A further consideration of the writings of Dr. Thomas Szasz, *Amer. J. Psychiat.*, 121; 1069–1074 [May] 1965; p. 1073.)

This intolerance is understandable. Doubt about the existence or dangerousness of mental patients would limit the methods permitted to institutional psychiatrists in combating mental illness, just as doubt about the existence or dangerousness of witches would have limited the methods permitted to inquisitors in combating witchcraft. The Inquisition thus flourished so long as its agents were entrusted with special powers by the society they served. Institutional Psychiatry now flourishes for the same reason. Only when these powers are curbed does such an institution wither away.

† This is true mainly for noncontagious illnesses, such as cancer, heart disease, or stroke. Contagious diseases, which I shall discuss presently, resemble both noncontagious illnesses and crimes, inasmuch as they threaten the individual as well as society.

diagnosis of his illness too vigorously, or not vigorously enough, his health may suffer, and hence he may suffer. It is therefore reasonable to leave the ultimate power for accepting or rejecting diagnostic procedures for disease in the hands of the patient himself. These ideas are contained in the legal concept of "informed consent."[44]

These two categories, described above in their pure form, coalesce in certain phenomena that exhibit the essential features of both—that is, the dangerousness to self, characteristic of illness, and the dangerousness to others, characteristic of crime. One such phenomenon, all too familiar to medieval and Renaissance man, was contagious illness. When, at last, toward the end of the thirteenth century, Europe was rid of leprosy, it was swept by successive epidemics of bubonic plague which decimated the population. Then, in the sixteenth century, syphilis assumed epidemic proportions.

Like leprosy and the plague, heretical beliefs and practices also spread through populations as if by contagion; and they too were regarded, by those who rejected them, as harmful to both self and others. Since contagious illness was understood to be harmful to both the sick person and others, it formed a ready conceptual bridge between ordinary, noncontagious illness (as something harmful to the self) and crime (as something harmful to others). Contagious illness thus became the model for religious heresy, fostering the imagery of witchcraft as a "condition" dangerous for both witch and victim alike. It was therefore considered justified to resort to special measures for controlling the epidemic spread of contagious illnesses and heretical ideas.

In modern society and the modern mind, contagious illness—now symbolized by syphilis and tuberculosis, rather than by leprosy and the plague—has continued to function as a conceptual and logical bridge between illness (as injury to self) and crime (as injury to others); and it became the model for secular heresy (mental illness).

Like syphilis and tuberculosis, nonconforming social beliefs and practices also spread through the population as if by contagion; and they too are regarded, by those who reject them, as harmful to both self and others. It is therefore still considered justified to resort to special measures for controlling contagious diseases (whose social significance has become negligible in industrially advanced nations) and dangerous ideas (whose social significance has skyrocketed in these countries). The result is a pervasive conceptualization of social nonconformity as a contagious disease—that is, the mythology of mental illness; a widespread acceptance of the institution which ostensibly protects the people from this "disease"—that is, Institutional Psychiatry; and popular approval of the characteristic operations of this institution—that is, the systematic use of force and fraud, disguised by the architecture of hospitals and clinics, the rhetoric of healing, and the prestige of the medical profession.

The fundamental parallels between the criteria of witchcraft and mental illness may be thus summarized as follows:

In the Age of Witchcraft, illness was considered either natural or demonic. Since the existence of witches as the analogues of saints* could not be doubted (save at the risk of incurring the charge of heresy), the existence of diseases due to the malefaction of witches could also not be doubted. Physicians were thus drawn into the affairs of the Inquisition as experts in the differential diagnosis of these two types of illnesses.

In the Age of Madness, illness is similarly considered either organic or psychogenic. Since the existence of minds as the analogues of bodily organs is not to be doubted (save at the risk of incurring vehement opposition), the existence of diseases due to the malfunction of minds also cannot be doubted.† Physicians are thus drawn into the affairs of Institutional Psychiatry as experts in the differential diagnosis of these two types of illnesses. This is why physicians and psychiatrists are so much concerned with the problem of the differential diagnosis between bodily illness and mental illness. This distinction seems simple only if we disbelieve

* In the theology and folklore of Christianity, saints are the agents of God, responsible for doing some of His good deeds, and witches are the agents of Satan, responsible for doing some of his evil deeds. Of course, good and evil, like beauty and ugliness, lie in the eye of the beholder. Thus, Joan of Arc, burned at the stake as a witch in 1431, was canonized as a saint in 1920. See Joan of Arc, *Encyclopaedia Britannica* (1949), Vol. 13, pp. 72–75.

† Illustrative is the following definition of "mind" by Stanley Cobb, the occupant, for more than thirty years, of a distinguished chair in neuropathology at Harvard, and one of America's most honored psychiatrists: "Mind . . . is the relationship of one part of the brain to another. Mind is a function of the brain just as contraction is a function of muscle or as circulation is a function of the blood-vascular system." (Stanley Cobb, Discussion of "Is the term 'mysterious leap' warranted?" in Felix Deutsch [Ed.], *On the Mysterious Leap from the Mind to the Body*, p. 11.)

in mental illness; but to most persons, who believe in it, making this differentiation is a difficult task. Moreover, the physicians and psychiatrists engaged in psychiatric "case-finding" carry out their work against a backdrop of a closely related problem that is very real indeed: they must distinguish between persons allegedly guilty of injurious acts, especially acts of violence against family members or famous personages, and those innocent of any wrongdoing, that is, ordinary citizens. By being considered simultaneously a male-factor (as mad), like the criminal, and a victim (as sick), like the sick patient, the mental patient helps to obliterate the sharp distinction between criminal and noncriminal, guilty and innocent person.

Moreover, in each of these situations, the physician must work with the classification imposed on him by his profession and his society. The medieval diagnostician had to distinguish persons afflicted with natural diseases from those afflicted with demonic diseases. The contemporary physician must distinguish persons afflicted with bodily diseases from those afflicted with mental diseases.* But in making this sort of differential diagnosis, the fifteenth-century physician did not distinguish between two types of diseases; instead he prescribed two types of interventions—one medical, the other theological. In effect, as diagnostician, such a physician was an arbiter deciding who should be treated by means of drugs and other medical methods, and who by means of exorcism and other inquisitorial methods. *Mutatis mutandis*, the contemporary physician does not distinguish between two types of diseases; instead, he prescribes two types of interventions—one medical, the other psychiatric. In effect, as diagnostician, such a physician is an arbiter deciding who should be treated by means of drugs, surgery, and other medical methods, and who by means of electroshock, commitment, and other psychiatric methods. This is why the methods of examination characteristic of Institutional Psychiatry

* My thesis regarding the relations between organic and mental illness thus both resembles and differs from Weyer's regarding the relations between natural and demonic illness. It resembles Weyer's in so far as he maintains that merely because physicians cannot cure a disease, they should not infer from this that the disease is due to witchcraft. It differs from his in so far as he proclaims his belief in witchcraft as a cause of illness and protests only that his colleagues make this diagnosis more often than they should. I hold that, like witchcraft, mental illness is a misconception which can "cause" neither bodily illness nor crime.

are compulsory: the power of consent is wrested from the "patient" and placed in the hands of medical authorities sitting in judgment on him.

The point we must keep in mind is that in the days of the *Malleus*, if the physician could find no evidence of natural illness, he was expected to find evidence of witchcraft; today, if he cannot diagnose organic illness, he is expected to diagnose mental illness.* In both situations, once the subject comes into the presence of the physician, he becomes a "patient" who cannot be left undiagnosed. The doctor often feels free to choose between two categories only: illness and witchcraft, physical illness and mental illness; he does not feel free—save at the cost of defining himself as professionally inept or socially deviant—to declare that the patient belongs in none of these categories.

In other words, the physician confronted with a person without demonstrable bodily illness is often baffled: Should he consider such a person a "patient"? Should he "treat" him, and if so, for what? In the past, the physician was generally reluctant to con-. clude that such an individual was neither sick nor possessed, and now he is reluctant to conclude that such a person is neither physically ill nor mentally ill. In the past, the physician tended to believe that such people ought to submit to the ministrations of either medicine or theology. Now he tends to believe that they ought to submit to the ministrations of either medicine or psychiatry. In short, physicians have avoided, and continue to avoid, the conclusion that the foregoing problem falls outside the scope of their expert knowledge and that they should therefore leave the person alone and unclassified—the master of his own fate.†

* In so far as the concept of mental illness functions as a classificatory label justifying the psychiatric denigration of nonconformists, it is logically faulty, not because it fails to identify a socially definable characteristic, but because it mislabels it as a disease; and it is morally faulty, not because the physicians and psychologists who use it are badly intentioned, but because it fosters social control of personal conduct without procedural protections of individual liberty. For detailed discussion, see Thomas S. Szasz, *The Myth of Mental Illness.*

† What, then, should the physician do when confronted with a "patient" without demonstrable bodily illness? How should he classify and treat him? From the standpoint of a dignified medical ethic—respecting equally the patient's and the physician's rights to self-definition and self-determination—the examiner may satisfy his need for classification by categorizing his professional role or the result of his diagnostic interventions; but he should not impose a categorization on the patient against his will. The physician may thus conclude that he could

These judgments are rendered impossible in principle by two assumptions concerning the therapeutic relationship. The first is that the person facing the medical or theological expert is a helpless, inferior being to whom the physician or priest owes a "responsibility" independent of his (the expert's) knowledge and skill, and which he cannot shirk. The second is that the institutional psychiatrist or inquisitor derives no "selfish" gains from his work with the patient or heretic, and that, were it not for his selfless devotion to healing or saving souls, he would be only too happy to leave the sufferer to his "horrible fate."* For these reasons, such messianic therapists feel that they must *do something*, even if what they do is harmful to the sufferer. The unfortunate outcome, until recent times, of most therapeutic interventions for the patient is therefore hardly surprising. In the first place, before the present century, the healing arts were in an exceedingly primitive state. Moreover, since the therapeutic interventions imposed on patients were prompted largely by the physician's (or priest's) own feelings of self-importance, obligations, guilt, and, of course, possible cravings for power and sadism, they were unrestrained by assessments of their curative value for the client or his informed consent to, or refusal of, the "service." These circumstances still characterize the purveyance of public (and sometimes even of private) psychiatric care, whose quality thus remains similarly unchecked by the free decisions of the ostensible recipients of its services.

It is consistent with this character of the wars on witchcraft and mental illness that vast efforts are made to refine the criteria of witchcraft and mental illness: but these labors only serve to confirm more securely the reality of these threats and the legitimacy of the defenses against them. Herein, as we have seen, lay the fatal

---

find no evidence of bodily illness, but not that he found evidence of mental illness; or that he cannot help the client, but not that the client should consult a psychiatrist. In this connection, see Thomas S. Szasz, The Psychology of Persistent Pain: A Portrait of L'Homme Douloureux, in A. Soulairac, J. Cahan, and J. Charpentier (Eds.), *Pain,* pp. 93–113.

* This is the myth of nonbenefits for coercive therapists; its corollary is the myth of immense benefits for those coercively helped (even if these benefits are temporarily unappreciated by them). Without this imagery, the social inequities of therapeutic exploitations—selfless helpers growing rich at the expense of their selfish victims, so obvious a feature of both the Inquisition and Institutional Psychiatry—could not be maintained; with it, they have been, and continue to be, readily justified.

weakness of Weyer's opposition against the "excesses" of the witch-hunts; and herein too lies the fatal weakness of the "moderate" contemporary opposition against the "excesses" of the Mental Health Movement.

Like Weyer before him, the "moderate" contemporary critic of involuntary mental hospitalization opposes only the "abuses" and "excesses" of Institutional Psychiatry. He wants to improve the system, not to abolish it. He too believes in mental illness and in the desirability of committing the insane; his main complaint against involuntary mental hospitalization is that patients are committed too often and too readily—for example, that patients with unrecognized bodily diseases (such as subdural hematoma, brain tumor, cancer of the pancreas, and so forth) are sometimes hastily categorized as psychotic and improperly confined in mental hospitals. This argument only serves to confirm the validity of Institutional Psychiatry's core-concept of mental illness, and the legitimacy of its paradigm intervention, involuntary mental hospitalization.[45]

The foregoing problems of "differential diagnosis" are bound to arise and will persist so long as physicians are entrusted with matters completely unrelated to medicine. A physician may, or may not, be able to ascertain that a patient suffers from bodily illness; but if he thinks the patient does not, he cannot infer from this that his symptoms are due to witchcraft or mental illness—if for no other reason than that there is no such illness.

These problems of "differential diagnosis" would disappear if we regarded the physician as an expert on diseases of the body *only*, and recognized mental illness as a fictitious entity similar to witchcraft. Were we to do this, the physician's evaluative function would be limited to making an organic diagnosis or concluding that he cannot make one; and his therapeutic function, to treating bodily diseases or abstaining from treatment.

The problem of who is a fit subject for commitment would likewise disappear if we regarded involuntary mental hospitalization as a crime against humanity. The question of who was a fit subject for burning at the stake was answered only when witch-hunting was abandoned. I believe that the question of who is a fit subject for commitment will also be answered only when we abandon the practice of involuntary mental hospitalization.[46]

Although the witch-hunts seem to us today an obvious crime, we must be cautious about passing judgment on the men who believed in witchcraft and fought against witches. "Those magistrates who persecuted witches and demoniacs and who lit so many bonfires," asks the noted French historian of psychiatry René Semelaigne, "should they be accused of cruelty, as they frequently are?" He answers: "They too were people of their time and thus had their prejudices, beliefs, and convictions; they thought in their souls and conscience that they were just when they struck the guilty in accordance with the law."[47]

The inquisitors who opposed and persecuted the heretics acted in accordance with their sincere beliefs, just as the psychiatrists who oppose and persecute the insane act in accordance with theirs. In each instance we may disagree with the beliefs and repudiate the methods. But we cannot condemn the inquisitors doubly—first for having certain beliefs, and then for acting upon them. Neither can we condemn the institutional psychiatrists doubly—first for holding that social nonconformity is mental illness, and then for incarcerating the mental patient in a hospital. In so far as a psychiatrist truly believes in the myth of mental illness, he is compelled, by the inner logic of this construct, to treat, with benevolent therapeutic intent, those who suffer from this malady, even though his "patients" cannot help but experience the treatment as a form of persecution.

Although the Inquisition and Institutional Psychiatry developed from different economic, moral, and social conditions, their respective operations are similar. Each institution articulates its oppressive methods in therapeutic terms. The inquisitor saves the heretic's soul and the integrity of his Church; the psychiatrist restores his patient to mental health and protects his society from the dangerously insane. Like the psychiatrist, the inquisitor is an epidemiologist: he is concerned with the prevalence of witchcraft; he is a diagnostician: he establishes who is a witch and who is not; and finally, he is a therapist: he exorcises the devil and thus ensures the salvation of the possessed person's soul. On the other hand, the witch, like the involuntary mental patient, is cast into a degraded and deviant role against her will; is subjected to certain diagnostic procedures to establish whether or not she is a witch; and finally, is deprived of liberty, and often of life, ostensibly for her own benefit.

Finally, as we have noted earlier, once the roles of witch and mental patient become established, occasionally people will seek, for reasons of their own, to occupy these roles voluntarily. For example, Jules Michelet writes that "Not a few [witches] seemed positively to want to go to the stake, and the sooner the better. . . . An English Witch on being led to the stake, tells the crowd not to blame her judges: 'I wanted to die. My family shunned me, my husband repudiated me. If I lived, I should only be a disgrace to my friends. . . . I longed for death, and I lied to gain my end.' "[48] Christina Hole offers the following interpretation of the motives that led men to incriminate themselves and others as witches: "To accuse an enemy of witchcraft was an easy method of revenge; to declare oneself bewitched was a short cut to that flattering attention so much desired by unbalanced and hysterical individuals. . . . Very often the accuser's main object was to draw attention to himself and to pose as the victim of some witch's peculiar malice. . . . In 1599 Thomas Darling, of Burton-on-Trent, confessed that his story of three years before was quite untrue and his fits a fake. His reason for the deception was one that might have been given by many other lying accusers. 'I did all,' he said, 'either of ignorance, or to get myself glory thereby.' "[49]

Since a desire for "flattering attention" is not confined to "unbalanced and hysterical individuals," but is, on the contrary, a basic human need, it is easy to see why, under certain circumstances, men will readily assume the roles of witch, criminal, or mental patient.

In sum, what we call modern, dynamic psychiatry is neither a glamorous advance over the superstitions and practices of the witch-hunts, as contemporary psychiatric propagandists would have it, nor a retrogression from the humanism of the Renaissance and the scientific spirit of the Enlightenment, as romantic traditionalists would have it. In actuality, Institutional Psychiatry is a continuation of the Inquisition. All that has really changed is the vocabulary and the social style. The vocabulary conforms to the intellectual expectations of our age: it is a pseudomedical jargon that parodies the concepts of science. The social style conforms to the political expectations of our age: it is a pseudoliberal social movement that parodies the ideals of freedom and rationality.

2

THE MALEFACTOR IDENTIFIED

> Our best and most experienced physicians work in
> the Operation Department under the direct super-
> vision of the Well-Doer himself. . . . About five
> centuries ago, when the work of the Operation
> Department was only beginning, there were yet to
> be found some fools who compared our Operation
> Department with the ancient Inquisition. But this
> is as absurd as to compare a surgeon performing a
> tracheotomy with a highway cutthroat. Both use a
> knife, perhaps the same kind of knife, both do the
> same thing, viz., cut the throat of a living man; yet
> one is a well-doer, the other is a murderer.
>
> *–Eugene Zamiatin*[1]

The identity of witches was established by three principal methods:
confession, examination for witch's marks with or without "pricking," and ordeal by water. We shall examine them separately and
compare each to contemporary psychiatric methods of identifying
mental patients.

Confession was believed to be the only sure way to prove
witchcraft. Since no one but a witch could witness many of the
prohibited acts in question—such as the devil's sabbat or pacts with
Satan—it was logical that the declaration of the only available
witness, the accused himself, was eagerly sought. That the confession was obtained under torture did not trouble the inquisitors
or the believers in the witch mania. Indeed, it was felt to be a
matter of fairness and justice that a witch should be convicted *only*
on the basis of her own confession.

"Common justice demands," say Sprenger and Krämer in the *Malleus*, "that a witch should not be condemned to death unless she is convicted of her own confession."[2] According to Robbins, "Once accused, the victim had to endure torture and inevitably make a confession of guilt."[3] Every witch trial had its confessions. Similarly, every sanity hearing has its psychiatric self-incrimination: the state-employed psychiatrist demonstrates to the court, from statements made by or attributed to the victim, that the "patient" is suffering from mental illness. The records of witch trials are as full of documented confessions of pacts with the devil and other evidences of witchcraft, as are the records of modern Institutional Psychiatry of "hallucinations," "delusions," and other evidences of insanity. One example of this should suffice here.[4]

In 1945, Ezra Pound was indicted for treason. Although he wanted to stand trial to exonerate himself, he was declared psychiatrically unfit to do so. This judgment was based on the reports of four psychiatrists, among them that of Dr. Winfred Overholser, the superintendent of St. Elizabeths Hospital in Washington, D.C., a mental hospital operated by the United States Government, which stated that: "He [Pound] insists that his broadcasts were not treasonable . . . He is abnormally grandiose, is expansive and exuberant in manner, exhibiting pressure of speech, discursiveness, and distractibility. In our opinion, with advancing years his personality, for many years abnormal, has undergone further distortion to the extent that he is now suffering from a paranoid state . . . He is, in other words, insane and mentally unfit for trial, and is in need of care in a mental hospital."[5] After imprisoning Pound for thirteen years, Dr. Overholser declared, in an affidavit dated April 14, 1958, that "Ezra Pound . . . is permanently and incurably insane."[6]

When reading accounts of the "confessions" of witches and of the "symptoms" of mental patients, we must always keep in mind that we are presented with documents written by victimizers purporting to describe their victims. The records of the witch-hunts were kept by the inquisitors, not the witches; the inquisitor thus controlled the language of clerical description, which was but a rhetoric for invalidating a person as a true believer and defining him as a heretic. Similarly, the records of psychiatric examinations are kept by the physicians, not the patients; the psychiatrist thus controls the language of clinical description, which is but a rhetoric for invalidating a person as a normal individual and defining him as a mental patient. This is why the inquisitor was, and the institutional psychiatrist is, free to interpret any behavior as a sign of witchcraft or mental illness.

Here are two accounts of the way confessions were obtained from those accused of witchcraft. "Thus these wretched women," writes Weyer in *De Praestigiis,* ". . . [are] constantly dragged out to undergo atrocious torment until they would gladly exchange at any moment this most bitter existence for death, [and] are willing to confess whatever crimes are suggested to them rather than be thrust back into their hideous dungeon and ever recurring torture."[7]

Some of the most damaging testimony about the day-to-day workings of the witch-hunter is provided by a German Jesuit who had himself assisted the Inquisition but later turned against it. Friedrich von Spee's *Cautio Criminalis (Precautions for Prosecutors),* published in 1631, was a major attempt to oppose the therapeutic program of the Church against alleged heretics. Spee, who had acted as confessor to hundreds of witches burned at the stake, writes: "Previously I never thought of doubting that there were many witches in the world; now, however, when I examine the public record, I find myself believing that there are hardly any."[8]

As to the use of confessions, Father Spee remarks: ". . . the result is the same whether she [the accused] confesses or not. If she confesses, her guilt is clear: she is executed. All recantation is in vain. If she does not confess, the torture is repeated—twice, thrice, four times. . . . She can never clear herself. The investigating body would feel disgraced if it acquitted a woman; once arrested and in chains, she has to be guilty, by fair means or foul."[9]

The person accused of mental illness is in much the same position. If he admits to the signs and symptoms of mental illness imputed to him by his denouncers, it proves that he is mentally ill: he recognizes the gravity of his illness and the need for its treatment in a mental institution. If he denies the "illness," it only proves that he lacks "insight" into his condition; this, even more than confession of illness, is thought to justify involuntary confinement and treatment.[10]

The basic similarity between the two situations is that the accusers can do no wrong, and the accused can do no right. For the victim, admission and denial of both witchcraft and mental illness lead to the same destructive end. As for the authorities, their attitude is illustrated by Father Spee's observation that "If the prisoner dies under so much torture, they say the Devil broke his neck."[11] Just so with the hospitalized mental patient today. If he regresses in the mental hospital, it is because he suffers from "incurable" chronic schizophrenia; if his back is broken by convulsions induced by electroshock, it is because "there is no medical treatment without risk." Like Father Spee, the man who discovered electroshock therapy later looked back in horror at what he had done. Toward the end of his life, recalling the first time he had tried the treatment on a human being, Professor Ugo Cerletti remarked to a colleague: "When I saw the patient's reaction, I thought to myself: This ought to be abolished!"[12]

Father Spee also confirmed Weyer's contention that the tortures were so severe that no prisoner could resist confessing. "The most robust who have thus suffered," he writes in *Cautio Criminalis*, "have affirmed to me that no crime can be imagined which they would not at once confess to, if it would bring ever so little relief, and they would welcome ten deaths to escape a repetition."[13] Although suicide is a grave sin for Roman Catholics, many persons accused of witchcraft killed themselves in prison to escape torture.

For the most difficult cases where, despite all the denunciations, threats, and tortures, the accused remains silent or protests his innocence, the *Malleus* suggests the following method of "ascertaining the truth":

. . . we must proceed to the extreme case, when after every expedient has been tried the witch still maintains silence. The Judge shall then loose her and, using the precautions which follow, shall take her from the place of punishment to another place . . . [L]et him cause her to be well treated in the matter of food and drink, and meanwhile let honest persons who are under no suspicion enter to her and talk often with her on indifferent subjects, and finally advise her in confidence to confess the truth, promising that the Judge will be merciful to her and that they will intercede for her. And finally let the Judge come in and promise that he will be merciful, with the mental reservation that he means he will be merciful to himself or the State; for whatever is done for the safety of the State is merciful.[14]

There are thus a number of good reasons why the ecclesiastic inquisitors (and their disciples, political as well as psychiatric) have

so regularly succeeded in eliciting confessions from those accused
of witchcraft (and of similar "crimes"). As a rule, the accused were
intimidated, isolated, and mystified by those who sat in judgment
of them. Hence, they were eager to see reality through the imagery,
and to articulate it in the vocabulary, of the admired and feared
authority: afraid of torture, they said whatever they thought might
help protect them from it; under torture, their self was emptied
of its old identity and filled with the new one—of repentant
heretic—ascribed to them by their interrogators.[15]

The secret police of modern totalitarian states have faithfully
copied this inquisitorial method. The Mental Health Movements of
modern Therapeutic States have improved upon it: Institutional
psychiatrists (and psychologists, social workers, etc.) act as and
believe themselves to be the individual's ally, friend, and therapist,
when, in fact, they are his adversary. Should the patient confide
his fears or suspicions to them, they will interpret these as signs of
"mental illness" and so report to their employer; should the patient
fail to "co-operate" with them, they will interpret his refusal as
itself a sign of "mental illness" and will again so report to their
employer.[16]

Besides eliciting confessions, the principal method for diagnosing
witchcraft was to find witch's marks on the body of the accused.
Witch's marks were supernumerary nipples, a common anatomical
variation, slightly more frequent in men than women, or any kind of
skin lesion, such as a birthmark, mole, scar, or hemangioma. The
mark was thought to indicate the spot on which the possessor was
branded by the devil, like an animal by its owner, and constituted
proof of a pact between that person and Satan. This made it easy
enough to diagnose almost anyone as a witch.

Those not taken in by the witch mania recognized, of course,
that these marks are both common and natural. "Very few people
in the world are without privy marks upon their bodies, as moles or
stains, even such as witchmongers call the devil's privy marks,"
wrote Thomas Ady,[17] an English critic of witch-hunts, in 1656.*

A direct line of progression can be traced from the witch's marks
to the so-called stigmata of the hysteric, and, most lately, to the
signs which schizophrenics are made to reveal through projective

---

* Ady also recognized that the confessions of witches were obtained by fraud or
were invented by the inquisitors.

psychological testing. Each of these "diagnostic" findings is used to incriminate the subject—as witch, hysteric, or schizophrenic; each is then used to punish him—by means of theological, medical, or psychiatric sanctions.

The fact that witch's marks were ubiquitous simplified the work of the diagnosticians of witchcraft. Witch-finders did not reject such "diagnostic signs" on this account any more than psychiatrists reject anxiety, depression, or suspiciousness, which are also ubiquitous, as "diagnostic signs" of mental illness.

Visible witch's marks were, however, not the only signs of a pact with Satan. It was also believed that a person could be branded by the devil in such a way as to leave only an *invisible* mark upon his body. These spots were supposed to have been bloodless and insensitive to pain, and hence could be located only by what was called "pricking." If a pin were stuck into such a spot, and it neither bled nor caused pain, the individual would be a witch.

The witch mania provided much work for physicians who often were entrusted with locating witch's marks. The persecutions also spawned a new profession, witch-pricking—and a new professional, the witch-pricker, some of whom were physicians.

The witch-finder's first task was to locate visible witch's marks. This explained the custom of shaving all hair off the suspect of witchcraft: the mark might be located in a hairy area and only thus could it be exposed. If no mark was found, pricking was employed.

The role of physicians in diagnosing witchcraft may be gleaned from the various accounts of "case finding" reported in the literature on witchcraft. Robbins mentions the case of a woman in Geneva, Michelle Chaudron, who had been accused of bewitching two young girls: "Michelle was searched by physicians for devil's marks, and long needles were stuck into her flesh, but blood flowed from each puncture and Michelle cried out in pain. Not finding a devil's mark, the judges ordered the woman tortured; overcome with agony she confessed everything demanded. After her confession, the physicians returned to hunt the devil's mark, and this time found a tiny black spot on her thigh. . . . she was condemned to be strangled and burned."[18]

The fundamental similarity, then, between the methods of witch-finders and psychopathologists is that each perpetrates a cruel hoax on his victim and deceives his audience.* Each plays by the rule, "Heads I win, tails you lose." An ancient method of ascertaining the guilt of an accused person, based on this principle, is the ordeal by immersion in water. This practice was revived and became popular during the witch mania.

Witch-finding by the water ordeal, or "swimming" as it was often called, became an accepted method in England during the first half of the seventeenth century, when it was recommended by King James. "So it appears," proclaimed James I, "that God has appointed, for a supernatural sign of the monstrous impiety of witches, that the water shall refuse to receive them in her bosom, that have shaken off them the sacred water of baptism and willfully refused the benefit thereof."[19]

The test by "swimming" consisted of restraining the accused witch's bodily freedom, by tying hands and feet in various manner—usually, "the right thumb on the left big toe, so that the witch was 'cross bound' "[20]—and throwing her into deep water, three times if necessary. If she floated, she was guilty; if she sank, she was innocent. In the latter case, she usually drowned, unless she was rescued in time by her torturers; since her soul went to heaven, however, this test was not considered absurd by either the practitioners or their clients. Indeed, accused witches occasionally volunteered for it, perhaps because it was one of the few "tests" through which, however great the odds against passing it, they could establish their innocence; or perhaps because, as a means of indirect suicide, they could bring an end to their tortures without incurring the sin of self-destruction.

The aims and results of several modern methods of psychodiagnosis resemble closely the ordeal by water. One is the use of projective tests—like the Rorschach or the Thematic Apperception Test. When a clinical psychologist administers this test to a person referred by a psychiatrist, there is the tacit expectation that the test will show some "pathology." After all, a competent psychiatrist would not refer a "normal" person for such costly and complicated testing. The result is that the psychologist finds some kind of

---

* Of course, inquisitors and institutional psychiatrists may also deceive themselves. However, their self-deception helps them: it authenticates them as conscientious priests and physicians. In contrast, their deception of the masses harms the people: it converts them into mystified victims.

psychopathology: the patient is either "hysterical," or "depressed," or "latently psychotic," or, if all else fails, "shows signs suggestive of organicity." All this pseudomedical hocus-pocus and jargon serves to confirm the subject in the role of mental patient, the psychiatrist in the role of medical doctor, and the clinical psychologist in the role of paramedical technician (who "tests" the patient's mind instead of his blood). In more than twenty years of psychiatric work, I have never known a clinical psychologist to report, on the basis of a projective test, that the subject is a "normal, mentally healthy person." While some witches may have survived dunking, no "madman" survives psychological testing.

I have discussed and documented elsewhere that there is no behavior or person that a modern psychiatrist cannot plausibly diagnose as abnormal or ill.[21] Instead of belaboring this subject, I shall cite a set of guidelines—conforming closely to the rule, "Heads I win, tails you lose"—offered by a psychiatrist for finding psychiatric problems in school children. In a paper advocating psychiatric services in public schools, the author lists the following types of behavior as "symptomatic of deeper underlying disturbance . . . : 1. Academic problems—under-achievement, over-achievement, erratic, uneven performance. 2. Social problems with siblings, peers—such as the aggressive child, the submissive child, the show-off. 3. Relations with parental and other authority figures, such as defiant behavior, submissive behavior, ingratiation. 4. Overt behavioral manifestations, such as tics, nail-biting, thumb-sucking . . . [and] interests more befitting to the opposite sex (such as tom-boy girl and effeminate boy). . . ."[22]

Clearly, there is no childhood behavior that a psychiatrist could not place in one of these categories. To classify as pathological academic performance that is "under-achievement," "over-achievement," or "erratic performance" would be humorous were it not tragic. When we are told that if a psychiatric patient is early for his appointment he is anxious, if late he is hostile, and if on time, compulsive—we laugh, because it is supposed to be a joke. But here we are told the same thing in all seriousness.

It is necessary to recall here the economic aspects of the witch-hunts. The persecution of witches was exceedingly profitable for both the ecclesiastic and secular authorities and for the individuals engaged in this business as well. The property of the condemned

person was confiscated and distributed among the witchmongers
and their institutions. In addition, towns and cities would pay witch-
hunters for their work, the remuneration depending on the number
of witches discovered. Just as the power and prestige of the witchmongers rose with the increasing incidence of witchcraft, so has the
power and wealth of psychiatrists with the increasing incidence of
mental illness. For a long time it did not occur to people that the
ecclesiastic epidemiologists of witchcraft had a vested interest in
a high, rather than a low, incidence of this disorder; indeed, as soon
as this was fully appreciated, the witch mania was at an end. For an
almost equally long time, it did not occur to people that the medical
and psychiatric "epidemiologists" of mental illness have also a vested
interest in a high, rather than a low, incidence of this disorder; indeed, this idea must be socially repressed—and the psychiatric
profession does all it can to make sure that it is—to insure that the
myth of mental illness is accepted as enlightened common sense.

Once the alleged facts of witchcraft are accepted, it becomes
necessary to locate, identify, and eliminate the witches responsible
for it. "One of the most terrifying features of the general witchcraft
belief was the fact," Christina Hole reminds us, "that no one knew
for certain who was, or was not, a witch."[23] The same may be said
for our present situation: No one knows for certain who is, or is
not, mentally ill. Hence, the former need for witch-finders, witch-
prickers, and inquisitors, and the present need for psychiatrists,
psychologists, and social workers.

"The most deplorable by-product of the general fear of witches,"
Hole continues, "was the professional witch-finder . . ."[24] Although
his activities were deplorable indeed, the witch-finder was no more
a by-product of the war on witchcraft than is the psychiatrist of the
war on mental illness. Aggressors, real or pretended, create their
opponents, whose defensive posture is, in turn, genuine or trumped-
up. Mackay thus relates that immediately after the publication of
the *Malleus,* "a class of men sprang up in Europe who made it the
sole business of their lives to discover and burn the witches."[25] They
were known as "witch-prickers." The lay prickers shared with physicians the task of discovering and identifying witches.

There is more than a slight similarity between the work of the
seventeenth-century witch-finder and that of the twentieth-century
finder of mental illness. Matthew Hopkins, one of the most famous

English witch-prickers, "had his own regular searcher, a woman named Goody Phillips, who went about with him from town to town . . ."[26] Just so do (male) psychiatrists have (female) psychologists or social workers for their assistants. Moreover, as befits our tastes for large-scale operations, today we also have mental hospitals, mental health clinics, mental health commissioners, and mental health workers scattered across the nation, and traveling psychiatric teams with headquarters in the big cities making periodic forays into the countryside—all engaged in "psychiatric case finding," and handsomely paid for it. This psychiatric busy-work does not help the persons identified as sick; by stigmatizing them, it more often harms them. But, then, psychiatric case finding or diagnosis is not really supposed to help the individuals identified as patients; it is supposed to help those *not* so identified. Consistent with this, the institutional psychiatrist is paid by the community (or by the mental patient's relatives), not by the freely contracting individual.

The source of the physician's compensation is, of course, an issue of the greatest importance for psychiatry. Except for a brief interlude—limited to Western countries and to the period from about 1900 to the present, during which psychiatric services rendered to private patients in the offices of physicians, and services rendered to involuntary clients in mental hospitals and other institutions have coexisted—psychiatric practice has been, and is now again becoming, synonymous with institutional practice.[27]

The laws of economics being what they are, witch-finding became a flourishing trade. In England and Scotland, the lay diagnosticians were known as "common prickers"; they received a fee for each witch discovered. The witch-pricking mania did not end until the common prickers became so numerous that they became a nuisance. In the end, the judges refused to accept their evidence. But before this inevitable exposure of their imposture, the common prickers enjoyed the support of the highest authorities of Church and State. "The parliaments had encouraged the delusion [in witchcraft] both in England and Scotland," writes Mackay; "and by arming these fellows [common prickers] with a sort of authority, had in a manner forced the magistrates and ministers to receive their evidence."[28]

All this has its parallel in the Mental Health Movement. Since the M'Naghten decision more than one hundred years ago, and increasingly in recent decades, the highest authorities of the State—through their legislators and judges—have encouraged the belief in mental illness, armed physicians with official authority on the subject, and persuaded the courts to receive their evidence.

Although witchcraft was defined as a theological offense, the task of ferreting out witches was entrusted to both professional theologians (inquisitors) and lay witch-finders ("common prickers"). Similarly, although mental illness is defined as a medical problem, the diagnosis of madness is entrusted to both medical psychopathologists (psychiatrists) and nonmedical mental health workers (psychologists, social workers). Today, each group tries to outdo the other in diagnosing mental illness. This is to be expected. For just as the witchmonger's social identity and prestige depended on his ability to find and identify witches, so does the psychopathologist's depend on his ability to find and identify mentally ill patients. The more witches and madmen found, the more competent is the witch-finder and the psychodiagnostician.

The fault, of course, does not lie with the deceiver only; those who want to be, who indeed demand to be, deceived, must share in it. Because the masses believed in witchcraft, and now believe in mental illness, the witch-finders had been, and the psychopathologists now are, under the irresistible pressure of popular expectation to deliver to society the properly identified and authenticated victims. Neither psychiatrists nor nonmedical mental health experts have disappointed their eager and credulous audiences.

During the Second World War, for example, the crusading spirit of American psychopathology was allowed to vent itself in the Psychiatric Division of the Surgeon General's office, then headed by Brigadier General William C. Menninger. Menninger devised a new system of classifying mental illnesses and psychiatric patients which was adopted by all branches of the Armed Forces and led to the development of what is now the official list of "mental diseases" catalogued in the American Psychiatric Association's *Diagnostic and Statistical Manual of Mental Disorders*.[29] Karl Menninger characterized this work as "a magnificent achievement."[30] Its effect was that more civilians were declared mentally unfit to serve in the Armed Forces, more soldiers were classified as mentally ill, and more veterans now receive compensation and "treatment" for mental illness than ever before in history. The actual figures are as follows. Between January 1942 and June 1945, out of approximately fifteen million examinations for induction into the Armed Services, nearly two million individuals were rejected for neuropsychiatric disability; that is, 12 percent of those examined were rejected for mental illness. Actually, the rate had been 9.7 percent in 1942, and rose to 16.4 percent in 1945. Moreover, out of every one hundred rejections for all causes, an average of 39.1 percent were for neuropsychiatric disability. This proportion rose from a low of 28.4 in 1942 to a high of 45.8 in 1944. Despite this screening—or possibly because of it, since it authenticated mental illness as so acceptable a ground for separating men from the Service—37 percent of all medical discharges from the Armed Forces were on the grounds of neuropsychiatric disability.[31]

If a psychiatrist's greatness is measured by the number of people he "diagnoses" as "mentally ill," then William Menninger was a very great psychiatrist indeed. Appropriately, his collected papers are published under the title, *Psychiatrist to a Troubled World.*[32] To the zealous psychiatrist all men are mad, just as to the zealous theologian all men are sinful.[33]

The prevalence of mental illness is a problem dear to the hearts of all modern mental health workers. Like the witchmongers of bygone days, contemporary psychiatrists never tire of emphasizing the prevalence of mental illness and the dangers to society of the mentally ill.[34] As a result, our ability to see signs of madness all around us now approaches—indeed, perhaps surpasses—that of the medieval inquisitor's ability to see signs of heresy all around him. Symptoms of madness appear with increasing frequency and in persons of all kinds—American and foreign, of high and low station, living and dead.*

---

* President Kennedy's assassination uncovered all the madness-mongering latent in this country. We may now reap the harvest of careful psychiatric plantings over the past quarter of a century. Thus we have been told by the most distinguished medical and psychiatric authorities, as well as by the most respected lay interpreters of human events, that not only was Oswald mad when he allegedly shot Kennedy, but also that Ruby was mad when he shot Oswald. "John F. Kennedy was killed," asserts Theodore H. White, "by a lunatic, Lee Harvey Oswald, who had momentarily given loyalty to the paranoid Fidel Castro of Cuba. And Oswald was, in turn, within two days, slain by another madman, Jack Ruby." (Theodore H. White, *The Making of the President, 1964*, p. 29.) In two brief sentences we are given three psychiatric diagnoses—Castro's thrown in gratis.

Today madness-mongering is carried on and is encouraged by the most respected and influential physicians and statesmen, just as witchmongering was a few centuries ago. Perhaps no one has carried a belief, at once naive and evangelical, in mental illness further than Karl Menninger. Denying the factual differences between bodily and mental illness, Menninger maintains that there are not several mental diseases but just one, and that everyone is sometimes afflicted with it. "We insist," writes Menninger, "that there are conditions best described as mental illness. But instead of putting so much emphasis on different kinds and clinical pictures of illness, we propose to think of all forms of mental illness as being essentially the same in quality, and differing quantitatively. This is what is meant when we say that all people have mental illness of different degrees at different times, and sometimes some are much worse, or better."[35]

Menninger's messianic views here find expression in the rhetoric of medicine. Everyone, Menninger says—no doubt in a well-intentioned, but nevertheless ill-conceived, effort to detoxify the malignant semantic powers of the term "mental illness"—is mentally ill. But then comes the specification: Some more than others. Presumably this means that the patients are more ill, and the psychiatrists less. How will all this help individuals deprived of their liberty by psychiatrists? Menninger does not say. Rather, he gloats over the notion that man is not only guilty with "original sin" but is also sick with "original mental illness": "Gone forever is the notion that the mentally ill person is an exception. It is now accepted that most people have some degree of mental illness at some time, and many of them have a degree of mental illness most of the time."[36]

As Karl Menninger, the dean of American psychiatry, supports the belief in the myth of mental illness and all that it implies socially for the individual incriminated as mentally ill, so, for example, did Sir Thomas Browne (1605–1683), the most eminent physician of his time, support the belief in witchcraft and encourage the punishment of witches. Testifying as an expert witness in a witch trial, he gave the opinion that "in such cases the devil acted upon human bodies by natural means, namely, by exciting and stirring up the superabundant humours; . . . these fits might be natural, only raised to a great degree by the subtlety of the devil, cooperating with the malice of these witches."[37]

Coercion, domination, and violence do not, of course, breed

decency, reciprocity, and sympathy. Although the witchmongers were generally safe from accusations of witchcraft, they were sometimes coerced to diagnose witchcraft against their will. Similarly, although psychiatrists are generally safe from accusations of mental illness, they are sometimes coerced to diagnose mental illness against their will.

Zilboorg reports an illustrative case. Describing the investigation for witchcraft of a young woman named Françoise Fontaine, who suffered from spells thought to be caused by possession, Zilboorg writes: "She was not delivered until the hair from her head and armpits had been shaven by the surgeon who himself was thoroughly frightened and, thrice begging to be excused from performing the task, finally had to be threatened by the provost with severe punishment, in the name of His Majesty the King!"[38]

In 1591, when this occurred, physicians generally treated medically sick patients with the consent of those treated; when they were called to examine or treat witches, however, they did not have the consent of their subjects. There has been no basic change from this situation. Today, too, physicians generally treat medically sick patients with the consent of those treated; when they are called to examine or treat mental patients, however, they often do not have the consent of their subjects. Many physicians like this arrangement; others get used to it; some must be compelled to yield to it. But whether physicians like it or not, the stubborn fact remains that psychiatric training is, above all else, a ritualized indoctrination into the theory and practice of psychiatric violence. The disastrous effects of this process on the patient are obvious enough; though less evident, its consequences for the physician are often equally tragic.

It is one of the few "laws" of human relations that not only those who suffer from arbitrary authority, but also those who wield it, become alienated from others and thus dehumanized. The oppressed tends to become a passive, thinglike object, and the oppressor a megalomaniacal, godlike figure. When the former realizes that he is but a mockery of man, and the latter that he is but a mockery of God, the result is often explosive violence, the victim seeking revenge in murder, the victimizer oblivion in suicide. I surmise that such considerations account, at least in part, for the fact that, in the United States, the highest incidence of suicide is among psychiatrists.[39]

3

THE MALEFACTOR AUTHENTICATED

> It is important, perhaps decisive, for the place madness was to occupy in modern culture, that *homo medicus* was not called into the world of confinement as an *arbiter*, to divide what was crime from what was madness, what was evil from what was illness, but rather as a *guardian*, to protect others from the vague danger that exuded through the walls of confinement.
>
> —*Michel Foucault*[1]

The denunciation of persons as witches, their examination for witch's marks, and their torture to extract confessions, served only to secure their formal, legal definition as witches and to justify their sentencing, usually to death by burning at the stake. We are now ready to examine the witch trial and compare it with contemporary legal proceedings to establish a person's status as mentally ill.

Of course, the witch trial was not a trial in the modern sense. Although its ostensible aim was to establish the innocence or guilt of the accused, its actual aim was to proclaim publicly the existence, prevalence, and dangerousness of witches and the power and mercy of the inquisitors and judges. Similarly, a sanity trial—for commitment, fitness to stand trial, or habeas corpus to gain release from a mental hospital—is also not a genuine trial. Although its ostensible aim is to establish the mental sickness or health of the "patient," its actual aim is to proclaim publicly the existence, prevalence, and dangerousness of insane persons and the power and mercy of the psychiatrists and judges.

Persons accused of heresy or witchcraft were treated differently from persons accused of ordinary—that is, nontheological—offenses. In the Middle Ages and the Renaissance, the proceeding against a person charged with an ordinary offense was "accusatorial": the defendant was permitted the aid of counsel; certain kinds of evidence against him were not admissible in court; and usually he was not forced to confess his alleged offense under torture. All such safeguards of the rights of the accused were abrogated in trials for heresy. "Those who defended the errors of heretics were to be treated as heretics," writes Lea. "[Moreover], although the evidence of a heretic was not receivable in court, yet an exception was made in favour of the faith, and it was to be held good against another heretic."[2]

The person accused of mental illness is in a similar situation. He too, instead of being treated as a respectable adult suspected of crime, is treated in a paternalistic fashion, as might a naughty child by a father who "knows best." Accounts of involuntary psychiatric interventions—and by this I mean any contact with a psychiatrist not actively sought by the patient—illustrate the similarities between the procedures characteristic of Institutional Psychiatry and of the Inquisition. A brief example should suffice here.

Mr. and Mrs. Michael Duzynski were displaced persons of Polish origin who emigrated to the United States after World War II and settled in a Polish-speaking neighborhood on Chicago's near-northwest side. On October 5, 1960, Mrs. Duzynski discovered $380.00 in cash missing from her apartment. The only other person with a key to the apartment being the janitor, she concluded that he took the money, accused him of theft, and demanded that he return the money. The janitor called the police, and when they arrived told them that Mr. and Mrs. Duzynski were "crazy." The police handcuffed the Duzynskis and took them to the Cook County Mental Health Clinic, where they were pronounced mentally ill. They were then promptly transferred to the Chicago State Hospital. During World War II, Mr. Duzynski had been imprisoned in a Nazi concentration camp. Then he knew why he was confined; now he did not. Six weeks passed, and the Duzynskis were still languishing in the Chicago State Hospital without any explanation of their status or hope of getting out. In desperation, Mr. Duzynski hanged himself. His death led to adverse publicity about commitment procedures in Illinois and the release of his wife.[3] However, Mrs. Duzynski's subsequent suit for compensation was unsuccessful.[4] Moreover, since the Duzynskis' commitment was "proper," in the sense that they had been diagnosed as "mentally ill" before hospitalization, the "reforms" generated by their case have not significantly altered the situation of individuals accused of mental illness.*

Consider how differently Mr. Duzynski would have been treated had he been an accused criminal instead of an accused mental patient: he would have been charged with a specific offense; arraigned promptly before a judge; allowed to post bond and go free on bail pending the outcome of his trial; tried before a jury of his peers; and, if found guilty, sentenced, in accordance with law, to the payment of a fine or to imprisonment for a definite term. In short, the alleged mental patient, as against the alleged criminal, is deprived of the following procedural safeguards provided by the Constitution: the right to be secure in his person, house, papers, and effects and against "unreasonable searches and seizures" (Fifth Amendment); the right to "a speedy and public trial, by an impartial jury," to be "informed of the nature and cause of the accusation; to be confronted with the witnesses against him; to have compulsory process for obtaining witnesses in his favor; and to have the Assistance of Counsel for his defense" (Sixth Amendment); the protection from "excessive bail" and "cruel and unusual punishment" (Eighth Amendment); and from deprivation of "life, liberty, or property, without due process of law" (Fourteenth Amendment).[5]

The protections of individual rights accorded the offender are thus abrogated for the insane (as they had been until recently for the juvenile), ostensibly to help him receive the treatment he needs. In effect, this leads to stripping him of any means of self-protection. Like the witch, the person accused of mental illness also cannot

---

* For a superb parody of the commitment procedure, see James Thurber, A Unicorn in the Garden, in James Thurber, *The Thurber Carnival*, pp. 268–269. The story, told by Thurber in less than five hundred words, is this:

One morning, a man announces to his wife that there is a unicorn in the garden. She replies: "You are a booby, and I am going to have you put in the booby-hatch." The husband, "Who had never liked the words 'booby' and 'booby-hatch,' [says] 'We'll see about that.'" The wife sends for the police and the psychiatrist. They arrive. She tells them her story. "'Did you tell your wife you saw a unicorn?'" they ask the husband. "'Of course not,' said the husband. 'The unicorn is a mythical beast.' 'That's all I wanted to know,' said the psychiatrist. . . . So they took her away, cursing and screaming, and shut her up in an institution. The husband lived happily ever after."

retain his own agents. If the state wishes to brand him insane, his relatives, lawyers, and psychiatrists will usually be helpless to intervene, and may themselves be subject to psychiatric harassment.[6] Nor is the person suspected of mental illness able to testify in his own behalf. Whatever evidence of his own sanity he may present will be discredited by the cloud of suspicion under which he stands. At the same time, although his testimony in his own favor is dismissed as unreliable, evidence given by him about his own mental disturbance is regarded as incontestable proof of insanity. In short, just as the accused witch could not, so the accused mental patient cannot, with his own arguments, convince his judges of his innocence—but only of his heresy or mental illness. "The major result of our study," writes Scheff, who studied the functioning of urban courts in processing petitions for commitment, "was the conclusion that in three of the four metropolitan courts, the civil procedures for hospitalizing and committing the mentally ill had no serious investigatory purpose, but were ceremonial in character. . . . Hospitalization and treatment appeared to be virtually automatic after the patient had been brought to the attention of the courts."[7]

Though most psychiatrists and a great many jurists object to this kind of interpretation of our mental hygiene laws, and instead maintain that such departures from the procedures used in criminal prosecutions serve the interests of the patient rather than of the State—it is obvious that these same methods made the Inquisition as irresistible as it was. "The right to abrogate any laws which impeded the freest exercise of the powers of the Inquisition," writes Lea, "was likewise arrogated on both sides of the Alps . . . This rendered the Inquisition virtually supreme in all lands, and it became an accepted maxim of law that all statutes interfering with the free action of the Inquisition were void, and those who enacted them were to be punished."[8] A more compelling similarity than between the sociolegal role of the Inquisition and that of contemporary Institutional Psychiatry would be hard to imagine. When Lea says that "In the exercise of this almost limitless authority, inquisitors were practically relieved from all supervision and responsibility,"[9] he utters a statement equally applicable to contemporary institutional psychiatrists.

The main similarity between the work of the inquisitor and that of the contemporary psychiatrist charged with ascertaining a person's sanity lies in the nature of the task. "The duty of the inquisitor," says Lea, "was distinguished from that of the ordinary judge by the fact that the task assigned to him was the impossible one of ascertaining the secret thoughts and opinions of the prisoner. External acts were to him only of value as indications of belief, to be accepted or rejected as he might deem them conclusive or illusory. The crime he sought to suppress by punishment was purely a mental one—acts, however criminal, were beyond his jurisidiction."[10] If we substitute psychiatric for theological terms, we have a description of the work of the contemporary psychopathologist.

In short, the inquisitor was not concerned with overt, antisocial acts; that was a problem for the secular courts. He was interested in heresy, which was a crime against God and the Christian religion, and was therefore defined in theological terms. The institutional psychiatrist is likewise not concerned with overt, antisocial acts; that is a problem for the criminal courts. He is interested in mental illness, which is an offense against the laws of mental health and the psychiatric profession, and is therefore defined in medical terms. Mental illness is the pivotal concept of institutional psychiatry, just as heresy was of inquisitorial theology.[11]

That both heresy and mental illness are thought-crimes, rather than act-crimes, helps to explain the repellent methods used to detect them. "We cannot wonder," remarks Lea with a rare note of sarcasm, "that he [the inquisitor] speedily emancipated himself from the trammels of recognized judicial procedure which . . . would have rendered his labors futile."[12] As a result, "The heretic, whether acknowledged or suspected, had no rights . . . there was no hesitation in employing whatever means were readiest to save and advance the faith."[13]

If we substitute psychiatric for religious terms, Lea's statement becomes a description of the legal situation of the hospitalized mental patient: "The mentally ill, whether diagnosed or suspected, has no rights. . . . there is no hesitation in employing whatever means are readiest to save his mental health and advance the faith in psychiatric medicine." "It is a feature of some illnesses," writes Francis J. Braceland, clinical professor of psychiatry at Yale University and a former president of the American Psychiatric Association, "that people do not have insight into the fact that they are sick. In short, sometimes it is necessary to protect them for a while from themselves. . . . If a man brings his daughter to me from California because she is in manifest danger of falling into vice or in some way disgracing herself, he doesn't expect me to let her loose in my home town for that same thing to happen."[14]

Since heresy was neither a social act nor a biological condition but a state of mind, the crime of witchcraft could never have been established if recognized judicial procedure had been followed. The vexing problems of proof were overcome by adopting what has since become known as the inquisitorial method of prosecution, colloquially called "witch-hunting." Lea describes the procedure as follows:

Of the three forms of criminal actions, accusation, denunciation, and inquisition, the latter necessarily became, in place of an exception, the invariable rule, and at the same time it was stripped of the safeguards by which its dangerous tendencies had been in some degree neutralized. If a formal accuser presented himself, the inquisitor was instructed to discourage him by pointing out the dangers of the *talio* to which he was exposed by inscribing himself; and by general consent this form of action was rejected in consequence of its being "litigious"—that is, because it afforded the accused some opportunities of defense. . . . The action by denunciation was less objectionable, because in it the inquisitor acted *ex officio*; but it was unusual, and the inquisitorial process at an early period became substantially the only one followed.[15]

Although more than five-hundred years old, the inquisitorial process did not really come into its own until the twentieth century. The fundamental difference between the accusatorial and inquisitorial procedures lies in the methods available to one person or institution (often the State), to impose a debased and degraded social role on another person (often the member of a minority group). The accusatorial process provides elaborate safeguards to the individual, protecting him from being placed in an ascribed role, such as criminal; in general, there must first be proof that he engaged in acts prohibited by law. The inquisitorial process removes such protection from the individual, and gives the prosecution unlimited power to cast the accused into the appropriate ascribed role, such as enemy of the state or mentally ill. In totalitarian states, the processes of criminal law enforcement are typically inquisitorial;

and so are the mental health laws and practices in nontotalitarian states.

In the evolution from religious (inquisitorial) to medical (psychiatric) methods of social control, there was an intermediate step consisting of the ostensibly therapeutic use of the powers of the king as benevolent despot or ruler: exemplified by the French *lettre de cachet,* this transitional—royal—form of social control was simultaneously religious and secular, magical and scientific. Inasmuch as the *lettre de cachet* is the immediate historical precursor of the contemporary petition for commitment, some comments about it are in order here.

A *lettre de cachet* (literally a letter bearing a seal) was a document bearing the seal of the king or of one of his officers, authorizing imprisonment without trial of the person or persons named in it. The uses of *lettres de cachet,* which enjoyed their greatest popularity from the beginning of the fifteenth to the end of the eighteenth centuries, are summarized in the *Encyclopaedia Britannica* as follows:

While serving the government as a silent weapon against political adversaries or dangerous writers, and as a means of punishing culprits of high birth without the scandal of a trial, the *lettres de cachet* had other uses. They were employed by the police in dealing with prostitutes, and on their authority lunatics were shut up. They were also often used by heads of families as a means of correction, e.g., for protecting the family honor from the disorderly or criminal conduct of sons; wives, too, used them to curb the profligacy of husbands, and vice versa.[16]

This statement constitutes an accurate description of the present-day uses of commitment petitions as well.

Social control by means of the *lettre de cachet* thus constitutes a transitional stage between control by means of the old, religious Inquisition and the new, psychiatric one. The procedures of all three institutions rest on the same principles of paternalism; only the identity of the father, in whose name control is exercised, differs. In the case of the Inquisition, it is the Holy Father, the Pope; in that of the *lettre de cachet,* it is the National Father, the King; and in that of Institutional Psychiatry, it is the Scientific Father, the Physician.

"In theory," explains Barrows Dunham, "the French king was father of the French family, and, on patriarchal principles, his will was absolute. Other parents could appeal to him, and he would put refractory children in the Bastille."[17] They could put their children —as did a woman her forty-year-old daughter—in the Salpêtrière as well![18] In the eighteenth century, Dunham continues, when "the times remained uneasy . . . the government began curbing intellectuals by frequent use of *lettres de cachet*. By such custom, it came to pass that, on the twenty-third of July, 1749, Louis XV, at Compiègne, signed a *lettre de cachet* which ran as follows: 'M. le Marquis du Châtelet: This letter instructs you to receive into my Chateau of Vincennes le Sieur Diderot [Denis Diderot, the French encyclopedist and philosopher] and to hold him there until some new order on my part. Further, I pray that God may have you, M. le Marquis du Châtelet, in his holy keeping,' "[19] Dunham comments: "Charming, this piety with which imprisonment was conferred."[20] This hypocritical religious piety of the *lettre de cachet* has been replaced by the hypocritical medical piety of the commitment paper.[21]

Today, in many of our states, physicians have the power to imprison a person in a mental hospital (in actuality, a jail) for as long as fifteen days *without* a court order; and for life with a court order, which, as we shall presently see, it is a mere formality to secure.[22] Ironically, this medicalization of commitment, whereby a physician can incarcerate a person in a mental institution without any recourse to the courts, is considered a "liberalization" of mental hospital procedures. The official position of the American Psychiatric Association on commitment, submitted to the Senate committee investigating the rights of mental patients in 1961 by Francis J. Braceland, M.D., and Jack R. Ewalt, M.D., both former presidents of the Association, may be noted here. "In recent decades," they stated, ". . . the new medical science of psychiatry, fighting an uphill battle, has sufficiently advanced that the public has become more sympathetic with the view that accepts mental illness as an illness. . . . In general, psychiatrists favor a simple commitment procedure entailing an application to the hospital by a close relative or a friend, and a certification by two qualified physicians that they have examined the subject and found him to be mentally ill."[23] The American Psychiatric Association thus favors commitment by means of medical *lettres de cachet*.

Furthermore, just as the inquisitor assumed that the person accused of witchcraft was a heretic, so the institutional psychiatrist
assumes that the person accused of mental illness is a mental patient.
These presumptions have been, and continue to be, justified by the
allegedly therapeutic aims of the respective interventions: saving
the soul of the heretic, and protecting and promoting the mental
health of the patient. Thomas J. Scheff investigated the assumptions of psychiatrists regarding persons processed for commitment,
and his findings confirm the foregoing contentions. After reviewing
existing studies on commitment, he noted that they "suggest that
there is a presumption of illness by mental health officials."[24] For
example, in two mental hospitals studied over a period of three
months, David Mechanic "never observed a case where the psychiatrist advised the patient that he did not need treatment. Rather,
all persons who appeared at the hospital were absorbed into the
patient population regardless of their ability to function adequately
outside the hospital."[25] Other studies amplify this impression. It is
"a fairly general understanding among mental health workers,"
Scheff remarks, "that state mental hospitals in the United States
accept all comers."[26]

Scheff observed the psychiatric screening procedures in four courts
in a Midwestern state with the largest volume of mental cases in the
state. He found that "interviews ranged in length from 5 minutes
to 17 minutes, with the mean time being 10.2 minutes. Most of the
examiners were hurried."[27] He concluded that "the behavior or
'condition' of the person alleged to be mentally ill is not usually an
important factor in the decision of officials to retain or release new
patients from the mental hospital. The marginal nature of the
majority of the cases, the peremptoriness and inadequacy of most
of the examinations, when considered in the light of the fact that
virtually every patient is recommended for commitment, would
appear to demonstrate this proposition."[28]

The psychiatrist has such discretionary powers because, like the
inquisitor before him, he is considered not a prosecutor or punisher,
but a healer or well-doer. The concept of the inquisitor as spiritual
healer followed, of course, inevitably from that of witchcraft as
spiritual deviation—just as the concept of the institutional psychiatrist as medical healer follows from that of madness as medical

deviation. The danger of so regarding social deviation and control was clear to students of the Inquisition, as Lea's comments show:

At best the inquisitorial process was a dangerous one in its conjunction of prosecutor with judge, . . . The danger was doubled when the prosecuting judge was an earnest zealot bent on upholding the faith and predetermined on seeing in every prisoner before him a heretic to be convicted at any cost; nor was the danger lessened when he was merely rapacious and eager for fines and confiscations. Yet the theory of the Church was that the inquisitor was an impartial spiritual father whose functions in the salvation of souls should be fettered by no rules.[29]

The identical dangers are inherent in the methods of Institutional Psychiatry. The pious inquisitor would undoubtedly have been enraged at the suggestion that he was the heretic's foe, not his friend. Likewise, the institutional psychiatrist angrily rejects the idea that he is the involuntary patient's adversary, not his therapist. In denying this interpretation, the inquisitor would have countered with the assertion that his ministrations—including burning the victim at the stake—were aimed at saving the heretic's soul from eternal damnation; while the psychiatrist replies that his efforts—including lifelong imprisonment, electric convulsions, and lobotomy—are aimed at protecting and promoting the patient's mental health. The following statements by psychiatric authorities are illustrative.

We would like our hospitals . . . to be looked upon as treatment centers for sick people, and we want to be, of course, considered as doctors and not jailers. . . . It is well known that there are legal safeguards against what is commonly called railroading people into mental hospitals, and we contend that people are well protected in all of the States. I have never in 30 years of constant living with this problem seen anyone whom I thought was being railroaded. . . . The opposite is true, however. People are railroaded out of mental hospitals before they should be, because these institutions are so crowded . . .[30]

. . . I wish to point out that the basic purpose [of commitment] is to make sure that sick human beings get the care that is appropriate to their needs . . .[31]

We, as doctors, want our psychiatric hospitals . . . to be looked upon as treatment centers for sick people in the same sense that general hospitals are so viewed.[32]

If psychiatrists really wanted these things, all they would have to do is to unlock the doors of mental hospitals, abolish commitment, and treat only those persons who, like in nonpsychiatric hospitals, want to be treated. This is exactly what I have been advocating for the past fifteen years.[33]

Lea describes the social function of the Inquisition thus: "The object of the Inquisition is the destruction of heresy. Heresy cannot be destroyed unless heretics are destroyed. . . . [T]his is effected in two ways, viz., when they are converted to the true Catholic faith, or when, on being abandoned to the secular arm, they are corporally burned."[34] This statement is readily converted into a description of the social function of the Mental Health Movement: "The object of Psychiatry is the eradication of mental illness. Mental illness cannot be eradicated unless the mentally ill are eradicated. . . . [T]his is effected in two ways, viz., when they are restored to mental health, or when, on being confined in state mental hospitals, they prove to be incurably sick and are therefore removed from contact with healthy society."

Perhaps more than anything else, the claim of a helping role by the prosecutor and the judge made the witch trial a vicious affair. "The accused was," Lea tells us, "prejudged. He was assumed to be guilty, or he would not have been put on trial, and virtually his only mode of escape was by confessing the charges made against him, abjuring heresy, and accepting whatever punishment might be imposed on him in the shape of penance. Persistent denial of guilt and assertion of orthodoxy . . . rendered him an impenitent, obstinate heretic, to be abandoned to the secular arm and consigned to the stake."[35]

The assumption of a therapeutic posture by the institutional psychiatrist leads to the same heartless consequences. Like the accused heretic, the accused mental patient commits the most deadly sin when he denies his illness and insists that his deviant state is healthy. Accordingly, the most denigrating diagnostic labels of psychiatry are reserved for those individuals who, although declared insane by the experts, and confined in madhouses, stubbornly persist in claiming to be sane. They are said to be "completely lacking in insight," or described as "having broken with reality," and are usually diagnosed as "paranoid" or "schizophrenic." The Spanish inquisitors also had a demeaning name for such persons: they called them *"negativos."* "The *negativo,*" Lea explains, "who persistently denied his guilt, in the face of competent testimony, was universally held to be a pertinacious impenitent heretic, for whom there was no alternative save burning alive, although . . . he might protest a thousand times that he was a Catholic and wished to live and die in the faith. This was the inevitable logic of the situation. . . ."[36]

One of the important differences between a person accused of crime and one accused of mental illness is that the former is often allowed bail, whereas the latter never is. This distinction too may be found in the Inquisition. The question of bail for suspected heretics was considered by the fifteenth-century inquisitors and was decided, according to Lea, as follows: "If one is caught in heresy, by his own confession, and is impenitent, he is to be delivered to the secular arm and to be put to death; if penitent, he is to be thrust in prison for life, and therefore is not to be let loose on bail; if he denies, and is legitimately convicted by witnesses, he is, as an impenitent, to be delivered to the secular court to be executed."[37]

In the same way, in procedures for mental illness bail is not allowed. If the accused admits mental illness, he is hospitalized, often for life; if he denies it and is found to be sick in a sanity hearing conforming to all the requirements of "due process," he is committed to a mental hospital and treated against his will by any means necessary until he "gains insight into his condition."

It cannot be emphasized too much that the idea of a therapeutic penology, hailed today as a fresh, humanitarian invention, attributable to the "scientific discoveries" of a "dynamic psychiatry," is neither novel nor psychiatric in origin. Instead, it is a characteristic feature of the Inquisition, and of the religious ideas and zeal which animated it. "In theory," says Lea, "the object of the Inquisition was the saving of souls. . . . The penalties inflicted on the repentant were not punishment but penance, and he was not a convict but a penitent; whatever statement he made during his trial, even in obstinately denying the charges, was a confession, and the penal prison to which he was consigned was a *casa de penitencia* or *de misericordia*. Even denunciations and the evidence of witnesses for the defense were sometimes called confessions."[38]

This therapeutic mythology and rhetoric was carried over into the penal or sentencing functions of the Inquisition, which, explains Lea, "were based upon a fiction which must be comprehended in order rightly to appreciate much of its action. Theoretically it had no power to inflict punishment. . . . Its sentences, therefore, were not, like those of an earthly judge, the retaliation of society on the wrong-doer, or deterrent examples to prevent the spread of crime; they were simply imposed for the benefit of the erring soul, to wash away its sin. The inquisitors themselves habitually speak of their ministrations in this sense. When they condemned a poor wretch to lifelong imprisonment, the formula in use, after the procedure of the Holy Office had become systematized, was a simple injunction on him *to betake himself to the jail* and confine himself there, performing penance on bread and water, with a warning that he was not to leave it under pain of excommunication, and of being regarded as a perjured and impenitent heretic. If he broke jail and escaped, the requisition for his recapture under a foreign jurisdiction describes him, with a singular lack of humor, *as one insanely led to reject the salutary medicine offered for his cure* and to spurn the wine and oil which were soothing his wounds."[39] (Italics added.)

Mental patients are confined and treated against their will for the same reasons and in the same ways. "This is the only court," intones a judge sitting in a Chicago court conducting commitment hearings, "where the defendant always wins. If he is released, it means he is well. If he is committed, it is for his own good."[40] Mental health workers now maintain, just as those assisting the Inquisition maintained formerly, that everything done to the victim is for his own good. This is what makes commitment procedures for prepatients and habeas corpus hearings for inpatients the awful mockeries they are. The following judicial decision is illustrative.

In an effort to gain his freedom, Stanley Prochaska, a patient confined against his will in the Iowa State Mental Hospital, petitioned for a writ of habeas corpus, charging that he had been deprived of due process of law because counsel appearing on his behalf at his sanity hearing did not consult with him. The Supreme Court of Iowa affirmed the decision of the trial court, dismissing plaintiff's suit. "It must be kept in mind," said the Court, "that

Appellant is not charged with a crime and is not so incarcerated. He is being restrained of his liberty in that he is not free to come and go at will but such restraint is not in the way of punishment, but for his own protection and welfare as well as for the benefit of society. Such loss of liberty is not such liberty as is within the meaning of the constitutional provision that 'no person shall be deprived of life, liberty or property without due process of law.' "[41]

Once this therapeutic view—whether of the Inquisition or of Institutional Psychiatry—is accepted, everything else follows logically. For example, Lea notes that "By a legal fiction, the inquisitor was supposed to look at both sides of the case and to take care of the defense as well as of the prosecution."[42] By the same legal fiction, the state hospital psychiatrist is supposed to look at both sides of the case and protect the community as well as the mental patient. Thus on the one hand, psychiatrists plead, as we saw earlier, that they want to be considered doctors, not jailers; on the other, they proudly assert that their duty is to protect society. "Tomorrow's psychiatrist will be, as is his counterpart today, one of the gatekeepers of the community," declares Robert H. Felix, dean of the St. Louis University Medical School and former director of the National Institute of Mental Health.[43]

We need not dwell here on the disastrous consequences of the widespread and unopposed practices of the inquisitors. It should suffice to re-emphasize that by combating witchcraft, the inquisitors actually created it. "The continuous teachings of the Church," observes Lea, "led its best men to regard no act as more self-evidently just than the burning of the heretic, and no heresy less defensible than a demand for toleration. . . . The fact is that the Church not only defined the guilt and forced its punishment, but created the crime itself."[44] The same, of course, may be said for Institutional Psychiatry.[45]

Finally, there is another similarity between heresy and mental illness, and also a difference. Once a person was cast into the role of heretic, the record of his deviance left a permanent mark on him. "[T]he inquisitorial sentence . . . always ended with a reservation of power to modify, to mitigate, to increase, and reimpose at discretion. . . . The inquisitor, however, had no power to grant absolute pardons, which was reserved exclusively to the pope."[46]

In the same way, once a person is cast into the role of mental patient, there is a permanent record of his deviance. Like the inquisitor, the psychiatrist can "sentence" a person to mental illness, but cannot wipe out the stigma he himself has imposed. In psychiatry, moreover, there is no pope to grant absolute pardon from a publicly affirmed diagnosis of mental illness.

4

THE DEFENSE OF
THE DOMINANT ETHIC

> The truth. No; by nature man is more afraid of the
> truth than of death—and this is perfectly natural:
> for the truth is even more repugnant than death
> to man's natural being. What wonder, then, that
> he is so afraid of it? . . . For man is a social animal—
> only in the herd is he happy. It is all one to him
> whether it is the profoundest nonsense or the
> greatest villainy—he feels completely at ease with
> it, so long as it is the view of the herd, or the
> action of the herd, and he is able to join the herd.
> —*Sören Kierkegaard*[1]

In the preceding chapters, we have examined the workings of the
Inquisition and of Institutional Psychiatry and have noted the similarities between them. However, dwelling on the details of the
inquisitor-witch and alienist-madman relationships, as we have
done, carries with it the usual hazard of focusing on detail: the
better one sees the trees, the more blinded one becomes to the forest.
The brutal oppression of the heretic by the priest and of the mental patient by the psychiatrist are, to be sure, important. They
illustrate some of the ways man's will to power, his urge to dominate
and degrade his fellow man, his greed for fame and fortune are
exercised in different ages. These are the trees without which there
can be no forests. But the forests—that is, the Inquisition and In-

stitutional Psychiatry—fulfill important social functions of their own.

The conduct of a society's business, as that of an individual's, may be likened to playing a game. The religions, laws, and mores of society constitute the rules by which people must play—or else they will be penalized, one way or another. Obviously, the simpler the games and the fewer in number, the easier it is to play them. This is why open societies and the freedoms they offer represent an onerous burden to many people. As individuals find it difficult and taxing to play more than a single game, or at most a few, at any one time, so societies find it difficult and taxing to tolerate the existence of a plurality of games, each competing for the attention and loyalty of the citizens. Every group—and this includes societies —is organized and held together by a few ideas, values, and practices which cannot be questioned or challenged without causing its disruption, or at least a fear of its disruption. This is why independent thought often undermines group solidarity, and group solidarity often inhibits independent thought. "We belong to a group," says Karl Mannheim, "not only because we are born into it, not merely because we profess to belong to it, nor finally because we give it our loyalty and allegiance, but primarily because we see the world and certain things in the world the way it does . . ."[2] To see the world differently than our group does thus threatens us with solitude; and to say that we see it differently, threatens us with ostracism. Hypocrisy, then, is the homage intellect pays to custom.

My thesis in this chapter is that the social function of the Inquisition and of Institutional Psychiatry lies in the service each renders its society: both provide an intellectually meaningful, morally uplifting, and socially well-organized system for the ritualized affirmation of the benevolence, glory, and power of society's dominant ethic. From without, or to the critical observer, these institutions might appear harsh and oppressive; but from within, or to the true believer, they are beautiful and merciful, flattering at once the masses and their masters. This is the secret of their success.

The Inquisition and Institutional Psychiatry thus fulfill the same sort of function as has been attributed to modern totalitarian movements: Each tranquilizes the massive anxieties mobilized by what is generally experienced as an excess of choices and a lack of worthwhile causes and trustworthy leaders.* What these seemingly diverse "therapeutic" movements have in common not only with one another but also with such modern totalitarian movements as National Socialism and Communism, is that each seeks to protect the integrity of an excessively heterogenous and pluralistic society and its dominant ethic. To accomplish this end, each represses certain individual and moral interests, and, in general, sacrifices the "one" for the "many," the "I" for the "we"; finally, to simplify the conceptual problem it faces, and to strengthen group cohesion, each channels—by systematic propaganda accompanied by the use of a brutal show of force—enmity toward a symbolic offender to whom the impending disintegration of the social order is attributed.[3]

The Inquisition, as we have seen, fulfilled this function by defining as heretics or witches those who rejected, or were alleged to oppose, the dominant ethic. The concept of witch, denoting alliance with the Devil rather than with God, thus served Catholic and Protestant societies equally well; each could, and did, define the other as the prototype of anti-Christ. Similarly, the concept of mental illness, denoting a state of disease rather than of health, serves Capitalist and Communist societies equally well (so long as they all adhere to a "scientific" view of human life); each can, and does, define the other as a paradigm of mental disease.

The central purpose of the Inquisition, as its name implies, was *inquisitio*—that is, inquiry—into heresy. In principle, heresy was always a serious crime in ecclesiastic law. When Christianity became the state church in the Roman Empire, Robbins reminds us, "the new religion extended the intolerance to which hitherto it had been subject. By A.D. 430, the civil code was ordering death for heresy . . ."[4] Such laws, however, were not enforced until some seven centuries later (for reasons we have noted earlier). The first formal inquisition was ordered by Pope Lucius III, in 1184: he directed bishops to make systematic inquiry into deviation from the official teaching of the Church. From its inception, then, the primary aim of the Inquisition was to insure adherence to a uniformity of religious belief and opinion. The *auto-da-fé* (literally, an act or pro-

---

* "It is interesting to notice that there were three peaks in the persecution of witchcraft. Each of them was at a period when new ideas were threatening the authoritarian framework of the Church, and there had been latitude of faith with the threat of disintegration." (Pennethorne Hughes, *Witchcraft*, p. 163.)

fession of faith) was the liturgy of this affirmation. It was a ceremonial occasion, held in the largest square of the city, attended by
clerical and secular officials and large numbers of people, at which
the accused—who had already been tried and convicted—would
publicly repent; would abjure Satan and embrace God; and would
then (usually) be burned. Every *auto-da-fé,* Lea tells us, was an
affair of "impressive solemnity which [would] strike terror on the
heretic and comfort the hearts of the faithful."[5] Great care was
taken not to produce any heretics at these ceremonies about whose
penitence there remained any doubt, lest they create a scandal by
denial.[6] In addition, "care was enjoined not to permit them to
address the people, lest sympathy should be aroused by their assertions."[7]

The ceremony began with pomp and circumstance, and was followed by sermon and prayer. Then "the oath of obedience was
administered to the representatives of the civil power, and a solemn
decree of excommunication was fulminated against all who should
in any way impede the operations of the Holy Office."[8] Actors and
audience now approached the climax of the dramatic enactment:
". . . the notary commenced reading the confessions one by one in
the vulgar tongue, and as each was finished the culprit asked if he
acknowledged it to be true . . . On his replying in the affirmative, he
was asked whether he would repent, or lose body and soul by per-
severing in heresy; and on his expressing a desire to abjure, the
form of abjuration was read and he repeated it, sentence by sentence.
Then the inquisitor absolved him from the *ipso facto* excommunication which he had incurred by heresy, and promised him mercy
if he behaved well under the sentence about to be imposed. The
sentence followed, and thus the penitents were brought forward
successively, commencing with the least guilty . . . Those who were
to be 'relaxed' or abandoned to the secular arm [to be burned] were
reserved to the last. . . ."[9]

Here, then, was a ceremony to symbolize the power and mercy of
the Grand Inquisitor and his all-powerful Church. The great sin
was defined: deviation from prescribed religious belief or opinion.
The deviant was forgiven and returned to the fold: he was converted
to the true faith. And the culprit was mercifully punished: he was
burned at the stake, having been strangled before being incinerated.
(The unrepentent heretic was burned alive.)

"We can readily picture to ourselves," Lea comments, "the effect produced on the popular mind by these awful celebrations, when, at the bidding of the Inquisition, all that was great and powerful in the land was called together humbly to take the oath of obedience and witness its exercise of the highest expression of human authority, regulating the destinies of fellow-creatures here and hereafter . . . The faith which could thus vindicate itself might certainly inspire the respect of fear if not the attraction of love."[10]

If anyone still entertained doubt about the existence or reality of a Christian God, and his great adversary, Satan, this ceremony must have sufficed to dispel it. The reality of the Devil and his "familiars" (the witches) was driven home by the ritualized destruction of the heretic. The transcendent significance of this ceremony is attested to by the following occurrence, presumably not an isolated one, reported by Huizinga: "The body of a heretic preacher of the sect of the Turpulins, who died in prison, before sentence was passed, was preserved in lime for a fortnight, that it might be burned at the same time with a living heretical woman."[11]

"A mentality, dominated like that of the declining Middle Ages by a lively imagination, by naive idealism, and by strong feeling," Huizinga comments, "easily believes in the reality of every concept which presents itself to the mind. When once an idea has received a name and form, its truth is presumed."[12] This mentality is, of course, not confined to the declining Middle Ages.

In the rhetoric of psychiatry, the basic aim of the Inquisition was to bring about "behavior change" in the heretic. In this respect, the inquisitors were superlatively successful: virtually all their subjects acquired "insight" and changed their personalities in the manner required. Kamen cites the inquisitorial therapy of a Judaizer (the name given to Jewish converts to Christianity who practiced their Jewish faith in secret), at an *auto* held in Spain in 1719. "We enter the picture," Kamen writes, "at the stage where the victim is already on the stake and a lighted torch is passed before his face to warn him of what awaits him if he does not repent. Around the Judaizer are a number of religious who 'pressed the criminal with greater anxiety and zeal to convert himself. With perfect serenity he said, "I will convert myself to the faith of Jesus Christ," words which he had not been heard to utter until then. This overjoyed all the religious who began to embrace him with tenderness and gave infinite thanks to God for having opened to them a door for his conversion. . . .' "[13] The Judaizer was then strangled and burned.

I have already suggested, and will presently document in greater detail, how the belief in witchcraft gave way to the belief in mental illness; and how the practices of the inquisitors were superseded by those of the institutional psychiatrists. The ritual sacrifice of the heretic, the *auto-da-fé,* was thus supplemented by the ritual sacrifice of the madman, the commitment of the insane.

The pomp and circumstances of the psychiatric *auto-da-fé* are, of course, no longer displayed in the city square; as befits a modern, secular society, they have been removed to the courtroom. Although the ceremony is conducted in relative privacy, knowledge of its existence is as common as was that of the burning of heretics. Indeed, the widespread publicity about the hearings and rehearings accorded to alleged mental patients to determine their sanity only serves to further authenticate the mental healthiness of the judges and the mental disability of those declared insane.

The mental patient's entry into and exit from the mental hospital are the climactic moments in this modern, pseudoscientific ritual. The patient enters as heretic and leaves as convert. Or he never leaves. Goffman puts it this way: "The key view of the patient is: were he 'himself' he would voluntarily seek psychiatric treatment and voluntarily submit to it, and, when ready for discharge, he will avow that his real self was all along being treated as it really wanted to be treated."[14]

In being authorized by society so to dispose over human destinies, the commitment proceeding—like the *auto-da-fé,* as Lea noted—symbolizes the "exercise of the highest expression of human authority, regulating the destinies of fellow creatures . . ." Who else exercises such vast discretionary powers over his fellow man as the contemporary psychiatrist? ". . . the psychiatric role is unique among servers, no other being accorded such power," observes Goffman.[15] Policeman and judge are constrained by the Rule of Law. They can punish only what the law forbids. Mental hygiene laws, like the orders of the Dominican inquisitors, recognize no such bounds.* Such awesome powers could not, and cannot, exist unless

---

* Institutional psychiatrists never speak or write about their power; they prefer to speak and write about their "responsibility" to "help" or "treat" "sick patients."

their legitimacy is widely respected and supported. Such, indeed, was the case with the Inquisition: to oppose it was tantamount to opposing the Church, Jesus, and God. In a religious society, who can be against God? Only a heretic! The same kind of logic and legitimacy supports Institutional Psychiatry: to oppose it is tantamount to opposing medical science, the physician, and nature. In a scientific society, who can be against health? Only a madman!

From this perspective, the classic, nineteenth-century view about the warfare between theology and science[16] appears in a somewhat different light. Intellectuals and scientists, especially of a materialistic and positivistic bent, have preferred to believe that this was a conflict between progress and the status quo—science standing squarely for informing and liberating man, religion for mystifying and oppressing him. Confrontations between Galileo and Bellarmine, between Darwin and his fundamentalist critics, were the leading symbols in this imagery. The traditional psychiatric interpretation of the movement from witchcraft to psychiatry adopts this same self-flattering view. The inquisitors were hateful men, full of irrational religious ideas, who did terrible injury to accused heretics; psychiatrists, in contrast, are loving men, informed by rational scientific ideas, who do great good for committed mental patients. Not only are these images badly out of focus, but, more importantly perhaps, they obscure an insight which modern man has gained at great cost and which he can ill afford to lose: The fundamental conflicts in human life are not between competing ideas, one "true" and the other "false"—but rather between those who hold power and use it to oppress others, and those who are oppressed by power and seek to free themselves of it.

To be sure, men like Galileo and Darwin were opposed by clerical authorities. And so were heretics and witches. But men like Semmelweis and Freud were opposed by clinical authorities. And so are the men and women we treat as involuntary mental patients. This is not surprising. In medieval society, the Church supplied the ideology, the State the power. Today, the Scientific Establishment supplies the ideology, the State the power. Formerly, the inquisitor accused the citizen of witchcraft and proved him to be a witch; he then "relaxed" the witch to the "secular arm"—that is, the State—and he was burned at the stake. Today, the institutional psychiatrist accuses the citizen of mental illness and diagnoses him as psychotic;

he then turns him over to the court—that is, the State—and he is committed to a prison called a mental hospital.

These considerations help us to appreciate the immense usefulness which inquisitorial clerical practices had in the past, and which inquisitorial clinical practices have at present. Each controls and counteracts the drift toward an anomie that seems to be the price which citizens of open and pluralistic societies must pay for their freedoms; and each furnishes a covert, extralegal system of penalties by means of which the ruling classes can maintain their social dominance. A few illustrations of the latter point should suffice here. Whistling could never be made illegal; but a Negro who whistled at a Southern white woman (or was said to have whistled at one) could be lynched. Lynch-law was thus an adjunct to Southern law on the books; it helped whites to keep the Negroes "in their place." So too is Institutional Psychiatry an implementation of the unwritten laws of power-maintenance in a society insufficiently committed to honoring the Rule of Law. Feeling sad cannot very well be made illegal; but a poor woman who is depressed (and refuses to play the role assigned to her in society) can be committed. Commitment-law is thus an adjunct to American law on the books; it helps the rich and well-educated to keep the poor and ill-educated in their place.

These considerations also help us understand why, despite the fact that many of the practices of Institutional Psychiatry are patently fraudulent, coercive, and harmful to "patients," the institution has received the support of all classes, groups, and organizations in our society, including those committed to the protection of civil liberties.* We thus live in a society in which far more people lose their liberty through psychiatric than through penal imprisonment. In 1964, the average daily census was 563,354 in hospitals for

---

* A Louis Harris survey reported in 1967 showed that 47 percent of the interviewees wanted to expand federal aid to mental health clinics, 39 percent wanted to keep aid on its present level, and only 5 percent wanted to reduce it. (*Seattle Times*, Apr. 3, 1967; quoted in James E. Beaver, The "mentally ill" and the law: Sisyphus and Zeus, *Utah Law Rev.*, 1968: 1–71 [Mar.], 1968; p. 2.)

A survey conducted in New York City revealed that "Most (nine out of ten) feel that 'the government should be raising more money for and spending more money on mental health services' "; and that "Five out of six (83 percent) agree that 'even if most patients do not get better there, state mental hospitals are needed because they do a job of protecting the community.' " (Jack Elinson, Elena Padilla, and Marvin E. Perkins, *Public Image of Mental Health Services*, pp. xv, 9.)

mental diseases, and 186,735 in institutions for the mentally retarded; in the same year, the census was 214,356 in federal and state prisons.[17] Ostensibly, some patients are in mental hospitals on a voluntary status; actually, however, all such patients are imprisoned, for even so-called voluntary patients cannot be sure of being allowed to leave at will. As to official figures, even those favorably disposed toward Institutional Psychiatry quote a figure of only 10 percent for psychiatric hospitalizations on a voluntary basis.[18] But in 1961, only 3.5 percent of the patients at St. Elizabeths Hospital in Washington, D.C., were on a voluntary status.[19]

In short, even without counting those persons who are deprived of liberty because of mental retardation, more than twice as many Americans lose their freedom on account of mental illness than on account of crime. This loss of freedom, moreover, cannot be morally justified as either protection for the community or as treatment for the "patient."[20] Nevertheless, the American Civil Liberties Union has not only failed to oppose this practice but, on the contrary, has actively supported it. In his book on the history of the Union, Charles Markmann relates, with what seems to me badly misplaced pride, that toward the end of the Second World War, "The [American Civil Liberties] Union . . . began to draft model statutes for the commitment of the insane. . . . Twenty years after the first Union draft of a model bill for commitments to mental hospitals, Congress enacted for the District of Columbia a law closely following the Union's proposals."[21]

Thus, the Union too accepts unquestioningly the concept of mental illness, whose "treatment," by imprisonment, it then delegates to psychiatrists. The position of the American Civil Liberties Union on civil commitment illustrates how enthusiastically, and how uncritically, all contemporary groups and organizations—clerical and secular, medical and legal, liberal and conservative, those for promoting stricter law enforcement and those for promoting stricter observance of civil liberties—agree on the desirability of civil commitment.

"A person who is involuntarily committed to a mental hospital," declares the Union, "is deprived of his freedom of movement and association and in many communities faces being branded with the stigma of 'insanity.' It is therefore essential that no one be committed without a careful hearing and jury trial which includes all constitutional protections of a jury trial in other types of civil proceedings."[22] The il-logic and il-liberality of this recommendation is shocking: if mental illness is undefined (or if it is what psychiatrists or the masses say it is), then what protection does a jury trial afford? If commitment entails the loss of liberty, why accept the legal hypocrisy that it is a "civil proceeding"? In what other civil proceeding can the losing litigant be incarcerated for life?

"A person, once committed," continues the recommendation of the American Civil Liberties Union, "is entitled to a periodic re-examination by a court . . . with a view to his release, when his condition so permits."[23] Is there a psychiatrist in the country, in the world, who would not claim that he is already doing just this? This, then, amounts to a complete approval of the psychiatric status quo. All that the American Civil Liberties Union asks for is that the courts release the patient when his "condition" permits. Not a word is said about the adversary relationship between the physician upon whose opinion the court bases its decision and the "patient" whose liberty needs defending.*

If the policy on civil commitment of the American Civil Liberties Union is ill conceived, its recommendations for further improvements are nothing less than terrifying: "Anyone hospitalized for mental illness," the statement asserts, "is entitled to medical and psychiatric care, appropriate to his particular case."[24] In making this declaration, the American Civil Liberties Union not only supports commitment on the basis of an undefined concept of mental illness and as a legitimate "medical" function, but also advocates psychiatric "treatment," regardless of whether or not the "patient" consents to it or of how dangerous or destructive such "treatment" might be. Does the American Civil Liberties Union really believe

---

* So-called psychiatric liberalism—in effect, psychiatric totalitarianism—has affected all of the policies of the American Civil Liberties Union bearing on matters of mental health. Thus, despite the clearly strategic—and often patently fraudulent—use of the insanity defense, the Union warmly endorses the adoption of what it calls "liberalized" tests of criminal responsibility. In adopting the new definitions of criminal insanity—in particular that embodied in the Durham Rule and in the proposal of the American Law Institute—the courts are, in the words of the American Civil Liberties Union, "liberalizing the 123-year-old M'Naghten rule in the light of modern psychiatry." (American Civil Liberties Union, *New Dimensions . . . New Challenges: 46th Annual Report* [July 1, 1965–Jan. 1, 1367], p. 35.) By adopting this view, the Union becomes a mouthpiece of the Mental Health Movement.

that involuntary mental hospitalization with involuntary treatment (especially if the treatment consists of electroshock or lobotomy) is preferable to involuntary mental hospitalization without such treatment? But, then, what is an *auto-da-fé* without a stake? Surely, the mental patient must have a right to treatment, just as the heretic must have a right to join his Maker. Truly, commitment ritualizes the legitimacy of involuntary mental hospitalization and, through it, the benevolence of Institutional Psychiatry and the Therapeutic Society it serves.[25]

"At the time of the Spanish Inquisition," observed Maurice Maeterlinck, "the opinion of good sense . . . was certainly that people ought not to burn too large a number of heretics; extreme and unreasonable opinion obviously demanded that they should burn none at all."[26] Today it is the same with involuntary mental hospitalization. The opinion of good sense now is that psychiatrists ought to commit only those mental patients who are "very ill," or "dangerous to themselves or others"; extreme and unreasonable opinion obviously demands that no one should be committed.

5

THE WITCH AS MENTAL PATIENT

> . . . the *Malleus Maleficarum* might with a little
> editing serve as an excellent modern textbook of
> descriptive clinical psychiatry of the fifteenth cen-
> tury, if the word *witch* were substituted by the word
> *patient*, and the devil eliminated.
>
> *—Gregory Zilboorg*[1]

Beginning with the works of such men as Rush[2] and Esquirol,
psychiatry shows an unmistakable tendency to interpret all kinds
of deviant or unusual behavior as mental illness. This tendency
was strongly reinforced by Freud and the psychoanalysts, who, by
focusing on the so-called unconscious determinants of conduct,
tended to interpret even "rational" behavior on the model of the
"irrational." Normal behavior was henceforth explained by reference to abnormal behavior. "Psychiatric research," Freud declares,
". . . cannot help finding worthy of understanding everything that
can be recognized in those illustrious models [of great men], and it
believes there is no one so great as to be disgraced by being subject
to the laws which govern both normal and pathological activity
with equal cogency. . . . Anyone who protests at our so much as
daring to examine him [Leonardo da Vinci] in the light of discoveries gained in the field of pathology is still clinging to prejudices
which we have today rightly abandoned. We no longer think that
health and illness, normal and neurotic people, are to be sharply
distinguished from each other . . ."[3]

Although Freud recognized some of the dangers inherent in the psychopathological interpretation of human behavior, he did not seem to understand the real nature of the problem, for he acted as if a verbal disclaimer would be enough to dispel it. "When psychiatric research, normally content to draw on frailer men for its material," writes Freud in his essay on Leonardo da Vinci, "approaches one who is among the greatest of the human race, it is not doing so for the reasons frequently ascribed to it by laymen. 'To blacken the radiant and drag the sublime into the dust' is no part of its purpose, and there is no satisfaction for it in narrowing the gulf which separates the perfection of the great from the inadequacy of the objects that are its usual concern."[4]

We see Freud remarking here—as if it were a regrettable fact rather than a debatable moral judgment—on ". . . the inadequacy of the objects that are its [psychiatry's] usual concern." He does not see the value judgment, and therefore cannot question it. He is satisfied, instead, with claiming that "We must expressly insist that we have never reckoned Leonardo as a neurotic or a 'nerve case,' as the awkward phrase goes."[5] While Freud does not wish to denigrate Leonardo da Vinci as a "nerve case," he evidently has no objection if others, less gifted and famous, are so degraded.

Perhaps unintentionally and unwittingly, the new vocabulary of psychoanalysis was thus combined with the traditional vocabulary of psychiatry, generating a rhetoric of rejection of hitherto unparalleled popularity and power.* The result was that everyone's conduct—living or dead, primitive or modern, famous or infamous—became a fit subject for the psychopathologist's scrutiny, explanation, and stigmatization.

To be sure, by adopting this approach, psychoanalysts threw fresh light on certain important similarities between dreams and mental symptoms, the behavior of primitive man and his civilized descendant, myth and madness. In these ways, the psychopathological perspective enriched and extended our understanding of human nature and personal conduct. There was, however, a serious

---

* Although Freud's "therapeutic" methods differed from those of his colleagues, his enthusiastic endorsement and use of a psychiatric vocabulary for denigrating people place him in the mainstream of psychiatric thought: By reclassifying witches as neurotics, he helped to replace theological by psychiatric methods of invalidating human beings. The result—which is contemporary history—is a justificatory rhetoric legitimizing man's inhumanity to man not by appeals to God but by appeals to Health.

danger in this approach, which soon manifested itself. Because the observers and interpreters were psychiatrists, and because they were impressed by a need to make psychopathological diagnoses, all kinds of human behaviors tended to be perceived and described as manifestations of mental illness; and various personalities, historical and living, tended to be seen and diagnosed as mentally sick individuals. The view that witches were mentally ill persons is an integral part of this psychiatric perspective.

The possibility that some persons accused of witchcraft were "mentally ill" was entertained already during the witch-hunts, notably by Johann Weyer. In his dedication of *De Praestigiis* to Duke William of Cleves, Weyer writes: "To you, Prince, I dedicate the fruit of my thought . . . none so agrees with my own [views on witchcraft] as does yours, that witches can harm no one through the most malicious will or the ugliest exorcism, that rather their imagination—inflamed by demons in a way not understandable to us—and the torture of melancholy makes them only fancy that they have caused all sorts of evil."[6]

Is it a coincidence that the suggestion that witches are mentally deranged comes from a physician opposed to their persecution? Or is this hypothesis itself a weapon in the struggle against the witch-hunts? The evidence strongly suggests that it is the latter: that, in other words, madness is an excuse for a wrongdoing (witchcraft), put forth by an authority (Weyer) on behalf of persecuted people (witches), to mitigate their suffering at the hands of oppressors (inquisitors) deaf to all pleas but this one (insanity).[7] Many contemporary psychiatrists openly profess this aim. Instead of protesting against the death penalty itself, they promote the concept of insanity as a "humanitarian" protection for defendants who, without the insanity defense, might be put to death.[8]

This ostensibly lofty aspiration of saving the defendant from execution was the motive behind the important M'Naghten decision, in 1843. Known as the M'Naghten rule, this decision has ever since provided the medicolegal basis for the insanity plea, the insanity defense, and the insanity verdict.[9] In modern psychiatric texts the insanity defense is thus invariably attributed to the "discoveries" of "scientific" psychiatry; and its recent burgeoning popularity, in this and other Western countries, to the long-overdue legislative and judicial appreciation of the supposed "contributions" of psychiatry to the administration of the criminal law. This view is completely at odds with the facts. More than three hundred years before M'Naghten, when there was no such thing as "modern medicine," much less anything that could even remotely be called "psychiatry," the insanity defense was an accepted plea in witch trials before the Spanish Inquisition.*

"The insane were recognized as irresponsible," writes Lea, "and were sent to hospitals. . . . In the enlightened view taken by the Inquisition regarding witchcraft, instructions of 1537 indicate a disposition to regard reputed witches as insane . . . Barcelona at the time had on hand a witch named Juanita Rosquells, whom the physicians and consultors considered to be out of her mind; not knowing what to do they referred to the Suprema, which ordered her discharge . . ."[10] This outcome, however, was unusual. As a rule, persons declared insane were incarcerated in a monastery or hospital.[11]

The physicians most responsible for classifying witches as mental patients were the celebrated French psychiatrists Pinel, Esquirol, and Charcot. They were the founders not only of the French school of psychiatry but of all of modern psychiatry as a positivistic-medical discipline. Their views dominated nineteenth-century medicine.

Philippe Pinel (1745-1826) believed that witches were mentally sick individuals; but he did not dwell on this subject. In his *Treatise on Insanity* (1801), he asserts, without discussion or demonstration, that "In a word, demoniacs of all description are to be classed either with maniacs or melancholics."[12] And he dismisses Weyer as a victim of the belief in witchcraft: "The credit attached to the

---

* The Spanish Inquisition was, as we shall discuss more fully in Chapter 7, opposed to the persecution of witches. It had its hands full with Jews, Judaizers, and Moriscoes, and it wanted no part of the witch-craze. It therefore discouraged the witch-hunts and, when the prosecution of alleged witches could, because of public pressure, not be avoided, took refuge in the dodge that witches were mad. This saved the Spanish Church from openly declaring the nonexistence of witches, a belief widely but discreetly held by its leading clergy, and protected it from the bad conscience which burning on the stake persons accused of witch-craft would have caused it. There are, then, obvious similarities between the use of the concept of insanity in witch-trials in sixteenth-century Spain and in criminal trials in twentieth-century America. In this connection, see Thomas S. Szasz, Moral conflict and psychiatry, *Yale Rev.*, 49: 555–566 (June), 1960; and Mind tapping: Psychiatric subversion of constitutional rights, *Amer. J. Psychiat.*, 119: 323–327 (Oct.), 1962.

impostures of demoniacal possessions in the writings of Wierus [Weyer] are not to be wondered at, when we consider that his works were published towards the middle of the seventeenth century, and bear as much reference to theology as to medicine. This author . . . appears to have been a great adept in the mysteries of exorcism."[13]

Jean Étienne-Dominique Esquirol (1772-1840), Pinel's student and intellectual heir, did more than any other man to establish the view that witches were mentally deranged persons. The most influential psychiatrist of his age, Esquirol believed not only that witches and sorcerers were mentally ill but also that (all or most) criminals were similarly afflicted; and he advocated that lawbreakers be treated by incarceration in mental hospitals rather than prisons. Modern psychiatric historians and forensic psychiatrists have borrowed these ideas from him. "These conclusions," writes Esquirol in 1838, "may appear strange today; some day, we hope, they will become popular truth. Where is the judge today who would condemn to the bonfire a deranged man or gypsy accused of magic sorcery? It has been a long time now that the magistrates have sent the sorcerer to an insane asylum; they no longer cause them to be punished as swindlers."[14]

Esquirol's views on witches were widely accepted by nineteenth-century scholars. Thus, Lecky, in his classic *History of European Morals*, repeats Esquirol's diagnoses as if they were self-evident truths. He characterizes witches as "decrepit in body and distracted in mind,"[15] and attributes their frequent suicide to "fear and madness [which] combined in urging the victims to the deed."[16] Describing a victim of the Spanish Inquisition in 1359, Lecky writes: "The poor lunatic fell into the hands of the Archbishop of Toledo and was burnt alive."[17] Commenting on the witch mania and on "epidemics of purely insane suicide," such as occurred sporadically in Europe between the fifteenth and seventeenth centuries, even Lecky blandly asserts that these problems "belong rather to the history of medicine than to that of morals."[18] Nothing, in my opinion, could be further from the truth.

In the hands of Jean-Martin Charcot (1825-1893), witchcraft became a problem of "neuropathology." In his obituary of his great teacher, Freud writes: "Charcot . . . drew copiously upon the surviving reports of witch trials and of possession, in order to show that the manifestations of the neurosis [hysteria] were the same in those days as they are now. He treated hysteria as just another topic in neuropathology . . ."[19] Like Esquirol, Charcot took the witches as he found them defined by their tormentors, and proceeded to study their "neuropathology."* And so did Freud. In his hands, however, witchcraft becomes a problem of "psychopathology."

In his obituary of Charcot, Freud proposes "the theory of a splitting of consciousness as a solution to the riddle of hysteria," and then reminds his readers that "by pronouncing possession by a demon to be the cause of hysterical phenomena, the Middle Ages in fact chose this solution; it would only have been a matter of exchanging the religious terminology of that dark and superstitious age for the scientific language of today."[20] This is an astonishing admission: Freud acknowledges that the psychoanalytic description of hysteria is but a semantic revision of the demonological one. He thus tries to legitimize his metaphors by claiming that they form a part of the language of science when, in fact, they do not.†

The demonological conception of hysteria, and Charcot's quasi-medical reinterpretation of it, made a profound impression on

---

* It is interesting that while Freud saw Charcot as intensely interested in witchcraft and its relation to mental illness, there is no reference to this subject in Georges Guillain's fine biography, *J.-M. Charcot, 1825–1893: His Life, His Work.*

The reason for this discrepancy is probably that Freud was a psychiatrist, and Guillain a neurologist. Guillain's biography is neurologically oriented and emphasizes Charcot's contributions to this field rather than to psychiatry. Perhaps because there is no longer anything creditable about the neuropathological conception of witchcraft, Guillain remains silent about it. Freud, on the other hand, had his ear tuned to Charcot's psychiatric and psychological views, and thus came away with lasting impressions of these aspects of his work.

† It would be unfair, however, to be excessively critical of Freud for his naive self-intoxication with "science." His foregoing views were written before Kraus, Wittgenstein, Orwell, and others elucidated the defining significance of language in both science and human affairs. Today, we know, or have scant excuses for not knowing, that the behavior of witches did not occur in a social vacuum: they behaved as they did partly because they were persecuted by their enemies (the inquisitors); and their conduct was described the way it was because the language for doing so was controlled by their persecutors (the theologians). *Mutatis mutandis,* the same is true for the "hysterics" Charcot and Freud encountered at the Salpêtrière: they behaved as they did partly because they were persecuted by their enemies (the neuropsychiatrists); and their conduct was described the way it was because the language for doing so was controlled by their persecutors (the physicians).

Freud. He returned repeatedly to this theme. "What would you say," he asks Fliess, in a letter dated January 17, 1897, ". . . if I told you that the whole of my brand-new primal theory of hysteria was well-known and had been published a hundred times over—several centuries ago? Do you remember how I always said that the medieval theory of possession, held by the ecclesiastical courts, was identical with our theory of a foreign body and a splitting of consciousness? . . . incidentally, the cruelties make it possible to understand some symptoms of hysteria which have hitherto been obscure."[21]

We see Freud here taking the decisive leap into psychopathology: he accepts the officially identified patient *as* a patient and proceeds to examine her for symptoms. First, he lays proprietary claims on the psychopathological interpretation of possession developed by the French school of psychiatry; then, he proceeds to disregard the cruelties inflicted on the witches as indications of the human character of the persecutors, and of the social nature of the times, and interprets them instead as part of the symptoms exhibited by the "patients."

Thirty years after publishing his obituary of Charcot, Freud returns to the similarities between the demonological theory of possession and the psychoanalytic theory of hysteria. "We need not be surprised," he writes in his essay on "A Seventeenth-Century Demonological Neurosis," "to find that, whereas the neuroses of our own unpsychological modern days take on a hypochondrical aspect and appear disguised as organic illnesses, the neuroses of those early times emerge in demonological trappings. Several authors, foremost among them Charcot, have, as we know, identified the manifestations of hysteria in the portrayals of possession and ecstasy that have been preserved for us in the productions of art. . . . The demonological theory of those dark times has won in the end against all the somatic views of the period of 'exact' science. The states of possession correspond to our neuroses . . . In our eyes, the demons are bad and reprehensible wishes, derivatives of instinctual impulses that have been repudiated and repressed."[22]

Here Freud asserts that the cultural climate in which people live determines the overt symbolic form of the "neuroses" they develop; but he stops short of entertaining the possibility that they also determine which persons assume dominant roles as persecutors, and which are cast into submissive roles as victims. He thus shuts the door on a broader, cultural-historical perspective, not only on "mental illness," but on psychiatry itself; and on the view that society not only shapes the symbolic forms of the madness it creates, but determines the very existence, direction, force, and output of this manufacturing process itself.

As we have seen, then, the psychopathological theory of witchcraft does not originate with Gregory Zilboorg. But Zilboorg was undoubtedly one of its most articulate and persuasive popularizers; what he lacked in originality, he made up in salesmanship. Moreover, Zilboorg was writing at a time when his audience had been prepared for his message by decades of psychiatric and psychoanalytic propaganda about mental illness. Perhaps for this reason as well, his views have been extremely influential. Virtually all contemporary psychiatrists and psychiatric historians who have expressed themselves on the subject of witchcraft subscribe to Zilboorg's interpretations.

The gist of Zilboorg's thesis is that most witches were mentally ill. Instead of their illness being correctly recognized, it was misinterpreted as a sign of witchcraft. "The *Malleus*," writes Zilboorg, "was a reaction against the disquieting signs of the growing instability of the established order, and hundreds of thousands of mentally sick fell victim to this violent reaction. Not all accused of being witches and sorcerers were mentally sick, but almost all mentally sick were considered witches, or sorcerers, or bewitched."[23]

Zilboorg does not question the mental health of the inquisitors. Nor does he present any evidence to show that the witches were mentally ill. Instead, he simply declares that they were ill and seeks to establish the validity of this interpretation by constantly repeating it. His recitation of the case of Françoise Fontaine (on whose inquisitorial "treatment" I have commented earlier[24]) is illustrative. How do we know that this woman was mentally ill? Here is Zilboorg's proof: "It would be idle, of course, to try to subject to modern scrutiny the symptoms of Françoise Fontaine in order to prove the obvious fact [sic] that she was a mentally sick girl."[25]

Zilboorg's method for establishing insanity is the same as the inquisitor's for establishing witchcraft: each proclaims that his subject suffers from the feared condition and uses his authority and power to transform his judgment into social reality. On the basis of this kind of "evidence" Zilboorg concludes that ". . . no doubt is left in our mind that the millions of witches, sorcerers, possessed and obsessed, were an enormous mass of severe neurotics, psychotics, and considerably deteriorated organic deliria . . . for many years the world looked like a veritable insane asylum without a proper mental hospital."[26] The mind boggles at such nonsense. Zilboorg cavalierly ignores facts with which he must have been familiar from his study of witchcraft, but which do not suit his purpose of selling psychiatry. Among these facts are, first, that many persons accused of witchcraft were criminals, for example, poisoners; second, that others were therapists, for example, midwives; third, that still others were of the wrong religion, for example, Protestants in Catholic countries or vice versa; and finally, that there were those—perhaps the majority—who were simply innocent men and women, falsely accused for a variety of reasons.

But to Zilboorg, and to other psychiatric imperialists eager to conquer all of the Middle Ages for medical psychology, the witches —whoever they might have been—are simply insane. "The fusion of insanity, witchcraft, and heresy into one concept," writes Zilboorg, "and the exclusion of even the suspicion that the problem is a medical one are now complete."[27] But what or where is the medical problem here? Heresy and witchcraft were defined and understood as religious and legal problems; hence the participation of the ecclesiastic and secular courts in witch trials. In suggesting that the problem of witchcraft was medical, Zilboorg not only ignores all this historical evidence, but also denies the role of social discrimination and scapegoating in the witch-hunts. For whatever else they were, the persons accused of witchcraft were oppressed and persecuted individuals. But oppression and persecution are not in themselves medical problems, though of course they may, and usually do, have medical consequences.

Commenting on the *Malleus*, Zilboorg observes that "The hallucinatory experiences, sexual or not, of the psychotic women of the time are well described by Sprenger and Krämer."[28] Again, Zilboorg simply labels the women "psychotic" and their experiences "hallucinatory." This is hardly proof. Actually, what Zilboorg calls "hallucinatory experiences" were usually lies and fabrications that persons accused of witchcraft were forced to utter under torture. Zilboorg not only ignores this, but insists that his purpose in analyzing the witch-hunts is "primarily to describe and to outline some of the forces at play, rather than to judge, approve, or disapprove . . . for the problem is scientific and clinical rather than moral."[29]

Zilboorg repeats his psychopathological interpretations of witchcraft in discussing Weyer's *De Praestigiis*: "He [Weyer] leaves no doubt that one conclusion is warranted: the witches are mentally sick people, and the monks who torment and torture the poor creatures are the ones who should be punished."[30] And again, "The confessions of witches and sorcerers . . . he [Weyer] insisted, were forms of madness, forms of abnormal fantasy, an indication and a part of a severe mental disease in which the whole personality was involved."[31]

Zilboorg thus distorts Weyer's views to suit his own argument. What Weyer most strongly emphasized was that the individuals accused of witchcraft usually were innocent of any wrongdoing. The issue of mental illness is neither crucial nor prominent in Weyer's argument. Above all else, *De Praestigiis* is an attack on the corruption and inhumanity of the inquisitors. "Of all the misfortunes which the various fanatical and corrupt opinions, through Satan's help, have brought in our time to Christendom," writes Weyer, "not the smallest is that which, under the name of witchcraft, is sown as a vicious seed . . . Almost all the theologians are silent regarding their godlessness, doctors tolerate it, jurists treat it while still under the influence of old prejudices; wherever I listen, there is no one, no one who out of compassion for humanity unseals the labyrinth or extends a hand to heal the deadly wound."[32]

Nor is this all. Weyer calls the witch-hunters "tyrants, sanguinary judges, butchers, torturers and ferocious robbers, who have thrown out humanity and do not know mercy."[33] He concludes his denunciation of the inquisitors and all who aid their work with these words: "So I summon you before the tribunal of the Great Judge, who shall decide between us, where the truth you have trampled under foot and buried shall arise and condemn you, demanding vengeance for your inhumanities."[34]

Are these the utterances of a "reverent, respectful, and religious man, [whose only goal was] to prove that witches were mentally ill and should be treated by physicians rather than be interrogated by ecclesiastics," as Alexander and Selesnick repeat Zilboorg and even exaggerate his efforts to "discover" Weyer as the founder of modern psychiatry?[35] Or are they the utterances of a social critic protesting against the unbridled power and immorality of the oppressors of his age?

We have seen how, in Zilboorg's hands, the psychopathological view of witchcraft begins as medical hypothesis, and ends as blinding bias. This bias has, in turn, become psychiatric dogma, so that today no "serious" student of psychiatry doubts that witches were insane. Albert Deutsch, the author of a standard text on the history of American psychiatry, thus takes it for granted that the witches were mad. "The records of the witch trials that have come down to us," he writes, "offer convincing evidence that a large percentage of those accused of witchcraft were really insane . . . What percentage of the victims of the witch mania were mentally unsound is of course beyond calculation, but on the basis of the records it would seem no exaggeration to judge that they comprised at least one-third of the total executed."[36]

But witch trials were, after all, *trials*. Hence, they were concerned with guilt and innocence, not with sickness and health. Zilboorg obscures this by constantly harping on mental illness. The fact is that witches had been severely punished for "crimes" that were poorly defined and not proven to the satisfaction of many honest observers. Yet, the mere fact that *they* were tortured and burned suffices to make *them* the subjects of special psychopathological interest: *their* social conduct and verbal productions are the "material" of psychopathology. "A witch," Alexander and Selesnick solemnly tell us, "relieved her guilt by confessing her sexual fantasies in open court; at the same time, she achieved some erotic gratification by dwelling on all the details before her male accusers. These severely emotionally disturbed women [sic] were particularly susceptible to the suggestion that they harbored demons and devils and would confess to cohabiting with the evil spirits, much as disturbed individuals today, influenced by newspaper headlines, fantasy themselves as sought-after murderers."[37]

The rhetoric of modern psychiatry is displayed here in its finest form. Alexander and Selesnick omit any reference to the tortures used to extract confessions from alleged witches. Indeed, they go so far as to compare the confessions of accused witches with the false claims to being criminals advanced by persons accused of nothing and laboring only under the influence of their own personal needs and stories printed in newspapers. The immorality of this analogy lies in equating the influence of brutal physical tortures with that of printed messages put forth without any coercion whatever. In this interpretation, the witch trial is transformed, from a situation where accused persons are tortured until they confess to crimes for which the penalty is burning at the stake, to one where unmolested citizens claim to have committed crimes of which they are easily proved innocent.

The full extent of the falsity and the immorality of this psychiatric interpretation of witchcraft becomes evident if we contrast it with the record of the Inquisition compiled and widely accepted by Christian historians and theologians. This historical interpretation, in contrast to the psychiatric, focuses on the persecutors, not the persecuted; it attributes intolerance to the former, not mental illness to the latter. For example, Henry Charles Lea, the great historian of the Inquisition, has this to say about the role of the Church in the persecution of nonconformists (here, of Jews):

Nor does the long record of human perversity present a more damning illustration of the facility with which the evil passions of man can justify themselves with the pretext of duty, than the manner in which the Church, assuming to represent Him who died to redeem mankind, deliberately planted the seeds of intolerance and persecution and assiduously cultivated the harvest for nearly fifteen hundred years. . . . Man is ready enough to oppress and despoil his fellows and, when taught by his religious guides that justice and humanity are a sin against God, spoliation and oppression become the easiest of duties. It is not too much to say that for the infinite wrongs committed on the Jews during the Middle Ages, and for the prejudices that are even yet rife in many quarters, the Church is mainly if not wholly responsible.[38]

Andrew Dickson White, a deeply religious historical scholar, the first president of Cornell University, and the author of the classic *History of the Warfare of Science with Theology in Christendom*, could also discover nothing wrong with the victims: they were simply scapegoats. And he, too, noted that among the victims, not only in Spain but also in the rest of Europe, the Jews often stood high. "Yet, as late as 1527," he writes, "the people of Pavia, being threatened with plague, appealed to St. Bernardino of Feltro, who during his life had been a fierce enemy of the Jews, and they passed a decree promising that if the saint would avert the pestilence they would expel the Jews from the city. The saint apparently accepted the bargain, and in due time the Jews were expelled."[39]

In short, the psychiatric perspective on witchcraft is objectionable because dwelling on the alleged mental derangement of the witches distracts the observer's attention from the activities of the witch-hunter. In this way, the social conduct of the oppressor is overlooked, explained away, or, in some cases, excused as also the product of madness.* Zilboorg calls the authors of the *Malleus* "two honest Dominicans."[40] Menninger, another enthusiastic advocate of the medical view of witchcraft, changes this to "two zealous but misguided Dominicans."[41] In like vein, Masserman calls the *Malleus* ". . . the result of the earnest friars' [Sprenger and Krämer's] research and codification . . .", and characterizes it as ". . . a medieval manual of clinical psychiatry, since it describes in great detail as the signs of wizardry and witchcraft the anesthesias, paresthesias, motor dysfunctions, phobias, obsessions, compulsions, regressions, dereisms, hallucinations, and delusions that today would be regarded as pathognomonic of severe neurotic or psychotic disorders."[42]

But what are the facts? Robbins, a considerably more trustworthy scholar of witchcraft than Zilboorg and his psychiatrist colleagues who copy him, tells us that Krämer, one of the authors of the *Malleus*, had "encouraged a dissolute woman to hide in an oven, making believe the devil lodged there . . . to justify his witch-hunts. Her voice denounced many people, whom Krämer cruelly tortured. The Bishop of Brixen finally managed to expel Krämer . . ."[43] As to Sprenger—that other "honest" but "misguided" Dominican—he was suspected of having forged a letter of approbation from the Theological Faculty of the University of Cologne in 1487 appended to the *Malleus*. At his death, Sprenger was not given a requiem mass by his colleagues, an omission which "may have been occasioned by his academic dishonesty."[44]

---

* The interpretation that both witch-hunters and witches were mad we owe to Deutsch. "The case of Mary Glover, of Boston, who was tried and executed in 1688," he writes, "served as a fitting prologue to the great Salem drama. In microcosm it illustrates very clearly the presence of mental illness in both accused and accusers." (Deutsch, *The Mentally Ill in America*, p. 33.) This passage shows how completely Deutsch, an astute and fine journalist, became enmeshed in and blinded by the mythology and rhetoric of his psychiatric mentors. He believes that he saw—"very clearly"—that not just the witches, but their accusers as well, were mentally ill; in short, that all of the *dramatis personae* in this tragedy were mad.

We may summarize the salient features of the psychopathological theory of witchcraft as follows: The idea that witches were mad was entertained by Weyer; it was fully developed by Esquirol and accepted by most nineteenth-century historians, physicians, and scholars; and it was finally elevated to unquestioned psychiatric dogma by Zilboorg and other mid-twentieth-century "dynamic psychiatrists."

The results were twofold. On the one hand, witches became the objects of endless psychopathological interest; their behavior was regarded as proof of the transhistorical and transcultural "reality" of mental illness. On the other hand, the inquisitors, judges, physicians, and witch-prickers were increasingly ignored by psychiatrists; their behavior was regarded as the unfortunate error of a bygone dark age. Illustrative is the opinion of Henry Sigerist, the eminent medical historian, who maintained that, "No doubt many women who ended their lives at the stake were psychopathic personalities, not so the men who persecuted them. It was society as a whole that believed in witchcraft as a result of a definite philosophy."[45] This view excludes the possibility that the phenomena in question—called witchcraft during the Renaissance and mental illness today—are actually created through the social interaction of oppressor and oppressed. If the observer sympathizes with the oppressor and wants to exonerate him, while he pities the oppressed but wants to control him, he calls the victim mentally ill. This is why psychiatrists declare that witches were mad. Conversely, if the observer sympathizes with the oppressed and wants to elevate him, while he loathes the oppressor and wants to degrade him, he calls the tormentor mentally ill. This is why psychiatrists declare that the Nazis were mad. I insist that both interpretations are worse than false; by interposing mental illness (or witchcraft, as was the case formerly), they conceal, excuse, and explain away the terrifyingly simple but all-important fact of man's inhumanity to man.

In short, we may conclude that although the psychiatric theory of witchcraft is worthless for our understanding of the witch-hunts, it is valuable for our understanding of psychiatry and its pivotal concept of mental illness. What is called "mental illness" (or "psychopathology") emerges as the name of the product of a particular kind of relationship between oppressor and oppressed.

6

THE WITCH AS HEALER

The doctors, who are in an even more true sense his [Satan's] lawful sons, who sprung from the popular empiricism known as Witchcraft, these his chosen heirs, to whom he left his noblest patrimony, are far too ready to forget the fact. They are basely ungrateful to the Witches who paved their way for them. They do more . . . they supply the mockers with some cruel weapons to use against him. . . . Satan, it would seem from them, is simply a form of disease!

—Jules Michelet[1]

The modern psychiatric view of the witch as a mentally ill person is not merely a false interpretation of the historical record; it is a perverse denial of the true role of the witch as benefactor or therapist as well as malefactor or troublemaker. Because psychiatric interpretations of the witch-hunts consistently neglect the figure of the good witch—also called the white witch (in contrast to the black one), or the wiseman or wisewoman—these accounts must be seen for what they are: psychiatric propaganda, not medieval historiography.

To understand the role of the witch as healer, we must remember that in the Middle Ages medicine, like other branches of learning, was in a state of arrest, dormant. "With the exception of Arab or Jewish physicians, hired at great cost by the rich, medical treatment was unknown—the people could only crowd to the church doors for aspersion with holy water."[2] Moreover, because of the religious misogyny characteristic of the age, woman was treated like an animal or worse. As a result, observes Michelet, "no woman in those days would ever have consulted a male physician, trusted to him, and told him her secrets. Sorceresses were the only observers in this field, and, for women in particular, were the sole and only practitioners."[3]

In short, the poor and powerless were utterly deserted: priest and Church curried favor with the feudal lord; the physician was the servant of princes and counts. Where could the wretched serf and his abused wife seek relief from their misery? Not within the fold of their faith, or from the court of their master, but only in magic, superstition, and sorcery. Hence, they turn to the magician, the sorceress, and the witch.

The sorceress interpreted and administered the magic rites of healing (to control disease) and of personal influence (to control malefactors). "For a thousand years," Michelet reminds us, as indeed historians of medicine and psychiatry need to be reminded, "the people had one healer and one only—the Sorceress. Emperors and kings and popes, and the richest barons, had sundry Doctors of Salerno, or Moorish and Jewish physicians; but the main body of every State, the whole world we may say, consulted no one but the *Saga*, the *Wise Woman*."[4] She was often called the Good Lady or the Beautiful Lady, Bella Donna—the name of one of her drugs, still used by physicians.

Indeed, the good witch was not only physician, but astrologer, necromancer, prophet, and sorceress as well. The study of anatomy, long prohibited by the Church, began with her; this is why she was accused of robbing graves and selling children to the Devil. The study of poisons, of chemistry and pharmacology, began with her as well. It is obvious why this had to be. Since secular healing had been forbidden by the Church, it could be practiced only by social outcasts: Jews or witches. As Pennethorne Hughes points out, "Jews were branded as usurers because no one but a Jew was permitted to lend money under the medieval system, and they were allowed few other professions. In the same way, witches had largely a monopoly of the powers of healing—the dual powers of healing and harming—because of the medieval injunction against medicine."[5]

Moreover, in the minds of the simple folk who sought her aid, the good witch was not (necessarily) an ally of the Devil; this inter-pretation was imposed upon her role by the Church during the Middle Ages.[6] Actually, the wiseman, or more often the wisewoman, was a kind of prescientific healer, combining the roles of medical practitioner, minister, and good neighbor. "The white witch, or wiseman," writes Christina Hole, "was the protector of the com-munity, as his criminal opponent was its enemy. Like the black witch, he relied on magic, but he used it principally for benevolent purposes, to cure disease, to defeat spells, detect thieves or find stolen goods, and to protect his neighbors from every kind of ill. . . . When doctors were few and not very highly skilled, he was often able to cure simple ailments by the use of herbs and common sense, garnished with charms. . . . The wisewoman filled the office of midwife. . . . Their [the white witches'] value to the community lay in the fact that they were known and trusted and were called upon in cases of illness and trouble when no stranger, however learned, would have been consulted."[7]

The white witch was thus truly a healer, a physician, a servant of the suffering individual. Her services ranged from curing disease and dispensing love-potions to forecasting the future and finding hidden treasures. The people who consulted her did so voluntarily, and paid for her services either in money or kind. Since her station was lowly, men did not fear her for her social power. Instead, they projected onto her all their magical expectations for cure of disease and relief of misery. This became a source of supernatural power which inspired awe and fear in her clients and often led to her being persecuted as a black witch. Midwives in particular were often suspected of being witches. "Because midwives so often were in bad repute," writes Forbes in *The Midwife and the Witch*, "even an innocent practitioner might be accused of witchcraft if the delivery had an unhappy outcome or if the non-obstetrical patients whom some midwives attempted to treat did not recover . . . Even more serious were the charges that midwives destroyed infants before or just after birth . . . the *Malleus Maleficarum* charged that witch-midwives destroyed the child in utero, causing an abortion, or found a moment of privacy in which to offer the newborn infant to Satan."[8]

Because of the nature of the human bond between suffering peasant and trusted sorceress, the good witch becomes endowed with great powers of healing: she is the forerunner, the mother, of the mesmeric healer, the hypnotist, and the (private) psychiatrist. In addition, because she is actually a combination of magician and empiricist, the sorceress acquires, by experimenting with drugs extracted from plants, a genuine knowledge of some powerful pharmacological agents. So advanced is her knowledge that, in 1527, Paracelsus, considered one of the greatest physicians of his time, burns his official pharmacopoeia declaring that "he had learned from the Sorceresses all he knew."[9]

It is important to emphasize that the magician (or sorcerer or witch—the distinction among these was frequently blurred) was a kind of scientist. His power lay not only in his authority, but also in his method. Basic to his method was the assumption, as Hole reminds us, "that, by careful study and right application of certain definite rules, the magician could always obtain the results he desired. For him, as for the scientist, the universe was governed by unchanging laws . . ."[10] For this reason, the magician's "outlook was not religious but scientific, however faulty the premises upon which it was based. The humility and supplication of the worshipper formed no part of his mental equipment. . . ."[11]

To be sure, not all of the white witch's methods of healing were scientific.* Some were decidedly magical, one of them being the transference of evil (disease) from the afflicted person to a mediating agent (the person of the witch). For example, in 1590, Agnes Sampson, a Scottish witch, was convicted of curing a certain Robert Kers of a disease "laid upon him by a westland warlock when he was at Dumfries, whilk sickness she took upon herself, and kept the same with great groaning and torment till morn, at whilk time there was a great din heard in the house."[12] The noise was made by the witch in her efforts to shift the disease from herself to a cat or a dog. However, the attempt miscarried, the disease missed the animal, and instead hit Alexander Douglas of Dalkeith, who died of it. The original patient, Robert Kers, recovered.

Because of her methods and popularity, the white witch was a challenge to the Church. Michelet suggests—and the suggestion is

---

* Some writers emphasize the magical, and others the scientific, aspects of the healing practices of witches. Actually, the sorceress was an embodiment of both folk wisdom and folk nonsense; she utilized magic rituals (for example, the recitation of incantations), as well as technical acts (the administration of drugs).

plausible—that the empiricism of sorcery and witchcraft was principally a revolt against the authority of the Church. "How come," he asks, "the great discovery [of scientific as opposed to religious principles of healing]?" And he answers: "No doubt by the simple application of the great Satanic principle *that everything should be done backwards,* precisely in the reverse way to that employed by the world of religion. The Church had a holy horror of all poisons; Satan utilizes them as curative agents."[13] Emphasizing that science always advances by skepticism of established authority, Michelet remarks: "Is there one science you can name that was not originally a revolt against authority? Medicine above all was truly and indeed Satanic, a revolt against disease, the merited scourge of an offended God. Plainly a sinful act to stay the soul on its road toward heaven and replunge it in the life of this world!"[14]

It is a serious mistake, therefore, to believe that the Church opposed witchcraft merely because it considered the witch a cause of disease and misfortune. The "early Christian Church," Hole writes, "denounced both black and white magic as equally sinful."[15] This opposition of Christianity—beginning with early Catholicism, through the Reformation, to our contemporary Fundamentalists—to science, and especially to healing by physical means mixed with magic rites, is not difficult to understand. "[Magic] was an appeal to a power other than that of God, a presumptuous attempt to compel by human arts what could be granted or denied only by the Divine Will. If any magical rite succeeded, it could only be by the help of devils, and whoever sought to do anything, even good, by such means must be God's enemy. Healing charms were condemned no less than darker sorceries . . ."[16] However, by aiding the weak, the white witch tended to undermine the established hierarchies of dominance—of priest over penitent, lord over peasant, man over woman. Herein lay the principal threat of the witch to the Church. And this is one of the reasons why, in the fifteenth century, the Church set out to crush her.

From the historical record, it is indeed clear that the Church resented the good witch even more than the bad. The wisewoman, the midwife who was an effective therapist, was an affront to the supremacy of the cleric. The inquisitors thus undertook the systematic repression of their nonprofessional competitors. The cure of bodies and souls, they declared, was the sole province of God and of his duly appointed vicars on earth, the priests. "With reference to the second point," write Sprenger and Krämer, "that a creature may be changed for better or for worse, it is always to be understood that this can only be done by the permission and indeed by the power of God, and that this is only done in order to correct or to punish . . ."[17]

Nor was the Church's prohibition of healing directed solely against sorcerers or witches; it was directed also against physicians. This was consistent with the premise that man was created by God, and belonged, body and soul, to his Creator. In this view, perhaps fashioned after the feudal model of agricultural economics, man is the land, God the feudal lord, and the priest the peasant who works the land. As land could be tilled only with the permission of the landowner and by those appointed by him, so man could be cured only with the permission of the Lord in heaven and by those appointed by Him. Trespassers—that is, nonclerical healers—were accordingly prevented from practicing their art, prosecuted, and, if necessary, killed. We see here the cure of man being placed under the exclusive jurisdiction of God and the priest; later, we shall see it placed under that of Nature and the physician.

In his classic account of the *History of the Warfare of Science with Theology in Christendom,* Andrew Dickson White emphasizes this fundamentally antimedical posture of the medieval Church: "Even the School of Salerno was held in aversion by multitudes of strict churchmen, since it prescribed rules for diet, thereby indicating a belief that disease arises from natural causes and not from the malice of the devil; . . . Hence it was, doubtless, that the Lateran Council, about the beginning of the thirteenth century, forbade physicians, under pain of exclusion from the Church, to undertake medical treatment without calling in ecclesiastical advice. This view was long cherished in the Church, and nearly two hundred and fifty years later Pope Pius V revived it. Not only did Pope Pius order that all physicians before administering treatment should call in a physician of the soul, on the ground, as he declares, that bodily infirmity frequently arises from sin, but he ordered that, if at the end of three days the patient had not made confession to a priest, the medical man should cease his treatment, under pain of being deprived of his right to practice, and of expulsion from the faculty if he were a professor, and that every physician and professor of medicine should make oath that he was strictly fulfilling these conditions."[18] Special prohibitions were directed by the Church against Jewish physicians.[19]

Significantly, the priests do not claim that Jewish physicians and wisewomen cannot heal; instead, they claim that their very cure is evil. For example, when, in the middle of the seventeenth century, the city council of Hall, in Württemberg, gave certain privileges to Jewish physicians, the clergy of the city protested, declaring that "it were better to die with Christ than to be cured by a Jew doctor aided by the devil."[20] Sprenger and Krämer complain similarly that "bewitched persons" consult sorceresses and are cured by them. "[T]he common method of taking off bewitchment," they write, "although it is quite unlawful, is for the bewitched person to resort to wise women, by whom they are very frequently cured, and not by priests or exorcists. So experience shows that such cures are affected by the help of devils, which it is unlawful to seek; therefore it cannot be lawful thus to cure bewitchment, but it must be patiently borne."[21]

As medieval clerics forbade nonclerics from healing, so modern clinicians (physicians) forbid nonclinicians (psychologists, social workers) from practicing psychotherapy independently.[22] As before, medical psychotherapists do not usually claim that nonmedical therapists are incompetent; instead, they assert that it is "irresponsible," and hence improper, for anyone but a physician to treat "sick patients."*

The view that the good witch represented a special affront to organized religion is further supported by her fate in Protestant countries: There, too, she was declared to be an even greater evil than the bad witch! Here is how William Perkins, perhaps the most famous English witch-hunter, explained why this had to be:

---

* The following resolution of the Executive Committee of the American Psychiatric Association, dated Mar. 7, 1954, is illustrative: "Mental illnesses are well-defined entities clearly described and delineated in the Standard Nomenclature; the diagnosis and treatment of mental illnesses remain a medical responsibility." (Quoted in Henry A. Davidson, The semantics of psychotherapy, *Amer. J. Psychiat.*, 115: 410–413 [Nov.], 1958; p. 411.) The American Psychoanalytic Association has likewise repudiated so-called lay analysis and prohibits the training of nonphysicians in its approved institutes. For further critical discussion, see Thomas S. Szasz, Psychiatry, psychotherapy, and psychology, *A.M.A. Arch. Gen. Psychiat.*, 1: 455–463 (Nov.), 1959, and Three problems in contemporary psychoanalytic training, ibid., 3: 82–94 (July), 1960.

". . . it were a thousand times better for the land if all witches, but specially the *blessing witch,* might suffer death. Men doe commonly hate and spit at the *damnifying sorcerer,* as unworthy to live among them, whereas they flie into the other in necessitie, they depend upon him as their God, and by this means thousands are carried away to their finall confusion. Death, therefore, is the just and deserved portion of the good witch."[23]

The English Witchcraft Act of 1542 specifically lists the good witch, describing her as a kind of unlicensed practitioner (of medicine and other useful skills), as among those whose activities are prohibited by law. The Act refers to persons who ". . . unlawfully have devised and practiced Invocations and conjurations of Spirits, pretending by such means to understand and get Knowledge for their own lucre in what place treasure of gold or silver should or might be found or had in the earth or other secret places . . . which things cannot be used and exercised but to the great offense of God's law, hurt and damage of the King's subjects, and loss of the souls of such Offenders, to the great dishonour of God, Infamy and disquietness of the Realm."[24]

Here we see, in astonishingly naked form, some of the economic motives behind the witch-hunts: Church and State, clerical and secular ruler, invoke moral arguments in defense of their monopolistic practices. Only the mighty leaders are supposed to "get knowledge" and so enrich themselves; when the lowly individual tries to do the same, he is castigated for selfishness, thinking only of his "own lucre," and offending against "God's law." In short, the English Witchcraft Act of 1542 articulates the argument for Communism (as State Capitalism) in surprisingly modern terms: Affecting the rhetoric of selfless collectivism, the authorities declare that only the "Realm" (the Ecclesiastic State) can rightly own knowledge and riches; for the individual, to have such possessions is theft—a sin against God and a crime against Society. To be sure, this is only a variation on the ancient theme of power and political inequality. *"Quod licet Jovi, non licet bovi"* ("What is permitted to Jove is not permitted to the cow") is the way the Romans put it. What the authorities really forbid is the subject's efforts at self-determination; what they fear most is a narrowing of the gap between ruler and ruled. How this gap is measured—whether in theological, economic, political, racial, sexual, or psychiatric terms—

is not especially important. Revolt against authority was, and remains to this day, the original sin, the classic crime, of the individual.

In 1563, twenty-one years after the passage of the English Witchcraft Act, a new Scottish witch law was enacted which, Trevor-Roper tells us, "abandoned the old humane distinction between 'good' and 'bad' witch . . . Obedient to the voice of Calvin, it prescribed death for all witches, good or bad, and for those who consulted with them."[25] Similarly, "In 1572, Augustus the pious, Elector of Saxony, introduced a new criminal code . . . according to which even the 'good witch' was to be burned, merely for having made a pact with the Devil, 'even if she has harmed nobody with her sorcery.' "[26] We see here clearly, once more, that the evil of witchcraft was not a specific, overt act, but a private, secret condition of the accused person.

When James I became the King of England, he did not like the mild Elizabethan laws against witches. He therefore "found a defect in the statute . . . by which none died for witchcraft but they only who by that means killed, so that such were executed rather as murderers than witches."[27] In other words, until then, alleged witches had been punished only for *what they did*; James had the law changed so that they were punished for *who they were*.

These facts about the medieval witch as healer divest the psychopathological theory of witchcraft of its last vestiges of plausibility. Indeed, to regard witches solely as aberrant, troublesome individuals, never as competent counselors and therapists, is a misinterpretation singularly limited to medical and psychiatric historians of witchcraft.* Other authorities, whose writings I have cited, recognize the significant role of the medieval witch as the mother, so to speak, not only of the modern physician, but of the astronomer and the chemist as well. The medical-psychiatric interpretation of the Church-witch relationship thus also serves to obscure the early, prescientific rivalry for dominance in the health professions. Catholic and Protestant clerics forbid the wisewoman to exercise her

---

* Redlich and Freedman's remarks constitute a notable exception to the usual psychiatric interpretation of the witch-hunts. They call the *Malleus* "infamous"; categorize Sprenger and Krämer's beliefs as "sadistic and misogynous"; and bewail the "vulgar and sadistic heritage" which the Middle Ages bequeathed "to psychiatric practice and thought." (Frederick C. Redlich and Daniel X. Freedman, *The Theory and Practice of Psychiatry*, p. 32.)

healing arts. In the West, only Jews and Mohammedans tolerate free competition between spiritual (religious) and secular (medical) healers. Hence the unchallenged supremacy, until the Enlightenment, of Arab and Jewish physicians throughout Europe and Africa.

Because the Medieval Church, with the support of kings, princes, and secular authorities, controlled medical education and practice, the Inquisition constitutes, among other things, an early instance of the "professional" repudiating the skills and interfering with the rights of the "nonprofessional" to minister to the poor. Contemporary physicians display the same intolerance toward medically untrained therapists; and psychiatrists, toward those not legitimized by their own guild.

The Church, Michelet writes, "declares, in the fourteenth century, that if a woman dare to cure *without having studied,* she is a witch and must die."[28] But the wisewoman had "studied." Her teacher, however, was Nature, not the Scriptures! In the age of Religion, to have "studied" meant to learn what the Church defined and taught as the true principles and correct practices of various disciplines, just as today it means to have learned what Science so defines.

In short, the medieval Theological State prohibited the practices of the white witch; similarly, the modern Therapeutic State prohibits the practices of the indigenous healer. For example, in 1967, the pastor of the First Church of Religious Science, in Hemet, California, was found guilty of the illegal practice of medicine for treating "emotional and weight problems" with hypnotism, because, in the opinion of the court, ". . . hypnosis could only be used when under the direction of a physician or surgeon, whether he is attempting to diagnose, treat, or prescribe."[29]

There is, of course, method in all this: The poor must not only be oppressed; they must also be kept in perpetual helplessness and dependence upon their masters. This explains the need to deny them their own indigenous healers, a process clearly discernible as early as the Middle Ages and, despite disclaimers to the contrary, in full sway today. Instead of allowing them access to their own helpers, the poor are supplied with physicians employed by the State. Insane asylums, public health facilities, and charity care in municipal teaching hospitals thus displaced the white witches who, though medically unaccredited, were frequently at least the genuine servants of the poor sick. No doubt, some white witches were self-serving frauds. This does not affect the thrust of my argument, however, which is that the white witch was, in principle, the servant of the sick individual, whereas the cleric was, in principle, the servant of God. Similarly, in our day the indigenous healer, however ineffective he might be technically, is the servant of the help-seeking individual, whereas the bureaucratic physician, however effective he might be technically, is the servant of the institution that employs him. Herein, I submit, lies the source of much of the popular dissatisfaction with physicians and medical care today.[30]

Moreover, just as the priest considered the white witch a theological charlatan and persecuted her in the name of the faithful, so the physician considers the unlicensed healer a medical charlatan and persecutes him in the name of the patient. To be sure, some people are, and will always be, more competent and skillful than others, whether in theology, medicine, or any other discipline; and, admittedly, medical incompetence poses an especially serious hazard for sick people. It is widely assumed nowadays that this hazard amply justifies the paternalistic intervention of the State—protecting the citizen from improper medical care by means of licensure regulations and criminal sanctions. This projects the State into the role of judging what is good medical care, who is competent to provide it, and how such competence is to be ascertained. Actually, not only is the State unequipped and unable to fulfill this responsibility, but in assuming the task it becomes an arbiter of what constitutes "scientific medicine," just as the medieval Church became an arbiter of what constituted "true faith."[31]

It is ironic, indeed, that despite the historical record summarized above, no male psychiatrist, no modern male psychiatric historian, acknowledges the witch as healer and therapist, the true mother of the modern, privately practicing physician and psychotherapist. Instead, as we have seen, Man (the Masculine Physician) robs Woman (the White Witch) of her discovery: he declares her mad, and himself the enlightened healer. This process is repeated over and over in the history of medicine. Semmelweis, protector of the parturient woman from the disease-producing hand of the physician, is likewise declared mad, and imprisoned in an insane asylum.[32] Anna O., Joseph Breuer's immortal patient, teaches her physician the human meaning of neurosis and the psychotherapeutic value of self-disclosure to a trusted and sympathetic authority;[33] nevertheless, persons with problems in living are henceforth defined as mentally ill, and their interlocutors as medical experts who know the "minds" of their "patients" better than do the patients themselves. The injustice and violence characteristic of Institutional Psychiatry, symbolized by the physician acting as jailer and torturer vis-à-vis a subject who does not want to be his patient, are thus compounded by the psychiatric historian's betrayal of his intellectual mandate. Such a historian chronicles, not the sufferings of victims, but the lies of oppressors; he serves, not truth, but power; not the patient, but the profession. His betrayal of historical fidelity is consistent with the political functions of psychiatry as an institution of social control, and with the methods characteristic of this institution, namely, force and fraud.[34]

In the modern psychiatric view, the medieval witch was a mentally diseased individual—a "patient" as yet unrecognized by medical science. In actuality, she was often a magician, a sorceress, and above all, a healer—a midwife and physician—an indigenous "professional" freely sought out for help by the people she served. This role-reversal—recasting the witch from healer to sufferer, from psychotherapist to mental patient—was imposed upon witches by historians of psychiatry creating the legend of their own prehistory. Herein lies one of the bitterest ironies of oppression: the victim, no matter how innocent, continues to exude an odor of error and dishonor; whereas the victor, no matter how unjust, continues to radiate an air of authority and benevolence. This is why the modern physician, and especially the psychiatrist, systematically repudiates his real medieval ancestor, the lowly and disreputable sorcerer and witch. Instead, he prefers to trace his descent directly from the Hippocratic physicians of ancient Greece, skipping over the embarrassment of the Middle Ages in silence; or, acknowledging that period, to claim as his predecessor the Roman Catholic priest, pointing to his work on behalf of the sick poor. His ancestors, he maintains, were the men of God; in fact, they were the women of Satan.

For this fundamental inauthenticity, the medical profession has paid the heavy price that such a bargain with falsehood invariably entails. By denying his origins—indeed, by identifying with those who have aggressed against his predecessors—the modern physician forfeits his identity as a modest but independent healer skeptical of the dogma of established social authority, and becomes instead a servile vassal of the State. Thus, in the course of about four centuries, the physician squanders away his Hippocratic mandate as servant of the suffering individual, and assumes instead the role of civil servant protecting the health of the bureaucratic State. In the official histories of contemporary medicine, the denial of the sorceress and witch as healer forms an important link in this fateful transformation of the physician's role from individual entrepreneur to bureaucratic employee.

7

THE WITCH AS SCAPEGOAT

> Honest folk give names to things, and the things
> bear these names. . . . [The scapegoat] is on the side
> of the objects named, not of those who name them.
>
> —*Jean-Paul Sartre*[1]

Psychiatrists are enthusiastic advocates of the psychopathological theory of witchcraft: they maintain that witches were mentally sick women who had been misdiagnosed by well-intentioned but ignorant inquisitors. Historians, on the other hand, are strong supporters of the scapegoat theory of witchcraft: they hold that witches were the sacrificial offerings of a society animated by the symbolism and values of Christian theology. The latter perspective on witchcraft is not new; its origins are readily traced to the middle of the last century. It is especially significant, therefore, that psychiatrists systematically neglect this interpretation of the witch-hunts.

According to the scapegoat theory of witchcraft, the belief in witches and their organized persecution represent an expression of man's search for an explanation and mastery of various human problems, especially bodily diseases and social conflicts. "If men had wanted an explanation of the ills of nature," writes Geoffrey Parrinder, an English anthropologist, "they found it in the diabolical activities of witches. They provided a scapegoat for the troubles of society, as the Jews had done at certain periods, and as they were to become again to the German Nazis in the twentieth century. Reginald Scot, who lived in the midst of the witch-fear and wrote so bravely against the whole superstition, gives the same picture. 'For if any adversity, grief, sickness, loss of children, corn, cattle, or liberty happen to them, by and by they exclaim on witches. . . . Insomuch as a clap of thunder or a gale of wind is no sooner heard, but either they run to bells, or cry out to burn the witches.' "[2] Parrinder compares the witch-hunts with anti-Semitism and with modern political mass movements, and concludes that "the belief in witchcraft is a tragic error, a false explanation of the ills of life, and one that has only led to cruel and baseless oppression in which countless innocent people have suffered."[3]

Many scholars have remarked on the similarities between the persecution of witches and Jews. For example, Andrew Dickson White calls attention to a seventeenth-century painting in the Royal Gallery at Naples depicting "the measures taken to save the city from the plague of 1656": it "represents the people, led by the priests, executing with horrible tortures the Jews, heretics, and witches who were supposed to cause the pestilence, while in the heavens the Virgin and St. Januarius are interceding with Christ to sheathe his sword and stop the plague."[4]

Pennethorne Hughes, an English historian, gives the same explanation for the activities of the inquisitors. "These [pre-Reformation] heresies," he writes, "are worth noticing very briefly because in the minds of the inquisitors they were closely allied with witchcraft, and did have features in common with the cult. Just as the right-wing Inquisitors of Nazism spoke comprehensively of Jews, intellectuals, and Marxists, so the Churchmen of the Middle Ages and of the Renaissance period spoke comprehensively of Jews, witches, and heretics."[5]

Adolf Leschnitzer, a Jewish historian of German origin, draws a close parallel between the persecution of Jews and of witches. "In the sixteenth and seventeenth centuries," he writes, "persecution of Jews was replaced by persecution of witches. Then the process was reversed in the nineteenth and twentieth centuries. In the late Middle Ages persecution of Jews can already be shown to have been staged as a device to divert attention . . . When, after the great persecutions, massacres, and expulsions from the fourteenth to the sixteenth century, . . . witches and sorcerers became the new subjects of persecution. With the disappearance of the Jews, they took their place as the desperately needed new outlet for emotional release."[6]

Although Leschnitzer's assertion about Jews and witches alternating as society's scapegoats does not fit the facts quite as neatly as he makes it seem, his general thesis is sound. "The witchcraft mania," observes Leschnitzer, "was a phenomenon not unlike the modern racial anti-Semitism produced by nineteenth-century Germany and brought to full intensity by twentieth-century Germany. The parallels are obvious: economic and emotional uncertainty, the apprehensions about physical security, and metaphysical fears for the salvation of the soul; deflection of turbulent antisocial impulses against a single defenseless group; denunciation of the enemy within and without as allies of the Devil; cruelty in combat—in the war against the Devil everything is permitted; spoliation of the enemy— the possessions of the witches were almost always confiscated; [etc.]."[7]

Leschnitzer correctly notes that the scapegoat is not a real person, but a type; or as the psychoanalyst would put it, he is a transference figure, upon whom the observer projects his own fears (or hopes). To those who feared them, witch and Jew thus appeared in a similar light. The terror "formerly attached to the witch was transferred to the Jew in the nineteenth and twentieth centuries. One learned to shudder in the presence of the Jew as one had once shuddered before the witch. The very word 'Jew' became charged with the same emotional values formerly inherent in 'witch.' And because the ridiculed word 'witch' became almost taboo and could hardly be used seriously any longer after the era of Enlightenment, one could all the more easily, irresponsibly and recklessly retain, or regain, the underlying archaic conceptions. In an age of half-education, many of the so-called educated went along with the rest."[8]

Although Leschnitzer's main emphasis is on the exploration of the parallels between the witch-hunts and Nazi anti-Semitism, he is not unaware of the equally important similarities between medieval and modern anti-Semitism. During the Middle Ages, he writes, "the Jews had been held responsible for the plague; now, no less absurdly, the Jews were made responsible for unemployment and economic crisis. 'The Jews are our misfortune!' This rallying cry, accompanied by a lusty program of Jew-baiting, had precisely the same effect as the baiting of the 'poisoners of wells' in the Middle Ages. The masses responded to the call."[9]

In much the same way, today all manner of misfortune is attributed to madness. And, as in earlier times, the masses respond to the call urging them to take up arms against the enemy—defined abstractly as mental illness, but embodied concretely in persons defined as mentally ill.

It is consistent with the scapegoat theory of witchcraft, but not with the psychopathological theory of it, that the individuals persecuted as witches were often helpless and poor; and that, in addition to witches, Jews, heretics of all sorts, Protestants, and scientists whose opinions threatened Church dogma, were also victimized by the Inquisition. In short, whereas psychiatric theory relates the belief in witchcraft and the persecution of witches to the mental diseases supposedly harbored by the witches, the scapegoat theory relates them to the specific conditions of the society in which such beliefs and practices occurred. Because of these different perspectives, psychiatric investigations of witchcraft concentrate on the witches and ignore the witch-hunters, while nonpsychiatric investigations of it reverse this focus.*

Although the passions of the people, receptive to the propaganda of the Church, made possible the spread of the witch craze, the inquisitors played a decisive part in it: they determined who was cast into the role of witch and who was not. When they pointed their fingers at women, women were burned; when at Judaizers, Judaizers were burned; and when at Protestants, Protestants were burned.

As witchcraft claimed its victims mainly from among certain classes, so does mental illness. The public madhouses of the seventeenth and eighteenth centuries were full of society's *misérables;* the state mental hospitals of the nineteenth and twentieth centuries have been full of poor and uneducated people.[10] Why? Because the social control and subjection of these people is one of the chief aims of Institutional Psychiatry. This, of course, is not the official psychiatric explanation. Spokesmen for the Mental Health Movement view the prevalence of lower-class persons in mental hospitals as an indication of the high incidence of mental illness in the lower classes; they thus construe it as justification for special psychiatric case-finding among these people. For example, the

---

* In the same way, the usual medical-psychiatric perspective on madness leads to an exclusive focus on the so-called mental patient and a corresponding neglect of the psychiatrist. For more than a decade, I have insisted that this perspective is in part insufficient, and in part totally false; and that, to understand Institutional Psychiatry (or the Mental Health Movement), we must study psychiatrists, not mental patients. In this connection, see Thomas S. Szasz, Science and public policy: The crime of involuntary mental hospitalization, *Med. Opin. & Rev.,* 4: 24–35 (May), 1968.

authors of a recent study on schizophrenia and poverty report that "The perusal of studies of the distribution of 'mental health' and psychological impairment leads us to conclude tentatively that the lowest socioeconomic strata have a lower proportion of mentally healthy individuals and a higher proportion of individuals with psychological impairment than the other social strata. . . . It appears reasonably safe to conclude that treated schizophrenia is concentrated in the lowest socioeconomic strata in large urban centers in the United States."[11] The authors then review eight theories claiming to account for this high incidence of schizophrenia among the poor, offer an "integrated explanation" of their own, but never consider the possibility that the lower-class "schizophrenic" is simply the scapegoat, cloaked in the diagnostic labels of modern psychiatry, of the upper and middle classes. Sprenger and Krämer interpreted the prevalence of women among those possessed of the Devil similarly, that is, as an indication of the high incidence of witchcraft among women; and they thus construed it as justification for directing special inquisitorial attention toward them.[12]

The psychopathological theory of witchcraft is, as we have seen, not the only available or possible explanation of the witch-hunts. The view that witches were society's scapegoats was held by Reginald Scot four hundred years ago, was articulated into a comprehensive and persuasive explanation by Jules Michelet more than one hundred years ago, and was massively documented from original sources by Henry Charles Lea more than fifty years ago. Why then do institutional psychiatrists and psychiatric historians ignore this competing explanation, and prefer instead the view that witches were madwomen? An effort to answer this question will help to clarify not only the practical import of these two theories of the witch-craze, but also the nature of Institutional Psychiatry as a modern mass movement.

All explanations fulfill a practical, strategic function.[13] The psychopathological theory of witchcraft is no exception. Its principal aim is to authenticate, as enlightened medical scientists, the physicians who propound it. The effect, if not the intent, of this explanation is to sidestep the competing explanation of witchcraft, namely, that persons alleged to be witches were not mentally sick but were society's scapegoats. In other words, the basic function of the medical theory of witchcraft—and, in my opinion, its basic immorality as well—lies in distracting attention from the persecutory practices of the institutional psychiatrists, and focusing it instead on the alleged disorders of the institutionalized mental patients. In both cases, the activities of those responsible for casting individuals into the roles of witch and mental patient are denied or ignored. This is why the medical interpretations of witchcraft advanced by psychiatrists systematically neglect to recognize the connection between the witch-hunts and the organized anti-Semitism of late-medieval and Renaissance Europe. This is true of all texts on the history of psychiatry which I have seen.

Consider, for example, Zilboorg's *History of Medical Psychology*.[14] First published in 1941, and widely accepted as a classic in medical and psychiatric historiography, it is a volume composed of 606 closely set pages, the last 16 of which make up the Index. Yet this Index lists no entry for "Jews," for "anti-Semitism," or for the "Spanish Inquisition." The single entry for "Spain" is a laudatory reference to the establishment of mental hospitals there in the fifteenth century.[15]

Alexander and Selesnick's *The History of Psychiatry*[16] not only repeats and exaggerates Zilboorg's misinterpretation of the witch-hunts, but also omits mentioning the Spanish Inquisition. The authors devote, in passing, one sentence to the persecution of Jews: "This age [the later Middle Ages] had to find its scapegoats, and severe persecution of the Jews did not seem to be enough to stem the tide."[17] Alexander and Selesnick do not say who persecuted the Jews or why. Indeed, not satisfied with playing down the Church's participation in these persecutions, they actually invert her role. "The thirteenth and fourteenth centuries," they write, "were marked by mass psychotic movements that terrified the Church because they could not be controlled."[18]

For works like Zilboorg's, and Alexander and Selesnick's, which range widely over the intellectual and political landscape of nearly all of mankind's history, these omissions speak eloquently through their silence. It is the premise of these authors that Institutional Psychiatry is an organization for providing medical care. It is not surprising, then, that they choose only that historical evidence which can be shaped to support this premise, and ignore that which indicates that Institutional Psychiatry is fundamentally an organization for the persecution of nonconformists; and that, in addition to omitting the entire story of medieval anti-Semitism and its connections with the persecution of witches, they also omit the vast chapter of nineteenth century psychiatry concerned with "masturbatory insanity."[19]

To be sure, all history is selective. My point is only that the standard histories of psychiatry—mixing as they do Institutional Psychiatry, psychoanalysis, and other social interventions considered "psychiatric"—blur the differences between procedures that help society (and often harm the patient), and those that help the patient (and sometimes harm society); and having blurred these differences, they emphasize the "therapeutic" value, to the so-called patient, of virtually all psychiatric methods. In contrast, my bias, which I have made explicit, has been to separate Institutional Psychiatry (which rests on coercion and whose function is to protect society) from Contractual Psychiatry (which rests on cooperation and whose function is to protect the individual client). I have therefore confined myself here to selecting materials relevant to the history of Institutional Psychiatry.

In short, psychiatrists and psychiatric historians systematically absolve the Catholic and Protestant churches of their responsibility for a social intolerance which theologians and nonpsychiatric historians have long recognized and acknowledged.[20] To demonstrate the validity of this interpretation—and to show how consistently psychiatrists distort the history of the witch-hunts by making it appear as if the inquisitors had persecuted only "hysterical," that is to say, strangely acting women—we shall briefly review the close relationship between the persecution of witches and Jews in the late Middle Ages and Renaissance, and of mental patients and Jews in the modern world.

In no medieval nation did the Jews rise so high in society as in Spain. For reasons that need not concern us here, discriminatory pressures against the Jews (and also against the Moors) increased commensurately. In Catholic Spain, as in other Christian nations before and since, deviation from the faith of Jesus became defined as heresy.* Persecution of the Jews was thus considered a well-justified sanction against them. This placed Jews and witches in the

* "To appreciate properly the position of the Jews in Spain," writes Lea, "it is requisite first to understand the light in which they were regarded elsewhere throughout Christendom during the medieval period. It has already been seen that the Church held the Jew to be a being deprived, by the guilt of his ancestors, of all natural rights save that of existence." (Henry Charles Lea, *A History of the Inquisition of Spain*, Vol. 1, p. 81.)

same category as deviants from prescribed social beliefs and conduct, in short, as heretics. This is no mere analogizing. "In medieval Hungary," writes Trevor-Roper, "witches were sentenced, for a first offense, to stand all day in a public place, wearing a Jew's hat."[21] While during the Renaissance it was believed that only Christians could be witches, before the sixteenth century witchcraft was a charge often leveled against Jews.[22] "Once we see the persecution of heresy as social intolerance," observes Trevor-Roper, "the intellectual difference between one heresy and another becomes less significant."[23]

The first consequence of Spanish anti-Semitism was the mass-conversion of Jews. The pressures for religious and social conformity continued to mount, however, and in 1492, all the remaining Jews were expelled from Spain. The incident that led to this is worth mentioning, since it was almost re-enacted five hundred years later in Russia. "The medical profession was virtually monopolized by Jews, and royal and aristocratic circles relied heavily on this race for physicians. . . . The unfortunate sequel . . . was that Jewish doctors were accused of poisoning their patients. This was given as a contemporary reason for the expulsion of the Jews in 1492, the royal physician, a Jew, being accused of having poisoned the Infante Don Juan, son of Ferdinand and Isabella."[24] In 1953, Stalin claimed that a group of physicians, many of them Jews, were poisoning him, and were plotting to kill him. After Stalin's death, the "plot" was branded a fabrication.[25]

In Spain, neither conversion nor expulsion sufficed to solve the "Jewish problem." If the Jew was an alien, so, perhaps, to a lesser extent, was the converted Jew. There remained in Spain in the fifteenth century tens of thousands of converted Jews, called *conversos,** who continued to dominate trade and capital. It therefore became necessary to distinguish old Christians from new, and more specifically, Jews whose conversion was "genuine" from those whose conversion was a matter of expediency and who continued, in secret,

---

* Converted Spanish Jews were called *conversos* or "converted ones," by the Spaniards, and *marranos*, the Spanish word for "swine" or "pigs," by the Jews. It is not known who coined the name *marrano*, Jew or Spaniard, why the name stuck, and why the Jews still call the Spanish crypto-Jews *marranos*. Persons accused by the Spanish Inquisition of practicing the Jewish faith in secret were called Judaizers. In this connection, see Max I. Dimont, *Jews, God, and History,* p. 220.

to practice some of the rituals of their old faith. The Spanish Inquisition was set up, by papal decree in November 1478, to discharge this function of "differential diagnosis": Its task was to examine the genuineness of the *conversos'* conversion. Judaizers thus became the principal scapegoats of Spanish society. Illustrative of the work of the Spanish Inquisition is the following case, related by Lea.

In 1567 a woman named Elvira del Campo was tried at Toledo as a Judaizer and was found guilty. She was of *converso* descent and married to an Old Christian. "According to witnesses, who had lived with her as servants, or were her near neighbors, she went to mass and confession and gave all outward signs of being a good Christian; she was kind and charitable, but she would not eat pork . . ." At her trial Elvira admitted not eating pork, but attributed this to medical advice "for a disease communicated to her by her husband, which she desired to conceal." She denied being a Judaizer and strenuously asserted her faith in the Catholic religion. Since the evidence against her was not conclusive, the court ordered her tortured. After having been tortured twice, she admitted "that when she was eleven years old her mother had told her not to eat pork and to observe the Sabbath . . ." On the strength of this confession, one of her judges voted for her "relaxation" (that is, burning at the stake), "but the rest agreed upon reconciliation with its disabilities, confiscation, and three years of prison and *sanbenito*, which were duly imposed in an *auto* of June 13, 1568, but, in a little more than six months, the imprisonment was commuted to spiritual penances, and she was told to go where she chose. Thus, besides the horrors of her trial, she was beggared and ruined for life, and an ineffaceable stain was cast upon her kindred and descendants."[26]

So inhuman does this proceeding seem to Lea that he cannot believe the inquisitors were sincere in believing what they professed. "Trivial as may seem the details of such a trial," he continues, "they are not without importance as a sample of what was occupying the tribunals of all Spain, and they raise the interesting question whether in truth the inquisitors believed what they assumed in the public sentence, that they had been laboring to rescue Elvira from the errors and darkness of her apostasy and to save her soul. The minute points on which the fate of the accused might depend are illustrated by the insistence with which they dwell on her abstinence from pork, on her refusal to eat buttered cakes, on her use of two stewing pots, and on the time at which she changed her chemise and baked her bread."[27]

The decisive role of the inquisitor as scapegoat-selector is displayed dramatically by the victims he chose in Spain as against the rest of Europe. In Spain, as we saw, the Inquisition was set up specifically to distinguish between Catholics and Jews. The Spanish inquisitors' scapegoats were accordingly Jews, Judaizers, and *conversos*. The need for scapegoats having been satisfied by this group, the Spanish Inquisition did not encourage the persecution of witches. Indeed, it frequently opposed the witch-mania, and this at a time when witch-burnings were commonplace elsewhere on the Continent. Among the Spanish inquisitors who combated the belief in witchcraft none is more famous than Alonzo Salazar de Frias. In 1610, after personally investigating an epidemic of witchcraft at Logrono, Salazar concluded that the phenomena had been provoked by the presence of inquisitors looking for witches. "I have not found," he writes in his report to the Suprema, "even indications from which to infer that a single act of witchcraft has really occurred . . . This enlightenment has greatly strengthened my former suspicions that the evidence of accomplices, without external proof from other parties, is insufficient to even justify arrest. Moreover, my experience leads to the conviction that, of those availing themselves of the Edict of Grace, three-quarters and more have accused themselves and their accomplices falsely. I further believe that they would freely come to the Inquisition to revoke their confessions, if they thought that they would be received kindly without punishment, for I fear that my efforts to induce this have not been properly made known."[28]

The differences between the Spanish and the Roman Inquisition with respect to witchcraft are consistently emphasized by historians and theologians, and equally consistently ignored by psychiatrists and medical historians. For the reasons of this omission we do not have far to seek. If the witches burned at the stake were mentally sick persons, and if there were hardly any witches burned in Spain, the psychiatric epidemiologist is faced with the need to explain why, with madmen so numerous throughout Europe, were there so few in Spain? Or were the Jews, Judaizers, and *conversos* persecuted by the Spanish Inquisition also mentally ill? Implicit in the reasoning of those who hold that witches were mentally sick is the presumption that an institution as lofty as the Roman Catholic Church would not hound people if there was nothing at all "wrong" with them. Where there is smoke, there is fire, says the proverb. The psychiatric historian adapts this for his purposes, and concludes that where there is fire there is mental illness. Instead of being a symbol of the Inquisition, the stake thus becomes a symptom of the witches' mental illness.* Only in this way can we explain why psychiatrists regard witches, and only witches, as a group of medieval individuals all of whom, though not selected by doctors, suffered from (mental) diseases. A remarkable coincidence.

In the Middle Ages, there were of course many well-identified classes: princes and priests, merchants and mercenaries, serfs and nobles—and, of course, Jews. None of these groups has been chosen by psychiatrists for special scrutiny, and none of them has been diagnosed as suffering, *en masse,* from mental illness. Why, then, the witches? And why not the Jews who, as we saw, were persecuted in much the same way as the witches, and, indeed, sometimes *as* witches?

The answer is simple. The persecution of Jews (and of Protestants and Catholics) is clearly and undeniably a religious persecution; Jews (and Huguenots and Catholics) are classified by terms familiar to us today; for these reasons, they cannot be easily reclassified, *en masse,* as mental patients. The persecution of witches, on the other hand, presents a very different picture to the modern mind. The witch—because of the semantic power of this word, whose significance we must not underestimate—is not recognized as practicing a legitimate religion whereas the Christian and the Jew are; because her behavior derives partly from pre-Christian, pagan sources, the witch readily appears as a strange and bizarre figure (save to the expert on medieval history or theology); for these reasons, she lends herself perfectly as a subject to psychiatric redefinition as insane. Moreover—and the importance of this final consideration can hardly be overestimated—of all the groups persecuted during the Middle Ages and the Reformation, only the witch can be psychiatrically denigrated without arousing the pro-

* Were we to apply this perverse logic to recent history, we would view the gas chamber not as a symbol of Nazi Germany but as a symptom of some incurable pandemic among European Jewry.

tective ire of a contemporary group. If psychiatrists were to diagnose as mad the Jews, the Protestants, or the Catholics burned at the stake by their enemies—their modern coreligionists would rightly regard this as adding insults to their injuries. And they would indignantly repudiate this fresh attack on their integrity and dignity, couched in—but, in this case, insufficiently disguised by—psychiatric jargon.* Witches, however, have no organized or identifiable successors; there is no group to protect their good name. Many of the things that made them ideal live victims for medieval inquisitors also make them ideal historical victims for contemporary psychiatrists.

By regarding witchcraft as a stigmatized status imposed on victims by their enemies, instead of as a condition or disease exhibited by or contained in discrete individuals, we can readily account for the differential incidence of witches—so troublesome to the psychiatric theory of witchcraft—east and west of the Pyrenees. The problem of the differential incidence of (hospitalized) mental patients among various social classes in the modern West likewise disappears if we regard mental illness as a stigmatized status imposed on citizens by their oppressors, instead of as a condition or disease exhibited by or contained in suffering patients. Thus, inquisitors, witchprickers, and their legal assistants were rarely burned at the stake; poor and unimportant people often were. Similarly, psychiatrists, psychologists, and lawyers are rarely committed to mental hospitals; poor and unimportant people often are. This, of course, is also why there are so many elderly persons in state mental hospitals. (In some hospitals they comprise 40 percent of the patient population.) Old people, especially if poor, occupy a position in our society most like that of women in medieval society. They can least protect themselves from invidious medical labeling; if unwanted, they are readily classified as suffering from "senile psychosis" or some other type of insanity, and confined in madhouses for the "care" and "treatment" of their "disease."

The view that the persecution of witches was stimulated by two

* In this connection, it is interesting to note that Albert Schweitzer devoted his medical dissertation to the task of proving wrong his medical colleagues who have diagnosed Jesus as paranoid, and to establishing, by what he calls an "impartial" examination of the historical record, that Jesus was mentally healthy. (Albert Schweitzer, *The Psychiatric Study of Jesus.*)

forces, the Church and the people, and that without either, but especially the former, there could be neither witches nor witch-hunts, is strikingly illustrated by the Spanish experience. There, the difference lay entirely with the Church. The people were as willing to believe in witches and persecute them as were their European neighbors. But the Spanish Inquisition, as Williams emphasizes, "struck at precisely the methods which had been, almost everywhere else, adopted. It forbade judges to ask leading questions; it forbade threats and hints of what confessions were wanted; it forbade—what the *Malleus* had encouraged—false promises; it commanded that sermons should explain how the destruction of crops was due to the weather, and not to witches; it continually imposed as sentence only the most formal abjuration; and finally, it even trained courts so well that before 1600 a woman who twice accused herself of having carnal relations with an incubus was discharged each time."[29]

Outside of the Iberian peninsula, the inquisitor's task was, in principle at least, similar to that of his Spanish colleague: he, too, sought to distinguish between genuine Christians and false or heretical ones. But the concept of heresy was more flexible east of the Pyrenees than west of them. In the Catholic parts of Europe, the heretic might be a Jew, a witch, or a Protestant; in the Protestant parts, he might be a Jew, a witch, or a Catholic. In the Wars of Religion, when Catholic and Protestant territories opposed each other, "it was natural," Trevor-Roper remarks, ". . . that witches should be found in Protestant islands like Orleans or Normandy [and] that by 1609 the entire population of 'Protestant' Navarre should be declared to be witches."[30] It was equally natural that "When Bishop Palladius, the reformer of Denmark, visited his diocese, he declared those who used Catholic prayer or formulas to be witches."[31]

There are other examples of groups of people having been defined as heretics—or "degenerates" or mentally ill. In 1568, the Spanish Inquisition declared the entire population of the Netherlands heretics and condemned it to death.[32] The Nazis declared whole groups of people whom they wanted to destroy—mainly Jews, Poles, and Russians—"racially degenerate." We, in the United States, have declared other groups—drug addicts, homosexuals, persons harboring anti-Semitic and anti-Negro prejudices—mentally sick *en-masse*.[33] Herbert Marcuse, leading ideologist and theoretician of the New Left, diagnoses the whole of American society as "insane": ". . . inasmuch as this society disposes over resources greater than ever before and at the same time distorts and abuses and wastes these resources more than ever before," he declares, "I call this society insane . . ."[34]

The modern physician, especially when he serves a racist or psychiatric ideology rather than an individual patient, may be enlisted in a similar task of scapegoat-selection. The Nazi physician, for example, was sometimes called upon to distinguish between genuine Aryans and false ones, that is, Jews. In his documentary novel on the German occupation of Kiev, Kuznetsov relates the story of a captured Russian soldier who was suspected of being a Jew. "He was taken to a conference room," writes Kuznetsov, "where German doctors examined him for Jewish traits, but their diagnosis was negative."[35] This twentieth-century physician looking for Jewish traits is hardly distinguishable from his nineteenth-century colleagues searching for hysterical stigmata, or from his sixteenth-century colleagues searching for witch's marks.* Similarly, the modern psychiatric physician is often called upon to distinguish between genuine patients, that is, persons suffering from bodily diseases—and false or heretical ones, that is, persons suffering from mental diseases.

To be sure, the scapegoat-selector—whether inquisitor or psychiatrist—does not work in a social vacuum. The persecution of a minority group is not imposed on a resistant population, but, on the contrary, grows out of bitter social conflicts. Nevertheless, the guiding mythology of such a movement is usually fabricated by a few ambitious individuals. Once fabricated, the mythology is spread by the propaganda arm of the movement. "This witch madness," writes Lea, "was essentially a disease of the imagination, created and stimulated by the persecution of witchcraft. Wherever the inquisitor or civil magistrate went to destroy it by fire, a harvest of witches sprang up around his footsteps. Every prosecution widened the circle, until nearly the whole population might become

---

* According to the Renaissance witch-hunter Guaccius, the witch's mark, imposed by the Devil, is designed to mock circumcision, the bodily mark which identifies the Satanic race of Jews. (Leschnitzer, *The Magic Background of Modern Anti-Semitism*, p. 223.)

involved, to be followed by executions numbered, not by the score but by the hundreds."[36]

Trevor-Roper is of the same opinion. "All the evidence makes it clear," he writes, "that the new mythology [of witchcraft] owes its system entirely to the inquisitors themselves. Just as anti-Semites built up, out of disconnected tidbits of scandal, their systematic mythology of ritual murder, poisoned wells, and the world-wide conspiracy of the Elders of Zion, so the Hammerers of Witches built up their systematic mythology of Satan's kingdom and Satan's accomplices out of the mental rubbish of peasant credulity and feminine hysteria; and the one mythology, like the other . . . [generates] its own evidence, and [is] applicable far outside of its original home."[37] The same may be said of the mythology of mental illness: it owes its system entirely to psychiatrists.*

In sum, witch and Jew in the past, madman and Jew today, represent two closely allied—sometimes indistinguishable but sometimes obviously distinct—enemies of society. Prior to her offense, the medieval witch was a full-fledged member of society; her crime was heresy—that is, rejection of the dominant religious ethic—and for this she was punished. The medieval Jew, on the other hand, was never a fully accepted member of society. Sometimes, when it was believed that his presence helped the community, he was tolerated as a guest; at other times, when it was believed that his presence endangered the community, he was persecuted as an enemy. What Christian witch and Jewish victim had in common was that the society in which they lived considered them both its enemies and hence sought to destroy them.

The same relationship obtains between the modern madman and the Jew. Prior to his mental illness, the (non-Jewish) mental patient is a member of society; his crime is madness—that is, rejection of the dominant secular ethic—and for this he is punished. The modern Jew, on the other hand, is not a fully accepted part of society. A Jew among Christians (or, worse, among atheists, as in Soviet Russia) is regarded as an outsider: sometimes, because it is believed that his presence is useful to the group, he is tolerated; at other times, because it is believed that his presence is injurious

---

* I have indicated the origins of this psychiatric mythology in Chapter 5, will trace its evolution further in Chapter 8, and shall discuss and document its recent history and present function in Chapters 9-13. See also Thomas S. Szasz, *The Myth of Mental Illness.*

to the group, he is persecuted.* Again, what madman and persecuted Jew have in common is that the society in which they live
considers them both its enemies and hence seeks to destroy them.
Moreover, the popular propensity for persecuting Jews and madmen has been fostered by similar techniques: for centuries, Christians have taught contempt for Jews;[38] and ever since psychiatry
was born as a medical specialty in the seventeenth century, physicians have taught contempt for mental patients.[39] But here the
similarity ends. For Christian religious instruction at least did not
pretend to have as its object the care of Jews, whereas "mental
health education" pretends to have as its object the care of mental
patients. Thus, officially, the history of psychiatry is presented as if
it were the story of the care and treatment of the insane; actually,
it is the story of their persecution.

In sum, the effect, if not the intent, of the modern psychiatric
interpretation of the witch-mania is the debasement, as insane, of
millions of innocent men, women, and children; the exoneration
from responsibility, as a virtual nonparticipant, of the Roman
Catholic Church and its executive arm, the Inquisition, for the
pogrom against Jews, heretics, and witches, and the similar exoneration of the Protestant churches and their leading spokesmen for
joining in the holy war against witchcraft; and, last but not least,
the exaltation, as medical scientist and healer, of the psychiatrist—
the sole possessor of an "enlightened" and "scientific" understanding of witchcraft and of the medical methods required for the
control of the public health hazards posed by human differences.[40]

The end of one ideology is thus the beginning of another: where
religious heresy ends, psychiatric heresy begins; where the persecution of the witch ends, the persecution of the madman begins.

---

* The specific danger which the Jew represents to the community has kept pace
with the historical changes in what the community values. In the Middle Ages,
the Jew was a traitor against Christianity: his ancestors, so it was believed, killed
Jesus, and he continued to reject the true Faith and the authority of the
Church. In the modern world, the Jew is a traitor against the Fatherland and
against the dominant political ideology. Dreyfus symbolizes the Jew as traitor
against the nation. Since the Russian Revolution, the Jew has emerged as the
prototypical enemy of Capitalism and Communism. In the West, the communist ideology is seen as Jew-inspired, with Marx and Trotsky as its leading
symbols. In the East, the capitalist ideology is seen as Jew-inspired, with the
Rothschilds and other "Jewish bankers" as its leading symbols.

8

THE MYTHS OF WITCHCRAFT
AND MENTAL ILLNESS

> It has become too easy to see that the luckless men
> of the past lived by mistaken, even absurd beliefs;
> so we may fail in a decent respect for them, and
> forget that the historians of the future will point out
> that we too lived by myths.
>
> —*Herbert J. Muller*[1]

The psychiatric interpretation of witchcraft suffers from many errors. Not the least among these is the claim that Johann Weyer discovered that witches were actually mentally sick women. Virtually all modern students of psychiatric history have accepted this view, popularized by Zilboorg, which traces the birth of psychiatry to the death of the witch-craze, and regards Weyer as the Columbus of madness. George Mora's following characterization is illustrative: "Johann Weyer [is] rightly considered today the father of modern psychiatry. . . . But Weyer was to remain isolated, a giant of psychiatry practically unknown until the beginning of our century . . ."[2]

This sort of statement makes it appear as if the psychiatric historian were a socially neutral person, discovering historical "facts"—when, in truth, he is a psychiatric propagandist, actively shaping the image of his discipline. Weyer has been canonized as the father of psychiatry because he was one of the few physicians who had opposed the persecution of witches. By claiming him as its founder, Institutional Psychiatry has tried, and largely succeeded, in concealing its oppressive practices behind a façade of liberational rhetoric.

It is significant that Weyer was "discovered" to be the "true" father of psychiatry in the twentieth century, and by American psychiatrists: this is when and where Institutional Psychiatry became a major social force in the Western world.

But Weyer did not discover the madness of witches. To be sure, he deserves credit for opposing the Inquisition, the principal oppressive institution of his time. But taking a courageous stand for human decency is not the same as propounding a fresh theory or making a new empirical discovery. The view that mental illness is not a disease and that the madhouse is a prison rather than a hospital is likewise not my discovery; it is merely a new articulation of insights and knowledge long available to men, both in and outside of medicine.*

The persecution of witches and of madmen is the expression of social intolerance and a search for scapegoats. Those who fight against such bigotry and oppression do not necessarily profess revolutionary beliefs or propound novel truths. On the contrary, their heresy all too often lies in their conservatism, that is, in their insistence on the validity of ideas and values long established and honored. In *The Plague,* Camus puts it this way: "But again and again there comes a time in history when the man who dares to say that two and two make four is punished with death."[3]

It seems to me that to maintain that what we call mental illness is not a disease is like asserting that two and two make four; and that to maintain that involuntary mental hospitalization is an immoral practice is like saying that three and three make six. I have

---

* Herein lies a fundamental difference between natural science and social science. In the former, we speak of a new discovery when something genuinely novel—usually both in a cognitive and practical sense—is added to man's knowledge of the world; the (physical) discovery of radioactivity is an example. In the human sciences, however, we often regard it as a discovery when man penetrates behind the mythology of his society or culture and "rediscovers" something that had been known in past ages; the (psychoanalytic) "discovery" of childhood sexuality is an example. To be sure, such advances, which consist essentially of the de-mythologizing of prevalent beliefs, also add something seemingly novel to man's knowledge of the world. But there is an important difference between these two kinds of scientific innovations. The former requires a cognitive breakthrough leading into new territory; the latter, self-emancipation from the dominant myths of one's group, often leading back to old wisdoms. This may be why the study of the social sciences, especially of history, often leaves one with the impression that, about human relations, everything important has been known and said before; whereas the history of science and technology provokes the very opposite impression.

held these views ever since, as John Stuart Mill says in *The Subjection of Women,* "I had formed any opinion at all on social and political matters . . ."[4]

For millennia, it has been convenient for men to believe that women were inferior, semihuman beings who needed to be subjugated and cared for. Sane men, for almost as long, have regarded insane men in the same way. Because the oppression of women by men was accepted as natural, it was difficult, Mill observed, to dispel this opinion by means of rational arguments: "So long as an opinion is strongly rooted in the feelings, it gains rather than loses in stability by having a preponderating weight of arguments against it."[5] Because the oppression of insane patients by sane psychiatrists appears similarly natural to us today, the correctness of this arrangement is likewise difficult to dislodge by means of rational arguments alone.

Perhaps the best way to understand the mythical character of certain beliefs is to examine their history. Why did medieval man choose to believe in witchcraft and seek the amelioration of his society in the compulsory salvation of witches? Why does modern man choose to believe in the myth of mental illness and seek the amelioration of his society in the compulsory treatment of mental patients? In each of these mass movements we are faced with two interlocking phenomena: a guiding myth (of witchcraft and of mental illness), and a powerful social institution (the Inquisition and Institutional Psychiatry); the former provides the ideological justification, the latter, the practical means for social action. Much of what I have said so far in this book, and particularly in Chapter 4, was an effort to answer the questions posed above. Since, in the discussion heretofore, my emphasis has been on institutional practices rather than on ideological (mythological) justifications, I shall concentrate, in this chapter, on what men believe and the imagery they use to express their belief, rather than on what they ostensibly seek and the means they employ to achieve it.

As historical research has shown, men entertained doubts about the existence of witches long before Weyer; indeed, long before the Enlightenment, some wise rulers even passed laws prohibiting their molestation. For example, as early as the eighth century, St. Boniface, the English apostle of Germany, declared that belief in witchcraft was "unchristian."[6] This is a remarkably enlightened view, inasmuch as it disregards the Biblical injunction, "Thou shalt not suffer a witch to live,"[7] invoked centuries later to justify the witch-hunts. Also in the eighth century, in newly converted Saxony, Charlemagne decreed the death penalty, not for witches, but for anyone who burned supposed witches. In eleventh century Hungary, the laws of King Solomon took no notice of witches, "since they do not exist."[8] Five hundred years later, Weyer, while protesting against the excesses of the witch-hunters, was sure that witches did exist.

It is shocking and sobering to contemplate that during the Renaissance, when learning flourished and experimental science was born, the laws against witch-hunting forged during the Dark Ages were forgotten, and former "ignorance" about witches was "corrected" by fresh theological and scientific insights. When the *Malleus* was published in 1486, it carried on its title page the epigraph: *"Haeresis est maxima opera maleficarum non credere"* ("To disbelieve in witchcraft is the greatest of heresies").[9] And, as a doctor of the Sorbonne wrote in 1609, the witches' sabat was an "objective fact, disbelieved only by those of unsound mind."[10]

Although the belief in witchcraft was widespread during the late Middle Ages and the Renaissance,* a careful reading of the *Malleus* suggests that many were skeptical about the evils attributed to witches, and critical of the methods used by the inquisitors. There is, however, no direct evidence that men doubted the reality of witchcraft or the existence of witches. Open expression of such doubt would, of course, have been tantamount to a self-imposed death sentence for heresy.

Men in power do not exhort their subjects to accept ideas they believe already. If, then, there is need to command belief and to threaten for disbelief, we may infer that the subjects lack faith or

---

* As late as 1775, Sir William Blackstone, the Father of English Law, said that "To deny the possibility, nay, actual existence, of witchcraft and sorcery is at once flatly to contradict the revealed word of God . . . and the thing itself is a truth to which every nation in the world hath borne testimony." (Quoted in Henry Charles Lea, *A History of the Inquisition of Spain*, Vol. 4, p. 247.) Soon the belief fell into disrepute. This change did not represent, however, a genuine advance of the human mind. "Men were terrified of behaving unfashionably," Williams remarks bitterly, "and those who would once have believed in witches now disbelieved for exactly the same reason—because everyone else did." (Charles Williams, *Witchcraft*, p. 301.) This might give pause to all who accept the popular belief in mental illness.

are beset by doubt. When clerical authorities warn that witchcraft is real and witches dangerous, and that to believe otherwise
is a grave sin; or when secular authorities declare that mental illness is real ("like any other illness . . ."), and that a contrary point
of view is a serious error—we may then assume that neither ex-
horters nor exhorted are convinced of the truthfulness of the
assertion. Indeed, this kind of "education," backed by threat and
force, betrays the strategic value of the proposition to be believed.[11]
Unless the contemporary reader keeps this implication of inquisitorial propaganda in mind, he may well miss—especially since he
takes his own skepticism about witchcraft for granted—the repeated
references in the *Malleus* to persons who do *not* believe in witchcraft. I infer from these admonitions that doubt about the reality
of witchcraft in late fifteenth-century Europe was far more prevalent than modern historians, looking vainly for overt declarations
of such an opinion, have led us to believe.

The second section of Part I of the *Malleus* is entitled "Whether
it be a Heresy to Maintain that Witches Exist." The peculiarly inverted phrasing of this sentence should be noted. Sprenger and
Krämer ponder whether the belief in witchcraft is a mistake—only
to conclude that to disbelieve it is a grave sin. "The question
arises," they ask, "whether people who hold that witches do not
exist are to be regarded as notorious heretics . . ."[12] They answer
yes. This is as if modern psychiatrists were to ask whether mental
patients exist, and would answer that to believe otherwise is a
serious error and a grave offense against the psychiatric profession.
Since I have dubbed mental illness a "myth," precisely this argument has been advanced by several psychiatrists critical of my
views.[13]

Priests and inquisitors in particular must not doubt the reality
of witchcraft. It is bad enough, say Sprenger and Krämer, for the
ordinary man to be "ignorant" about witchcraft; "those who have
the cure of souls [sic] cannot plead invincible ignorance, nor that
particular ignorance, as the philosophers call it, which by the
writers on Canon Law and by the Theologians is called Ignorance
of the Fact."[14] In the same way, it is considered permissible for
laymen to be "ignorant" about the facts of mental illness; physicians
and psychiatrists, however, must display unswerving allegiance to
this concept and its practical implications (such as limiting the

treatment of mental illness to physicians and justifying commitment of the insane as a medical measure.)*

In another passage Sprenger and Krämer describe witchcraft in astonishingly modern terms; they attribute the following view—which we would consider correct—to many of their contemporaries, and declare them heretics for holding it. "And the first error which they [the Theologians] condemn," they write, "is that of those who say that there is no witchcraft in the world, but only in the imagination of men who, through their ignorance of hidden causes which no man yet understands, ascribe certain natural effects to witchcraft . . . Doctors condemn this error as a pure falsehood, . . . St. Thomas impugns it as actual heresy . . . therefore such deserve to be suspected as heretics."[15]

The fulminations of the *Malleus* and of the inquisitors notwithstanding, there were brave and honest men who, throughout the many centuries of witch-persecution, expressed doubts about the victims' guilt and condemned the methods of their accusers. Thomas Ady, Cornelius Agrippa, Salazar de Frias, Friedrich von Spee, and Johann Weyer are among the best-known critics of the witch-hunts. Salazar, a Spanish inquisitor to whose work we have referred earlier,[16] was, more than any other man, responsible for preventing the persecution of witches in Spain. He examined charges of witchcraft with an open mind and found, in 1611, "that some sixteen hundred persons had been falsely accused. At one place he found tales of a Sabbath held at the very place where his own secretaries had been harmlessly on the night named. He had women who confessed to carnal intercourse physically examined by women; they were found to be virgin."[17]

Thomas Ady was a foremost English critic of the witch-hunts. His book, *A Candle in the Dark* (1655), was quoted vainly by the Reverend George Burroughs at his trial in Salem.[18] Ady's attack on the witch mania was two-pronged. On the one hand, he tried to show that contemporary proofs of witchcraft were not based on

---

* Thus, Robert H. Felix, former director of the National Institute of Mental Health and dean of the Saint Louis University Medical School, asserts flatly that "We [psychiatrists] *do* deal with illnesses of the mind." (Italics in the original.) (Robert H. Felix, The image of the psychiatrist: Past, present and future, *Amer. J. Psychiat.*, 121: 318–322 [Oct.], 1964, p. 320.) Criticism of this position is considered psychiatric heresy. See, for example, Frederick G. Glaser, The dichotomy game: A further consideration of the writings of Dr. Thomas Szasz, *Amer. J. Psychiat.*, 121: 1069–1074 (May), 1965; p. 1073.

the Bible. "Where is it written in all the Old and New Testaments," Ady asks, "that a witch is a murderer, or has the power to kill by witch-craft, or to afflict with any disease or infirmity? Where is it written that witches have imps sucking off their bodies?"[19] And so he goes on in an effort to undermine the Biblical authority for the persecution of witches.

On the other hand, Ady also denounced the examination of alleged witches as brutal and fraudulent. "Let any man that is wise and free from prejudice," he writes, "go and hear but the Confessions that are so commonly alleged, and he may see with what catching and cavelling, what thwarting and lying, what flat and plain knavery, these confessions are wrung from poor innocent people, and what monstrous additions and multiplications are afterwards invented to make the matter seem true, which yet is most damnably false."[20] That such arguments failed indicates the subsidiary role reason plays in the acceptance or rejection of beliefs which motivate mass-movements. Moreover, in Spain, where the persecution of witches was opposed by the ecclesiastic authorities, the witch-craze was stemmed without such arguments. These facts point to the determining role of authority and power in making or breaking such movements. The Spanish Inquisition successfully restrained the witch-hunts, whereas individuals battling the Roman Inquisition and the Protestant witch-craze failed to do so.

In 1640, for example, the Spanish Inquisition "suspended the case of Maria Sanz of Triqueros, against whom there was testimony of witchcraft, and, in 1641, it discharged with a reprimand Maria Alfonsa de la Torre, accused of killing cattle, although witnesses swore to seeing her at midnight riding on a stick over a rye-field, with a noise as though accompanied by a multitude of demons."[21] From cases such as these, Lea infers that ". . . it is evident that the Inquisition had reached the conclusion that witchcraft was virtually a delusion, or that incriminating testimony was perjured. This could not be openly published; the belief was of too long standing and too firmly asserted by the Church to be pronounced false . . ."[22] The idea that mental illness does not exist, except as a myth, likewise cannot be openly acknowledged. The doctrine that mental illness is a disease has been too firmly established by science to be pronounced false. The prestige and tradition of the medical profession thus stand in the way of the rapid correction of this monumental error.

True to the life of bureaucratic organizations, the Spanish Inquisition never admitted that any of its teachings had been false or its practices misguided. "It did not," as Lea points out, "deny the existence of witchcraft, or modify the penalties of the crime . . . ; [instead], it practically rendered proof impossible, thus discouraging formal accusations, while its prohibition of preliminary proceedings by its commissioners and by the local officials, secular and ecclesiastical, was effectual in preventing the outbreak of witchcraft epidemics. So far as the records before me show, cases became very few after . . . 1610."[23]

The ideologies of witchcraft and madness may perhaps be thrown into even bolder relief by focusing on the moral ideals and images characteristic of their times. In the thirteenth century, the symbol of nobility is the knight-in-armor, and of depravity, the black witch; benevolent motivation is chivalrous, malevolent is Satanic. This imagery embodies and expresses the sexocidal hatred of woman; the knight, the symbol of good, is male; the witch, the symbol of evil, is female. At the same time, the battle between the sexes, the treachery among the nobles, the oppression of the poor by the rich—none of these things is presented directly; on the contrary, social reality is portrayed as if it were a dream in which symbols signified their opposites. Woman is not debased; she is exalted. The nobles are not brutal and treacherous; they are refined and chivalrous. Huizinga puts it this way:

Froissart, himself the author of a super-romantic epic of chivalry, *Meliador,* narrates endless treasons and cruelties, without being aware of the contradiction between his general conceptions and the contents of his narrative. Molinet, in his chronicle, from time to time remembers his chivalrous intention, and interrupts his matter-of-fact account of events, to unbosom himself in a flood of high-flown terms. The conception of chivalry constituted for these authors a sort of magic key, by the aid of which they explained to themselves the motives of politics and of history. The confused image of contemporaneous history being much too complicated for their comprehension, they simplified it, as it were, by the fiction of chivalry as a moving force . . .[24]

The reason for this imagery is not hard to find. In seeking explanations for events, and especially for their own actions, men always try to flatter themselves or their superiors. Since, in the Middle Ages, poetry, literature, and history were written either by or for the oppressor, it is not surprising that we hear so much about the glory of princes and the chivalry of knights.

By this traditional fiction [Huizinga observes], they succeeded in explaining to themselves, as well as they could, the motives and the course of history, which thus was reduced to a spectacle of the honour of princes and the virtue of knights, to a noble game with edifying and heroic rules. As a principle of historiography, this point of view is a very inferior one. History thus conceived becomes a summary of feats of arms and of ceremonies. The historians *par excellence* will be heralds and kings-at-arms—Froissart thinks so— for they are the witnesses of these sublime deeds; they are experts in matters of honour and of glory, and it is to record honour and glory that history is written.* 25

Although the mentality of modern man may be more advanced than that of his medieval ancestor, it shows the same credulity toward authority and the same tendency to explain complicated situations or events by a single motive. As the Middle Ages had their ideal types of good and evil, we have ours. Theirs were the knight-in-armor and the black witch. Ours are the doctor-in-white-coat and the dangerous psychotic. They had Sir Lancelot; we have Rex Morgan, M.D. They had sorceresses who poisoned men of high station; we have madmen who kill political personages. The symbols of good and evil again signify two warring classes of human beings, the victors and the victims.

In the Middle Ages, the imagery of chivalry disguised the conflict between man and woman. Today, we conceal the conflict between doctor and patient, expert and layman, behind the imagery of therapy. The lyricism of chivalry dulled their sense of reality; the lyricism of therapy dulls ours. They repressed the truth about

* What Huizinga says here about the Middle Ages applies, *mutatis mutandis*, to our age as well. Then, the historian had to be an expert "in matters of honour and glory"; now, he must be an expert in matters of mental health and emotional maturity. Then, history was written to "record honour and glory"; now, it is written to record mental health and emotional maturity. Evidence and observation thus are subordinated to ascribing Christian virtue or mental health to the heroes, and Satanic sin or mental illness to the villains. For an example of this type of modern historiography, see Meyer A. Zeligs, *Friendship and Fratricide.*

heresy and inquisitorial salvation; we repress the truth about mental illness and coerced psychiatric treatment. The poetry of chivalry focused on knights, tournaments, pomp, and the self-sacrifice of Jesus. The dungeons, the torture, and the stake did not have to be described. Everyone knew of them and indeed approved and enjoyed their proper application for saving the heretical soul of the Other. In the same way, the poetry of therapy focuses on doctors, medical research, the vast funds expended on psychiatric services, and the psychiatrist's selfless devotion to healing. The state mental hospital, the commitment procedure, the social degradation of the mental patient need not be dwelled upon. Everyone is familiar with them and indeed approves their proper application to curing the mentally sick mind of the Other.

Medieval history, as Huizinga remarked, was in this way reduced to "a spectacle of the honour of princes and the virtue of knights." Modern history, at least in the hands of psychiatrists, stands in danger of being similarly reduced to a spectacle of the honour of rulers and the virtue of doctors. In Nazi Germany, this dramatic imagery was acted out in the deification of the ruler and the glorification of doctors as his servants. Physicians thus fought against "vermin" (Jews), and "useless eaters" (old or incurably sick people), and, so doing, transformed, in Justice Robert Jackson's words, "the sanatorium Hadamar [a German mental hospital in which such patients were killed] . . . from a hospital [in]to a human slaughter-house."[26] In nontotalitarian nations, the same dramatic imagery is acted out in only slightly less violent forms. Democratic leaders are not deified, but are hailed as the paragons of mental health; their opponents are not liquidated, but are degraded as mentally sick. Confronted with great and disturbing events, such as the assassination of a president, the people eagerly accept madness (as they did sorcery before) as their explanation, and look to psychiatrists (as they did to inquisitors before) for containing the threat of this transcendent evil.[27]

In short, myth—whether of witchcraft or mental illness—functions as justificatory imagery and rhetoric for both the group and the individual. Myth, says Bronislaw Malinowski, "can attach itself not only to magic but to any form of social power or social claim. It is used always to account for extraordinary privileges or duties, for great social inequalities, for severe burdens of rank, whether this be very high or very low."[28]

The myth of witchcraft was thus used to account for the extraordinary privileges and duties of the inquisitor; similarly, the myth of mental illness is used to account for those of the institutional psychiatrist. Myths are not artistic embellishments, fairy stories men make up to amuse themselves and their fellows; they are the very heart and brain, as it were, of the social organism, necessary for its survival—as *that* particular society.

Indeed, anthropologists have no difficulty in discovering myths in primitive cultures, and social critics have none in discovering them in their own. Thus, Barrows Dunham cautions that "Myths abound concerning the nature of society; these myths will be found, stretched screaming over many a long volume, in the very heart of the science itself. There can be few tasks more important than to remove these myths, and thus to instill health and vigor into man's most valuable study—that of his own nature and destiny."[29]

Let us now examine the history of witchcraft and mental illness from points of view other than those supplied by their own ideologies and see what we find.

The idea that madness is not less meaningful than sanity—indeed, that the madman, like the so-called genius, sees reality more accurately than the ordinary person—occurs frequently in Western literature. A striking illustration of this view is contained in the Gospel according to Mark, where, we are told, the first man to recognize the divinity of Jesus is "a man with an unclean spirit," that is, a madman. In the idiom of modern psychiatry, correct reality-testing is here equated with mental illness. I shall cite the relevant passages.

The opening sentence of the Book of Mark, the second chapter of the New Testament, defines the essential aim of this Gospel as the identification of Jesus as the son of God: "The beginning of the gospel of Jesus Christ, the son of God."[30] Then, the story unfolds. "In those days Jesus came from Nazareth of Galilee and was baptized by John in the Jordan. And when he came out of the water, immediately he saw the heavens opened and the Spirit descending upon him like a dove; and a voice came from heaven. 'Thou art my beloved Son; and with thee I am well pleased.' "[31]

Jesus then spends forty days in the wilderness resisting Satan's temptations, returns to Galilee to preach the gospel of God, and gathers around him the first of his followers with whom he travels to Capernaum. "And they went into Capernaum; and immediately on the Sabbath he entered the synagogue and taught. And they were astonished at his teaching, for he taught them as one who had authority, and not as the scribes. And immediately there was in their synagogue a man with an unclean spirit; and he cried out, 'What have you to do with us, Jesus of Nazareth? Have you come to destroy us? *I know who you are, the Holy one of God.'* "[32] (Italics added.)

This "madman," then, is the first mortal to recognize Jesus' true identity. But this identification, Jesus feels, is premature. He commands silence: "But Jesus rebuked him, saying, 'Be silent, and come out of him!' And the unclean spirit, convulsing him and crying with a loud voice, came out of him."[33]

This theme is repeated several times. Thus, as Jesus' fame as a healer spreads, ". . . all who had diseases pressed upon him to touch him. And whenever the unclean spirits beheld him, they fell down before him and cried out, 'You are the Son of God.' And he strictly ordered them not to make him known."[34] And again: "They came to the other side of the sea, to the country of the Gerasenes. And when he had come out of the boat, there met him out of the tombs a man with an unclean spirit, who lived among the tombs; and no one could bind him any more, even with a chain . . . no one had the strength to subdue him; and crying out with a loud voice, he said, 'What have you to do with me Jesus, Son of the Most High God?' "[35]

The ancient Romans viewed madness much as did the authors of the Book of Mark. *"In vino veritas"* ("In wine there is truth"), said their proverb. They did not deceive themselves, as our modern jurists do, about the nature of drunkenness, by attributing irrationality or meaninglessness to it. Instead, they believed, I think correctly, that when a man is under the influence of alcohol, his conduct, far from being meaningless, expresses his true or authentic aspirations. But to treat the drunkard thus is to treat him with the same dignity as his sober fellows. For the Puritan who wants to demean and punish the "self-indulgent" toper, for the physician who wants to humiliate and treat the "self-destructive" alcoholic, this will not do. What better way is there, then, for degrading the culprit than to declare him incapable of knowing what he is doing—either when taking to drink or while intoxicated? This is the general formula for the dehumanization and degradation of all those persons whose conduct psychiatrists now deem to be "caused" by mental illness. The behavior of such men is considered "meaningless." The alcoholic, the addict, the homosexual—all these and many more are said to be mentally ill. Our foremost psychiatrists and highest judges tell us so. In arriving at this opinion—which happens to be so very convenient both for them and for our society—they no doubt follow Lewis Carroll's formula. "If there is no meaning in it," says the King in *Alice*, "that saves a world of trouble, you know, as we needn't try to find any."[36] But if the task of the humanist is to reveal meaning, not to conceal it, we cannot rest content with this solution, tempting though it may be.

The proposition that the madman does not know what he is talking about, or that his utterances are untrue, is explicitly contradicted by an old German proverb which asserts that "Only children and madmen tell the truth" (*"Nur Kinder und Narren sagen die Wahrheit"*).

In the English language, we have Shakespeare's famous phrase about the "method in madness."* I believe it is significant that Shakespeare did not find it necessary to explain or defend this opinion. This suggests that the idea was commonplace in his day. If so, it would mean that in Elizabethan England men understood not only that there is a difference between bodily disease and spiritual disharmony, but also that insane behavior, no less than sane, is goal-directed and motivated; or, as we might say today, that it is tactical or strategic. In short, Shakespeare and his audiences regarded the behavior of the madman as perfectly rational from the point of view of the actor or affected individual—a perspective which psychoanalysis and existential psychology had to rediscover and defend against the powerful pretensions of a positivistic, organically oriented psychiatry.

To John Perceval, son of a Prime Minister of England, who, in 1830, was immured in a mental hospital by his family, the distinction between physical illness and mental illness, the treatment of bodies and the cure of souls, was equally clear:

---

* "Polonius: Though this be madness, yet there is method in't." (*Hamlet*, Act II, Scene 2, Line 211.)

For a perceptive analysis of Shakespeare's understanding of Hamlet's madness, see Howard M. Feinstein, Hamlet's Horatio and the therapeutic mode, *Amer. J. Psychiat.*, 123: 803–809 (Jan.), 1967.

For by what right can a doctor presume to pry into the secrets of a patient's conscience . . . ? They [the doctors] confess themselves ignorant of the nature of the disease they handle; they show themselves willfully so. . . . The clergymen of the established church ought to have the superintendence of the mental wants and infirmities of the deranged members of their communion, and the two offices of *physician to the body and the physician to the soul, distinctive in nature, should be equally respected.* Sovereigns in this country, their ministers, and the people have been guilty of a great crime in *neglecting this important distinction,* and the hierarchy have betrayed their office."[37] [Italics added.]

This distinction—between bodily diseases and problems in living —was equally clear to Leo Tolstoy in 1889. Indeed, even so early in the history of psychiatry—when Charcot rather than Freud was the world-renowned medical expert on mental illness—Tolstoy saw that the physician who conceptualizes difficulties in living as illnesses mystifies rather than clarifies the problem, and harms rather than helps the sufferer. In *The Kreutzer Sonata,* whose protagonist is a husband who is the victim of the tragically unequal, mutually exploitative relationship between men and women, Tolstoy expresses the following view about psychological medicine and psychiatry:

"I see you don't like doctors," I said, noticing a peculiarly malevolent tone in his voice whenever he alluded to them.

"It is not a case of liking or disliking. They have ruined my life and they have ruined and are ruining the lives of thousands and hundreds of thousands of human beings, and I cannot help connecting the effect with the cause. . . . Today one can no longer say: You are not living rightly, live better. One can't say that, either to oneself or to anyone else. If you live a bad life, it is caused by the abnormal functioning of your nerves, etc. So you must go to them, and they will prescribe eight penn'orth of medicine from a chemist, which you must take! You get still worse: then more medicine, and the doctor again. An excellent trick!"[38]

In a later passage, Tolstoy points specifically to unhappy marriage as a phenomenon often misinterpreted by physicians as illness, and blames Charcot for it. This is a very different appraisal of

Charcot's achievement as a medical psychologist than that found in textbooks of psychiatric history.

We were like two convicts [writes Tolstoy, speaking through the husband who is finally driven to murdering his wife], hating each other and chained together, poisoning one another's lives and trying not to see it. I did not then know that ninety-nine per cent of married people live in a similar hell to the one I was in and that it cannot be otherwise. I did not then know this either about others or about myself. . . . Thus we lived in a perpetual fog, not seeing the condition we were in. . . . Those new theories of hypnotism, psychic diseases, and hysterias are not a simple folly, but a dangerous and repulsive one. Charcot would certainly have said that my wife was hysterical, and that I was abnormal, and he would no doubt have tried to cure me. But there was nothing to cure.[39]

It would be difficult, indeed, to find more penetrating insight into the mythological character of mental illness than this one.

Freud, as we know, reconstructed the diverse meanings of various "mental illnesses" not only, or even primarily, from what he learned from his patients (who, of course, were not "patients" in the medical sense of the word), but also from what he learned from the works of men of letters. Those who believe that the "adaptational" point of view in psychiatry is something new—a great scientific discovery by Harry Stack Sullivan or Sandor Rado, and an important advance over Freud—ought to consider the following passage from *The Way of All Flesh* by Samuel Butler:

All our lives long, every day and every hour, we are engaged in the process of accommodating our changed and unchanged selves to changed and unchanged surroundings; living, in fact, is nothing else than this process of accommodation; when we fail in it a little we are stupid, when we fail flagrantly we are mad, when we suspend it temporarily we sleep, when we give up the attempt altogether we die.[40]

One of the earliest critics of the coercive medical treatment of insanity, writing long before the advent of the systematic confinement of madmen, is Caelius Aurelianus, a second-century, A.D., Roman physician of African birth. He complains that

They [his medical colleagues] seem mad themselves, rather than disposed to cure their patients, when they compare them to wild beasts, to be tamed by deprivation of food and the tortures of thirst. Doubtless led by the same error, they want to chain them up cruelly, without thinking that their limbs may be bruised or broken, and that it is more convenient and easier to restrain them by the hand of man than by the often useless weight of irons. They go so far as to advocate personal violence, the lash, as if to compel the return of reason by such provocation.[41]

When, fifteen hundred years later, Pinel advanced similar ideas, he was hailed as a great psychiatric innovator. When, about the same time, Benjamin Rush advocated and practiced "therapeutic" brutalities far worse than those denounced by this ancient Roman physician, he was hailed as a great physician and humanitarian.* Pinel, as the writers of official psychiatric history would have it, launched the First Psychiatric Revolution. Rush, for his part, is canonized as the Father of American Psychiatry.†

The idea that the mental hospital is harmful for the inmates, serving primarily the interests of the patient's relatives or those of society, is more easily traced to specific individuals in the history of psychiatry than is the idea that mental illness is not a disease. This is because the mental hospital system is only about three hundred years old, whereas man's views on madness are as old as recorded history.

A study of the origin of European madhouses in the seventeenth century makes it abundantly clear that when these institutions were founded, they were not considered medical or therapeutic facilities.[42] Rather, they were regarded as prisonlike structures for the confine-

---

* The path of progress in psychiatry is circular, periodically returning to its starting point. In 1754, the following entry appears in the record book of the Pennsylvania Hospital, the oldest hospital in the United States, the first to care for mental patients, and the pride of the historiographers of American psychiatry: "John Cresson, blacksmith, against ye hospital, 1 pair handcuffs, 2 legg locks, 2 large rings and 2 large staples, 5 links and 2 large rings and 2 swiffels for cells, £ 1.10.3. Paid for 7 yds. of Thicken for Mad Shirts, £ 0.16. 4-½." (Edward A. Strecker, *Beyond the Clinical Frontiers*, p. 155.) With modern advances in the technology of psychiatric violence, mental hospitals have replaced the handcuffs with electroshock, and the mad shirt with tranquilizers.

† The vast majority of books on the history of psychiatry suffer from the same distortions as do histories of slavery written before the Civil War by men favorable to the pro-slavery position. Standard texts on the history of psychiatry are accounts of the glories of Institutional Psychiatry. A history of psychiatry from the point of view of the "patient" has yet to be written.

ment of socially undesirable persons. Out of this nucleus grew an ever larger institutional system of both public and private hospitals and madhouses, confinement in which gradually became justified on the grounds of insanity. But no sooner was this idea articulated than it was assailed as unsound and untrue.

An early criticism of involuntary mental hospitalization—in terms almost identical to those of modern writers—came from the pen of Andrew Harper, a surgeon on the staff of the Royal Garrison Battalion of Foot, at Fort Nassau in the Bahamas.

The custom of immediately consigning the unfortunate victims of insanity to the cells of Bedlam, or the dreary mansions of some private confinement [wrote Harper in 1789], is certainly big with ignorance and absurdity. This practice, 'tis true, may answer the purpose of private interest, and domestic conveniency, but at the same time it destroys all the obligations of humanity, robs the sufferer of every advantage, and deprives him of all the favourable circumstances which might tend to his recovery. . . . I am convinced that confinement never fails to aggravate the disease. A state of coercion is a state of torture from which the mind, under any circumstance, revolts.[43]

Sixteen years later, in 1815, Thomas Bakewell, the lay owner of a private madhouse in England, protested, in a letter addressed to the Chairman of the Select Committee of the House of Commons appointed to inquire into the state of madhouses, that "The general treatment of the insane is incontestably wrong; it is an outrage to the present state of knowledge, to the best feelings of enlightened humanity, and to national policy. . . . Large Public Asylums for the Insane are certainly wrong, upon system; for nothing can be more calculated to prevent recovery, from a state of insanity, than the horrors of a large Mad House . . ."[44]

John Reid, an English physician and author of the classic psychiatric text, *De Insania* (1789), anticipated by nearly two centuries the contemporary psychiatric view that individuals confined in mental hospitals are taught to act crazy and may become mad in this way.

It is principally on account of the barbarous and unphilosophical treatment . . . of mental indisposition [wrote Reid in 1816], that the receptacles are too often found to be the nurseries of insanity, where any, however small an aberration from the ordinary and healthy standard of nervous excitement may, in due time, be matured and expanded into the full size and frightful monstrosity of madness. . . . Many of the depots for the captivity of intellectual invalids may be regarded only as nurseries for and manufactories of madness.[45]

The modern ideas that "sanity" and "insanity" are categories created and used for the purpose of segregating, and thus injuring, persons classified as insane, and that the aim of confining people in mental hospitals is not to cure them of an illness but rather to authenticate them as insane, were clearly set forth by John Conolly almost 150 years ago. Conolly was a professor of medicine in the University of London and a prominent psychiatrist in his time. In his classic work, *An Inquiry Concerning the Indications of Insanity, With Suggestions for the Better Protection and Care of the Insane,* published in 1830, Conolly writes:

They [medical men] have sought for, and imagined, a strong and definable boundary between sanity and insanity, which has not only been imaginary, and arbitrarily placed, but, by being supposed to separate all who were of unsound mind from the rest of men, has unfortunately been considered a justification of certain measures against the portion condemned, which, in the case of the majority, were unnecessary and afflicting . . . Once confined, the very confinement is admitted as the strongest of all proofs that a man must be mad. . . . It matters not that the certificate is probably signed by those who know little about madness or the necessity of confinement; or by those who have not carefully examined the patient; a visitor fears to avow, in the face of such a document, what may be set down as mere want of penetration in a matter wherein nobody seems in doubt but himself; or he may even be tempted to affect to perceive those signs of madness which do not exist.[46]

Although I have cited the opinions mainly of physicians and hospital managers, it would be false to believe that theirs were the sophisticated insights of a scientific *avant-garde.* On the contrary. These ideas about madness and madhouses were commonplace. For example, it was obvious to John Stuart Mill that people were committed to insane asylums to punish them for deviance, not to treat them for illness: ". . . the man and still more the woman, who can be accused either of doing 'what nobody does,' or of not doing 'what everybody does,' is . . . in peril of a commission *de lunatico* . . ."[47] It required a long "educational campaign," which was crowned with success only in our day, before the public as well as the medical profession came to accept insanity as an illness and the insane asylum as a hospital.*

John Perceval, whose views on mental illness were cited earlier, was a contemporary of John Conolly's. Being a layman who experienced confinement in several private mental institutions at first hand, his observations on commitment deserve attention.

I will be bound to say [wrote Perceval in 1830] that the greatest part of the violence that occurs in lunatic asylums is to be attributed to the conduct of those who are dealing with the disease, not to the disease itself; and that the behavior which is usually pointed out by the doctor to the visitors as the symptoms of the complaint for which the patient is confined, is generally more or less reasonable, and certainly a natural result, of that confinement, and its particular refinements in cruelty; for all have their select and exquisite moral and mental, if not bodily tortures.[48]

Perceval is thus quite clear that, in the mental hospital, doctor and patient are locked in a struggle for power, the doctor being cast in the role of oppressor, the patient in that of victim.[49] He is equally clear, moreover—and in this respect, too, modern psychiatry has yet to catch up with him—on the role of the mental patient's relatives: it is they who empower the physician to control and restrain the patient.

But when the lunatic doctors say that the presence of friends is hurtful to lunatic patients [Perceval observes], they are not aware of the fact—at any rate they do not acknowledge it—that the violent emotions and disturbance of spirit, which takes place on their sudden meeting with them MAY arise from their being overcome by a sense of their relations' conduct toward them, in neglecting

* "Why had the mental health movement, as it is called now, been as successful as it had during the half century since 1900?" asks Robert H. Felix. (*Mental Illness*, p. 32.) He gives the credit for this to Clifford Beers and the mental health propaganda machinery he built. The "success" of the Mental Health Movement to which Felix refers is not measured, however, by the development of effective "treatments" for "mental illness," but by the profession's ability to find many cases of the disease, and to channel into its coffers commensurately huge portions of the federal and state tax levies.

and abandoning them to the care and control of strangers, *and from the treatment of the doctors themselves.* The doctors naturally do not acknowledge this, for if they are acting from stupidity, their pride refuses correction, and will not admit the suspicion of being wrong; if they are acting with duplicity and hypocrisy, they necessarily preserve their character, and cannot in consistency confess that there is any error on their part—who can expect it of them? You cannot gather grapes from thorns. Nevertheless, it is true.[50] [Italics in the original.]

Perceval also calls attention to some parallels between the Inquisition and Institutional Psychiatry. To be sure, Perceval's analogy is not Zilboorg's, but its mirror image. It is not that witches and mental patients are alike; on the contrary, it is because inquisitors and psychiatrists are alike that they treat their victims similarly. "Where," asks Perceval, "is the boast of the Protestant religion—where is liberty of conscience, if the lunatic doctor is allowed to be supreme judge over his patients in these matters, when lunatic asylums supply the place of the Inquisition, and in a form so dreadful?"[51]

The parallel between the Inquisition and Institutional Psychiatry was put in more complete form by Mrs. E. P. W. Packard, who was committed to the Jacksonville State Hospital in Illinois, in 1860, by her clergyman husband. This commitment, as best one can reconstruct the case, was based on disagreements between the Reverend Packard and his wife over matters of religious faith and observance. After Mrs. Packard secured her release—through what must be one of the earliest writs of habeas corpus sustained by a mental patient in the United States—she published an account of her experiences in the hospital. In it she wrote:

Had I lived in the sixteenth instead of the nineteenth century my husband would have used the laws of the day to punish me as a heretic for this departure from the established creed—while under the influence of some intolerant spirit he now uses this autocratic institution as a means of torture to bring about the same result— namely *a recantation of my faith.* In other words, instead of calling me by the obsolete title of heretic, he modernizes his phrase by substituting insanity instead of heresy as the crime for which I am now sentenced to endless imprisonment in one of our Modern Inquisitions. . . . Much that is now called insanity will be looked upon by future ages with a feeling similar to what we feel toward those who suffered as witches in Salem, Massachusetts.[52] [Italics in the original.]

The similarities between Mrs. Packard and the Salem witches are perhaps even greater than Mrs. Packard realized. In both cases, the victims were persecuted on the grounds of an ideology held unquestioningly by experts and laity alike; and in both, the accused never challenged the logical basis of the accusation, their complaint being limited to the claim that they had been erroneously identified as members of the "offending" class. Mrs. Packard did not doubt that insanity existed and that it was proper to confine madmen in mental hospitals, even against their will. But she was not one of them, she insisted. Others who have reviewed her case—even as careful a student of psychiatric history as Albert Deutsch—thought that she was probably mentally ill. "Whether Mrs. Packard was mentally sound or not at the time of her commitment or confinement," writes Deutsch, "is a moot question. It appears to be established that she suffered from certain delusions, and had been a patient at the Worcester State Hospital in Massachusetts for a brief period when a girl."[53]

Deutsch gets caught here in the same trap that ensnares all who treat the rhetoric of oppression as if it were a dialogue between equals. The accused—witch, Jew, mental patient—must be at fault or guilty, or else he would not be accused by "honest" men. What such "reasonable" critics of mental health practices as Deutsch fail to see is that in a relationship where one party controls another by brute force, the former forfeits all possibility of a dialogue with the latter; and, before a critical observer not subject to his power, he forfeits all claim to credibility as well.

Nothing shows the hold of an ideology upon the mind of men more clearly than this stubborn adherence, by both accusers and accused, to the identical imagery and vocabulary. The history of witchcraft abounds in the same kinds of charges and refutations of being a witch, accusers and defenders alike having not the slightest doubt about the existence of witches. The same basic acceptance of the existence of mental illness characterizes contemporary accounts of the "railroading" of "sane" men and women into insane asylums.

In the annals of witchcraft, the case of Mary Easty parallels closely that of Mrs. Packard. In 1692, in Salem, Massachusetts, Mary Easty was accused of witchcraft and was put to death. In an Introduction to a reprinting of her "Petition," Edmund S. Morgan notes that "She might easily have escaped the punishment [of death] by admitting guilt and throwing herself on the mercy of the court. To have done so would have been to belie her conscience and jeopardize her soul. Mary Easty did not share our enlightenment about the nonexistence of witchcraft. She knew that Satan was abroad in the world and that the court which condemned her was doing its best to combat him. She wished her judges well. But she knew she was not guilty, and she did not dare lie to save her life."[54]

Mary Easty was, indeed, a tragic victim. Naive and trusting, she respected her executioners to the minute of her death. "I question not," she writes in her "Petition" to her judges, "but your honours does the utmost of your Powers in the discovery and detecting of witchcraft and witches and would not be guilty of innocent blood for the world . . . the Lord in His infinite mercy direct you in this great work if it be His blessed will that no more innocent blood be shed."[55]

Mary Easty argues that she is not a witch; Mrs. Packard, that she is not insane; and the victims of our Mental Health Movement, that they are not mentally ill. None denies the reality of witchcraft, or of mental illness.

Trevor-Roper emphasizes this great power of the dominant ideology on the minds of men, as seen in the history of witchcraft.

To the end of the witch-craze [he writes], although we always hear it said that there are some who deny the very existence of witches, we never actually hear the denials. To the last, the most radical argument against the witch-craze is not that witches do not exist, not even that the pact with Satan is impossible, but simply that the judges err in their identification. The "poor doting women," as Scot called them, . . . They were "melancholic." This was a very tiresome doctrine. . . . It could not be refuted. But equally it could not refute the witch-craze. Logically, it left it untouched.[56]

Trevor-Roper's observation on the absence of fundamental criticism of the doctrine of witchcraft during the witch-hunts is well taken. The same may be said, however, about the mythology of any popular mass-movement. Dissent from such ideologies is both conceptually difficult and personally hazardous. Ideologies couched in a salvational or therapeutic vocabulary are particularly resistant to criticism. Such belief-systems command not only obedience to the truth, as revealed to priests or physicians, but also define skepticism as heresy or madness.* The real significance of the therapeutic rhetoric thus lies in its power to disarm both victim and critic. For, in a Christian society, who can be opposed to God? Only a heretic. And in a scientific society, who can be opposed to mental health? Only a madman.† In the days of the witch-mania, the popular consensus supported the Inquisition: ". . . none dared to raise a voice against what was everywhere regarded by pious souls as supplying the most urgent need of the time," comments Lea.[57] There is a similar consensus in the United States today that, next to national defense, the gravest social problem is mental illness. This justifies not only vast expenditures of public funds, but also the use of extrajudicial methods of social control.

Who can criticize such popular excesses? Julien Benda felt that this was the fundamental moral duty of the intellectuals.[58] But it

* Historians of the witch-hunts have seen this. Thus, Pennethorne Hughes writes: "For the Faithful it was an Age of Faith and, as such, all embracing. Criticism was madness, and heretics and witches were lynched with the terrified cruelty with which animals will dispatch one of their own kind which suffers from a deformity. If Totality admits toleration, its case is lost." (Pennethorne Hughes, *Witchcraft*, p. 59.)

Persecutions in the name of science (or, better, scientism) have emulated and even outdone those waged in the name of religion. No one disputes this any longer. The only disagreement that remains is between the optimists, who see the scientistic witch-hunts largely behind us, in such things as Nazism and Stalinism; and the pessimists, who see the worst possibly still ahead of us, in such things as the progressive dehumanization of man through the unopposed powers of massive central governments.

† If a person disagrees with and disobeys authority, when that authority is religious, then he is the Devil or is possessed by the Devil. Likewise, if a person disagrees with and disobeys authority, when that authority is scientific, then he is insane or mad. In the last analysis, this is a matter of definition. The Devil, the heretic, the witch are defined as rebels against God and his vicars on earth—that is, the Church and the priest. Similarly, the insane, the madman, the psychotic are rebels against Nature and her experts on earth—that is, Medicine and the physician.

would be a mistake to believe that the intellectuals as a group, or any other group, could maintain such a posture and survive in a society overwhelmingly hostile to it. It seems to me, therefore, that the task of social criticism must remain forever in the hands of individuals. Harassed or persecuted, an individual can more easily survive than an organization.

There is no historical evidence that any group of intellectuals—whether it be clergymen, lawyers, physicians, or educators—resisted the popular beliefs of its time. Individuals often have. Robbins errs, therefore, when he asserts that "What makes witchcraft so repellent, and morally lower than fascism, is that throughout civilized Europe, in every country (with the possible later exception of Holland), the clergy led the persecutions and condoned them in the name of Christianity, while the lawyers and judges and professors abetted them in the name of reason."[59] The identical criticism of "lawyers and judges and professors"—and of clergymen and physicians as well—could be made in the case of Negro Slavery[60] or Institutional Psychiatry.

The lesson taught by the Inquisition and its ideology of spiritual salvation is one that modern man, faced with the new Inquisition of Psychiatry and its ideology of secular salvation, can ignore only at his own peril. The lesson is that man must forever choose between liberty and such competing values as health, security, or welfare. And if he chooses liberty, he must be prepared to pay its price—not only in eternal vigilance against malevolent tyrants, bent on enslaving their subjects; in eternal skepticism of benevolent priests and psychiatrists, bent on curing souls and minds; but also in eternal opposition to enlightened majorities, bent on reforming misguided minorities.

PART II

THE MANUFACTURE
OF MADNESS

[The Grand Inquisitor:] Oh, we shall persuade
them that they will only become free when they re-
nounce their freedom to us and submit to us. And
shall we be right or shall we be lying? They will be
convinced that we are right . . .

–John Stuart Mill[2]

In former days, when it was proposed to burn
atheists, charitable people used to suggest putting
them in the madhouse instead; it would be nothing
surprising now-a-days were we to see this done, and
the doers applauding themselves, because, instead
of persecuting for religion, they had adopted so
humane and Christian a mode of treating these
unfortunates, not without a silent satisfaction at
their having thereby obtained their deserts.

–John Stuart Mill[2]

9

THE NEW MANUFACTURERS—
BENJAMIN RUSH, THE FATHER
OF AMERICAN PSYCHIATRY

When the Jeffersonian came upon the concept of
evil in theology or moral philosophy, he naturalized
it into just another bodily disease: a disease, indeed,
of the moral sense, but essentially no different from
others. To reproach a man because his moral sense
was corruptible was like blaming him for suscep-
tibility to yellow fever—like reproaching a wagon
for its broken wheel.

–*Daniel J. Boorstin*[1]

The metamorphosis of the medieval into the modern mind entailed
a vast ideological conversion from the perspective of theology to
that of science. My thesis is that the development of the concept
of mental illness is best understood as part of this change. The
conditions or behaviors we now call mental diseases were not discovered as diseases such as diabetes mellitus or myocardial infarction
were. Instead, they had formerly been known by other names, such
as heresy, buggery, sin, possession, and so forth—or had been accepted as customary and natural and were therefore not designated
by special names. In the eighteenth and nineteenth centuries, a host
of such phenomena—never before conceptualized in medical terms
—were renamed or reclassified as illnesses. This process, which led to
the creation of the discipline known as psychiatry, is an integral part

of the larger process which substituted scientific concepts for religious ones. Nature thus displaced God; the State, the Church; and mental illness, witchcraft.

In the natural sciences, we have thus witnessed a profound change in ideas and practices: we use fertilizers, not animal sacrifices, to improve our crops; drugs and surgery, not sympathetic magic, to cure diseases; and energy, derived from the movement of water, the burning of fossil fuels, and the reaction of fissionable materials, not prayer, to move the seas and smite our enemies. There has been no comparable change, however, in the "social sciences."* Descriptions and explanations of human behavior and social control are, more often than not, merely a papering over, with a fresh, scientific-sounding vocabulary, of earlier religious descriptions and explanations. This is especially clear, as we have seen,[2] in the replacement of the theological concept of heresy with the medical concept of mental illness, and of the religious sanctions of confinement in a dungeon or burning at the stake with the psychiatric sanctions of confinement in a hospital or tortures called treatments.

This change in the conceptualization and control of personal conduct, from the religious and moral to the medical and social, is dramatically displayed in the ideas and practices of most of the psychiatrists of the Enlightenment. An outstanding exemplar is Benjamin Rush. His ideas and work will illustrate my propositions about the origin, nature, and uses of the concept of mental illness.

Benjamin Rush (1746-1813), was Physician General of the Continental Army and served as Professor of Physic and Dean of the Medical School at the University of Pennsylvania. He is the undisputed Father of American Psychiatry: his portrait adorns the official seal of the American Psychiatric Association. What kind of man was he? What were his psychiatric ideas and practices?

Rush is hailed as the founder of American psychiatry because he claimed that there is no difference between mental and bodily

---

* I have placed quotation marks around the term *social sciences* to indicate the scientifically dubious character of the disciplines usually subsumed under this heading or, at least, their fundamental differences from the physical sciences. These differences stem from the subject matter of each—persons or human beings, in the case of social science, things or nonhuman beings, in that of natural science. Although my following remarks are directed mainly toward psychiatry, they apply generally also to history, psychology, political science, sociology, and social work.

diseases, and because, through his great personal influence as a successful physician and friend of the Founding Fathers, he was able to implement his ideas on mental illness. In short, he was the first American physician to urge the medicalization of social problems and their coercive control by means of "therapeutic" rather than "punitive" sanctions. As we shall see, Rush's ideas still sound remarkably fresh. This is because the social problems Rush tried to control are still with us, and because we are still trying to control them through medical sanctions.

In 1812 Rush published his *magnum opus,* titled *Medical Inquiries and Observations upon the Diseases of the Mind,*[3] a work that went through many editions, was translated into several languages, and helped establish psychiatry as a medical specialty. In a letter to his friend John Adams, Rush writes: "The subjects of [mental diseases] have hitherto been enveloped in mystery. I have endeavored to bring them down to the level of all other diseases of the human body, and to show that the mind and the body are moved by the same causes and subject to the same laws."[4]

Rush's evidence for his belief that so-called mental patients were physically ill was, of course, woefully inadequate. He based this view on such observations as that ". . . seven-eighths of all the deranged patients in the Pennsylvania Hospital in the year 1811 had frequent pulses . . ."[5] Coupled with Rush's personal authority, however, this "symptom," interpreted as ". . . an unequivocal mark of intellectual derangement," sufficed to obtain a Presidential pardon for a convicted murderer.[6] Unable to prove empirically that mental and physical illnesses were the same, Rush tried to "prove" it strategically, by treating both in the same way: "I infer madness to be primarily seated in the blood-vessels, from the remedies which most speedily and certainly cure it, being exactly the same as those which cure fever or disease in the blood-vessels from other causes, and in other parts of the body."* [7]

In contrast to the discoveries of his contemporaries in the physical sciences, Rush, the much-hailed medical scientist, discovered nothing. To be sure, he innovated. He used the concept of insanity in a novel way. For example, Rush believed that after the Peace of

---

* Contemporary psychiatrists employ the same strategy. By treating mental patients with hospitalization and drugs, they "prove" that such individuals are sick and suffer from an illness.

1783, the people of the United States were not prepared for their new situation; and he gave the following explanation for their behavior: "The excess of the passion for liberty, inflamed by the successful issue of the war, produced, in many people, opinions and conduct, which could not be removed by reason nor restrained by government. . . . The extensive influence which these opinions had upon the understandings, passions, and morals of many of the citizens of the United States, constituted a form of insanity, which I shall take the liberty of distinguishing by the name of *anarchia*."[8]

This was not an isolated psychiatric interpretation of the popular mood—a poetic metaphor in medical idiom—that Rush allowed himself. On the contrary, it was a fixed point of view, truly a pair of ideological glasses, through which Rush gazed at the world. His eyes thus beheld the world in terms of sickness and health. He categorized opposition to the Revolution as illness; support of it, as therapy. Americans loyal to the British Crown "tended to suffer from a disease which Rush christened 'revolutiona.' . . . [Whereas] women who favored the Revolutionary cause were cured of hysteria."[9]

Rush was a master of the medical metaphor, recasting moral and social problems in medical terms. Illustrative of this is a kind of dictionary he devised, called *A Moral and Physical Thermometer*, which gave the medical equivalents of moral terms. "At the top of the scale," explains Carl Binger, "is temperance, which leads to health and wealth. This is compatible with drinking water, milk, and small beer. Cheerfulness, strength, and nourishment can also be had with cider and perry, wine, porter, and strong beer when taken only in small quantities, and at meals. Then the scale descends rapidly to a freezing 70° below zero, beginning with punch and passing through toddy and egg rum, grog, flip and shrub, bitters infused in cordials . . . ,"[10] and so on. In a letter to Jeremy Belknap, Rush writes: "In the year 1915, a drunkard I hope will be as infamous in society as a liar or thief, and the use of spirits as uncommon in families as a drink made of a solution of arsenic or a decoction of hemlock."[11]

In other words, Rush was composing propaganda against alcohol, making full use of the rhetoric of medicine. Binger believes that "it is to his credit that, in spite of his moral outrage, Rush recognized addiction to strong drink as a medical and public health problem of the first magnitude, which it still unfortunately remains."[12] What one thinks of Rush's tactics depends, of course, on what one thinks of the ideology of psychiatric imperialism and its attendant quasi-medical sanctions. Binger, himself a prominent figure in the American mental health movement, hails Rush for "recognizing" drinking as a medical problem. But Rush did not *recognize* that drinking was a medical problem; he *defined* it as one.*

With regard to the obscene talk of so-called madmen, Rush held that their words had no meaning and hence were "as devoid of impiety as an epileptic fit . . ."—a view he attributed to the "teaching . . . of the science of medicine . . ."[13] To hold such an opinion, it was necessary for Rush to treat men as inanimate objects. He did just that, comparing "The apparent vices of such deranged people . . . to the offensive substances that are sometimes thrown upon the surface of the globe by an earthquake . . ."[14] Having started to march down the road of reinterpreting social deviance as mental illness, Rush was prepared to go all the way. Just how far he actually went will seem incredible, even to the contemporary reader accustomed to viewing all kinds of undesirable conduct as the manifestation of mental disorder.

"Chagrin, shame, fear, terror, anger," Rush declares without any qualifications, "unfit for legal acts, are transient madness. . . . Suicide is madness."[15] And he fearlessly defines sanity and insanity: "Sanity—aptitude to judge things like other men, and regular habits, etc. Insanity a departure from this."[16] Rush thus equates social conformity with mental health, and social nonconformity with mental illness. But who should judge whether the individual conforms or not? "Physicians best judges of sanity,"[17]

---

* In an effort to humanize the law through psychiatry, the American Civil Liberties Union is now mistaking, as Rush had mistaken nearly two hundred years ago, promotive rhetoric for descriptive assertion. After hailing the Supreme Court's 1962 decision declaring narcotic addiction a disease, not a crime, Markmann notes with approval that the Union "has begun a similar campaign against the parallel callousness that treats the alcoholic as a criminal he is not rather than as the sick man he is . . . the Union will attempt to bring the law abreast of medicine and justice." (Charles Lam Markmann, *The Noblest Cry*, p. 406.) For a critical discussion of the disease concept of alcoholism, see Thomas S. Szasz, Alcoholism: A socioethical perspective, *Western Med.*, 7: 15–21 (Dec.), 1966.

Rush answers, as if anticipating the question. It is not surprising that he is the patron saint of the American Psychiatric Association, and of historians of psychiatry forever trying to persuade people that social nonconformity is illness, not deviance, and that psychiatry is a branch of medicine, not of the police. It is remarkable, too, how Rush—who signed the Declaration of Independence and was on friendly terms with many of the Founding Fathers—viewed the legal and political status of the alleged madman. "Absence of reason," he opined, "annuls a man's social compact, disfranchises him, takes away testimony, morality, etc."[18] Psychiatrists still employ this figure of speech in justifying their violence against the so-called mental patient. But Rush, an exceptionally well-educated man with fine command of the English language, must have known that this was deceitful rhetoric. "Absence of reason" cannot annul a man's social compact, nor can it disfranchise him; it can only render him stupid or ill equipped for citizenship. It is individuals (who wield power), not diseases (that impair mental faculties), that impose legal and political limitations, such as Rush enumerates, on other men.

Rush also maintained that crimes were diseases. This idea is often credited, falsely, to modern psychiatrists. One of the classes of mental illnesses he devised he called "derangements in the will." Murder and theft are "symptoms" of this disease-complex. "I have selected," Rush writes, "those two symptoms of this disease (for they are not vices) from its other morbid effects, in order to rescue persons affected with them from the arm of the law, and to render them the subjects of the kind and lenient hand of medicine."[19] Just how kind and lenient Rush's hand was we shall see presently. It is worth noting that in the foregoing passage Rush admits, perhaps unwittingly, that he considers murder and theft diseases not because they *are* diseases, but *to justify* the transfer of murderers and thieves from the control of policemen and judges to that of physicians and the keepers of madhouses.

Rush regarded lying as also a disease, indeed, "a corporeal disease. . . . Persons thus diseased cannot speak the truth upon any subject . . . "[20] The fact that most of the diseases Rush "discovered" were incurable apparently did not bother him. "Lying, as a vice, is said to be incurable. The same thing may be said of it as a disease, when it appears in adult life."[21]

Most revealing of Rush's blueprint for a psychiatric inquisition is his "discovery" of the mental disease he calls "Derangement in the Principle of Faith, or the Believing Faculty."[22] "This faculty of the mind," Rush asserts, "is subject to disorder as well as to disease; that is, to an inability to believe things that are supported by all the evidence that usually enforces belief."[23] Among examples of patients suffering from this mental disease, Rush lists "persons who deny their belief in the utility of medicine, as practiced by regular bred physicians, believing implicitly in quacks; [and] persons who refuse to admit human testimony in favour of the truths of the Christian religion, believing in all the events of profane history."[24]

So starkly put, the aim of the semantic conversion from morals to medicine is embarrassingly clear. *Cui bono?* Who profits from it? The patient? No. The clergyman? No. The physician? Yes.

That Rush's medical conceptualization of social problems— or of personal conduct of which he disapproved—served to justify their medical control is made unmistakably clear by his own writings and utterances. "If he was irritated and distressed by the follies of his fellows," Binger tells us, "he tried to explain them away by saying that most men were 'madmen at large.' "[25] Rush was a fervent advocate of psychiatric confinement as a method of "treatment" and would evidently have preferred to have his enemies behind psychiatric bars, or worse. For "lying . . . as a disease," for example, he prescribes, as "its only remedy . . . bodily pain, inflicted by the rod, or confinement, or abstinence from food."[26]

The same principles and methods—medical diagnosis, followed by coercive controls based on it—characterize Rush's position on alcoholism. He not only proclaims that the "use of strong drink" is a disease; he also advocates its coercive medical control. To exercise such control, he unhesitatingly enlists the police power of the State. It is not hard to understand why American psychiatry claims him as its founding father. "They [the users of strong drink] are as much the objects of public humanity and charity," asserts Rush, "as mad people. They are indeed more hurtful to society, than most of the deranged patients of a common hospital would be, if they were set at liberty. Who can calculate the extensive influence of a drunken husband or wife upon the property and morals of their families . . ."[27] Thus did the protection of property and morals become a medical problem. Binger, we may note, is in unqualified agreement with Rush's views on alcoholism. He comments that "After more than a century and a half we can only echo and applaud these sentiments. . . . Society has not, as yet, followed his advice nor met this still imperative need."[28]

The Puritan ethic is thus disguised as a medical concern based on scientific facts about diseases and their cures. The results are the psychiatric rhetoric of diagnosis and treatment, and the psychiatric practice of coercion and oppression in the name of mental health. In assuming this posture, the zealous medical man has replaced the crusading clergy. Even Binger acknowledges that Rush was an evangelistic reformer, characterizing him as "never the pure scientist who could look at human folly with cool detachment, he was a Savanarola rather than a Leonardo."[29]

Not surprisingly, we find that "Rush also turned his reformer's zeal against the habitual use of tobacco, which he thought led to a desire for strong drink and was injurious to both health and morals. He found smokers generally offensive."[30] In his battle against tobacco,* as in that against alcohol, Rush's weapon was not argument based on information, but intimidation based on threat. It was the old brimstone and hell-fire tactic, expressed in the language of medicine. Rush threatened his would-be patients—and he considered all of society to be his patients—with the dreadful medical consequences of drinking and smoking, just as his brethren of the cloth threatened their parishioners—and everyone else they could lay their hands on—with eternal damnation.

Binger says that Rush "regarded himself as a doctor not only to sick men and women but also to the ills of society."[31] Moreover, "the 18th century physician was an authoritarian figure and Rush,

* There was apparently no conflict between Rush's war on smoking and his cordial friendship with Jefferson and other landowners whose income was often derived largely from growing tobacco. In the year 1799, for example, Jefferson's crop of tobacco totaled 43,433 pounds. (Nathan S. Schachner, *Thomas Jefferson,* p. 643.) This contradiction between condemning tobacco as a danger to health while at the same time encouraging its cultivation and profiting from its sale, Benjamin Rush bequeathed to the nation he helped create. Long neglected, this heirloom has been rediscovered of late; the upshot is that the United States Government now condemns smoking through its Department of Health, Education, and Welfare, but subsidizes tobacco farming through its Department of Agriculture.

because of his extraordinary personal magnetism and intelligence and his reputation as America's greatest doctor, was the very embodiment of authority. He did not hesitate to exploit this by the use of moral and emotional persuasion."[32]

Binger tries to whitewash Rush's autocratic methods which included far more than "persuasion." Binger himself reports, for example, that "if his patient thought he had a snake in his stomach, Rush would not hesitate to have one placed in what he calls his close-stool."[33] Nor was this an isolated lie. On the contrary, it was an instance of systematic deception in the service of what Rush considered psychiatric therapy. "Cures for patients who suppose themselves to be glass," Rush advises, "may easily be performed by pulling a chair upon which they are about to sit from under them, and afterwards showing them a large collection of pieces of glass as the fragments of their bodies."[34] In like vein, Rush relates with approval the cure of a patient "who believed himself to be a plant. One of his companions, who favored his delusion, persuaded him he could not thrive without being watered, and while he made the patient believe, for some time, he was pouring water from the spout of a teapot, discharged his urine upon his head."[35] Another treatment which Rush recommends, he describes as follows: "I have heard of a person afflicted with this disease [madness], who supposed himself to be dead, who was instantly cured by a physician proposing to his friends, in his hearing, to open his body, in order to discover the cause of his death."[*][36]

These episodes illustrate the essential relationship between alienist and mental patient and the attendant concepts of madness and cure. If the citizen tells a falsehood, he is a sick patient suffering from a mental illness; if the psychiatrist does, he is a magnanimous therapist performing a cure.[†]

Binger recognizes that "Control was the essence of Rush's therapeutic activity,"[37] but, once again, he minimizes Rush's zeal, intrusiveness, and outright brutality. The "control" Binger speaks

---

[*] For a story of a similar psychiatric "cure," see Spitzka's description of the recovery of a young man suffering from "masturbatory insanity" upon discovering the family plot to commit him to an insane asylum (Chapter 11).

[†] Rush solved the moral problem inherent in the physicians' deception of the patient by asserting that the ends justify the means: ". . . the deception [of the patient] would be a justifiable one if it served to cure him of his disease." (Rush, *Medical Inquiries,* p. 109.)

of was directed exclusively toward the patient. Self-control was not a part of Rush's therapeutic "armamentarium." It continues in short supply in that of the contemporary psychiatrist. To do nothing was anathema to Rush. Since I believe the kinds of "therapeutic" measures Rush used on psychiatric patients reveal the kind of man he was (a connection equally valid for psychiatrists today), we must pay special attention to them.

Rush believed that to cure madness, the physician had to gain complete control over the person of the madman. He was not alone in subscribing to this view, which, indeed, was held by most contemporary physicians. The great Philippe Pinel—who is always thought of as having removed the chains from the insane—was himself an uncompromising advocate of psychiatric coercion. In fact, he opposed chains and bodily assaults on mental patients, not because he wanted to restore them to liberty, but because he believed that, in a properly run madhouse, the patients should be so impressed with the overwhelming authority and power of the keepers that such crude methods of control should be unnecessary. Pinel's *Treatise on Insanity* abounds with the praise of "intimidation" and "coercion," as the following excerpts show: "If [the madman is] met, however, by a force evidently and convincingly superior, he submits without opposition or violence." "In the preceding cases of insanity, we trace the happy effects of intimidation, without severity; of oppression, without violence; and of triumph, without outrage."[*38]

For his part, Rush advocated not only conscious deceptions and lies, but a variety of other interventions—and especially involuntary hospitalization—as "therapeutic" methods. "It will be necessary,"

---

[*] This view is still exceedingly popular among institutional psychiatrists. Masserman, for example, frankly states that psychiatry can be better practiced in the military service than in civilian life because in the former setting the physician can exercise an "authority . . . over them [the patients]" which he lacks in the latter. (Jules H. Masserman, *The Practice of Dynamic Psychiatry*, p. 634.) In a like vein, Glasser considers coercive control over the patient a technical asset, not a moral liability. When a ". . . wealthy, young, overindulged, satisfactorily married mother of two whose only obvious problem was overweight . . ." tauntingly asks Glasser why he can't help her and contrasts this with his ability to "help" institutionalized delinquent girls, he retorts: "Because I can't lock you up. If I could, you know as well as I do that you would change." (William Glasser, *Reality Therapy*, p. 142.)

writes Rush, "to mention the means of establishing a complete government over patients afflicted with it [madness], and thus, by securing their obedience, respect, and affections, to enable a physician to apply his remedies with ease, certainty, and success."[39]

One of Rush's favorite remedies was "terror," which, he believed, "acts powerfully upon the body, through the medium of the mind, and should be employed in the cure of madness."[40] To terrorize the patient properly, it was necessary to remove him from his home and incarcerate him in a madhouse. This Rush considered therapeutic: "The effect of thus depriving a madman of his liberty has sometimes been of the most salutary nature . . ."[41] In Rush's day, such incarceration was easily accomplished. Until the middle of the nineteenth century, the American physician had uncontested power to compel the medical detention of any individual whom he considered in need of care for mental disease. To arrange for the admission of a patient, all Rush had to do was to write, "on a chance scrap of paper," as Deutsch tells it, that " 'James Sproul is a proper patient for the Pennsylvania Hospital,' and append his signature."[42]

It would be wrong to believe, however, that Rush was oblivious to the deprivation of personal liberty inherent in medical or psychiatric incarceration. He simply thought, as do many modern psychiatrists, that such loss of liberty was amply justified by the protection of society so afforded. The psychiatric perspective on civil commitment has not advanced one inch beyond Rush's position on this subject. "Let it not be said," declares Rush about his proposal to incarcerate drunkards, "that confining such persons in a hospital would be an infringement upon personal liberty, incompatible with the freedom of our governments. We do not use this argument when we confine a thief in a jail, and yet, taking the aggregate evil of the greater number of drunkards than thieves into consideration, and the greater evils which the influence of their immoral example and conduct introduce into society than stealing, it must be obvious that the safety and prosperity of a community will be more promoted by confining them than a common thief. To prevent injustice or oppression, no person should be sent to the contemplated hospital, or SOBER HOUSE, without being examined and committed by a court, consisting of a physician, and two or three magistrates, or commissioners appointed for that purpose."*[43]

Once the patient was psychiatrically imprisoned and rendered incapable of resisting his physician's therapeutic efforts, Rush employed a number of measures which were exceedingly unpleasant for the subject; indeed, even in Rush's days, some of these methods would have been indistinguishable from tortures had they been used outside of a medical setting. Rush's own words give him away. After recommending some of the measures reviewed above, he declares that "If all the means that have been mentioned should prove ineffectual to establish a government over deranged patients, recourse should be had to certain modes of coercion."[44] Then, having surveyed the full panoply of his psychiatric interventions, Rush notes, with evident satisfaction, that "By the proper application of these mild and terrifying modes of punishment, chains will seldom, and the whip never, be required to govern mad people. I except only from the use of the latter, those cases in which a sudden and unprovoked [sic!] assault of their physicians or keepers may render a stroke or two of the whip, or of the hand, a necessary measure of self-defense."[45]

Sometimes Rush classifies his methods as "treatments," and at other times as "punishments." The following example makes unmistakably clear how Rush thought of madmen: he compares them to untamed animals whom it is the physician's duty to subdue. In his list of therapeutic recommendations—among which we find "confinement by means of a strait waistcoat, . . . privation of their customary pleasant food, . . . pouring cold water under the coat sleeve . . . ,"[46] blood-letting, solitude, and darkness—Rush includes "an erect position of the body." This method works as follows: "There is a method of taming refractory horses in England, by first impounding them, as it is called, and then keeping them from lying down or sleeping, by thrusting sharp pointed nails into their bodies for two or three days and nights. The same advantages, I have no doubt, might be derived from keeping madmen in a stand-

---

* The principles and practices of psychiatric justice here advocated by Rush not only characterize the administration of Soviet law, but are also becoming steadily more influential in the administration of English and American law. The resultant political organization I have named the "Therapeutic State." (Thomas S. Szasz, *Law, Liberty, and Psychiatry,* and *Psychiatric Justice.*)

ing posture, and awake, for four and twenty hours, but by different and more lenient means."[47]

One of Rush's most celebrated therapeutic inventions was a contraption he called the "tranquilizer." Deutsch describes this apparatus as follows: ". . . the tranquilizer consisted of a chair to which the patient was strapped hand and foot, together with a device for holding the head in a fixed position. This mechanism was intended to reduce the pulse through lessening the muscular action . . . of the patient's body. Although it would be viewed by moderns as a device of fiendish torture, it was really invented by Rush out of humane considerations."[48] It would seem that Rush's contemporaries must have regarded this device as a form of torture, too, for there is no evidence that they ever submitted to its use voluntarily.*

Like many psychiatric discoveries and inventions, Rush's tranquilizing chair was an adaptation of an inquisitorial device for dealing with witches, called the witch-chair. This contraption was "an iron chair, with blunt studs all over it, in which the accused was fastened, while fire was lit below the seat. . . . The idea of torture had been that it helped the truth. Pain brought the human spirit to its last point of mortal existence; there, in its nakedness, it was asked and answered the question."[49]

The second of Rush's psychiatric-therapeutic inventions was a machine he called the "gyrator." This consisted of "a rotating board to which patients suffering from 'torpid madness' were strapped with the head farthest from the center. It could be rotated at terrific rates of speed, causing the blood to rush to the head . . ."[50]

It is ironic, indeed, that in our day, when psychiatrists and social scientists coldly reject "patriotism" as a justification for violence against external enemies, they warmly embrace "therapeutism" as

---

* With the development of modern pharmacological techniques, psychiatrists turned to barbiturates for extracting truth from mental patients, and to phenothiazines for subduing them. The "armamentarium" (as medically oriented psychiatrists like to refer to their methods) of the psychiatric therapist has indeed kept pace with advances in the technology of violence. As soldiers need no longer be bayoneted to death in hand-to-hand combat, but may be killed instead by rockets from airplanes, so mental patients need no longer be wrapped in strait jackets but may be injected instead with drugs, which, if necessary, may be shot into them from guns specifically designed for the purpose. See, Bringing violent psychotics back alive; gun that fires drug-filled syringe is aimed at subduing patients safely. (*Med. World News*, Sept. 8, 1957, p. 71.)

justification for violence against mental patients. As we just saw, Deutsch tells the reader that Rush invented the "tranquilizer" out of "humane considerations." Actually, we cannot be certain *why* he invented it. We know only that Rush *claimed* to have been motivated by benevolence. In a letter dated 1810, he described the purpose of his invention thus: "To obviate these evils [of the strait waistcoat], and at the same time to *retain all the benefits of coercion*, I requested an ingenious cabinetmaker . . ."[51] (Italics added.) Binger, however, consistently defends Rush's actions as fully justified by his motives.

Psychiatry will not abandon its coercive and violent methods until it repudiates them in its heroes. This is why I criticize not only Rush's treatment of the insane, but also contemporary psychiatrists' and social scientists' acceptance of it and apologies for it.* The facts are no longer in dispute. Even Deutsch recognizes them, although he writes about them without incriminating Rush or other "great" psychiatric well-doers. "Strangely enough," he comments, "tortures and terrors that had been applied as outright punishments in previous ages received in this particular age the blessings of respectable medical theory as praiseworthy therapeutic measures.

---

* The following brief quotations should suffice to show how psychiatric propagandists idolize Rush. "It was his heart that revolted at the inhumane treatment of the insane." (Sarah R. Riedman and Clarence C. Green, *Benjamin Rush*, p. 233.) "[Rush was] laboring to do good even when behaving at his worst . . . [He] always sought, however violent his therapeutic methods, to be humane." (James Thomas Flexner, He sought to do good, *New York Times Book Review*, Nov. 13, 1966, p. 60.)

Although psychiatrists and psychiatric historians have only glowing tributes for Rush as a great humanist, physician, and scientist, others, not identified with the Mental Health Movement, see him as the very opposite. Thus, Thomas Jefferson, who knew Rush well and considered him a friend, nevertheless recognized him for the medical menace he was. "In his theory of bleeding and mercury," writes Jefferson in a letter to Dr. Thomas Cooper in 1814, "I was ever opposed to my friend Rush, whom I greatly loved; but who had done much harm, in the sincerest persuasion that he was preserving life and happiness to all around him." (Quoted in Maurice B. Strauss [Ed.], *Familiar Medical Quotations*, p. 425.)

William B. Bean, a professor of medicine at the University of Iowa and a noted scholar of medical history, reaffirms Jefferson's judgment of Rush. "The heroic aspects of Benjamin Rush [he writes] . . . have made us forget the harm he did. His willingness to follow the guttering candle of ignorance, his dogmatic convictions that he was right, his consummate ability to fool himself consistently helped to kill an unmeasured plenty of his patients in Philadelphia." (William B. Bean, Bring out your dead [Editorial], *Arch. Intern. Med.*, 117: 1–3 [Jan.] 1966; p. 3.)

. . . Physicians specializing in the care of the insane outdid themselves in devising ingenious mechanisms for terrorization."[52] But this is strange only if we insist on viewing mental illness as a disease rather than as a successor notion to heresy; psychiatrists as physicians rather than as successor-enforcers to the inquisitors; and psychiatric interventions as treatments rather than successor-punishments to inquisitorial tortures.*

The "tranquilizer" and the "gyrator" did not exhaust Rush's therapeutic methods. He used "ducking," which consisted of immersing the patient in water and telling her that she will be drowned. Deutsch defends this crude adaptation of the witchhunter's ordeal by water by declaring that Rush's therapies "were truly gentle when compared with the methods sanctioned by many of his most celebrated contemporaries,"[53] while Binger calls "ducking" a "kind of ingenious intimidation."[54]

The father of American psychiatry thus emerges as an autocratic, domineering, violent, and zealous person who saw mental disease wherever he looked, and who was ready to use the most terrifying measures to control this desperate scourge. We recognize in this posture the very origin of the harm against which the protector supposedly guards us. This kind of "diagnostician"—whether he be priest or physician—does not find witches or madmen; he creates them. How many victims Rush created, no one, of course, could say. There is one, however, whose fate deserves brief mention. I refer to Rush's son, John.

It may seem uncharitable to discuss the family life of the psychiatrist whose ideas and practices one is considering. Like most people, I, too, regard *ad hominem* arguments as repugnant; I do not intend to employ any. There is, however, an important difference, especially in the study of human behavior, between efforts

---

* An anonymous Spanish inquisitor is said to have remarked, apropos of the terrors of the Inquisition, that "It is no great matter whether they that die on account of religion be guilty or innocent, provided we terrify the people by such examples." (Herbert J. Muller, *Freedom in the Western World*, p. 173.)

This comment applies equally to the methods of prescientific medicine and of Institutional Psychiatry. The psychological connections between helpfulness and cruelty have, of course, often been noted. Russell had this to say on the subject: "When we pass in review the opinions of former times which are now recognized as absurd, it will be found that nine times out of ten they were such as to justify the infliction of suffering . . . I cannot think of any instances of an erroneous medical treatment that was agreeable rather than disagreeable to the patient." (Bertrand Russell, *Unpopular Essays*, p. 148.)

to disqualify a man's ideas and achievements by pointing to some unedifying feature of his personal life, and noting some aspect of his personal life for the bearing it has on him, as an individual, both private and public. The latter use of personal information about psychiatrists, psychologists, politicians, artists, and others can, I believe, be both legitimate and instructive.

It is not difficult to see that the first-born son of such a man as Benjamin Rush might have some difficult problems building an identity of his own. This, apparently, was the case. John Rush began to study medicine, dropped it in favor of a naval career, resumed it and got his degree, only to drop it again. On December 11, 1802, Benjamin Rush made this note in his *Commonplace Book*: "This day my son John resumed the study of medicine. So anxious was he to return to my house and business that he said 'he would supply the place of one of my men servants, and even clean my stable rather than continue to follow a sea life.' "[55] We are left to wonder why the son had to, or felt that he had to, humiliate himself before his father so much before he could return home; and why the elder Rush recorded his son's abjection in his diary.

John returned home and took his medical degree in 1804. His dissertation was dedicated to his father. Then, instead of accepting an appointment at the Philadelphia General Hospital—where he would have been under his father's shadow—he re-entered the Navy as a sailing master. His naval career lasted less than four years. In 1807, John Rush fought a duel with Benjamin Taylor, one of his closest friends, in which he killed Taylor. Within a year, he attempted suicide. In February, 1810, John was returned to the parental home. His father described him thus: "Neither the embraces nor tears of his parents, brothers or sisters could prevail upon him to speak to them. His grief and uncombed hair and long beard added to the distress produced by the disease of his mind . . ."[56]

It is neither possible nor necessary to reconstruct here John Rush's predicament.[57] It should suffice to record what happened to him: he was locked up in his father's hospital where he remained, except for one short "remission,"* until he died twenty-seven years later.

---

* Entry in the *Commonplace Book* for September 2, 1810: "This day my son John came home from the hospital somewhat better, but not well. He returned six days afterward, much worse." (In *The Autobiography of Benjamin Rush*, p. 294.)

On January 2, 1811, Rush writes to Jefferson: "My son is better. He has become attentive to his dress, now and then opens a book . . . He is now in a cell in the Pennsylvania Hospital, where there is too much reason to believe he will end his days."[58] "This prognosis," Binger dryly comments, "was an accurate one."[59]

But, surely, this does not do justice to what happened. Rush did not simply "prognosticate" that his son would be confined for life; he actually initiated the confining. Binger makes no comment about the fact that Rush was in charge of the Pennsylvania Hospital and was, therefore, not only John's father but also his doctor, psychiatrist, and jailer. In Rush's day, no less than in ours, it was customary for physicians not to treat members of their own families.

This portrait of Rush as physician and psychiatrist would be incomplete without touching on his attitude toward the Negro. As a signer of the Declaration of Independence and an early abolitionist, Rush is generally thought of as a great liberal, that is, a lover of liberty. This is far from the truth. While he loved liberty, he loved power far more.* His ideas on Negroes bear out this contention in a surprising way.

Binger hints that there was a similarity, perhaps a connection, between Rush's opposition to slavery and to drinking: "There were two subjects that continued to plague Rush and to give him no rest," he writes. "One was the existence of slavery in the United States . . . ; the other was the abuse of spiritous liquors and widespread drunkenness."[60]

Negroes, Rush claimed, aroused a special emotion in him. "I love even the name of Africa," he wrote to Jeremy Belknap, "and never see a Negro slave or free man without emotions which I seldom feel in the same degree toward my unfortunate fellow creatures of a fairer complexion."[61] It is significant that Rush calls his fellow white citizens "unfortunate," a term usually applied by physicians to incurably sick patients. Rush's attitude toward Negroes betrays his deep-seated paternalism. Like many a modern liberal, Rush discriminates in reverse: He considers the Negro specially worthy, thus implicitly defining himself as specially generous and protective.

* "The love of power and the love of liberty are in eternal antagonism," observed John Stuart Mill. (In *The Subjection of Women*, p. 313.)

More surprising than Rush's self-proclaimed love for the Negro is his theory of Negritude. Rush does not believe that God created the Negro black; nor that the Negro is black by nature. Instead, he believes that Negritude is a disease! This theory—so consistent with and supportive of his pan-medical perspective on life and his therapeutic zeal toward all that he disliked or considered inferior—merits our closest attention.

Rush's generation was torn between the assertions of the Declaration of Independence and the realities of Negro slavery. The heart of the Declaration was the "self-evident truth . . . that all men are created equal." The heart of slavery was the deep-seated belief that the Negro is racially inferior to the white man. Americans ached in their souls for a reconciliation of this bitter contradiction. Rush tried to find a way out. The solution he offered—like so many psychiatric solutions of moral dilemmas—provided a scientific justification for the *status quo*.

The exact origins of Rush's disease concept of Negritude were these. About 1792, white spots began to appear on the body of a Negro slave named Henry Moss. In three years, he was almost entirely white. Moss had the symptoms of an hereditary disease we now know as vitiligo. This condition, characterized by progressive loss of skin pigmentation, occurs in both white and colored people. In the United States, approximately one person in a hundred suffers from it.

In 1796, armed with letters of introduction, Moss went to Philadelphia, advertised himself in public prints, exhibited himself for the then substantial admission price of "one Quarter of a Dollar each person," and used the proceeds to purchase his freedom.[62] Evidently, this was too much for Rush. Like the inquisitor who sees heresy wherever he looks, this was all Rush needed to see illness. What is striking, however, is that he regarded the Negro's biologically normal color as a disease, and Moss's skin disorder as a "spontaneous cure."

At a special meeting of the American Philosophical Society held on July 14, 1797, Rush read a paper entitled "Observations intended to favour a supposition that the black Color (as it is called) of the Negroes is derived from the LEPROSY."[63] In this paper, Rush reasoned, as Daniel Boorstin summarizes it for us,

. . . toward the conclusion that the so-called black color of the Negro was the effect not of any original difference in his nature, but of the affliction of his ancestors with leprosy. This disease, he noted, was accompanied in some instances by a black color of the skin. The big lips and flat nose typical of Negroes were actually symptoms of leprosy, which Rush himself had more than once observed. The inhabitants of the leper islands of the South Pacific possessed thick lips and woolly hair, and albinism (also found among American Negroes) was not unknown there. The same morbid insensibility of the nerves which was induced by leprosy was found peculiarly in Negroes, who, compared to white people, were able to endure surgical operations with ease. Rush recalled cases where Negroes had actually held the upper part of a limb during amputation. Such pathological insensibility was also apparent in the apathy with which Negroes exposed themselves to great heat, and the indifference with which they handled hot coals. Lepers were remarkable for their strong venereal desires; and so strong were these desires in Negroes that even the depressing circumstances of slavery had not prevented their extraordinary fruitfulness. When asked to account for the duration of the Negro's color through long centuries, Rush answered that leprosy was of all diseases the most permanently inherited. According to Rush, the fact that in the eighteenth century Negroes seldom infected others with the disease could not be held against his theory, because by now leprosy had nearly ceased to be infectious.[64]

The gist of Rush's theory was that the Negro suffered from congenital leprosy which ". . . appeared in so mild a form that excess pigmentation was its only symptom."[65] Henry Moss, Rush claimed, was undergoing a spontaneous cure.

With this theory, Rush made the Negro a medically safe domestic, while at the same time called for his sexual segregation as a carrier of a dread hereditary disease. Here, then, was an early model of the perfect medical concept of illness—one that helps the physician and the society he serves, while justifying social maltreatment as medical prophylaxis.*

* If a so-called mental patient were to entertain such a patently self-serving theory, we would call his explanation a "projection," and we would call him "paranoid." But as a Hindu saying has it, "It is all a question of whose guru is being gored."

Remarkably, in his lengthy biography of Rush, dealing especially with Rush's

"Having determined that the Negro's color was a symptom of endemic leprosy," writes Stanton, Rush drew three conclusions. "First, whites should cease 'to tyrannize over them,' for their disease 'should entitle them to a double portion of our humanity.' However, by the same token, whites should not intermarry with them, for this would 'tend to infect posterity' with the 'disorder' . . . Finally, attempts must be made to cure the disease."[66]

It is not clear whether Rush believed that the Negro should have a voice in deciding if he wanted to be cured, or whether he thought that for the treatment of the Negro, as for that of the madman, "doctor knows best." In any case, Rush announced that "Nature has lately unfurled a banner upon this subject. She has begun spontaneous cures of this disease in several black people in this country."[67] Here he was referring to the case of Henry Moss, already mentioned.

Rush hoped that attempts to treat the Negro for his leprosy would be encouraged when philosophers understood how much it would increase human happiness. Such a cure, Rush argued, "would produce a large portion of happiness in the world [by destroying] one of the arguments in favor of enslaving the Negroes, for their color has been supposed by the ignorant to mark them as objects of divine judgments . . ."[68] The replacement here of a harsh religious explanation with a benign scientific one is worth noting. Clearly, Rush got out of his medical ideology—whether he applied it to alcoholism, smoking, insanity, or Negritude—what he had put into it: the Bible. Perturbed by slavery, Rush's contemporaries found justification for the enslavement of the black man in the Scriptures: God had marked the Negro to show his inferior status in the eyes of the Creator.[69] Rush looked to science and found what

---

medical activities, Binger manages to remain completely silent on Rush's theory of the black skin of the Negro. The leprosy theory and Binger's omission of it reveal the strategic function of the disease-rhetoric in psychiatry. Rush's theory was intended to help Americans accept the Negro as a man, while rejecting him as an infectious patient. Presumably, Binger's omission of it has a similar aim—namely, to help Americans accept mental illness as a medical problem, while rejecting the mental patient as a social outcast. Were Binger to dwell on Rush's theory of Negritude, he would encourage the reader to think Rush's views on mental illness no better than those on Negritude, thus throwing doubts on the very foundation of the Mental Health Movement. Nor is Binger alone in thus rewriting psychiatric history. None of the standard texts on psychiatric history mentions Rush's leprosy theory of Negritude.

he wanted: It was not God but nature that marked the black man; his blackness, moreover, is a sign, not of his "congenital sin," but of his "congenital illness."*

Such a cure would also add to the happiness of the Negro himself, Rush believed, for "however well they appear to be satisfied with their color, there are many proofs of their preferring that of the white people."[70]

In his attitude toward the Negro, Rush thus adheres to the fundamental principle of Institutional Psychiatry, namely, that the "patient" does not know, and hence cannot protect, his own best interests. He needs the medical man to do this for him. In 1796, the psychiatrist knew that the Negro would have preferred to be white. Today, the psychiatrist knows that the alleged drug addict would prefer not to take drugs; that the homosexual would prefer to be heterosexual; and that the suicidal person would prefer to live.† The upshot is the psychiatric discreditation of human experience and the therapeutic destruction of human differences.

Rush makes us realize how unoriginal, but yet how enduring, are the therapeutic posturings of the modern psychiatrist. Since the Inquisition, oppressors have insisted on wearing the uniforms of helpers. First, they donned the garb of the cleric. Today they will not show themselves without their white medical coats. Benevolent paternalism (if one wants to so mislabel human evil) was the basic article of faith and the fundamental strategic weapon for the clergyman's domination of those he deemed sinners; and so it has con-

---

* Defining as a disease what for the Other is physiologically natural (for example, the Negro's black skin), or personally desirable (for example, the beliefs of so-called madmen), and as treatment the physician's efforts to change these into conditions and beliefs more attractive to the medical profession or society, have always been, and still are, the characteristic strategies of Institutional Psychiatry.

† Almost any article or book on the "care" of the involuntary mental patient may be used to illustrate the contention that physicians fall back on paternalism to justify their demands for coercive controls in situations where the patient, or alleged patient, disagrees with them. "Certain cases [not individuals!]"— writes Solomon in a recent article on suicide—". . . must be considered irresponsible, not only with respect to violent impulses but also in all medical matters." In this class, which he labels "The Irresponsible," he places "Children," "The Mentally Retarded," "The Psychotic," and "The Severely or Terminally Ill." Solomon's conclusion is that "Repugnant though it may be, he [the physician] may have to act against the patient's wishes in order to protect the patient's life and that of others." (Philip Solomon, The burden of responsibility in suicide, *J.A.M.A.*, 199: 321–324 [Jan. 30], 1967.)

tinued for the psychiatrist's domination of those he deems mad. In Rush, the characteristics of these two types of oppressors were perfectly blended in a single identity. He was the immigrant from religion who spoke faultless medicine. In propounding leprosy as an explanation for the Negro's black skin, he let it slip that he did not advocate this hypothesis merely because he believed it to be true, but, more importantly, because he considered it socially useful. Rush thus argues that, by accepting the leprosy theory of Negritude, "We shall render the belief of the whole human race being descended from one pair easy and universal, and thereby not only add weight to the Christian revelation, but remove a material obstacle to the exercise of that universal benevolence which is inculcated by it."[71]

We see here Rush urging adherence to his theory because it adds "weight to the Christian revelation," and because it helps his fellow white Americans "to exercise . . . universal benevolence" toward the Negro. What this flowery rhetoric disguises is Rush's advocacy of the separation of the races, justified not by the outworn shibboleths of the traditional proslavery position, but by the latest discoveries of "medical science." This is not merely my interpretation of Rush's intentions; he himself says so. "If the color of the Negroes be the effect of a disease," he writes, "the facts and principles which have been here delivered should teach white people the necessity of keeping up that prejudice against such connections with them as would tend to infect posterity with any portion of their disorder."[72]

The chauvinistic, indeed racist, character of this theory did not escape the historians. Through Rush's whole argument about the Negro, Boorstin remarks, "ran the assumption (the more significant because not explicitly avowed) that the norm for the color of a healthy member of the human species was *white*. It was inconceivable to Rush that when the Negro had been cured of his affliction and returned to his pristine condition, he would have the red complexion of the American Indian or the yellow of the Asiatic. One of his final arguments for redoubling the effort to perfect a cure was that the Negro might have the happiness of wearing the proper white color of the human skin."[73]

The leprosy theory of Negritude—a forerunner of modern psychiatric theories of a wide variety of behaviors—is truly an Orwellian parody of medicine in the service of behavioral control. Rush used it mainly as an outlet for his reforming passion, which was as boundless in its intolerance of human differences as in its therapeutic zeal. Like the inquisitor who accepts the heretic if he recants and embraces the true faith, so Rush accepts the Negro if he is cured of his blackness and becomes white!

This is precisely what characterizes Everyman as the enemy of human differences. He accepts the Other in so far as the Other conforms to his image and conduct. However, if he and the Other differ, he defines the Other as defective—physically, mentally, or morally—and accepts him only if he is able and willing to cast off those of his features that set him apart from the normal. If the Other recants his false beliefs, or submits to treatment for his illness, then, and only then, will he be accepted as a member of the group. If he fails to do these things, the Other becomes the Evil one—whether he be called the Stranger, the Patient, or the Enemy.

This principle, so clearly enunciated by Benjamin Rush, has become the hallmark of Institutional Psychiatry; and the strategies implicit in it, so enthusiastically employed by him, have become the therapeutic methods of the institutional psychiatrist.

10

THE PRODUCT CONVERSION—
FROM HERESY TO ILLNESS

> The most prejudiced must admit that this religion
> without theology [positivism] is not chargeable with
> relaxation of moral restraints. On the contrary, it
> prodigiously exaggerates them.
>
> *–John Stuart Mill*[1]

In the work of Benjamin Rush, we have traced the manifestations
of the great ideological conversion from theology to science. We
saw how Rush had redefined sin as sickness, and moral sanction
as medical treatment. In this chapter I shall analyze this process
in broader terms and shall show that as the dominant social ethic
changed from a religious to a secular one, the problem of heresy
disappeared, and the problem of madness arose and became of
great social significance. In the next chapter I shall examine the
creation of social deviants, and shall show that as formerly priests
had manufactured heretics, so physicians, as the new guardians of
social conduct and morality, began to manufacture madmen.

The change from a religious and moral to a social and medical
conceptualization and control of personal conduct affects the entire
discipline of psychiatry and allied fields. Perhaps nowhere is this
transformation more evident than in the modern perspective on
so-called sexual deviation, and especially on homosexuality. We
shall therefore compare the concept of homosexuality as heresy,

prevalent in the days of the witch-hunts, with the concept of homo-sexuality as mental illness, prevalent today.

Homosexual behavior—like heterosexual and autoerotic behavior —occurs among higher apes and among human beings living in a wide variety of cultural conditions. Judging by artistic, historical, and literary records, it also occurred in past ages and societies. Today it is part of the dogma of American psychiatrically en-lightened opinion that homosexuality is an illness—a form of mental illness. This is a relatively recent view. In the past, men held quite different views on homosexuality, from accepting it as a perfectly natural activity to prohibiting it as the most heinous of crimes. We shall not explore the cultural and historical aspects of homosexuality;[2] instead, we shall confine ourselves to a com-parison of the attitude toward homosexuality during the witch-hunts and at the present time. Since late medieval and Renaissance societies were deeply imbued with the teachings of Christianity, we shall first survey the principal Biblical references to this subject.

The Bible prohibits almost every form of sexual activity other than heterosexual, genital intercourse. Homosexuality is prohibited first in Genesis, in the story of Lot. One evening, two angels come to Sodom, disguised as men. Lot meets them at the gates and invites them into his house. First, the angels refuse Lot's hospitality, offer-ing instead to spend the night in the street; but at Lot's urgings, the Old Testament tells us, "they entered his house; and he made them a feast, and baked unleavened bread, and they ate. But before they lay down, the men of the city, the men of Sodom, both young and old, all the people to the last man, surrounded the house; and they called to Lot. 'Where are the men who came to you tonight? Bring them out to us, that we may know them.' "[3]

The men of Sodom wanted to use the travelers as sexual objects. Among the ancient Israelites, however, he who gave shelter to strangers was obligated to protect them from harm. Because of this, Lot offered his daughters as substitute objects: "Lot went out of the door to the men, shut the door after him, and said, 'I beg you, my brothers, do not act so wickedly. Behold, I have two daughters who have not known man; let me bring them out to you, and do to them as you please; only do nothing to these men, for they have come under the shelter of my roof.' "[4]

As this suggests, homosexuality was considered a serious offense. This story also makes clear the abysmal devaluation of women as human beings in the ethics of ancient Judaism. Lot values the dignity of his male guests more highly than that of his female children. The Christian ethic did not raise the worth of female life much above the Jewish; nor did the clinical ethic raise it much above the clerical. This is why most of those identified as witches by male inquisitors were women; and why most of those diagnosed as hysterics by male psychiatrists were also women.

The episode in Sodom is undoubtedly the earliest account in human history of the entrapment of homosexuals, a strategy widely practiced by the law enforcement agencies of modern Western countries, especially those of the United States. In effect, the men of Sodom were entrapped by the two strangers, who in truth were not travelers but angels, that is to say, God's plain-clothesmen. These agents of the Biblical vice-squad wasted no time punishing the offenders: ". . . they struck with blindness the men who were at the door of the house . . ."[5] The angels then warn Lot of God's plan to destroy the wicked city, giving him time to flee with his family. God's terrible punishment follows: "Then the Lord rained on Sodom and Gomorrah brimstone and fire from the Lord out of heaven; and he overthrew those cities, and all the valley, and all the inhabitants of the cities, and what grew on the ground."[6]

Homosexuality is again prohibited in Leviticus. "You shall not lie with a male as with a woman; it is an abomination."[7] Adultery, incest, and bestiality are also forbidden. The punishment for transgression is death: "If a man lies with a male as with a woman, both of them have committed an abomination; they shall be put to death, their blood is upon them."[*] [8]

It is important to note that only male homosexuality is forbidden: "You shall not lie with a male as with a woman . . ." God addresses males only. He does not command woman not to lie with a female as with a man. Here by omission and implication, and elsewhere by more explicit phrasing, woman is treated as a kind of human animal, not as a full human being. The most up-to-date legal statutes of Western nations dealing with homosexuality continue

* For further Biblical references to homosexuality, condemning it in essentially similar terms, see Judges 1: 22–30; 1 Kings 22: 46; 2 Kings 23: 7; Romans 1: 27; 1 Corinthians 6:9; and 1 Timothy 1:10.

to maintain this posture toward women: Though homosexual intercourse between consenting adults continues to be prohibited in many countries, nowhere does this apply to women.* The inference about the less-than-human status of women is inevitable. No wonder that in his morning prayer, the Orthodox Jew says, "Blessed be God . . . that He did not make me a woman," while the woman says, "Blessed be the Lord, who created me according to His will."[9]

Biblical prohibitions against homosexuality had of course a profound influence on the medieval equation of this practice with heresy; on our contemporary criminal laws and social attitudes, which regard homosexuality as a hybrid of crime and disease; and on the language we still use to describe many so-called sexually deviant acts. Sodomy is an example.

Webster's *Unabridged Dictionary* (Third Edition) defines sodomy as "The homosexual proclivities of the men of the city as narrated in Gen. 19: 1–11; carnal copulation with a member of the same sex or with an animal or unnatural carnal copulation with a member of the opposite sex; specif.: the penetration of the male organ into the mouth or anus of another." This definition is pragmatically correct. In both psychiatric and literary works, the term "sodomy" is used to describe sexual activity involving contact between penis and mouth or anus, regardless of whether the "passive" partner is male or female. Fellatio is thus a type of sodomy. Because human beings frequently engage in these and other nongenital sexual acts, Kinsey correctly emphasized that there are few Americans who, in their everyday sexual lives, do not violate both the religious prohibitions of their faith and the criminal laws of their country.[10]

In short, the Church opposed homosexuality not only, or even primarily, because it was "abnormal" or "unnatural," but rather because it satisfied carnal lust and yielded bodily pleasure. This condemnation of homosexuality, says Rattray Taylor, "was merely

* Kinsey and his coworkers have fully documented the differential social treatment, throughout the ages, of male and female homosexual acts. The Talmud, they observe, is relatively lenient regarding women, classifying female homosexual activity as a "mere obscenity," disqualifying the offender from marrying a rabbi. (Alfred C. Kinsey, Wardell B. Pomeroy, Clyde E. Martin, and Paul Gebhard, *Sexual Behavior in the Human Female*, p. 484.) "In medieval European history there are abundant records of death imposed upon males for sexual activity with other males, but very few recorded cases of similar action against females." (Ibid.)

an aspect of the general condemnation of sexual pleasure and indeed of sexual activity not directly necessary to ensure the continuation of the race. Even within marriage, sexual activity was severely restricted, and virginity was declared a more blessed state than matrimony."[11] It is no accident, then, that carnal lust, leading to nonprocreative sexual practices and pleasure of all kinds, was a characteristic passion of witches. They were supposed to satisfy their cravings by copulating with the Devil, a male figure of superhuman masculinity, equipped with a "forked penis," enabling him to penetrate the woman at once vaginally and anally.[12]

As we turn to a consideration of the Church's attitudes toward sex during the witch-hunts, we discover a concrete connection between notions of religious deviance and sexual offense: Heresy and homosexuality become one and the same thing.* For centuries, no penological distinction is made between religious unorthodoxy and sexual misbehavior, especially homosexuality. "During the Middle Ages," says Westermarck, "heretics were accused of unnatural vice [homosexuality] as a matter of course. . . . In medieval laws sodomy was also repeatedly mentioned together with heresy, and the punishment was the same for both."[13]

In thirteenth-century Spain, the penalty for homosexuality was castration and "lapidation" [execution by stoning].[14] Ferdinand and Isabella changed this, in 1479, to "burning alive and confiscation, irrespective of the station of the culprit."[15] In other words, then the crime was subject to punishment by both secular and ecclesiastic courts—just as now it is subject to punishment by both penal and psychiatric sanctions. In 1451, Nicholas V empowered the Inquisition to deal with it. "When the institution [Inquisition] was founded in Spain," Lea writes, ". . . the Seville tribunal made it [homosexuality] the subject of a special inquest; there were many arrests and many fugitives, and twelve convicts were duly burnt."[16] The Spanish Inquisition, whose principal enemies, as we have seen,[17] were Judaizers and Moriscoes, was thus also hard on homosexuals.†

* The concept of evil, especially in so far as it functions mainly as a rhetorical device justifying the expulsion of the source of danger, absorbs many cognitive distinctions. Thus, in the Middle Ages, heretic, sorcerer, sodomist, and witch were often subsumed under a single category.

† This was not true of the Roman Inquisition, whose principal enemies were witches and Protestants. ". . . throughout Italy," Lea tells us, "the crime

In Portugal, too, the Spanish prohibitions against homosexuality were strictly enforced. "In 1640, the Regulations prescribe that the offence is to be tried like heresy, and the punishment is to be either relaxation [burning] or scourging [flogging] and the galleys. In a case occurring in the Lisbon *auto* of 1723, the sentence was scourging and ten years of galley-service."[18]

In Valencia, the usual punishment for homosexuality was burning at the stake. There was, however, some disinclination to inflict this penalty because these offenders ". . . could not escape, as heretics could, by confession and conversion."[19] In this connection it is interesting to note that homosexual clerics were treated more leniently than laymen exhibiting the same conduct. "Many authorities . . . ," says Lea, "held that clerics were not to be subjected to the rigor of the law for this offense, and it was common opinion that incorrigibility was required to justify the ordinary penality."* [20]

The frequency of prosecutions for homosexuality in Spain was appreciable. From 1780 to 1820, Lea records, "the total number of cases coming before the three tribunals [in Valencia] was exactly one hundred."[21]

In English-speaking countries, the connection between heresy and homosexuality is expressed through the use of a single word to denote both concepts: buggery. The double meaning of this word persists to this day. Webster's *Unabridged Dictionary* (Third Edition) defines "buggery" as "heresy, sodomy"; and "bugger" as "heretic, sodomite." The word is derived from the medieval Latin *Bugarus* and *Bulgarus*, literally Bulgarian, "from the adherence of the Bulgarians to the Eastern Church considered heretical."

---

was everywhere treated with a leniency wholly inadequate to its atrocity. The Roman Inquisition, moreover, took no cognizance of it." This tolerance, indeed approval, of homosexuality in Italy is attested to by the fact that, in 1664, some Conventual Franciscans actually "rendered themselves conspicuous by sounding the praises of the practice . . ." (Lea, *A History of the Inquisition of Spain*, p. 365.)

* Physicians now enjoy similar lenience with respect to such typical psychiatric "offenses" as depression and the threat of suicide. Laymen are severely punished for such conduct: they are hospitalized and treated against their will. Although the incidence of suicide is higher in physicians than in any other group— and is highest among psychiatrists—medical men exhibiting such conduct are rarely punished for it with involuntary mental hospitalization and treatment.

This connection, at once semantic and conceptual, between unorthodoxy and sodomy, was firmly established during the late
Middle Ages, and has never been severed. It is as strong today as
it was six hundred years ago. To be stigmatized as a heretic or
bugger in the fourteenth century was to be cast out of society.
Since the dominant ideology was theological, religious deviance
was considered so grave an offense as to render the individual a
nonperson. Whatever redeeming qualities he might have had
counted for nought. The sin of heresy eclipsed all contradictory,
personal characteristics, just as the teachings of God and the Church
eclipsed all contradictory, empirical observations. The disease called
"mental illness"—and its subspecies "homosexuality"—plays the
same role today. The late Senator Joseph McCarthy thus equated
the social sin of Communism with the sexual sin of homosexuality
and used the two labels as if they were synonymous. He could not
have done this had there been no general belief that, like medieval
heretics, men labeled "homosexual" are somehow totally bad. They
can have no compensating or redeeming features: They cannot be
talented writers or patriotic Americans. Given this premise—which
McCarthy did not invent, but only appropriated for his use—it
follows that homosexuals must also be politically deviant, that is,
Communists. The same logic applies in reverse. If Communists
are the modern, secular incarnations of the Devil—political incubi
and succubi, as it were—then it follows that they, too, can have no
redeeming features. They must be completely bad. They must be
homosexuals.*

We are ready now to consider the problem of homosexuality in its

---

* In using the term "mental illness" (and its variants) we follow the same
principle. When we call men like Ezra Pound or Lee Harvey Oswald mad,
we establish, by ascription, a characteristic of that person which overshadows
with transcendent badness the individual whom it is supposed to describe. Once
the characterization is accepted, it negates the individual's other human—
especially good—qualities. He is thus degraded and dehumanized. We then
no longer worry about him as a person with rights and talents. If he is a poet,
we can dismiss him as an artist; if he is an accused criminal, we can ignore his
guilt or innocence; and if he is a suspected presidential assassin, murdered in
jail, we can simplify a hopelessly unresolved event with far-reaching political
and international implications by attributing everything about it to the madness of a single, virtually unknown, individual. In short, psychiatric heresy,
like religious heresy, is a functional concept. It is useful for the society that
employs it; were it not so, the concept would never have evolved and would
not continue to receive popular support.

contemporary form: that is, is homosexuality a disease? In a recent authoritative volume on "sexual inversion," Judd Marmor, the editor, raises this question, and answers that "Most of the psycho-analysts in this volume, except Szasz, are of the opinion that homo-sexuality is definitely an illness to be treated and *corrected*."[22] (Italics added.) The correctional zeal of the modern psychiatric therapist shows itself here in a way that cannot be mistaken. Disease as a biological condition and as a social role are confused. Cancer of the bladder is a disease; but whether it is treated or not depends on the person who has the disease, not on the physician who makes the diagnosis![23] Marmor, like so many contemporary psychiatrists, forgets or ignores this distinction. There is, to be sure, good reason why he, and other "mental health workers," do so: By pretending that convention is Nature, that disobeying a personal prohibition is a medical illness, they establish themselves as agents of social control and at the same time disguise their punitive inter-ventions in the semantic and social trappings of medical practice.

René Guyon, a French student of sexual customs, has recognized this characteristic tendency of modern psychiatry to brand as sick that which is merely unconventional. "The trouble to which the psychiatrists have gone," he observes, "to explain . . . nature in terms of convention, health in terms of mental disease, is scarcely to be believed. . . . The distinctive method of its system is that every time it comes across a natural act that is contrary to the prevailing conventions, it brands this act as a symptom of mental derangement or abnormality."[24]

The question of whether or not homosexuality is an illness is therefore a pseudo problem. If by disease we mean deviation from an anatomical or physiological norm—as in the case of a fractured leg or diabetes—then homosexuality is clearly not an illness. Still, it may be asked if there is a genetic predisposition to homosexuality, as there is to a stocky body build; or is it entirely a learned pattern of behavior? This question cannot be answered with assurance. At present, the evidence for such predisposition is slim, if any. The biologically oriented person may argue, however, that more evidence for it might be discovered in the future. Perhaps so. But even if homosexuals were proven to have certain sexual preferences be-cause of their nature, rather than nurture, what would that prove? People who are prematurely bald are sick, in a stricter sense of this word, than homosexuals could possibly be. What of it? Clearly, the question that is really being posed for us is not whether a given person manifests deviations from an anatomical and physiological norm, but what moral and social significance society attaches to his behavior—whether it be due to infectious illness (as was the case with leprosy in the past), or to learned preference (as is the case with homosexuality today).

Psychiatric preoccupation with the disease concept of homosexuality—as with the disease concept of all so-called mental illnesses, such as alcoholism, drug addiction, or suicide—conceals the fact that homosexuals are a group of medically stigmatized and socially persecuted individuals. The noise generated by their persecution and their anguished cries of protest are drowned out by the rhetoric of therapy—just as the rhetoric of salvation drowned out the noise generated by the persecution of heretics and their anguished cries of protest. It is a heartless hypocrisy to pretend that physicians, psychiatrists, or "normal" laymen for that matter, really care about the welfare of the mentally ill in general, or the homosexual in particular. If they did, they would stop torturing him while claiming to help him. But this is just what reformers—whether theological or medical—refuse to do.*

The idea that the homosexual is "sick" only in the sense that he is so categorized by others, and himself accepts this categorization, goes back at least to André Gide's autobiographical work, *Corydon*, and perhaps earlier. First published anonymously in 1911, the narrative is set in the form of a series of dialogues between the author and his younger friend Corydon. The following excerpt illustrates Gide's conception of the homosexual as a victim of an overzealously heterosexual society.

"I am . . . preparing a fairly important study on the subject [of homosexuality]" [says the author].

"Aren't the works of Moll, Krafft-Ebing, and Raffalovitch enough for you?" [replies Corydon].

* For many decades, but especially since the days of Senator Joseph McCarthy, the insinuation of homosexuality about one's adversaries has become an accepted strategy in American political life. If homosexuality is an illness—"like any other"—then why do psychiatrists not protest its use as a means of social degradation and political disqualification? For a further discussion of the hypocrisy of the disease concept of homosexuality, see Chapter 13.

"They are not satisfactory. I would like to approach it differently. . . . I am writing a *Defense of Homosexuality*."

"Why not a *Eulogy,* while you are about it?"

"Because such a title would force my ideas. I am afraid people will find even the word '*Defense*' too provocative . . . the cause lacks martyrs."

"Don't use such big words."

"I use the words needed. We have had Wilde, Krupp, Macdonald, Eulenburg . . . Oh, victims! Victims as many as you please. But not a single martyr. They all deny it; they always will deny it."

"There you are! They all feel ashamed and retract as soon as they are faced with public opinion, the press, or the courtroom."

". . . Yes, you are right. To try to establish one's innocence by disavowing one's life is to yield to public opinion. How strange! One has the courage of one's opinions, but not of one's habits. One can accept suffering, but not dishonor."[25]

Here Gide unmasks homosexuality as a socially stigmatized role, like witch or Jew, which, under the pressure of public opinion, its bearer is likely to disavow and repudiate. The homosexual is a scapegoat who evokes no sympathy. Hence, he can be only a victim, never a martyr. This is as true today in the United States as it was in France a half century ago. The same applies, moreover, to the mentally ill; he, too, can only be a victim, never a martyr.

The next excerpt illustrates Gide's penetrating insight into the disease concept of sexual inversion, and, *mutatis mutandis,* into mental illness generally.

"If you had been aware of it [homosexual inclination], what would you have done?" [asks Corydon].

"I believe I would have cured the boy" [replies the author].

"You said a moment ago that it was incurable . . ."

"I could have cured him as I cured myself. . . . By persuading him he was not sick . . . that there was nothing unnatural in his deviation."

"And if he had persisted, you would naturally have yielded to it."

"Ah! That is an entirely different question. When the physiological problem is resolved, the moral problem begins."[26]

Gide thus shows that the "diagnosis" of homosexuality is in actuality a stigmatizing label which, to protect his authentic identity, the subject must reject. To escape from medical control, the homo-sexual must repudiate the diagnosis ascribed to him by the physician. In other words, homosexuality is an illness in the same sense as we have seen Negritude described as an illness. Benjamin Rush claimed that Negroes had black skin because they were ill; and he proposed to use their illness as a justification for their social control.[27] Rush's modern follower asserts that men whose sexual conduct he dis-approves of are ill; and he uses their illness as a justification for their social control.

Only in our day have Negroes been able to escape from the semantic and social trap in which white men have held them fast after their legal shackles had been cast off a century ago. So-called mental patients, whose fetters—forged of commitment papers, asylum walls, and fiendish tortures passed off as "medical treat-ments"—have a strangle hold on their bodies and souls are only now learning how to properly abase themselves before their psychia-tric masters. It seems probable that many more people will have to be injured by means of psychiatric labeling and its social conse-quences than have been so far, before men will recognize, and pro-tect themselves from, the dangers of Institutional Psychiatry. This, at least, is the lesson which the history of witchcraft suggests.

So long as men could denounce others as witches—so that the witch could always be considered the Other, never the Self—witch-craft remained an easily exploitable concept and the Inquisition a flourishing institution. Only loss of faith in the authority of the inquisitors and their religious mission brought an end to this practice of symbolic cannibalism.* Similarly, so long as men can denounce each other as mentally sick (homosexual, addicted, in-sane, and so forth)—so that the madman can always be considered the Other, never the Self—mental illness will remain an easily ex-ploitable concept, and Coercive Psychiatry a flourishing institu-tion. If this is so, only loss of faith in the authority of institutional psychiatrists and their medical mission will bring an end to the Psychiatric Inquisition. This day is not imminent.

My contention that the psychiatric perspective on homosexuality is but a thinly disguised replica of the religious perspective which it displaced, and that efforts to "treat" this kind of conduct medically

---

* The concept of symbolic cannibalism is discussed fully in Chapter 15.

are but thinly disguised methods for suppressing it, may be verified by examining any contemporary psychiatric account of homosexuality. The handling of the subject by Karl Menninger, widely recognized as the most "liberal" and "progressive" of modern psychiatrists, is illustrative. In *The Vital Balance,* Menninger discusses homosexuality under the general rubric of "A Second Order of Dyscontrol and Dysorganization," immediately following an analysis of "Perverse Sexual Modalities."[28] "We cannot, like Gide, extol homosexuality," writes Menninger. "We do not, like some, *condone* it. We regard it as a *symptom* with all the functions of other symptoms—aggression, indulgence, self-punishment, and the effort to forestall something worse."[29] (Italics added.) Menninger, like other medical writers on moral topics, gives himself away by the choice of his words: If homosexuality is a "symptom," what is there to "condone" or not "condone"? Menninger would not speak of "condoning or not condoning" the fever of pneumonia or the jaundice of biliary obstruction—but he does speak of "not condoning" a psychiatric "symptom." His "therapeutic" recommendations for homosexuality bear out the suspicion that his medical role is but a cloak for that of the moralist and social engineer.

A "married man, a church member, a director of a bank, the father of three children"—in short, a pillar of the community—consults Menninger and confides his secret to him: He is a homosexual. The man asks: "But what can I do?" Menninger's answer: "Of course one thing he could do would be to live continently; there are millions of heterosexually inclined people who are continent for one reason or another, and this should be no more difficult for a homosexually inclined individual."[30] True. But would not the possibility of sexual continence have occurred to a man who is the successful director of a bank?*

Menninger's second recommendation is "to get treatment for the condition. Treatment can be efficacious if the afflicted one is not too strongly entrenched in despair or in the rationalizations that there was something wrong with his hereditary genes, that he

---

* In this connection, see Guyon, who writes: "Finally, the medical profession, prostituting science to the service of taboo (and taking the latter for granted), has endeavored to show that it is possible to forgo the sexual act without injury to health. . ." (René Guyon, *The Ethics of Sexual Acts,* p. 204.) Guyon is here referring to heterosexual acts, but, *mutatis mutandis,* the same also applies to homosexual and autoerotic acts.

is condemned to be this way and must make the best of it."[31] To Menninger, the "treatment" can have only one goal: to convert the heretic to the true faith, to transform the homosexual into a heterosexual. The possibility of helping the client accept his existing inclinations with greater equanimity, to help him value his own authentic selfhood more than his society's judgment of it—these therapeutic alternatives are not even mentioned by Menninger. Indeed, he castigates the homosexual by reversing an old accusation against him: Only a few years ago—after giving up the "theory" that homosexuality was caused by masturbation, which was standard psychiatric dogma toward the end of the nineteenth century— psychiatrists insisted that sexual inversion was a genetic disease; it was due to "bad heredity." Despite this, Menninger flatly accuses the homosexual of "rationalizing" if he believes that heredity may have something to do with the nature of his sexual interests, and is not eager to change them in the direction approved by society. Perhaps one reason for Menninger's intellectual intransigence is that he has no doubt that he knows what homosexuality—its "essence"—really is: It is "aggression"—the psychiatric name for Satan. "But the fact remains," he writes, "that as we see homosexuality *clinically* and *officially* it nearly always betrays its *essentially* aggressive nature."[32] (Italics added.) Of course, when Menninger looks at any other sexual or social behavior "clinically and officially [sic]," he sees their "essence" also in aggression.* Like the devout theologian seeing the Devil lurking everywhere, Menninger, the devout Freudian, sees aggression and the death instinct.

Occasionally, however, Menninger forgets his clinical lines and speaks in explicitly clerical terms. In his Introduction to *The Wolfenden Report*, for example, he asserts that "Prostitution and homosexuality rank high in the kingdom of evils"[33]—surely a remarkable statement from a leading psychiatrist in the second half of the twentieth century. Nor does calling prostitution and homosexuality grave sins prevent Menninger from regarding these activities as mental illnesses as well. "From the standpoint of the psychiatrist," he writes, "both homosexuality and prostitution—and

---

* Menninger offers the same explanation for masturbation: ". . . in the unconscious mind it [masturbation] always represents an aggression against some one." (Karl Menninger, *Man Against Himself,* p. 69.) For further discussion, see Chapter 11.

add to this the use of prostitutes—constitutes evidence of immature sexuality and either arrested psychological development or regression. Whatever it be called by the public, there is no question [sic] in the minds of psychiatrists regarding the abnormality of such behavior."[34] Menninger seems to believe that entertaining no doubts about one's opinions is a special virtue, a sure sign of psychiatric grace.*

Contemporary psychiatrists will not admit to the possibility that they might be wrong in categorizing sexual inversion as an illness. "In a discussion of homosexuality, psychiatrists would probably agree unanimously on at least one point: the belief that the homosexual is a sick person."[35] This statement appears in the introduction to a pamphlet on homosexuality, distributed free to the profession by Roche Laboratories, one of the principal manufacturers of so-called psychopharmacologic drugs. Like the inquisitor, the psychiatrist defines, and thereby authenticates, his own existential position by what he opposes—as heresy or illness. In stubbornly insisting that the homosexual is sick, the psychiatrist is merely pleading to be accepted as a physician.†

As befits the ministrations of a modern inquisitor, the persecutory practices of the institutional psychiatrist are couched in the vocabulary of medicine. Pretending to be diagnosing a measles-like illness during its incubation period in order the better to treat it, the psychiatrist actually imposes pseudomedical labels on society's scapegoats in order the better to handicap, reject, and destroy them. Not satisfied with diagnosing overt homosexuals as "sick," psychiatrists claim to be able to discover the presence of this supposed

* The righteous convictions of mankind's self-appointed benefactors has moved Russell to observe that "Most of the greatest evils that man has inflicted upon man has come through people feeling quite certain about something which, in fact, was false." (Bertrand Russell, *Unpopular Essays*, p. 162.)

† Since true belief—whether in the mythologies of Christianity or of Psychiatry —is difficult to establish, especially to the satisfaction of a skeptical judge, hostility against the heretic becomes the hallmark of the genuineness of belief. Speaking through Sancho Panza, Cervantes puts it this way: "Yet the historians ought to take pity on me and treat me kindly in their writings, if only because I've always believed in God and all the tenets of the Holy Roman Catholic Church, and because I am a mortal enemy to the Jews." (Miguel de Cervantes Saavedra, *The Adventures of Don Quixote*, p. 516.) In other words, as the faithful Spaniard living at the height of the Inquisition proved his religious orthodoxy by hating Jews, so the scientific psychiatrist living today proves his medical orthodoxy by hating mental illness.

disease (in its "latent" form, of course), in persons who show no outward sign of it. They also claim to be able to diagnose homosexuality during childhood, while it is incubating, as it were. "We have noted," write Holemon and Winokur, "that this [effeminate behavior] often antedated homosexual orientation and homosexual relations. In these patients effeminacy seems to be the primary problem and the sexual behavior is secondary. From this one should be able to predict which children will develop effeminate homosexuality by selecting those with objective signs of effeminacy."[36] In a similar vein, Shearer declares that "excessive clinging to the parent of the opposite sex, especially between father and daughter, should also alert the physician to the possibility of homosexuality."[37] What constitutes "excessive clinging"? How much affection between child and parent of the opposite sex is permitted without it signifying the presence of the dread disease, homosexuality?

From the foregoing we may safely conclude that psychiatric opinion about homosexuals is not a scientific proposition but a medical prejudice.* It is pertinent to recall here that the more attention the inquisitors paid to witchcraft, the more the witches multiplied. The same principle applies to mental illness in general, and to homosexuality in particular. Zealous efforts to eradicate and prevent such "disorders" actually create the conditions in which the assumption and ascription of such roles flourish.

With the penetrating insight of the literary artist, William S. Burroughs has described just this process—that is, the manufacture of madness through a "medical examination" for the "early detection" of homosexuality. An episode in *Naked Lunch*, called "The Examination," begins with Carl Pederson finding "a postcard in his box requesting him to report for a ten o'clock appointment

---

* In one of those ironic reversals of roles which occur every so often in human history, the homosexual is now persecuted by physicians, and defended by clergymen. In an article published in the influential *National Catholic Reporter*, Father Henri Nouwen of Utrecht, in the Netherlands, recasts the problem of homosexuality in the light of modern Christian and phenomenological teaching. His essential thesis is that homosexuality is neither a sin nor a disease, but a medical, and especially psychiatric, prejudice. "If a man has chosen the homosexual way of life, prefers homosexual circles and homosexual friends, and does not show any desire or willingness to change," writes Father Nouwen, "it does not make any sense to punish him or try to change him." (Henri J. M. Nouwen, Homosexuality: Prejudice or mental illness? *Nat. Cath. Rep.*, Nov. 29, 1967, p. 8.) See also Lars Ullerstam, *The Erotic Minorities*, especially p. 24.

with Doctor Benway in the Ministry of Mental Hygiene and Prophylaxis . . ."[38] As the examination gets underway, Pederson realizes that he is being tested for "sexual deviation." The doctor explains that homosexuality is "a sickness . . . certainly nothing to be censored or uh sanctioned any more than say . . . tuberculosis. . . ."[39] However, since it is a contagious disorder, it must be treated compulsorily, if necessary. " 'Treatment of these disorders [says Doctor Benway] is, at the present time, hurmph symptomatic.' The doctor suddenly threw himself back in his chair and burst into peals of metallic laughter. . . . 'Don't look so frightened young man. Just a professional joke. To say treatment is symptomatic means there is none . . .' "[40] After subjecting Pederson to a series of humiliating "tests," the doctor finally says, "And so Carl will you please oblige to tell me how many times and under what circumstances you have uh indulged in homosexual acts???"[41] As the scene ends, Pederson is going mad: "The doctor's voice was barely audible. The whole room was exploding out into space."[42]

It is clear that psychiatrists have a vested interest in diagnosing as mentally ill as many people as possible, just as inquisitors had in branding them as heretics. The "conscientious" psychiatrist authenticates himself as a competent medical man by holding that sexual deviants (and all kinds of other people, perhaps all of mankind, as Karl Menninger would have it) are mentally ill, just as the "conscientious" inquisitor authenticated himself as a faithful Christian by holding that homosexuals (and all kinds of other people) were heretics. We must realize that in situations of this kind we are confronted, not with scientific problems to be solved, but with social roles to be confirmed.* Inquisitor and witch, psychiatrist and mental patient, create each other and authenticate each other's

---

* One prominent psychiatric expert on homosexuality classifies bachelorhood itself as a form of mental illness. "Failure to marry in either sex is the consequence of the fear of it," says Irving Bieber. "There is increasing recognition that bachelorhood is symptomatic of psychopathology . . ." (*Time*, Sept. 15, 1967, p. 27.) While failure to marry may, of course, be due to fear of the other sex or of marriage as a social institution, the urge to marry may be due to fear of loneliness or of homosexuality. To Bieber, bachelorhood signifies psychopathology. To me, his widely shared view signifies the intense dread of a sexual role frowned upon by society. In contemporary America, the urge for social acceptance as normally heterosexual is as strong as was the urge, in Renaissance Spain, for acceptance as faithfully Catholic. Playing the former role requires, in Bieber's judgment, that one classify bachelorhood and homosexuality as diseases, just as playing the latter role required, in the judgment of earlier experts, that one classify Judaism and Mohammedanism as heresies.

roles. For an inquisitor to have maintained that witches were not heretics and that their souls required no special effort at salvation would have amounted to asserting that there was no need for witchhunters. Similarly, for a psychopathologist to maintain that homosexuals are not patients and that neither their bodies nor their minds require special efforts at cure would amount to asserting that there is no need for coercive psychiatrists.

It is necessary to keep in mind here that most people diagnosed as physically ill *feel* sick and *consider themselves* sick; whereas most people diagnosed as mentally ill *do not feel* sick and *do not consider themselves* sick. Consider again the homosexual. As a rule, he neither feels ill, nor considers himself ill. Hence, he usually does not seek the help of a physician or psychiatrist. All this, as we have seen, parallels the situation of the witch. As a rule, she, too, neither felt sinful, nor considered herself a witch. Hence, she did not seek the help of the inquisitor. If, then, a psychiatrist is to have a patient of this kind, or a priest such a parishioner, each must have the power to impose his "care" on an unwilling subject. The State gives this power to the psychiatrist, just as the Church gave it to the inquisitor.

But these are not the only possible, or indeed actually existing, relationships between psychiatrists and patients, or priests and parishioners. Some of their relationships are, and were, wholly voluntary and mutually consensual. The discussion about the disease concept of homosexuality (and mental illness generally) narrows down to two questions, and our answers to them. First, should psychiatrists have the right to consider homosexuality a disease (however defined)? I say: Of course they should. If that concept helps them, they will be wealthier; if it helps their patients, the patients will be happier. Second, should psychiatrists have the power, through alliance with the State, to impose their definition of homosexuality as a disease on unwilling clients? I say: Of course they should not. I have presented my reasons for this opinion elsewhere.* [43]

* I do not claim originality for my position on homosexuality. Nor is it held by me alone. Robert Lindner, a well-known nonmedical psychoanalyst writes: ". . . when the veneer of our contemporary system of defenses against the age-old conflict over sex is stripped away, there is to be discovered the same hostility for the invert and his way of life and the same abhorrence of him as a person that have been traditional in Western society. That we now employ

Psychiatrists and others who like, and plead for the adoption of, the disease concept of homosexuality (and of other types of human behavior) often seem to be talking about the first question—that is, what kind of disease the alleged "patient" has. But, as a rule, consciously or unwittingly, they are concerned with the second question—that is, how to control or "correct" (to use Marmor's term) the patient's alleged "sickness." The president of the Mattachine Society, the nation's largest organization of homosexuals, rightly warns that "when doctors rush into print with wild claims of 'cures' for homosexuality they are not serving the homosexual. Indeed, they are doing just the opposite; they are increasing social pressure on him. . . . A 'cure' would be a sort of 'final solution' to the homosexual problem."[44]

Our position on the disease concept of homosexuality and its social control through medicine could be vastly clarified were we to apply to it our experience with the heresy concept of homosexuality and its social control through religion. Indeed, the parallels between these two sets of theoretical concepts and social sanctions need to be extended only to include one additional consideration—the legitimacy or illegitimacy of combining religious and medical *ideas* and *practices* with political *power*.

If it is true that God rewards faithful Christians with eternal bliss in a life hereafter, is this not inducement enough to insure true belief? Why should the State use its police power to impose religious faith on nonbelievers, when, if left alone, such heretics are sure to suffer eternal damnation? In the past, the zealous Christian countered this challenge by affirming his boundless love for his "misguided" brother whom it was his duty to "save" from his horrible fate. Since the heathen could usually not be saved by persuasion alone, the use of force—justified by the lofty theological goal—was in order.

Witnessing the tragic consequences of this logic translated into everyday life, the Founders of the American Republic reasserted

---

such terms as 'sick' or 'maladjusted' to the homosexual appears to me to make little difference so far as basic attitudes and feelings are concerned. As a matter of fact, I suggest that precisely these designations reveal the ugly truth of our actual animus toward homosexuals and the sham of modern social-sexual pretensions; for in the current lexicon such words reflect the nonconformism of their referents—and nonconformism is the major, perhaps the only, sin of our time." (Robert Lindner, *Must You Conform?*, pp. 32–33.)

the classic distinction between truth and power, and sought to embody this distinction in appropriate political institutions. The Founding Fathers thus reasoned that if the Christian religions were "true" (as many of them believed they were), then their value (or the value of other religions) ought to become manifest to rational men (and they treated men generally as rational). Entertaining the possibility of religious falsehood, they refused to endorse any particular faith as the only true one. In short, they held that should there be error in religion, men should be left unhampered to discover it for themselves and to act freely on their discoveries. The upshot was the uniquely American concept of religious freedom and pluralism, based on a separation of Church and State. This concept, which depends wholly on the blocking of the official guardians of religious dogma from access to the police power of the State, is embodied in the First Amendment to the Constitution, which states that "Congress shall make no law respecting an establishment of religion, or prohibiting the free exercise thereof . . ."

Inasmuch as the ideology that now threatens individual liberties is not religious but medical, the individual needs protection not from priests but from physicians. Logic thus dictates—however much expediency and "common sense" make this seem absurd— that the traditional constitutional protections from oppression by a State-recognized and supported Church be extended to protections from oppression by a State-recognized and supported Medicine. The justification now for a separation of Medicine and State is similar to that which obtained formerly for a separation of Church and State.

As the Christian concept of sin carries with it its own deterrent of suffering in hell, so the scientific concept of disease carries with it its own deterrent of suffering on earth. Moreover, if it is true that nature rewards faithful believers in medicine (and especially those who seek prompt and properly authorized medical care for their illnesses) with a long and healthy life, is this not inducement enough to insure true belief? Why should the State use its police power to impose medical dogma on nonbelievers, when, if left alone, such heretics are sure to suffer the ravages of bodily and mental deterioration? Today, the zealous psychiatrist counters this challenge by affirming his limitless medical obligation to his "sick" brother whom it is his duty to "treat" for his dread disease. Since the madman cannot usually be cured by persuasion alone, the use of force—justified by the lofty therapeutic goal—is in order.

Witnessing the tragic consequences of this logic translated into everyday life, we ought to emulate the wisdom and the courage of our forebears and trust men to know what is in their own best medical interests. If we truly value medical healing and refuse to confuse it with therapeutic oppression—as they truly valued religious faith and refused to confuse it with theological oppression—then we ought to let each man seek his own medical salvation and erect an invisible but impenetrable wall separating Medicine and the State.*

* A new Constitutional Amendment, extending the guarantees of the First Amendment to medicine, would have to state that "Congress shall make no law respecting an establishment of medicine, or prohibiting the free exercise thereof . . ." At this time in our history, anything even remotely resembling such a declaration would seem to be quite impossible, for Organized Medicine is now as much a part of the American government as Organized Religion had been of the government of fifteenth-century Spain. Still, a small beginning in this direction might perhaps be made.

11

THE NEW PRODUCT—
MASTURBATORY INSANITY

All certain tyrants over souls wish for the men
they teach is that they should have unsound minds.

—Voltaire[1]

Nature, Spinoza said, abhors a vacuum. This adage is one of those
poetic projections that tells us more about the speaker than about
the subject. While Nature neither loves nor abhors a vacuum, men
assuredly abhor phenomena without explanations, problems without solutions. This is why magic and religion are the true ancestors
of rationalism and science. It is also why, under the name of rationalism and science, many explanations of problems have been pro-
pounded and widely believed that are no less erroneous, and often
more harmful, than those held in prescientific times.[2]

With the decline of the power of religious beliefs and institutions
toward the end of the seventeenth century, and the corresponding
rise in the power of secular thought and of the rulers of nation-
states, the explanatory force and usefulness of the concept of
witchcraft rapidly diminished. The Devil and his disciples no longer
sufficed as the cause of otherwise inexplicable misfortunes. A new
explanation of comparable scope was needed. Where could it be
found? In one source only: the authorities who were succeeding the
priests and whose explanatory fables, called science, were displacing
those of religion. Among the new scientists, the medical men, being
the experts on the welfare of man's most indispensable possession,

his body, were in an especially favorable position to advance a fresh explanation for many of the things previously ascribed to witchcraft. Moreover, if the new theory is but a revised edition of the old one, so much the better; people can feel that they have a fresh truth, without having to make any serious change in their mental or worldly habits.

The concept of insanity was admirably suited to replace the concept of witchcraft. But, just as witchcraft had to have a cause, and was given one in the pact with the Devil, so madness also had to have a cause. The question thus arose: What caused madness, and how could madness be prevented and cured? Now, for the kind of theory-building we are here considering—that is, one which is wholly strategic and nonempirical—it is important that the "causative agent" be omnipresent: This allows the theorist—who is actually a covert enforcer of social rules and values—to apply his explanation to any problem he chooses, and to make it fit; and it also allows him not to apply his explanations when he, or his powerful agents, so choose. Since witchcraft was a consequence of a pact with Satan, and since the Devil was omnipresent, acts which one wanted to repudiate or punish could always be attributed to witchcraft. This explanation had to be replaced by one equally universal in its potential application, but more worldly in its imagery. If necessity is indeed the mother of invention, this time she gave birth to a full-fledged genius: She proposed that madness is due to another heinous act—masturbation. So, I submit, was the myth of masturbatory madness born. The "illness" known from the eighteenth century on as "masturbatory insanity" thus constitutes the new product manufactured by the new breed of manufacturers of degraded humanity, the physicians, and particularly, the alienists (or psychiatrists).

Although a large number of sexual practices are mentioned in the Bible, masturbation is not among them.* Nevertheless, the ob-

---

* Although onanism is a synonym for masturbation, Onan's crime was not masturbation, a practice to which there is no reference in the Bible. The Biblical story is this:

Er, Onan's older brother, was wicked and God slew him. "Then Judah [their father] said to Onan, 'Go to your brother's wife, and perform the duty of a brother-in-law to her, and raise up offspring for your brother.' But Onan knew that the offspring would not be his; so when he went in to his brother's wife he spilled the semen on the ground, lest he should give offspring to his brother.

jections to masturbation, like those to other types of nonprocreative sexual acts, originate from Judeo-Christian religious sources. "In Orthodox Jewish codes," Kinsey notes, "masturbation constitutes a major sin and, at times in Jewish history, a sin which was penalized with death."[3] Indeed, Kinsey claims that "few other peoples have condemned masturbation as severely as the Jews have. The Talmudic references and discussions make masturbation a greater sin than nonmarital intercourse. There were excuses for premarital intercourse and for extramarital intercourse with certain persons under the Jewish code, but no extenuation for masturbation. The logic of this proscription depended, of course, upon the reproductive motive in the sexual philosophy of the Jews. This made any act which offered no possibility of a resulting conception unnatural, a perversion, and a sin."[4]

This view was adopted, virtually unaltered, first by the Church, and then by Medicine. The result is, that, as Kinsey puts it, "the proscriptions of the Talmud are nearly identical with those of our present-day legal codes concerning sexual behavior."[5]

The word "masturbation" does not appear in English usage before the middle of the eighteenth century; the first citation of it in the *Oxford English Dictionary* is dated 1766.[6] The etymology of the term is significant: it is a corruption of the Latin word *manustupration* or manual stupration, meaning to defile by hand. The use of the word "onanism" as a synonym for masturbation was introduced in 1710, by the anonymous author of the important text *Onania*, to be discussed presently; this term was generally preferred in medical writings during the eighteenth and nineteenth centuries, the word "masturbation" displacing it only in the present century.

The credit for inventing masturbation as a grave medical hazard belongs to an anonymous clergyman who became a physician and, in about 1710, published a treatise entitled *Onania, or the Heinous Sin of Self-Pollution*. In his excellent study of "masturbatory insanity," Hare suggests that the author was "certainly . . . not a

---

And what he did was displeasing in the sight of the Lord, and he slew him also." (Genesis, 38: 8–10.)

In other words, Onan's act was not masturbation but *coitus interruptus*, withdrawal of the penis from the vagina before ejaculation. His crime was not "self-abuse" or sexual self-satisfaction, but refusal to comply with the law of the Levirate and beget a son with his brother's widow.

reputable physician. His book is concerned more with the sin than the harm of masturbation."[7] This distinction was, however, not one usually made by physicians in those days, or by psychiatrists even today. In any case, *Onania* must have met a great popular need— perhaps the need to be deceived, this time by medical rather than by religious authorities—for by 1730 it reached its fifteenth edition, and by 1765 its eightieth.

Although the author of *Onania* might have been a quack, he set the stage on which reputable physicians soon played leading roles. In 1758, Tissot, a prominent Lausanne physician, published a book entitled *Onania, or a Treatise upon the Disorders Produced by Masturbation.* With the appearance of this work, the status of masturbation as a major etiological factor in disease was placed on what might be called solid medical foundation: Lofty medical authorities said it was so! Tissot's book is important, not only as one of the works that launched the myth of masturbatory madness, but also as an example, commonplace today in psychiatry, of disguising moral arguments in medical rhetoric. Tissot is not content with warning his reader that sexual excesses of all types, but masturbation in particular, can cause a host of serious disorders, both bodily and mental, among them, "consumption, deterioration of eyesight, disorders of digestion, impotence, . . . and insanity";[8] he also castigates the masturbator as a "criminal," calls the practice a "flagrant crime," and speaks of the victim's deteriorated condition as one "which more justly entitles him to the contempt than the pity of his fellow creatures";[9] and he concludes that the patient's punishment by disease in this world is only a prelude to his punishment by eternal fire in the next.[10]

Tissot's book was translated into English in 1766. Soon thereafter, the idea of masturbational insanity was transformed from hypothesis into dogma. From about 1800 until the early decades of this century, physicians threaten patients with the disastrous consequences of masturbation in a manner hardly distinguishable from the way their clergymen-predecessors threatened parishioners with the disastrous consequences of heresy. Moreover, they not only threaten, they also punish—though they call their punishment "treatment." Indeed, it is the punishment for masturbation that defines the role of this new professional, the alienist or psychiatrist. The penalty for masturbation is future insanity, begetting children who will go insane, and last but not least, incarceration in the madhouse for present insanity. Thus from the beginning of his historical career, the institutional psychiatrist plays simultaneously the roles of accuser, judge, and warden. As befits a secular moralist, he replaces the threat of brimstone and hellfire with the threat of insanity and tainted heredity, and the punishment of eternal damnation in a hell in the hereafter with the punishment of life-long imprisonment in a hell on earth, called the madhouse.

In the first half of the nineteenth century, masturbation grad-ually becomes defined as a psychiatric problem; in the second half of the century, first surgeons, and then pediatricians become an-cillary specialists, the former as experts in curing the "disease," the latter as experts in preventing its development. Though it is of dubious pride for American psychiatry, the first definite statement about masturbation as a cause of insanity appearing in a text on mental diseases is in Benjamin Rush's *Medical Inquiries upon Diseases of the Mind.** [11] "Four cases of madness occurred, in my practice, from this cause between the years 1804 and 1807," writes Rush. "It is induced more frequently by this cause in young men than is commonly supposed by parents and physicians. The morbid effects of intemperance in a sexual intercourse with women are feeble, and of a transient nature, compared with the train of phys-ical and moral evils which this solitary vice fixes upon the body and mind."[12] Onanism, Rush goes on to say, "produces seminal weakness, impotence, dysury, tabes dorsalis, pulmonary consumption, dyspepsia, dimness of sight, vertigo, epilepsy, hypochondriasis, loss of memory, manalgia, fatuity, and death."[13]

Without doubt, Rush was a pioneer in the manufacture of mad-ness, and particularly in the manufacture of masturbatory madness. Hare points out that Pinel does not mention masturbation in the first edition of his epoch-setting *Traité médico-philosophique sur l'aliénation mentale,* published in 1801; and although he dis-cusses the subject in the second edition, published in 1809, he does

---

* Johann Frank, the acknowledged founder of public health, claimed masturba-tion for his specialty more than thirty years before Rush did for his. Onanism had become so widespread in schools, Frank declared in 1780, that the authori-ties "cannot take too much care to stamp out this plague." (Quoted in E. H. Hare, Masturbatory insanity: The history of an idea, *J. Ment. Sci.,* 108: 1–25 [Jan.], 1962, p. 23.)

not say that masturbation causes insanity. By 1813, however, Pinel is becoming more enlightened: he declares that masturbation causes nymphomania.[14]

In French psychiatry, which played so crucial a part in the history of this discipline, it was Esquirol who embraced the masturbatory hypothesis and placed upon it the stamp of his authority. We should recall here that Esquirol was also responsible for popularizing the view that witches were mentally sick.[15] As to the pathogenic effects of masturbation, Esquirol claimed no originality for having discovered them. On the contrary, in 1816 he expresses himself in such a way as to imply that no reputable medical authority can doubt the harmfulness of the practice: "Masturbation is recognized in all countries as a common cause of insanity." In 1822, he writes: "Onanism is a grave symptom in mania; unless it stops at once, it is an insurmountable obstacle to cure. By lowering the powers of resistance it reduces the patient to a state of stupidity, to phtisis, marasmus, and death."[16] These views are repeated and extended in his classic textbook, *Des maladies mentales,* published in 1838. Masturbation, he writes, "may be a forerunner of mania, of dementia, and even of senile dementia; it leads to melancholy and suicide; its consequences are more serious in men than in women; it is a grave obstacle to cure in those of the insane who frequently resort to it during their illness."[17]

Backed by the authority of men like Rush and Esquirol, the "masturbatory hypothesis," as Hare calls it, soon spread across the face of the "civilized" world. The first reference to masturbation as a cause of insanity appears in England in 1828, and in Germany in the 1830s. Before long, not only are there few critics of the myth of masturbation, but even physicians who believe that its harmfulness is exaggerated are put on the defensive. "I hope I shall not be accused of having written an apologia for self-abuse," writes a German physician in 1838; "my object has simply been to question the correctness of the view that self-abuse is so very often the only or the principal cause of mental disorder."[18] By the mid-nineteenth century, however, there were, Hare notes, "incipient doubts and general softening of views [on masturbation as a cause of insanity] . . . among Continental alienists . . . [but these] were not yet paralleled in the English-speaking world."[19] England and the

United States had, indeed, the dubious honor of leading the crusade against masturbatory insanity.*

Rush's pioneering work in this regard was followed by that of his equally revered successor, Isaac Ray. Ray considered the "insanity of masturbation" a form of "moral insanity," its particular features being "a tendency to dementia, loss of self-respect, a mischievous and dangerous disposition, and an irritable, depressed state of mind."[20]

Illustrative of mid-nineteenth-century American medical opinion on masturbation is the position taken by an editorial in the *New Orleans Medical and Surgical Journal* (1854–1855). The editor begins by pointing out that morality among American women is much higher than among women in other countries, an assertion supported by noting that most of the prostitutes in New Orleans are foreigners. He then turns to his main subject, masturbation, which he describes as "very injurious to the health of both males and females." Men, the editor observes, occasionally admit to the practice, but not women. "To ask or expect information from adult females concerning this practice is altogether useless and vain," he writes, "although many of their diseases, as leucorrhea, uterine hemorrhage, falling of the womb, cancer, functional disorders of the heart, spinal irritation, palpitation, hysteria, convulsions, haggard features, emaciation, debility, mania—many symptoms called nervous—*un triste tableau,* have been referred to masturbation as the cause. Even if these affections did not originate with masturbation, its practice would certainly aggravate them." The editorial concludes with this warning from a French physician: "In my opinion, neither plague, nor war, nor smallpox, nor a crowd of similar evils, have resulted more disastrously for humanity than the habit of masturbation: it is the destroying element of civilized society."[21]

The same view is expressed in 1876 by the French physician Pouillet, who declares that "Of all the vices and of all the misdeeds which may properly be called crimes against nature, which devour humanity, menace its physical vitality and tend to destroy its in-

---

* Nineteenth-century psychiatrists did not believe that masturbation was the sole, or necessarily even the most important, cause of insanity. They probably emphasized it so strongly in their writings, especially in addressing the laity, because they thought they could control it the best. Syphilis as well as hereditary (or constitutional) predisposition were also popular explanations for the cause of mental disorder.

tellectual and moral faculties, one of the greatest and most wide-spread—no one will deny it—is masturbation."[22]

The dangerousness of masturbation, which medical science claims to have firmly established, was duly appreciated in all Western nations. In his book, aptly titled *The Sneaking Enemy,* published in Stockholm in 1887, E. J. Ekman warns that "self-pollution" is apt to transform a young man into a "destroyed and emaciated ruin, swaying toward either the grave or the madhouse cell," and to make him sink into the "dark and bottomless night of insanity." In addition, masturbation also causes the child's "growth to be interrupted, while the development of the muscular system, the voice, the growth of the beard, courage and energy, all are slowed down, if not completely stunted."[23]

We may wonder how learned men and the public alike could believe such nonsense, flagrantly contradicted by observations easily made among both men and animals. This human tendency to embrace collective error—especially error that threatens harm and commands specific protective action—seems to be an integral part of man's social nature. Thus, when man is faced with important mass-beliefs—like that in witchcraft, the harmfulness of masturbation, or mental illness—he is more interested in preserving popular explanations which tend to consolidate the group than in making accurate observations which tend to divide it. This is why most men most of the time attend only to those of their observations that confirm the accepted theories of their age, and reject those that refute them.*

It is therefore necessary, in every historical period, to pay careful attention to the dominant world view through which men observe their physical surroundings, their society, and themselves. The nineteenth century was an age of physical preconceptions. It was an age, when, as Wayland Young puts it,

---

* This is no less dramatically true for the falsity of the concept of mental illness than it is for that of masturbatory insanity. The National Association for Mental Health asserts, and American presidents endorse and repeat, that "Mental illness is like any other illness." The facts are that American citizens may be hospitalized and treated against their will for mental illness, but not for any other; may plead mental illness as an excuse to crime, but not any other; and may obtain a divorce from their spouses disabled by mental illness, but not by any other. Yet, these facts have not weakened—indeed, perhaps they have strengthened—the psychiatric and popular view that "mental disorders" are medical diseases requiring care by physicians in hospitals.

the concepts of energy . . . clothed the Augustinian asceticism, the theological doubts and inhibitions of an earlier time, in a physical form. It was then that the possibility of regarding man as a machine became a normal part of people's minds, and in certain respects the new mechanical blueprint of man fitted very neatly over the former theological one. . . . It is easy to see the analogy. The more energy you draw from a machine, the less there is left; you must not overload it. The more money you draw from a bank or a firm, the less there is left: it must not overspend. Therefore the more a man fucks, the weaker he gets.[24]

The religious idea that sexual pleasure is sinful was thus easily transformed into the medical idea that losing sperm is harmful. That is to say, ". . . loss of semen whether in intercourse or not, . . . is loss of vigor, health, and ultimately sanity."[25] The masturbatory hypothesis is simply the traditional Christian ethic translated into the language of modern medicine.

The American psychiatric view on masturbation typical of the 1880s is exemplified by Spitzka's textbook on *Insanity,* a work its author characterized as "the first systematic treatise on insanity published on this side of the Atlantic since the days of the immortal Rush."[26]

The functional abuse of the male sexual apparatus [Spitzka declares] is of more general importance to the alienist than its organic affections. Excessive venery and masturbation have from time immemorial been supposed to be the direct causes of insanity. Unquestionably they exert a deleterious influence on the nervous system, and may provoke insanity partly through their direct influence on the nervous centres, partly through their weakening effect on the general nutrition. . . . Melancholia, stuporous insanity, katatonia, and insanity of pubescence are the forms most frequently found in masturbators, and the essential characters are always recognizable under these circumstances. The ordinary characteristics of the masturbator are, however, found in addition. Thus such lunatics are usually retired, sly, suspicious, hypochondriacal, indolent, mean, and cowardly. They are capital simulators, and develop an art in concealing and in practicing their vice which is in remarkable contrast with their stupidity, apathy, and feeble-mindedness in other respects. The prognosis of the psychoses associated with masturbation in males is bad. A variety of primary deterioration marked by moral perversion is observed in young victims of the habit, which yields to treatment if the habit is abolished.* [27]

But the British were not to be outdone. It was the Scottish physician David Skae who apparently first claimed that there was a *specific* type of insanity due to masturbation. Here was scientific advance: masturbation could not cause *any* kind of mental illness, but only *one particular type*! That Skae had not a shred of evidence for this view did not matter; it was enough that the idea appeared scientifically more sophisticated than those previously advanced.

Henry Maudsley, a foremost British psychiatrist often considered the father of English psychiatry, lent important support to the masturbation myth. In 1867 he writes: "The habit of self-abuse notably gives rise to a particular and disagreeable form in insanity, characterized by intense self-feeling and conceit, extreme perversion of feeling and corresponding derangement of thought, in earlier stages, and later by failure of intelligence, nocturnal hallucinations, and suicidal and homicidal propensities."[28] A year later he devotes an article solely to "that kind of insanity which is brought on by self-abuse"; in it he writes:

A later and still worse stage at which these degenerate beings arrive is one of moody and morose self-absorption, and of extreme loss of mental powers. They are sullen, silent, and indisposed to converse at all. . . . It is needless to say that they have lost all healthy human feeling and every natural desire. . . . [T]hough they often last for a longer period than might be thought possible, they finally

---

* In a remarkable footnote, Spitzka relates how his efforts to manufacture madness in a young man were foiled by the victim's discovery of the plans to commit him. A young man "of bad hereditary antecedents, who for days had not quitted his bed, and who exhibited feeble-mindedness and moral perversion, as a result of this habit [writes Spitzka], was about to be sent to an institution by the writer. The following day, he, suspicious as these subjects are, made a search and found the commitment papers. After perusing them, he immediately turned over a new leaf, went into his father's store, did the best he could, abandoned his bad habits, and to this day, that is, during a period of nearly two years, has filled his position in life with average ability, being remarkable only on account of his taciturnity." (Spitzka, p. 379.)

In other words, when this young man realized that the physician was not his ally, but his adversary, he became promptly cured of his "mental illness." This episode illustrates one of the ways in which psychiatrists create mental illness, and in which individuals who accept the role of mental patient help confirm the psychiatrist in his role as psychodiagnostician and therapist.

totter on to death through complete prostration of the entire system, if they are not carried off by some intercurrent disease. Such, then, is the natural history of the physical and mental degeneracy produced in men by self-abuse. It is a miserable picture of human degradation, but it is not overcharged. . . . I have nothing to add concerning treatment; once the habit is formed, and the mind has positively suffered from it, the victim is less able to control what is more difficult to control, and there would be almost as much hope of the Ethiopian changing his skin, or the leopard its spots, as of his abandoning the vice. I have no faith in the employment of physical means to check what has become a serious mental disease; the sooner he sinks to his degraded rest the better for himself, and the better for the world which is well rid of him. It is a poor and sad conclusion to come to, but it is an unavoidable one.[29]

Hare, an English psychiatrist, seems embarrassed to remind his readers that the great Maudsley, whose name is the most venerated one in English psychiatry, should have held such views. "This article [on masturbation]," Hare remarks, "is not one on which admirers of Maudsley could wish to dwell, but it may profitably be read as a warning example of that besetting sin of psychiatrists—a tendency to confuse the rules of mental health with those of morality."[30] But, as I have tried to show, and as Maudsley's example makes abundantly clear, it is Hare who is confused, not Maudsley: since psychiatry deals with personal and social conduct, and since such conduct cannot be described, much less evaluated, without anchoring it in a matrix of values, there is nothing to confuse between rules of mental health and rules of morality. The two are one and the same; they are two different sets of terms, two different languages, for describing and influencing human relations and personal conduct.[31]

Although Maudsley condemned masturbation and excoriated masturbators, at least he did not advocate destructive medical interventions defined as "treatments" for this "illness." This is more than can be said for his successors. Indeed, in the second half of the nineteenth century, when belief in the myth of masturbatory madness was diminishing, the popularity of surgical treatments for the condition was increasing. This is clearly related to the development of surgical skills and of aseptic operating techniques, which allowed safe surgical mutilations of patients—not to any newly discovered medical indications for the treatment of masturbation. No discussion of masturbatory insanity would be complete without some mention of the "treatments" employed for this "illness" after about 1850.

To treat masturbation in girls and women, Dr. Isaac Baker Brown, a prominent London surgeon who later became the president of the Medical Society of London, introduced, around 1858, the operation of clitoridectomy. To cure this "disease," he removed the organ which it "affects"—because he believed, or claimed that he believed, that masturbation caused hysteria, epilepsy, and convulsive diseases.[32] A. J. Block, a visiting surgeon at the Charity Hospital in New Orleans, called female masturbation a form of "moral leprosy" and advocated clitoridectomy for it as late as 1894.[33] Apparently, neither he nor his colleagues thought there was anything amiss, either logically or morally, in treating a moral condition by surgical means. Male masturbators fared not much better. For example, J. L. Milton, an English physician, recommended that they wear locked chastity belts by day, and spiked or toothed rings by night, the latter to awaken them in case of nocturnal erection.* Milton's book on *The Pathology and Treatment of Spermatorrhea* (1887) went through twelve editions—which gives a further idea of the popularity and influence of such works as these.†[34]

In 1891, James Hutchinson, president of the Royal College of Surgeons, published a paper *On Circumcision as Preventive of Masturbation*; in it, he not only advocated circumcision for the treatment and prevention of this "shameful habit," but proposed that ". . . if public opinion permitted their adoption, . . . measures more radical than circumcision would . . . be a true kindness to many patients of both sexes."[35] Had Hutchinson lived a few years later, he, instead of Egas Moniz, might have received the Nobel Prize for the treatment of insanity.‡

---

* As late as 1897, the U. S. Government granted a patent—number 587,994—to one Michael McCormick of San Francisco, for a "male chastity belt" for fathers to put on their adolescent sons to prevent masturbation. (*Playboy*, Dec., 1967, p. 79.)

† Like Rush and other messianic physicians, Milton was also opposed to smoking; in 1857 he published a book entitled *Death in the Pipe*. (Comfort, *The Anxiety Makers*, p. 97.)

‡ As surgical skills and techniques became perfected, more difficult and more destructive operations were devised and employed to cure new iatrogenic diseases. The progression from clitoridectomy to colectomy and thence to lobotomy—as methods of "treatment" not only for insanity but also for a host of other iatrogenic diseases—illustrates this principle. We may thus distinguish between

In 1895, T. Spratling, also an English surgeon, recommended for the treatment of masturbation among "adult insane males, . . . the complete section of the dorsal nerves of the penis"; for females, "nothing short of ovariotomy will be found to deserve even the term palliative."[36]

In a critical review of the myth of masturbation, Alex Comfort notes the popularity of drastic surgical treatments of masturbation in the period between approximately 1850 and 1900, and has this to say about them:

Over this period there was a truly remarkable upsurge of what can only be termed comic-book sadism. The advocacy of these bizarre therapies was not confined to eccentrics. By about 1880 the individual who might wish for unconscious reasons to tie, chain, or infibulate sexually active children or mental patients—the two most readily available captive audiences—to adorn them with grotesque appliances, encase them in plaster of paris, leather or rubber, to frighten or even castrate them, to cauterize or denervate their genitalia, could find humane and respectable medical authority for doing so in good conscience. Masturbational insanity was now real enough—it was affecting the medical profession.[37]

Comfort's point is well taken. Yet, to categorize masturbational insanity as a madness affecting the doctors is like calling Hitler or Stalin mentally sick. Physicians, like political leaders, possess a

---

two basic principles of identifying diseases and their causes. One, the empirical, is based on observation and sometimes on experimentation; for example, the identification of syphilis and gonorrhea as venereal diseases. The other, the strategic, is based on the availability of plausible means for medical intervention; for example, moral suasion and intestinal purgation, when these were the main possibilities for therapy.

A functional—or strategic—theory of iatrogenic diseases and noxious treatments may thus be constructed. According to it, physicians discover diseases and attribute them to causes depending on how they would like to *intervene* in the patient's life. Thus, when moral authority was a powerful therapeutic weapon, the physician attributed insanity to masturbation and used suggestion for its treatment; when surgical skills were embryonic, he attributed the disease to the same cause, but treated it with circumcision and clitoridectomy. As surgical skills improved, the physician attributed insanity to the (anatomically intact) colon and treated it with colectomy; when neurosurgical techniques were perfected, he attributed the disease to malfunctioning frontal lobes and treated it with lobotomy. The current fashion of treating mental illness with psychopharmacological agents may be interpreted similarly.

measure of real social power. Power is power. It does not really matter—especially to the victim—who wields it. Pope or prince, politician or physician, each can oppress, persecute, and kill those subject to his power. Politicians wage war against enemies, and in the process sacrifice their own people. Physicians wage war against diseases, and in the process often degrade, injure, and even kill persons who voluntarily surrender to them as patients or who, as in pediatrics and Institutional Psychiatry, are surrendered to them by their families and the State. There is no significant difference between the former persecution of masturbators and the present persecution of homosexuals; nor is clitoridectomy as a treatment for masturbational insanity more "bizarre," "sadistic," or "insane"— the adjectives are Comfort's—than is lobotomy for schizophrenia. I shall have more to say about this later.

Toward the end of the nineteenth century there begins a slow decline in the belief that masturbation causes psychosis. But the myth of masturbation dies hard. Psychiatrists now begin to claim that although masturbation does not cause insanity, it causes milder forms of mental illness, that is, neurosis, and also homosexuality. Maudsley, for example, abandons, by 1895, his earlier views on masturbatory insanity, only to attribute a fresh class of mental diseases to this practice; these, he claims "preserve certain tolerably distinctive features," among them being obsessional thoughts, compulsions, ruminations, and phobias.[38] Kraepelin, the great German psychiatrist whose *Textbook* was perhaps the most influential of all modern psychiatric works, lists masturbation, in the sixth edition of his work published in 1899, under the main heading of "Mental conditions of constitutional origin," and under the subheading of "Sexual abnormalities," where it is followed by such other mental diseases as exhibitionism, fetishism, masochism, sadism, and homosexuality.[39]

To fully appreciate the role played by the medical profession in the manufacture of masturbatory insanity, I shall cite the advice given by an American woman physician in 1903 to mothers regarding the "sex education" of their male children. "Go, teach your boy," exhorts Mary Melendy, "that which you may never be ashamed to do, about these organs that make him specially a boy. Teach him they are called sexual organs, that they are not impure, but of

special importance, and made by God for a definite purpose. . . .
Impress upon him that if these organs are abused, or if they are put
to any use besides that for which God made them—and He did
not intend they should be used at all until man is fully grown—
they will bring disease and ruin upon those who abuse and disobey
those laws which God has made to govern them."* [40]

The psychoanalytic movement lent strong support to the survival,
albeit in a muted form, of the masturbatory hypothesis. Indeed,
Freud gave the hypothesis a fresh lease on life just as it was becoming generally accepted that masturbation does not cause *psychosis*, by claiming that it causes *neurosis*! Preoccupied as they were
with the sexual "etiology" of mental illnesses, the early psychoanalysts were staunch defenders of the idea that masturbation was a
harmful activity.

There are countless passing references to, and several extended
discussions of, masturbation in Freud's writing. A few of his comments must suffice to indicate his position. In 1894, analyzing the
symptoms of "a girl [who] suffered from obsessions of self-re-
proaches," he offers the following explanation: "Close questioning
then revealed the source from which her sense of guilt arose. Stimulated by chance voluptuous sensation, she had allowed herself to be
led astray by a woman friend into masturbating, and had practiced
it for years, fully conscious of her wrong-doing and to the accom-
paniment of the most violent, but, as usual, ineffective self-re-
proaches. An excessive *indulgence* after going to a ball had
produced the intensification that led to the psychosis. After a few

* Looking at such advice as Melendy's through the comfortable distance of
more than a half century, we are likely to assume that this was a medical mistake, made in good faith and without malicious intent. But how can we be sure
that it was? Might it not, instead, have been a falsehood asserted at least half-
knowingly in the interest of bringing about the required behavior of mothers
and children? The latter supposition is strengthened, in Melendy's case, by her
erroneous advice not only about masturbation but also about birth control.

"It is a law of nature," she writes, "that conception must take place at about the
time of menstrual flow. . . . It may be said with *certainty*, however, that from
ten days after the cessation of the menstrual flow until three days preceding
its return, there is very little chance of conception, while the converse is equally
true." (Italics added.) (Mary R. Melendy, *Perfect Womanhood*, pp. 263–265.)

Melendy here declares that the woman's period of greatest fertility is the
"safe period," and vice versa. Since she acknowledges being opposed to birth
control, one wonders if her "facts" here, as with masturbation, are not strategic
falsehoods.

months of treatment, and the strictest *surveillance,* the girl recovered."* [41] (Italics added.)

In 1897, in a letter to Fliess, Freud writes: ". . . It has dawned on me that masturbation is the one major habit, the 'primal addiction,' and that it is only as a substitute and replacement for it that the other addictions—for alcohol, morphine, tobacco, etc.—come into existence."[42] Calling masturbation an "addiction" is really no different than calling it a sinful or bad habit: the former is to condemn it in the language of medicine, the latter in that of morals.

In *The Psychopathology of Everyday Life* (1901), Freud relates being asked by a mother to come to her house "to examine a young man," her son. Freud notices a stain on the boy's trousers and inquires about it. The boy replies that he had spilled raw egg-white on it. Of course, Freud was not fooled. ". . . when his mother had left us alone," he comments, "I thanked him for making my diagnosis so very much easier, and without more ado took as the basis of our discussion his confession that he was suffering from the troubles arising from masturbation."[43] I would only remark here that, from the little that Freud relates about this case, one would have to conclude that he was wrong: The young man did not send for Freud and there is no reason to believe that *he* was suffering from anything at all; the person who was suffering was the *mother,* presumably from the son's maturing sexuality. It is interesting that Freud here accepts the mother's definition of the situation, and treats the son as a patient "suffering from the troubles arising from masturbation."†

Freud's most detailed comments on masturbation are contained in his contribution to a discussion on this subject held in the

---

* Here Freud is hardly the libertine his contemporary critics believed him to have been. Freud remained opposed to masturbation throughout his life. The views of other psychoanalysts, as we shall see, remain ambivalent and hesitant on this subject to this day.

† Freud soon learned not to make this mistake. Psychiatry has never learned this lesson, and many psychoanalysts are fast forgetting it. The point I am making here is that when a person does not complain to a psychiatrist and indeed wants to be let alone, it is illogical and unwise to claim that he is "suffering" from an illness or problems, and that he wants "help." In such cases, those who suffer are the people whom such an "involuntary patient" disturbs. Thus, addicts, homosexuals, psychopaths, juvenile delinquents, and so forth, do not suffer from anything; they make others suffer. This statement does not mean, of course, that I approve of their behavior; or that I disapprove. That is another matter.

Vienna Psychoanalytic Society from November 22, 1911, to April 24, 1912. In these remarks he shows himself deeply committed to the view that masturbation is harmful, if not somatically then certainly psychically, and that it causes mental illness. "We are all agreed," Freud writes in his "Concluding Remarks" to this discussion, "(a) on the importance of the phantasies which accompany or represent the act of masturbation, (b) on the importance of the sense of guilt, whatever its source may be, which is attached to masturbation, and (c) on the impossibility of assigning a qualitative determinant for the injurious effects of masturbation. (On this last point agreement is not unanimous)."[44] Freud does not here, or anywhere else, mention, much less criticize, either the religious or the medical factor in masturbation—that is, the feeling of anxiety and guilt attached to it because the priests say it is wicked and the doctors say it drives you crazy. Instead, Freud builds much of his theory of "castration fear" on the anxieties he finds in his patients, which he prefers to attribute to their own phantasies rather than to the religious and medical atmosphere in which they are brought up.

Next, Freud turns to certain, "unresolved differences of opinion" in the group, and speaks—the choice of words is significant—of a "denial [sic] of the injurious effects of masturbation."[45] He then briefly summarizes his own view on masturbation. Perhaps most interesting is what he does not say: "I have," he writes, ". . . divided masturbation according to the subject's age into (1) masturbation in infants . . . (2) masturbation in children . . . and (3) masturbation in puberty . . ."[46] Masturbation in adults is not listed. It is clear, however, that Freud regards adult masturbation as a pathologic and pathogenic practice. He writes: "On the question of the relation of masturbation and emissions to the causation of so-called 'neurasthenia,' I find myself, like many of you, in opposition to Stekel . . . I maintain, as against him, my former views [that masturbation is harmful]."[47]

Freud thus comes down squarely on the side of the true believers in the myth of masturbatory mental illness. "I must confess that here again I am unable to share Stekel's point of view. . . . As he sees it, the injuriousness of masturbation amounts to no more than a senseless prejudice which, purely as a result of personal limitations, we are unwilling to cast off with sufficient thoroughness. I believe, however, that . . . to take up such a position contradicts our fundamental views on the aetiology of the neuroses. Masturbation corresponds essentially to infantile sexual activity and to its subsequent retention at a more mature age."[48] Here we have it. The clergymen said masturbation was wicked and God punished you for it in Hell; the pre-Freudian psychiatrists said it drove you mad and were ready to treat you for it with mutilating operations; and Freud says it is infantile, causes "actual neuroses" such as neurasthenia, anxiety neurosis, and hypochondriasis, and is prepared to shame you out of it. This progression reminds one of changes in the severity of punishments prescribed for certain offenses in Anglo-American criminal law. Pickpockets, for example, used to have their hands cut off; then they were sentenced to long terms at hard labor; now they draw short sentences of imprisonment. The analogy is, I think, a close one. The gradual lessening of the punishment for picking pockets does not mean that the act has become acceptable. It is still regarded as criminal. Only our ideas about how severe a *punishment* it justifies have changed. So too with masturbation. The gradual lessening of sanctions for masturbation—from brimstone and hellfire, through mutilating surgical operations on the penis, to demeaning psychoanalytic diagnoses—indicate that the attitude toward masturbation, both professional and popular, has not changed fundamentally. It was deemed an undesirable activity in the past and it still is; only our ideas about how severe a *treatment* it justifies have changed.

Freud's claim that masturbation is harmful seems curiously insistent. He had, of course, no real evidence for it. Rather, his evidence was his own theory of the pathogenesis of neurosis. Hence, in standing up for the masturbatory hypothesis, Freud was, in effect, defending his own—to be sure well-disguised—reformulation of this theory. However great Freud's accomplishments might be, in this case he was clearly more interested in protecting his theories than his patients. The kind of evidence Freud adduced to support his view is interesting. One proof lies in his "medical experience": On the basis of it, he says, "I cannot rule out a permanent reduction in potency as one among the results of masturbation . . .";[49] another lies in his "judgment": "Yet, however much we may trace things further back, our judgment on the causation of the illness [actual neurosis] will nevertheless rightly remain attached to this activity [masturbation]";[50] and a third lies in an as yet undiscovered "organic injury": "Organic injury may occur by some unknown mechanism."[51] On this flimsy evidence—but with his feet planted firmly on the solid rocks of psychiatric tradition and Victorian morality—Freud concludes that masturbation *is* (not might be) damaging: "We are therefore brought back once more from arguments to clinical observation, and we are warned by it not to strike out the heading 'injurious effects of Masturbation.'"[52] Freud never gave up these ideas.

Psychoanalysts continued to condemn masturbation, albeit in increasingly softer terms. In 1918, for example, Ernest Jones still believes that ". . . true neurasthenia . . . will be found to depend on excessive onanism or involuntary seminal emissions."[53] In 1923, he writes that "It is known that phantasies preceding or accompanying masturbation are predominantly incestuous in origin, hence a feeling of guilt attaches to them . . ."[54]—a view that strangely ignores the effects of medical threats as a source of anxiety and guilt.

We must cut short our review of the psychoanalytic aspects of the myth of masturbation and will conclude by citing the views of Otto Fenichel, whose book, *The Psychoanalytic Theory of Neurosis*, is considered the definitive modern text on psychoanalysis. Fenichel is considerably less opposed to masturbation than Freud had been. But he, too, tries to present moral criteria of what are desirable and undesirable attitudes toward masturbation as if they were scientific psychoanalytic criteria of mentally healthy behavior. "Masturbation," Fenichel writes, ". . . is normal in childhood; and under present cultural conditions is also normal in adolescence, and even in adulthood as a substitute when no sexual object is available. . . . Masturbation is certainly pathological under two circumstances: (a) whenever it is preferred by adult persons to sexual intercourse, and (b) when it is done not occasionally for the purpose of relieving sexual tension but at such frequent intervals that it reveals a disfunction with respect to the capacity for sexual satisfaction."[55]

In the sexual ethic advocated by Fenichel, it is desirable that one allow oneself sexual pleasure. If one does not, it is pathological; not masturbating may therefore also be an abnormality. "If a person whose sexual activites are blocked by external circumstances absolutely refuses to make use of this way out"—a phrasing that makes masturbation a kind of moral equivalent to therapeutic abortion—"analysis always reveals some unconscious fear or guilt feeling as the source of the inhibition."*[56]

Our review of the story of masturbatory insanity is almost complete. All that remains is to fill in its recent history and present status. Gradually, the myth becomes attenuated: the harm attributed to masturbation becomes progressively vaguer; the practice is condemned in increasingly milder terms; occasionally, but very rarely, it is even declared to be completely harmless.

It is astonishing until how very recently masturbation was considered an "illness" requiring "medical treatment" by physicians. In an extensive bibliographical study of this subject, René A. Spitz found that as late as 1926 a German physician, Werner Villinger, in an article published in the prestigious *Zeitschrift für Kinderforschung*, speaks of masturbation as "a snake that has to be throttled."[57] Spitz also notes that, until its 1940 edition, one of the standard American textbooks on pediatrics, Holt's *Diseases of Infancy and Childhood*, condemns the practice as medically harmful. "Between 1897, when the first edition [of Holt's work] appeared," writes Spitz, "and 1940, eleven revised editions were published of this standard work. . . . In the early editions, the treatment recommended is mechanical restraint, corporal punishment in the very young, circumcision in boys even if phimosis does not exist 'because of the moral effect of the operation'; in girls, separation of the preputial hood from the clitoris or complete circumcision, cauterization of the clitoris; blistering the inside of the thighs, the vulva, or the prepuce.

---

* Fenichel's psychoanalytic definition of what makes masturbation "pathological" (that is, "bad") points unmistakably to the true reasons why this practice is condemned, especially for adults. The sinfulness of autoeroticism lies simply in the fact that the masturbating person engages in a sexual act in which he validates, as a desirable partner, only his own body. The Don Juan, the homosexual, the pervert, even the necrophiliac—these and all others who engage in alloerotic sexual practices—validate as necessary and hence valuable some person other than themselves, or at least some body other than their own. But not the masturbator: his self and body are, or act as if they were, the perfect couple, gratifying each other. He is the very antithesis of the contemporary sexual ideal, the considerate lover for whom the partner's orgasm is more important than his own. In short, by validating only himself, the masturbator implicitly invalidates all others. Masturbation thus symbolizes the individual's separateness from, or rejection of, the group. This is why, psychologically, it is the gravest of all "crimes." Hence too, I surmise, its remarkable neglect in *belles lettres*.

This therapy is recommended up to and including the 1936 edition, but the tone becomes slowly more uncertain."[58]

Another standard American pediatric text of the same vintage, Griffith and Mitchell's *Diseases of Infants and Children* (Second Edition, 1938), expresses similar views. Under the general heading of "Functional Nervous Disorders," the authors devote nearly three pages to masturbation. "It is remarkable," they observe, "how little damage seems to result in some instances, even in the case of masturbation in young children carried on to an extreme degree." This does not prevent them, however, from devoting a whole page to treatment, and to recommending, among other measures, the following: "In bad cases, and especially if the act occurs during sleep, some appliance must be employed which will mechanically make friction impossible. A small pillow may be placed between the thighs and a bandage applied around them; or the knees kept separate by a rod terminating at each end in a leather collar fastened around the thigh just above the knees . . . where the hands are employed, it may be necessary to confine these, as by elbow splints or in other ways. . . . Circumcision is . . . sometimes curative in older children through the soreness produced by the operation, and the consequent breaking in upon the habit . . . if necessary, circumcision of the clitoris [must be] performed."[59]

During the years of the Second World War, masturbation no longer causes insanity in patients, but it still causes embarrassment to doctors. For example, *Cecil's Textbook of Medicine* (Fifth Edition, 1942), one of the standard texts used in American medical schools, asserts, with characteristic ambivalence, that masturbation both is and is not a perversion. Listing masturbation under the heading of "perversions," Israel S. Wechsler, professor of clinical neurology at Columbia University, the author of the chapter on nervous diseases, writes: "Masturbation, while not a perversion in itself, may become so if practiced inveterately and as an end in itself."[60] This is illustrative of the last rationalization of the anti-masturbation forces: the practice is normal in moderation, but excess—always undefined—renders it pathological.*

* Kinsey has made the same point. In the contemporary medical and psychiatric literature, he wrote, "It has become customary to admit that earlier teachings greatly exaggerated the possible harms of masturbation; but the conclusion is nevertheless reached that no manly youth will want to accept such a habit. . . . The boy is advised that a limited amount of masturbation may do him no

A sex hygiene manual of the U.S. Public Health Service for 1937 and the *Boy Scout Handbook* for 1945 exhort the youth to avoid "wasting" the vital fluids.[61] The medical regulations of the U.S. Navy Department for 1940 go even further, prescribing that candidates for the U.S. Naval Academy at Annapolis "be rejected by the examining surgeon for . . . evidence of masturbation."[62]

Writing in 1953, René Spitz, a psychoanalyst, remarks: "In psychoanalytic circles one does not always realize how extremely cruel the persecution of the masturbator has been up to our day; nor is it generally known that these sadistic practices found support among authoritative physicians and that they were recommended up to almost a decade ago in official textbooks."[63] Spitz's comment is well taken, but it curiously exempts the psychoanalyst from responsibility for perpetuating the belief in the harmfulness of masturbation. Since analysts make no use of medical and surgical interventions, they hardly deserve special credit for eschewing the destructive methods of their nonpsychoanalytic colleagues for "treating" masturbation. Nor was their psychopathological orientation intellectually clarifying or helpful to patients: As Esquirol and Charcot had ignored the witch-hunters and classified the witches as insane, so Freud and the early analysts ignored the physicians (who persecuted "masturbators" with tortures called treatments), and classified the victims as neurotics (suffering from "castration anxiety"). Indeed, the last remaining opponents of masturbation on psychopathological grounds are the psychoanalysts.

Thus, Karl Menninger, perhaps the most influential contemporary psychoanalyst, sees in masturbation aggression against others and oneself. "Closely related to the exhibitionistic motive in suicide is its connection with masturbation," he writes in 1938. "It has been observed that suicidal attempts sometimes follow the interruption of an individual's habitual autoerotic activities. This interruption may

---

harm, but in excess it is something which needs the attention of a physician. Since the point at which excess begins is never defined, the conscientious boy is left uncertain whether his own rate is going to harm him. . . . Many of the persons who are responsible for the compromised attitudes found in the sex literature cited above are physicians. Even psychiatrists are divided on this question." (Alfred C. Kinsey, Wardell B. Pomeroy, and Clyde E. Martin, *Sexual Behavior in the Human Male*, pp. 514–515.) Kinsey's critical attitude toward medical men because of their anti-sexual opinions couched in medical terms may partly explain the hostile reaction of many psychiatrists to his work.

come in the form of a prohibition from external forces or from the person's own conscience. In either case the mechanisms by which the suicide is precipitated are the same; the masturbation occasions a heavy burden of guilt, because in the unconscious mind it *always* represents an aggression against someone."[64] (Italics added.) This is one of the most remarkable reformulations of the original masturbatory hypothesis: Menninger does not claim that masturbation is physically harmful; he claims, rather, that it is psychologically harmful because it represents an unjustified attack on another person, and therefore provokes guilt in the actor.

Joseph B. Cramer, also a psychoanalyst and a professor of child psychiatry at the Albert Einstein College of Medicine in New York, writing in the authoritative *American Handbook of Psychiatry* (1959), distinguishes between two types of "childhood neurosis"—types A and B. "Type A," he writes, "may be thought of as a pure type. . . . Symptomatically, this type is characterized mainly by fears and phobias. Masturbation, nightmares, and enuresis are other frequent symptoms."[65] Masturbation is here considered a "symptom" of a "mental illness" of children.

Today, then, the myth of masturbatory madness is rarely held in anything resembling its original form. According to authoritative psychiatric thinking, the harmful effects of masturbation are not due to the act itself but to worry over "exaggerated opinions" of its consequences. "By the irony of history," Hare observes, "this view—that masturbation is harmful only if, from ignorance or misinformation, the patient worries about it—is all that now survives of the masturbatory hypothesis. Two centuries of indoctrination have taught the public a lesson which it can forget less quickly than can its teachers; and today the principal concern of medical writers on the subject is to persuade the public that its fears of the consequences of masturbation are groundless."[66]

How are we to interpret the widespread belief in the dreadful harm caused by masturbation and the medical persecution of masturbators which it spawned and justified? To Hare, on whose excellent study I have relied heavily, it was due to a failure of science and logic, an explanation that does not really explain. Comfort dismisses Hare's suggestion as inadequate and offers an explanation of his own. This hypothesis—which compares the persecution of masturbators with that of witches—is one which I not only share with Comfort but which I have extended to cover a much larger area.* At the same time, I disagree with Comfort, who relates both the witch-hunts and the persecution of masturbators to the mental illness of the persecutors. "Seen from the present," concludes Comfort, "the outbreak of masturbational insanity . . . came close[r] to the pattern of witch finding, a *true endemic paranoid reaction* spread by example and propaganda, and quite unarrested by *saner* comment until it had run its course."[67] (Italics added.)

The passion to interpret as madness that with which we disagree seems to have infected the best of contemporary minds. Even Comfort considers it "an endemic paranoid reaction." This interpretation suffers from the same errors as does the interpretation of the Inquisition as an expression of madness. As I have tried to show throughout this volume, it is tempting to dismiss, to explain away, the horrors of oppressor-victim relationships by diagnosing either the former (as Comfort does for masturbation), or the latter (as Zilboorg does for witchcraft), as mentally ill. I reject this as a kind of autotherapy for both the author and his readers. I believe it is the writer's responsibility to tell it the way it is (or was), and not the way it makes him appear safe from the errors and sins he is describing; likewise, the reader has the responsibility to hear it the way it is (or was), and not the way it makes him feel secure from the errors and sins he is reading about.

By failing to make connections between the story of masturbatory insanity and current psychiatric practices, Comfort himself becomes a victim of the mythology of mental illness. "One has the uncomfortable feeling," he writes, "of the multiplicity and uncontrollability of such reactions [as those of physicians toward masturbation here reviewed], and the utter inability of those involved in them to acquire more than a limited insight, and one begins to look for the counterpart of witchcraft mania and masturbation anxiety in our own, in public irrationalities of which all but a few unusually detached observers are unaware today." In our contemporary world, Comfort sees such "irrationalities" in "the Bomb, the

* In other words, I regard the psychiatrist-masturbator relationship as a typical example of the social relations between institutional psychiatrists and (involuntary) patients, the latter category including not only individuals formally defined as patients but also the general public subject to and deceived by the official propaganda of the Mental Health Movement.

space race, . . . [and] the Cold War . . . These too have their maniacs and their *pathologically driven* quacks, but, as with the persecution of witches, homosexuals, Jews, or masturbators, it is in the spread of such thinking to the humane and *apparently balanced* that it becomes most sinister."[68] (Italics added.)

By attributing the "persecution of witches, homosexuals, Jews, and masturbators [to] irrationalities," Comfort misses the crucial moral, political, and social-psychological features of these phenomena. I hold that in each of the foregoing persecutory situations we are confronted with a relationship between oppressor and oppressed; the oppressor invariably resorts to both force and fraud in subduing and exploiting his antagonist; frequently he develops a therapeutic rhetoric, justifying his domination by claims of selflessness and a desire to help the victim; criticism of the oppressive practice is rendered impossible by persecution of the critic as a traitor to the existing social order; finally, the ideology of helpful coercion is institutionalized, stabilizing and perpetuating the persecutory practices over long periods of time.

Thus, while Hare, Comfort, and Spitz emphasize modern psychiatry's enlightenment and rise above the errors of the past, I maintain that the situation in psychiatry today is virtually the same as it was when masturbatory madness was the reigning dogma. To be sure, the rhetoric has changed: the magic words are no longer "masturbation," "bad habit," and "insanity," but rather "mental illness," "not blaming sick patients," and "understanding"; and the therapeutic interventions have changed: the magic treatment is no longer clitoridectomy or section of the dorsal nerves of the penis, but electroshock or thorazine. But these are only changes in psychiatric fashion; the basic social structure and function of Institutional Psychiatry have remained unaltered. (Its scope and power have, however, steadily increased during the past one hundred years.) The result is that a century after the cruel hoax of masturbatory insanity reached its height, psychiatrists still employ the same kind of rhetoric as they did formerly, and still command the attention, and often even the trust, of a public eager to be led— and deceived—by psychiatrists posturing as medical scientists. Then, the psychiatrist was saving the "patient" from masturbation, even though he did not wish to be saved from it. Now, the psychiatrist is saving the "patient" from drug addiction, homosexuality, suicide, and a host of other terrifying "mental illnesses," even though, again, the victim makes it unmistakably clear, by word and act, that he does not wish to be saved.

In short, the shifts from witchcraft to masturbatory insanity, and from masturbatory insanity to the modern concept of mental illness, may perhaps be best understood as changes in Western man's imagery and concept of personal badness. This changing imagery and understanding of evil reflect, in turn, the changing cultural conditions. For example, in the Middle Ages and Renaissance, the quintessence of evil is the pact with Satan; its symbol is the witch on a broomstick flying to celebrate the sabbat. From the Renaissance until the beginning of the twentieth century, the quintessence of evil is masturbation; its symbol is the madman masturbating in the asylum. As heresy is an offense against the authority of God and priest, so madness is an offense against that of Nature and physician. With the displacement, in our day, of the authority of both God and Nature, priest and physician, by that of popular opinion and mass man, the quintessence of evil becomes personal autonomy, that is, conduct in defiance of the wills and ways of the "enlightened majority"; and the symbol of evil becomes the non-conformist rejecting accepted belief or custom. Man's partner in crime thus shifts, over a period of time, from the devil, to his own penis, and thence to his self. His "offense" is always a kind of "self-abuse"—of his soul, sex organs, or personality. Thus, the concept of mental illness has replaced the devil and the genital organs as the *mediator* of the individual's offense against society. It is as if man-kind were unable to accept the reality of human conflict. It is never simply man who offends against his fellow man. Someone or some-thing—the devil, masturbation, mental illness—always intervenes, to obscure, excuse, and explain away man's inhumanity to man.

The story of masturbatory insanity, which spans the entire history of psychiatry, illustrates several of the arguments I have advanced in this book. In conclusion, let me briefly summarize them.

First, the invention of the masturbatory hypothesis and its medi-cal, and especially psychiatric, uses exemplify the spirit of therapeu-tic imperialism and messianism. As the goal of the evangelistic mis-sionary is to conquer more and more souls for Christianity, so the goal of the evangelistic doctor is to conquer more and more bodies for medicine. In Christianity, this is done by defining all men as sinful (the doctrine of original sin), whose redemption can be achieved only through the aid of the Christian churches; in medicine, it is done by defining all men as sick (the masturbatory hypothesis, recently reformulated as the 100 percent incidence of mental illness), whose cure can be achieved only through the aid of the medical profession.

Second, the masturbatory hypothesis illustrates a fundamental tactic of medical and psychiatric imperialism. In order to conquer an area of human life for medical expertise and intervention, it is necessary first to define its normal functioning as the manifestation of disease. Once this is accomplished, the next step may be taken: this consists in defining destructive interventions by doctors as medical treatments. The third and final step, typical of psychiatry, is the imposition of the destructive intervention on the patient against his will. The triumph of medical imperialism is complete when the laity regards normal bodily and mental functions as diseases, and harmful interventions—even against the patient's will—as treatments.

Third, the masturbatory hypothesis—or, more precisely, its treatment by modern psychiatric authorities—supports my thesis about the role of deception and oppression in the work of the institutional psychiatrists. Zilboorg, Alexander, and Menninger—to mention only three outstandingly influential protagonists of the Mental Health Movement—have been prolific writers on the history of psychiatry. Yet in all these millions of words, not one is devoted to masturbatory insanity. It is clear that these authors knew about this "syndrome."* Their failure to discuss it, then, must be construed as an effort to protect psychiatry from embarrassment. Their "authoritative" histories of psychiatry that do not mention masturbatory insanity may thus be compared to the Constitution of the United States, which does not mention Negro slavery. Such rigged histories—which fail to alert the victims of an oppressive relationship to their exploited status, thus facilitating their continued deception and degradation— serve only the interests of the oppressors, whether they be priests, politicians, or psychiatrists.

* The omission of masturbatory insanity in Menninger's *The Vital Balance* is especially significant because, in the Appendix, Menninger lists David Skae's system of psychiatric classification in which "Insanity of Masturbation" appears in fourth place. Menninger neither comments on this, nor does he list the "syndrome" in the index. (Menninger, *The Vital Balance*, p. 453.)

12

THE MANUFACTURE OF MEDICAL STIGMA

PARPALAID: You may think me too much of a stickler for ethical standards, but doesn't your method subordinate the interest of the patient just a bit to that of the doctor?

KNOCK: Dr. Parpalaid, you're forgetting that there is an interest which is greater than either.

PARPALAID: What?

KNOCK: The interest of medicine. I serve that interest and that alone . . . You've given me a township inhabited by several thousand neutral individuals, individuals without direction. My function is to direct them, to lead them into a life of medicine. I put them to bed and see what can be made of them: tuberculosis, neurasthenia, arteriosclerosis, whatever you like, but *something*, for God's sake. Nothing gets on my nerves like that indeterminate nonentity called a healthy man.

—Jules Romains[1]

Today, Americans live under two sets of laws: one applicable to the sane, the other, to the insane. The legal regulations binding on the former—with respect to hospitalization for illness, marriage or divorce, standing trial for crime, or the privileges of driving a car or practicing a profession—do not apply to the latter. In short, individuals categorized as mentally ill labor under the handicap of a stigma imposed upon them by the State through Institutional Psychiatry.

Like earlier processes of stigmatization and the discriminatory legislation based upon them—such as those authorizing the persecution of witches and Jews—statutes discriminating against psychiatric minorities are not imposed on an unwilling public by a few scheming tyrants. On the contrary, the people and their leaders feel equally caught up in an "irresistible" historical and social demand for certain kinds of "protective" laws. In every one of these situations, the leading crusaders, and the masses, whom, by turns, they appease, deceive, and dominate, have the same two-pronged explanation for their actions. First, they deny that the affected minority is seriously mistreated, and defend the "mild" repression they acknowledge by stressing the need for social protection from malefactors. Second, they proudly proclaim their aim to destroy the accused minority, and justify it on the grounds of self-defense against a diabolically dangerous and vastly powerful adversary bent on undermining the fabric of existing society. This imagery animated those who waged wars on heresy in the past, and it animates those who wage wars on mental illness today. Since heresy could be destroyed only by destroying heretics, and mental illness can be controlled only by controlling people alleged to be mentally ill, both social movements involve curtailing the liberties, or taking the lives, of the stigmatized members of the group. The most cursory glance at our mental hygiene laws would suffice to support this claim. Statutes authorizing the special legal treatment of "sexual psychopaths"—and most recently, of "drug addicts"—are the most glaring examples.

I have already commented on the situation of the homosexual, and will have more to say about it presently.[2] As for the so-called addict, he is the target of a major "war on addiction," fought by powerful troops on many fronts. In New York State, a new anti-addiction law, enacted in 1967, authorizes the incarceration, for up to five years, not only of proven addicts, but also of persons "in imminent danger of becoming dependent upon narcotics."[3] This far-reaching repression of the addict is again justified on the grounds that addicts are "physically and emotionally sick . . . [and] must be treated as if they were the victims of a contagious and virulent disease."[4]

There is a fundamental similarity between the persecution of individuals who engage in consenting homosexual activity in private, or who ingest, inject, or smoke various substances that affect their feelings and thoughts—and the traditional persecution of men for their religion, as Jews, or for their skin-color, as Negroes. What all of these persecutions have in common is that the victims are harassed by the majority not because they engage in overtly aggressive or destructive acts, like theft or murder, but because their conduct or appearance offends a group intolerant to and threatened by human differences.

There is, of course, nothing new in the veneration, even by "intellectuals," of popular opinion or the will of the masses. The moral error of mistaking the "popular will" for what is right, and the political error of equating it with liberty or justice, have been exposed by thinkers since antiquity, but especially since the French Revolution, by such men as Edmund Burke, Alexis de Tocqueville, Ortega y Gasset, and George Orwell. More than a hundred years ago, Kierkegaard anticipated and saw clearly what was wrong with arguments justifying the "democratic" suppression of conduct not directly injurious to majorities but offensive to them, as exemplified by our mental hygiene laws. Observing that for centuries men have fought against the tyranny of popes and kings, thus associating oppression with them, Kierkegaard warned that "It does not occur to people that historical categories change, that now the masses are the only tyrant and at the bottom of all corruption. . . . Nowadays, when a man is censured for some trifling wrong but, be it noted, by the King, by someone in authority, he has the sympathy of everyone, he is a martyr. But when a man is, intellectually speaking, persecuted, ill-treated, insulted day in and day out by the stupidity, inquisitiveness, and impertinence of the plebs, then it is nothing at all and everything is as it should be."[5]

To illustrate in depth the ways in which Institutional Psychiatry serves the function of stigmatizing individuals as mentally ill, thus producing psychiatric scapegoats, I shall review some representative medical, journalistic, legal, and psychiatric writings on the nature of mental illness, psychiatric care, and mental health services. I shall begin with the views of an important authority in public health, a discipline often taken as the model of modern socially oriented psychiatry,* and work my way toward specifically psychiatric contributions.

* "[C]ommunity psychiatry and public health psychiatry are the same. Specifically, the latter involves using the public health approach to the problems of emotional disturbance, with the basic premise being that the extensiveness of emotional disturbance in the population makes it essentially a public health problem." (Stephen E. Goldston [Ed.], *Concepts of Community Psychiatry*, p. 201.)

Milton I. Roemer, a professor of public health at the University of California at Los Angeles, extols "social medicine" as the answer to all health problems. "The importance of the hospital," he writes, ". . . will continue to grow in the foreseeable future not because it contains beds for the seriously sick, but because it is a practical locale for the increasing organization of health services in general."[6] By "organization," Roemer means organization under the auspices of the State, not of voluntary, mutually competing, groups. At least Roemer is frank about the goal he seeks: "Just as hospitals are acquiring the status of public utilities, the whole range of health manpower is increasingly recognized as an essential corps for the public welfare. Physicians, dentists, nurses, pharmacists, technicians, therapists, and others are seen not merely as members of the healing arts *selling* their wares to the sick. They are viewed increasingly as essential *servants required by society* for its effective functioning—therefore, increasingly subject to both public support and public control."[7] (Italics added.)

Roemer does not, however, spell out the moral and social consequences of the arrangement he so enthusiastically supports. If the physician is an "essential servant required by society," then his role is comparable to that of the policeman or the soldier; as such, his duty is to obey the commands of his superiors, whether they order him to cure or to kill. If, like Roemer, physicians wish to repeal the Hippocratic ethic that has so far governed the practice of medicine in the United States, it would seem desirable—not, to be sure, for the attainment of their goals, but for an intelligent public appreciation of the competing interests and values at stake—that they plainly say so.[8] Many advocates of medical collectivism do.*

Donald Gould, a British journalist writing in the *New States-*

---

* Medical collectivists now speak and write about the coming Golden Age of medicine, in which private practice will be abolished and all medical services will be dispensed by the State, in terms identical with those Marxists and Communists have long used in economics and politics. For example, Dr. Oscar Creech, Jr., professor and chairman of the department of surgery at the Tulane Medical Center in New Orleans before becoming its dean, "forecast that [by 1990] the private practice of medicine as doctors know it today will no longer exist. Instead, physicians will be full-time employees of community medical centers or of the federal government. . . . This was not an idealized vision but a view of what is likely to be." (Lofty career cut short at its peak, *Med. World News*, Jan. 19, 1968, p. 30.) This was not a situation that Creech merely predicted, but one that he also tried to bring about and whose arrival he eagerly anticipated.

man, pleads for a frank revision in the definition of the physician's role.[9] Commenting on the problem of medical secrecy in the administration of the National Health Service, he asks if "we [may] not be making altogether too much fuss about the right of citizens to a secret life"? He answers—and we must keep in mind that this is an Englishman writing in an independent liberal magazine—that, "Surely, *in an ideal society, made up of thoroughly well-adjusted people, there would be no need for secrets.* Their very existence spells out the presence of greed, fear, inequity, fraud or any one of a long list of attitudes and activities, all of which are *universally recognized as properties of the Devil.*"[10] (Italics added.)

One does not know whether to laugh or to weep. Gould is, let us make no mistake about it, in deadly earnest. He really believes that mental health is the same as good adjustment; that a society made up of such people would be "ideal"; and that it is "universally recognized" that a desire for personal secrets connotes evil. The publishers of the *New Statesman* must consider this a respectable view to give it as much space as they do. The essay may thus fairly be taken as a sign of our times.

Having established that all personal secrets are bad secrets, Gould condemns the Roman Catholic confessional: "The secrecy of the confessional makes priests conspirators in the covering-up of countless crimes."[11] He then turns his wrath against the medical secrecy commanded by the Hippocratic Oath. "So firmly is this principle [of medical secrecy] established, that no doctor with any sense of self-preservation will blurt out confidences of the consulting room, even in a court of law, unless the judge specifically commands him to do so. I suggest that this obsessional reticence on the part of the medical profession is unreasonable, and that it constitutes a positive encumbrance to the advance of public health."[12] Gould, as we see, not only holds the beliefs characteristic of medical collectivism, he also speaks its language: physicians who wish to protect their patient's confidences are labeled "obsessional" and "unreasonable."

"We do not argue that a more or less adequate statement of our financial affairs should not be made available at regular intervals to the inspector of taxes," continues Gould. "Why then," he asks, "should we jibe at the idea that a full, accurate, and regular account of our physical (and, indeed, mental) state should be rendered to some central authority? . . . Ideally, our medical record cards should be sent to the Ministry of Health, say once a year, and all the information on them should be fed into a computer. Moreover, these cards . . . should list our jobs, past and present, our travels, our relatives, whether and what we smoke and drink, what we eat and do not eat, how much we earn, what sort of exercise we take, how much we weigh, how tall we are, even, perhaps, the results of regular psychological tests, and a host of other intimate details."[13]

Like the zealous inquisitor intoxicated with the glory of God and the supreme good of man's salvation, for whom personal liberty was a subsidiary value (if not a positive evil)—so the zealous medical collectivist, intoxicated with the glory of Science and the supreme good of man's health (bodily and mental, of course), regards personal liberty as a subsidiary value (if not a positive evil).

"Proper records, analyzed by a computer," Gould concludes in a burst of enthusiasm enough to frighten anyone but the truest of believers, ". . . could even reveal the people who ought not to be allowed to drive a motor-car, or have a seat in the cabinet. Ah! But what about the sacred freedom of the individual? Freedom, my foot. We survive as a community or not at all, and *doctors to-day are as much servants of the state as of their patients. Away with humbug, and let us admit that all secrets are bad secrets.* It is time we were shown for what we are—warts and all."[14] (Italics added.)

"Warts," surely, must be a misprint. Gould must mean witch's marks. And who will ascertain that the psychological testers and the interpreters of these dossiers of personal information will have no bad secrets to hide? That is a foolish question. Modern physicians and psychiatrists are the perfect and infallible interpreters of Science and of Nature, just as Renaissance popes had been of the Bible and of God.*

In a subsequent article, Gould elaborates his concepts of the doctor as an agent, and of the citizen as the property, of the State.[15] "How far," he asks, "should a government assume the responsibility of protecting its people from their own folly, or of deciding, on

---

* It may be worthwhile here to contrast Gould's totalitarian philosophy with the libertarian view of the framers of the Constitution. "There is no greater fallacy," declares Brant, "than the belief that government can or ought to separate truth from error. Error, protected by freedom of speech, may outlive truth. But freedom dies when error is repressed by law, and error multiplies when freedom dies." (Irving Brant, *The Bill of Rights*, p. 506.)

behalf of the individual citizen, when a risk is justifiable and when it is not?"[16] Suppose, he suggests, that contraceptive pills turn out to be harmful to health. "Present indications are that a real risk will finally be proved. And if it turns out to be so, what action [by the government] should be taken?"[17] Gould ponders the alternatives between the government providing people with information and leaving them free choice to act as they deem best, or proscribing such substances and "sending the immoral weaklings who use them to prison."[18] He firmly rejects the former, classically libertarian posture. He does so, moreover, not because he thinks that the State might, in all its scientistic wisdom, be mistaken, or that the citizen might take better care of himself than could the State of him; these things never occur to him (or at least he does not mention them). He rejects the proposition that the citizen owns his body, because he believes that "People are part of the wealth of the community. The community puts a lot of money into them in terms of education, subsidized housing, subsidized farm produce for their bellies, and in a whole host of other fashions. That investment is only recovered if the men and women . . . live an active and productive life, of reasonable length."[19]

Not even Marx or Lenin went this far. Gould here carries the logic of a materialistic Statism (or State Capitalism) to its inexorable conclusion, especially so far as medical matters are concerned. The State owns everything, people included. People are at once an investment and a product. The investment is into young and unhealthy bodies; the product is mature and healthy ones. Surely, these healthy bodies cannot be allowed to govern themselves, make themselves sick, perhaps even kill themselves. That would be destroying State property. "So," Gould triumphantly concludes, "hasn't the state the right—nay, the *duty* [his italics]— to see that its citizens stay healthy, and to stop them, by law [sic], from doing unhealthy things? . . . it is time the problem was faced, and that our masters [sic] got round to working out some sort of rules concerning their responsibility for the manner in which we handle our bodies. They are, after all, just as much a part of the national wealth as the steel mills."[20]

Our bodies are like steel mills; they are part of the national wealth; they belong to the State, and we must, therefore, take good care of them. It all sounds vaguely familiar. Our bodies, we used to be told, are like temples; they are part of the Grand Design; they belong to God, and we must, therefore, not tamper with them. Gould's vision, then, is but a rewarming of the hoary, positivistic doctrines of the Jacobins, of Comte, of the modern liberals and behavioral scientists.[21] When such bureaucratic and totalitarian principles and methods are applied to mental health planning and organization—as indeed they are both in England and the United States—the psychiatric physician emerges as a political evangelist, social activist, and medical despot. His role is to protect the state from the troublesome citizen. All means necessary to achieve this are justified by the loftiness of this aim. The situation in Germany under Hitler offers us a picture—horrible or idyllic depending on our values—of the ensuing political tyranny concealed behind an imagery of illness, and justified by a rhetoric of therapy.

It should be recalled that psychiatrists in Nazi Germany played a leading role in developing the gas chambers whose first victims were mental patients.[22] Even in occupied territories, where soldiers were used for the mass murder of civilian populations, the inmates of mental hospitals—in Kiev, for example—were killed by doctors.[23] In Poland alone, about 30,000 mental hospital patients were put to death.[24] All this was done in the name of protecting the health of the sane members of the population. The Nazis had pioneered, however, not only in developing new technics of mass murder, but also—and this apparently has largely been forgotten, if indeed its significance was ever appreciated—in perfecting a fresh rhetoric of hygiene to justify their programs. For example, Heinrich Himmler, chief of the Nazi S.S., explained that "Antisemitism is exactly the same as delousing. Getting rid of lice is not a question of ideology. It is a matter of cleanliness."[25] Similarly, Paul Otto Schmidt, press chief of the Nazi Foreign Office, declared that "The Jewish question is no question of humanity, and it is no question of religion; it is solely a question of political hygiene."[26] In the postwar world, this imagery has been inverted, so that instead of the Jew, the anti-Semite is defined as posing a problem in hygiene; and instead of being incarcerated in a concentration camp, he is incarcerated in a mental hospital.*

* The present tendency to attribute anti-Semitism and Nazism in West Germany to mental illness differs little from the earlier tendency to attribute Capitalism and Communism to Jews. "In a report on right-wing radicalism," the *New York Times* informs us, "Mr. Lucke [West German Minister of the Interior Paul Lucke] noted that there were 521 confirmed cases of pro-Nazi or anti-

As I have stressed throughout this book, the de-moralization and de-politicalization of social problems, and their transformation into problems of medicine and treatment, is a characteristic modern totalitarian states (both National Socialist and Communist) share with modern bureaucratic states. Moreover, although the degree and the directness of the destructiveness which such therapeutic rhetoric justifies may vary from one political system to another, its essential aim is always the same: to identify, stigmatize, and control particular segments of the population.

In Germany, the imagery of the Jews as vermin led to their extermination by gassing. "The most dramatic application of this theory [of the Jew as insect]," writes Hilberg, led to "a German fumigation company, the Deutsche Gesellschaft für Schädlingsbekämpfung [being] drawn into the killing operations by furnishing one of its lethal products for the gassing of millions of Jews. Thus the destruction process was also turned into a 'cleansing operation.' "[27]

In America, the justification of commitment, based on the imagery of the mental patient as a person so sick that he does not even know he is sick, rests on a similar hygienic rhetoric. Its consequences are only slightly less horrendous.

One of the earliest, and most instructive, parallels between the Nazi concentration camp and the American state mental hospital is that drawn by Harold Orlans in 1948. As a conscientious objector, Orlans worked in a state hospital during the war. "It is in the murder by neglect of decrepit old men," he writes, "that, I believe, the closest analogy is to be found with death camp murders. The asylum murders are passive; the Auschwitz murders active . . . but otherwise their logic is the same."[28] We may note here that at present approximately 40 percent of the patients in New York State mental hospitals are sixty-five years old or over. "The round-about manner," Orlans remarks in an exchange of letters with Dwight MacDonald, "in which the asylum kills inmates strikes one at first as irrational (a gas chamber would be more efficient); but

Semitic incidents in the Federal Republic during 1965, compared with 171 in the previous year. . . . The Interior Minister reported that much of the right-wing activity could be traced to apolitical symptoms such as drunkenness and insanity." (Philip Shabecoff, Rightist activity rises in Germany: Neo-Nazi and anti-Semitic action up sharply in '65, *New York Times*, Mar. 2, 1966, p. 14.)

knowledge (or hindsight) of American society makes it apparent that no shorter course is, at present, practicable; indeed, a longer course may one day be adopted."[29] Orlans' basic thesis, amply confirmed in the twenty years since the publication of his article, is summed up in these sentences: ". . . I [do not] assert that there is an identity between the American asylum and the German death camp. I am, instead, interested in certain similarities of social process in both institutions, and my thesis is that the American asylum manifests, in embryo, some of the same social mechanisms which in Germany matured into death camps . . ."[30]

The medical rhetoric of Nazism was, morever, not just a ruse for the murder of Jews (any more than the medical rhetoric of Institutional Psychiatry is just a ruse for the coercive control of helpless or troublesome individuals). On the contrary, it was an integral part of the health-consciousness of the scientistic Nazi society. In case of victory, Hannah Arendt tells us, "they [the Nazis] intended to extend their extermination politics into the ranks of 'racially unfit' Germans . . . Hitler contemplated during the war the introduction of a National Health Bill. 'After national X-ray examination, the Fuehrer is to be given a list of sick persons, particularly those with lung and heart diseases. On the basis of the new Reich Health Law . . . these families will no longer be able to remain among the public and can no longer be allowed to produce children. What will happen to these families will be the subject of further orders of the Fuehrer.' It does not need much imagination [adds Arendt]to guess what these further orders would have been."[31]

Thus, what happened in Germany to Jews and mental patients foreshadowed what was to happen to other minorities. Similarly, what hapened in the United States to Negroes and mental patients foreshadowed what was to happen to other minorities, in particular, the medically ill, the aged, the homosexual, and the drug addict.

Unlike the Nazis, the Communists do not exterminate their mental patients; they only make them behave. "In general, because of the social system, there is total acceptance of the problem of mental illness in Russia," said B. A. Lebedev, a former director of the Bekhterev Psychoneurological Research Institute in Leningrad, and now a medical officer of the World Health Organization, at a lecture at the University of Oklahoma Medical Center.[32] *Mental illness* may be accepted in Russia, but the *mental patient,* as we shall see, is not. "Russia does not have the problem of educating the public that America has . . . since recommended therapy and treatment are obligatory," explained Lebedev. "Putting patients in mental hospitals is kept to a minimum in Russia," Lebedev noted; however, "when discharged from a hospital, a patient *has to come* to the dispensary (community mental health center) where a psychiatrist *decides* what kind of medical care he will receive and how often."[33] (Italics added.) The coercion of the patient by the bureaucratic physician is accepted here as the most natural and appropriate medical arrangement possible. Lebedev then goes on to say that while Freudian psychoanalysis is not practiced in Russia, "treatment measures generally are the same types of therapy used in the U.S." Furthermore, "Russia's social structure has enabled psychiatry to go out into communities and actively search for persons in need of treatment . . ."[34]

This adaptation to modern conditions of the methods of witch-finding plays an important role, not only in Russian psychiatry, but, as we shall presently see, in the American community mental health movement as well. Indeed, in his lecture, Lebedev emphasized that "community mental health centers were begun in Russia as early as 1923. [Whereas the] community mental health center concept has gained headway in the U.S. only in the last few years."[35] It is worth noting in this connection that Russian physicians frankly acknowledge that their primary duty and loyalty is to the State, not the individual. A Soviet medical publication, *Meditsinskaya Gazeta (Medical Gazette)*, asserts that "the Soviet doctor is bound to co-operate actively with the government, Party, Komsomol, and professional organizations in measures aimed at safeguarding the health of the population. This means that he can have no secrets from the State."[36] This, as we saw, is precisely the arrangement Donald Gould advocates for British medicine.

In such a medical system, there can, of course, be no restraints on the use of psychiatric incarceration as a method of social control. Indeed, in Russia, there are none. We thus find that the authorities, especially since Stalin's death, make frequent use of psychiatry and mental hospitals for discrediting and disposing of politically embarrassing or otherwise unwanted individuals. In the West, the writer Valeriy Tarsis is perhaps the best-known victim.[37] But there are many others, among them the mathematician-logician Aleksander Yesenin-Volpin, the painter Yuri Titov, the school-girl-poet Yulia Vishnevskaya, and the interpreter Zhenya Belov.[38]

Despite the blatantly political, and repressive, character of Russian psychiatry, many prominent American psychiatrists have gone on record with unstinting praise for Soviet-styled community psychiatry. An article by Lawrence C. Kolb, chairman of the department of psychiatry at Columbia University College of Physicians and Surgeons and director of the New York State Psychiatric Institute, is illustrative.

Kolb describes the dispensary system of psychiatric care in the Soviet Union without ever mentioning patient coercion, and concludes that "Other advantages of the Soviet system are: the guarantee of employment of patient on discharge; the provision that hospitals may pay families to care for the patient at home; the attachment of the psychiatrists to the dispensaries; the facility with which effective decisions and actions are made in regard to the economic, social, legal, and vocational life of the patient."[39]

The religious inquisitor, let us not forget, never burned heretics; he "relaxed" them to the secular courts. Similarly, the psychiatric inquisitor never coerces conformity or imposes punishment; he makes "effective decisions and actions . . . in regard to the . . . life of the patient." In short, what Kolb extolls are simply the political "advantages," as he sees them, of a collectivistic ideology over an individualistic one, and of a closed society over one that is relatively open.

In a companion article, Isadore Ziferstein, a research psychiatrist at the Psychiatric and Psychosomatic Research Institute at Los Angeles, confirms and amplifies Kolb's findings and views. "The distinctive features of Soviet psychotherapists," he writes, "include informality, availability, and activity."[40] Again, power over the patient—frankly acknowledged by Soviet psychiatrists—is not mentioned. A brief description of what the Soviet psychiatrist in a Russian "community mental health center" (the one visited by Ziferstein happens to be the Bechterev Institute, the same clinic where Lebedev worked) actually does, should suffice here: "More and more they [the psychiatrists] were undertaking the duties of psychiatric public health officers. These duties included the inspection of factories and other places of work, to ferret out any working conditions which might have deleterious effects on mental health."[41] One such "working condition . . . with deleterious effects on mental health"—another Soviet study implies—might be having a boss who goes to church.[42]

It should be apparent from this discussion that Soviet principles of medical ethics are an integral part of the collectivist ethic of Communism, just as the Hippocratic principles are of the individualist ethic of the Free West. Each of these moral codes reflects a different solution of the perennial problem of the conflict between the individual and society. Each prescribes a different code of conduct for the physician, especially in those cases where the interests of the citizen and of the state conflict. Accordingly, in totalitarian countries, the physician is often compelled to act as the patient's adversary; whereas in free countries, he need almost never do so.[43]

The crime of the Nazi physicians was an offense only from the point of view of a nontotalitarian medical ethic. It was to reaffirm the primacy of the patient-physician relationship over the state-physician relationship that the Geneva version of the Hippocratic Oath was formulated shortly after the Nuremberg trials. This oath, adopted by the World Medical Organization, explicitly commands the physician to honor the following principles:

The health and life of my patient will be my first consideration. I will hold in confidence all that my patient confides in me . . . I will not permit considerations of race, religion, nationality, party, politics, or social standing to intervene between my duty and my patient . . . Even under threat I will not use my knowledge contrary to the laws of humanity. These promises I make freely and upon my honor.[44]

In actuality, the Hippocratic Oath, whether in its original or revised form, is like other declarations of moral principles; it is no stronger than the will of the people to respect and uphold it. The Declaration of Independence proclaimed that liberty is an inalienable human right; this did not prevent Americans from holding the Negro in bondage. Similarly, the Hippocratic Oath proclaims that the physician's primary loyalty is to the patient; this did not prevent physicians from betraying this loyalty—to the Church in the Middle Ages, and to the State in the modern world. Thus, in a competition between Soviet and Western medical ethics, the prospects for our side are not bright. This time, of course, we cannot blame an external enemy. The Communists are not imposing their medical ethic on us by force of arms. The conflict is within our society, in our own unwillingness to shoulder the responsibilities of political freedom and personal autonomy. Indeed, the erosion of the individualistic medical ethic antedates the Russian revolution. As early as 1912, apropos of the enactment, in England, of the Lloyd George Insurance Act (the first compulsory insurance program for workers in Britain), the *Journal of the American Medical Association* noted that this law marked the beginning of a new era for society and physicians. The modern physician had become a "health officer for the State, working for the general good rather than as a private, professional or business man."[45]

Furthermore, Institutional Psychiatry—which always claimed to be a part of medicine, and was in turn always eagerly accepted by it as one of its specialties—was created, and has always been, a quasitotalitarian, collectivistic enterprise, in which the physician served the State, not the patient. As the institution of Negro slavery had corrupted the libertarian ethic of American democracy, so Institutional Psychiatry has corrupted the individualistic ethic of Western medicine. Medicine adhered to this ethic only when it served its purposes—that is, when the patient willingly availed himself of the physician's services. When the alleged patient refused to do so, and was instead delivered up to the doctor for "treatment" by the State—the physician accepted this new role without protest.[46] This, of course, is past history. Today, in addition to the momentum of this tradition, there are other forces, which need not concern us here, propelling Western medicine in a collectivistic direction. It should suffice to remind and warn the reader, that, as Oliver Garceau has remarked, "the logic of events is clearly to bureaucratic rather than entrepreneurial practice, with rapidly diminishing scope for free choice on the part of either patient or doctor . . . [T]he transformation of the doctor from *petit bourgeois* to bureaucrat is inevitable . . . In a centrally organized society, the morality of medicine will necessarily be judged in different terms than the doctor-patient and doctor-doctor relations of the traditional codes of medical ethics."[47]

The significance of these considerations for our present concerns lies in the fact that, in a "centrally organized society" (which is really a euphemism for "bureaucratic" or "totalitarian society"), the psychiatrist can only be the agent of the State. Hence, his views on mental health and mental illness will depend on which government's payroll he happens to be on. His consequent partisanship in moral and political conflicts must, however, be concealed, both from himself and others. The vocabulary of psychiatry, as we have seen, is singularly useful for this purpose.

Although many psychiatrists have implied that the aim of psychiatry should be to replace morality by an ostensibly value-free mental health technology, G. Brock Chisholm, former director-general of medical services in the Canadian army, former head of the World Federation of Mental Health, and former director of the World Health Organization, has stated this so clearly and directly that his words deserve to be quoted. "The only lowest common denominator of all civilizations," Chisholm asserts, ". . . is morality, the concept of right and wrong, the position long ago described and warned against as 'the fruit of the tree of knowledge of good and evil.'"[48] This concept, he believes, must be psychiatrically destroyed: "The reinterpretation and eventual eradication of the concept of right and wrong . . . are the belated objectives of practically all effective psychotherapy."[49] Incredible? Chisholm can't mean it? His conclusions and recommendations should leave the reader in no doubt about how deadly in earnest he is. "If the race is to be freed from its crippling burden of good and evil," Chisholm continues, "it must be psychiatrists who take the original responsibility. This is a challenge which must be met."[50] His conclusion is: "With the other human sciences, psychiatry must now decide what is to be the immediate future of the human race. No one else can. And this is the prime responsibility of psychiatry."[51]

And what is to be the future of the human race, as arranged by psychiatrists? Well, of course that will really depend on their masters. "Give us a healthy world, in the full sense," declares Sargent Shriver, former director of the Peace Corps, and subsequently director of the Office of Economic Opportunity, "and Communism will disappear from the earth in every sense."[52] This, of course, is not the goal of Lebedev and his Soviet employers. Nor, as we shall see, is it the goal of the American community mental health workers. Indeed, by juxtaposing Shriver's views on mental health and those of a contemporary Chinese psychiatrist, we shall see that what is "health" to the one is "disease" to the other.

In an interview with Italian novelist Goffredo Parise, Professor Suh Tsung-hwa, who is described as Communist China's foremost psychiatrist, observed that

". . . neuroses and psychoses do not exist here, not even paranoia. At the bottom of these neuroses—a bourgeois sickness—is egoism. In the West, egoism is necessary for survival . . ."

"There is no egoism in China, then?" [Parise asks.]

"Of course, it exists, but we are fighting to destroy it. I will say, however, that in China even before the liberation it was the privilege of the few . . . The Chinese family has always been very large and very complex in its hierarchical structure. The single individual had little chance to express his private egoism. Already this collective condition, together with the teachings of Confucius, mitigated against an individualistic egoistic concept of life, ceased to exist in China when the Chinese began to work, live, and be nourished in a Marxist society, free of the class system. The conclusion? Egoism equals neurosis equals class struggle."*[53]

Troubled by the liquidation of "neuroses" and "psychoses" by Mao's thoughts, Parise asks: "If, as you say, neuroses do not exist here, what about depression?" Professor Suh's answer shows how the psychiatrist's ideological orientation—in his case, toward collectivism, in mine, toward individualism—shapes the psychiatrist's judgment of human behavior.[54]

"There are some forms of depression which might be called remorse [Suh replies]. Many workers, students, and peasants feel a kind of guilt toward the Socialist society. They think that perhaps they have not dedicated enough faith and revolutionary energy to the Socialist construction of China. For example, they come to me and say 'The Party does so much for me, and I do too little for the Party and my colleagues.' This idea sometimes becomes obsessive

* The view that individualism is "the disease of the Western world" was first proposed by August Comte (1791–1857), founder of Positivism and father of modern sociology. (Robert A. Nisbet, *The Sociological Tradition*, p. 273.)

Maine de Biran, a contemporary of Comte's, believed that "The individual, the human being, is nothing; society alone exists. It is the soul of the moral world. It alone has reality, while individuals are only phenomena." (Quoted in Albert Salomon, *The Tyranny of Progress*, p. 100.)

and even in some cases a mania. At this point melancholia can result, which is still not a true neurosis."

Here I could no longer restrain myself [Parise writes]. "The statements you have made seem paradoxical to a European. Quite honestly it is difficult for me to believe them."

The professor bowed. "I understand perfectly. But first of all I will say to you that in spite of my scientific and cultural background in Europe, I am a Chinese, a Marxist Chinese. I love the Chinese people much more than I do myself. These patients are my children and I am a father to them."*[55]

Shriver's "healthy world" and Suh Tsung-hwa's are clearly not the same: in the former, Communism disappears; in the latter, Capitalism. In the past, Holy Wars were fought with the rhetoric of salvation and the threat of the sword; now they are waged with the rhetoric of mental health and the threat of the bomb. The scientific advance in the weaponry is incontestable; the moral advance in the rhetoric is doubtful.

Significantly, though Shriver and Suh were not actually addressing each other, each equates the promotion of mental health with the destruction of his political opponent. We saw how Suh did this; let us now see how Shriver does it. In the address quoted above, which Shriver delivered at the Albert Einstein College of Medicine in the Bronx, he amplified his remark as follows: "Let universal health education become a reality, and the Chinese Communists will have more than a headache. We do this not to make the Communists sick but to make the world's people well."[56]

Like Mr. Shriver, I, too, oppose Communism, whether Chinese or Russian. But I think we ought to resist it as a moral and political evil, not as a medical or psychiatric illness; and, I think, we should implement our convictions with economic, political, and, if necessary, military sanctions, rather than with a psychiatric rhetoric sure to deceive us, but certain to leave our enemies unharmed—and smiling.

The crusading ideology of utopian reform, long typical of Institutional Psychiatry, and exemplified by the views of Chisholm, Shriver, and Suh, now animates the proponents of the movement for

---

* In his "love" of the patient as a child, the Communist Chinese psychiatrist and his American institutional colleague stand shoulder to shoulder on the common ground of paternalism.

community mental health centers. Their spirit is characterized by boundless benevolence and reforming zeal, together with stubborn insistence on treating mental patients, and sometimes even medical patients, as defective objects in need of repair by omnicompetent technocrats. The alleged patient is thus transformed from a *person,* who also happens to be sick and seeks treatment from a physician of his choice, into a *thing,* whose malfunctioning is diagnosed by experts commissioned and paid by the State. Implicit in this perspective is a demand from the physician for the same unswerving loyalty to the modern state as the priest owed to the medieval church. We know that this obedience is already being exacted from the physician in totalitarian countries; what we are now being asked, and told, is to accept it as a great leap forward in medical ethics for free societies as well. For only in this way, so this argument runs, can the "health" of the entire community, rather than that of only a few "capitalists," be safeguarded.[57] We touch here on a large and complex historical and social problem--namely, on the tendency toward the bureaucratization of all social functions in modern industrial societies, whether they be "capitalist" or "communist"; and on the implications of this process for medical, and especially psychiatric, services. When Americans encounter this process under the aegis of National Socialism or Communism, they bewail it as "dehumanizing totalitarianism" and coldly reject it; but when they meet it under the aegis of democratic social reform, they hail it as "humanitarian liberalism" and warmly embrace it.[58]

In open as well as in closed societies, the institutional psychiatrist has long been in the business of putting under lock and key deviant citizens categorized as mentally ill. The community mental health centers movement proposes to expand and extend this traditional police power of the psychiatrist. It does so by asserting that the mental health worker has a responsibility, not only to the patient who comes for help, but also to those who do not come because they do not consider themselves sick but who must nevertheless be "serviced." For example, Harold Visotsky, Commissioner of Mental Health for the State of Illinois, asserts that "a benignly aggressive approach should be made to reach out and seek these people rather than sit and wait for them to come through [our psychiatric] programs."[59] Gerald Caplan, a professor of psychiatry at the

Harvard Medical School, declares that the community psychiatrist "differs from his traditional colleagues in having to provide services for a large number of people with whom he has had no personal contact, and of whose identity and location he has no initial knowledge. He cannot wait for patients to come to him, because he carries equal responsibility for those who do not come."[60] And Norman Lourie, executive deputy secretary of the Pennsylvania Department of Public Welfare, insists that "Mental health services can no longer rely upon patients asking for help. Potential patients must be sought out to achieve early detection and prevention . . ."[61] It is no exaggeration to say that these modern psychobureaucracies are being set up for the express purpose of manufacturing mental patients.

This plea for augmenting Institutional Psychiatry's already momentous powers of social control is echoed and re-echoed by all of the advocates of this modern psychiatric barbarism. Illustrative are the pronouncements of Leopold Bellak, a psychoanalyst, a professor of psychiatry in the New York School of Psychiatry, and a leading spokesman for community psychiatry.

Bellak looks to public health medicine as the model for community psychiatry. He observes that "the community has long recognized the need for legal measures which will safeguard its physical health, and such measures have been instituted . . . Yet, in many instances, those members of the community who need psychiatric care most, refuse such treatment, and there are so far no ways of enforcing psychiatric care where it is most needed."[62] Bellak then lists compulsory public health measures, such as the reporting of contagious diseases, vaccination against smallpox, sanitary inspection of public dining facilities, et cetera, and suggests that "certainly, similar legislation designed to protect the community against emotional contamination, to provide the necessary minimum protection for the many from the severe mental illness of the relatively few, would be equally appropriate."[63] Since "mental illness" may, however, be manifested by such things as the espousal of Communism, Nazism, anti-Semitism or anti-Negroism—the political implications of such public mental health measures are painfully obvious.

However, by never deviating from the rhetoric of health and disease, Bellak pretends that his proposals are morally and politi-

cally value-free. "Thus," he writes, "the enactment of legal measures which provide for the compulsory care of the public's physical
health problems has established a precedent which may serve as
a model for our efforts to diminish its psychiatric problems . . . If
public health workers have been successful in implementing legislation to make treatment of contagious diseases obligatory, the
difficulties we encounter in the course of our parallel efforts on
behalf of enforced psychotherapy should not prove insurmountable."[64] Keeping in mind the definitions and treatments of mental
illness used in psychiatry, it seems to me fair to conclude, as I have
done, that the "beneficiaries" of such "enforced psychotherapies"
would in fact be society's scapegoats—selected, to be sure, not on
racial, religious, or national grounds, but on psychiatric.

Bellak is, moreover, not satisfied with the idea of community
psychiatry becoming a kind of public health activity. He wants it
to be a more significant part of a collectivistic system of government. He urges psychiatrists to embrace the view that "it has to
be part of our armamentarium to make ego alien what was ego
syntonic, and to provide motivation where there was none to begin
with. A court order for psychotherapy might be as good as a motivation for a start as any. *Legislated psychotherapy* has a role to
play." [65] (Italics in the original.)

Bellak's premises and arguments, summarized above, lead him
to the following conclusions: "A new executive arm of the government which will concern itself with the every-day problems of child-
rearing as well as the emotional state of the community may have
to be developed. On a broader basis, psychiatric awareness will
have to enter political considerations and the soundness of legislators and executives in a way that would be inappropriate to spell
out at this occasion. No doubt, though, that by a broad scope of
activities, community psychiatry will increasingly have to be able
to protect society as a whole, and simultaneously assure each individual as much chance for happiness as possible."[66]

There is, of course, nothing new in such schemes to make men
happy. "For fifteen centuries we have been wrestling with thy
freedom," declares Dostoyevsky's Grand Inquisitor, "but now it is
ended and over for good . . . For now . . . for the first time it has
become possible to think of the happiness of men."[67] The modern
Grand Inquisitor would not, as indeed Bellak does not, make the
mistake of using such words as "freedom."

Significantly, Bellak does refer to the Magna Charta. He views it, however, not as a contract protecting subject from ruler, but as a license for the ruler to exercise unlimited authority "on behalf" of the subject. "Most important," declares Bellak in his *Handbook of Community Psychiatry,* "the stated goals . . . [of the] enlightened program President Kennedy outlined recently [in his Message Relative to Mental Illness and Mental Retardation, February 5, 1963] . . . are to seek out and eradicate the causes of mental illness, and to strengthen the knowledge and the manpower to sustain the attack. Thus, this measure might be considered to constitute the Magna Charta of Community Psychiatry, for it is designed to guarantee and safeguard, to a degree previously undreamed of, a basic human right—the privilege of mental health."*[68] This, too, the Grand Inquisitor knew and said better: "We have corrected Thy work and founded it upon *miracle, mystery, and authority.* And men rejoiced that they were again led like sheep, and that the terrible gift [of freedom], that had brought them such suffering, was, at last, lifted from their hearts."[69] (Italics in the original.)

Bellak's writing exemplifies the crusading spirit of Community Psychiatry. He is ready to wage war against "mental illness" and "emotional contamination"; believes psychiatry should "protect society," and simultaneously work toward the individual's "happiness" by means of "legislated psychotherapy"; and, revealingly, dedicates his book to President Kennedy, not because he fought for liberty or justice—but because he was "sane." "Among his [Kennedy's] many contributions," writes Bellak in his Dedication, "is to have given the United States of America a Magna Charta of Community Mental Health. The campaigns of his lifetime as

---

* Incredibly, as eminent a legal authority as Abe Fortas uses the expression, "a bill of rights for psychiatry." "In my opinion," he writes, "the importance of the [Durham] decision cannot be judged by a semantic exercise. Its importance is not due to the new standard that it established for adjudicating the defense of insanity. *Durham* is not a charter of liberty for the insane. Rather, as I shall show, its importance is that it is a charter, a bill of rights, for psychiatry and an offer of a limited partnership relationship between criminal law and psychiatry." (Abe Fortas, Implications of Durham's case, *Amer. J. Psychiat.,* 113: 577–582 [Jan.], 1957; p. 579.)

But it is the defendant, or alleged mental patient, not the psychiatrist, that stands accused in the courtroom; it is he, not his adversary, who needs a bill of rights. It is difficult to understand how Fortas could disregard these elementary facts. Most likely, he does so because he considers those who persecute mental patients their protectors. Through this twist of logic and fact, increased power for the oppressor becomes increased protection for the victim.

well as his tragic death bear testimony that we can ill afford political lunacy of any kind."[70]

Without doubt, Bellak's book has at least one element of novelty about it: It must be the first time in history that an ostensibly scientific work has been dedicated to a political leader because he possessed the virtue of sanity.* The suggestion that the leader's death was caused by the insanity of his assassin compounds the psychiatric glorification of the leader, and the psychiatric vilification of his (alleged) assassin, in a way hard to distinguish from the death of the crusading Christian at the hands of the barbarous infidel. But with this difference: To be killed by an insane man is to rob the victim's death of any meaning. Was this President Kennedy's idea of how the concepts and methods of psychiatry should be deployed? Or was he, himself, deceived—as indeed I suspect he might well have been—by the ideology and rhetoric of the Crusade for Mental Health?

Like Bellak, community psychiatrists generally look to public health and preventive medicine both for a theoretical model of their activities and for a moral justification of their use of the police power of the State. "If the preventive [community] psychiatrist can convince the medical authorities in the clinics that his operations are a logical extension of traditional medical practice," writes Caplan, for example, "his role will be sanctioned by all concerned, including himself."[71] In fact, however, community mental health work is not an extension of traditional medical practice. This is evident from Caplan's own definition of the preventive psychiatrist's main task, which he identifies as the provision of more and better "socio-cultural supplies" to people. And how is this accomplished? By offering "consultation to legislators and administrators and [by] collaborating with other citizens in influencing governmental agencies to change laws and regulations."[72] In psychiatric jargon, this is medical practice; in plain English, it is lobbying for the Mental Health Movement.

Stanley Yolles, director of the National Institute of Mental Health, also appeals to the public health model as a justification for community mental health programs. "Through community

---

* The first line of Bellak's dedication reads: "To—JOHN F. KENNEDY, President of the United States, who was the rare political leader to be literate and intellectual, courageous as well as sane." (Bellak, p. xi.)

planning on a comprehensive basis," he writes, "through crisis intervention and other methods, mental health professionals can share with other community leaders in environmental manipulations to eliminate *known producers* of *stress* such as urban slums and rural depressed areas—potential breeding grounds of mental disease. All of these are perfectly legitimate methods of *treatment* . . . These are some of the public health approaches which are being adapted to the community mental health program."[73] (Italics added.)

But what or who might be "producers of stress"? Negroes? Jews? Communists? Fascists? Members of the Ku Klux Klan or the John Birch Society? These possibilities are by no means farfetched. We need only to recall the Supreme Court's landmark decision in the school desegregation case, handed down in 1954.[74] That opinion was based largely on the allegedly harmful effects of racially segregated schools on the mental health of Negro children. "To separate them [Negro school children] from others of similar age and qualifications solely because of their race," the Court held, "generates a feeling of inferiority as to their status in the community that may affect their hearts and minds in a way unlikely ever to be undone . . . Whatever may have been the extent of *psychological knowledge* at the time of *Plessy* v. *Ferguson,* this finding is amply supported by *modern* authority."[75] (Italics added.). The justices then cite a number of well-known studies showing the harmful effect of segregation on Negroes.

In this decision, and also in the Boutilier case,[76] to be discussed in the next chapter, the Supreme Court shows itself to be of a piece—perhaps as it ought to be—with American public opinion. The justices, too, like to transform moral problems into medical or psychological ones; they prefer to do the "right thing" medically or psychologically, rather than morally. While I agree with the aims of the Court in the Brown decision, and with the ruling itself, I disagree with the reasoning used to justify it. Racial segregation, and the systematic victimization of the American Negro, is a grave moral wrong. But what has "psychological knowledge" allegedly not available at the time of the Plessy decision (in 1896) to do with it? Didn't we know that segregation was bad for the Negro before Gunnar Myrdal wrote about it in 1944?[77] In short, I consider the psychological support marshaled for the desegregation decision objectionable on moral grounds: in its tacit ranking of human values, it places health values above moral values. The Court held that since segregation was harmful to the "hearts and minds" of Negro children, segregated schools cannot be considered "separate but equal," and are hence unconstitutional. But let us assume—as a kind of mental experiment—that psychologists were to show that, by shielding Negro children from harassment and humiliation by white pupils, segregated schools may actually be favorable to their development. Would such a finding make segregated schooling, enforced by the police power of the states, morally acceptable? Would such segregation be any less immoral? I say No. It makes no difference whatever how segregation or integration affects the education of children in *public* schools. Such schools, supported by tax monies, should not—on moral grounds alone—make distinctions among children on *racial* or *religious* grounds. Schools should, however, make such distinctions on *educational* grounds. But that is another story.

I have cited the *Brown* decision here as another example of the way we use medical explanations to justify and rationalize our moral and social policies, just as our forebears used theological explanations to justify and rationalize theirs. Those who approve the Supreme Court's reliance on sociological and psychological studies in *Brown* v. *Board of Education* might consider the implication of similar studies conducted by Soviet sociologists showing the adverse effects on mental health, not of segregation, but of religion. In an article entitled "Personality and Religion," Russian sociologist A. Krasilov asserts that "By and large in the Soviet Union the atheist leads a happier, more 'spiritually satisfying' life than does the believer." He supports this conclusion by data from empirical studies showing that "Among peasants, those with job satisfaction included 75 percent of the atheists, 64 percent of nonbelievers, 58 percent of those observing religious rites, and only 39 percent of the 'convinced believers.'" Krasilov concludes that "religion does not bring happiness and consolation to believers, even in their personal, family life."[78]

The American reader will perhaps dismiss this kind of study as basically corrupt: the investigator "discovers" what he believes ought to be the case in the first place, and what he also knows to be in harmony with the dominant ideology of his society. But are the studies demonstrating the benefits of school integration in the United States any different? Sociologists "discovering" the evils of segregation, from Gunnar Myrdal on, have harbored the same hostility to racial prejudice as do Soviet sociologists to what they might very well call religious prejudice. Such sociologic studies, then, are either venal or strategic: they produce "data" as ammunition with which to fight a battle for some social goal. This is one way of showing that the "social sciences" (or at least a great deal of what passes under that rubric) are not sciences at all. American mathematicians or physicists would not hesitate to use data from Russian studies in their own work. But would the Supreme Court consider tax exemption to churches unconstitutional because they foster mental illness? An absurd question, of course. But it is no more absurd than are the arguments used in the Brown case and in much of our social legislation based on considerations of mental health.

It is in forensic psychiatry, finally, that we find the best examples of how preoccupation with the "mental health" of victimized individuals or groups—Negroes, persons accused of crime, old people —actually works to their detriment, serving only to confirm them in their debased roles as defective objects, and to elevate their caretakers to the exalted position of loving parents. I have discussed this subject in other publications.[79] A brief critical examination of the views of one of the leading exponents of what I have called "psychiatric justice" should suffice here.

In an essay revealingly entitled "Justice Stumbles over Science," David L. Bazelon, Chief Judge of the U.S. Court of Appeals for the District of Columbia, describes how a psychiatrically "informed" jurisprudence should try to "understand" and deal "humanely" with the "man in the dock."[80] I will try to show how, by looking only at the man in the dock, and ignoring the man on the bench, Bazelon succeeds in authenticating the defendant as a psychiatric scapegoat. Bazelon begins by emphasizing his concern for the victim: ". . . as a judge I am primarily troubled by the man in the dock—about how the behavioral sciences are used in our criminal courts."[81] But if, as I suggested, the person incriminated as mentally ill is a scapegoat, then it is the duty of a humanistic behavioral science to focus attention not on him but rather on those responsible for casting him in that role. This would require that judges scrutinize their own behavior, rather than that of defendants alleged to be mentally ill. This is precisely the lesson psychoanalysis has tried—but failed—to teach psychiatry: To understand the patient, the therapist must first scrutinize his own behavior and role; moreover, to succeed in understanding the patient, the therapist must purge from his behavior and role those elements that interfere or hinder understanding or render it completely impossible. Most important are the power and ability to inflict harm on the subject.[82] Our contemporary (so-called) psychiatrically enlightened criminology shows not the slightest tendency to adopt this self-critical posture. It prefers, instead, the posture of condescending benevolence and righteous paternalism.[83]

Bazelon asserts that he and his like-minded colleagues in law and psychiatry "are all troubled by punishing people who suffer from mental and emotional disorders."[84] This is pure rhetoric. If it were true, they would have to advocate the abolition of involuntary mental hospitalization; to the subject, who can be the only arbiter in this matter, such confinement is a form of punishment. But they do nothing of the sort. On the contrary, they assiduously manufacture more and more madmen by shifting more and more individuals from prisons, where they serve determinate sentences, to mental hospitals, where they serve indeterminate ones.

Believing that "Scientists now generally agree that human behavior is caused rather than willed,"[85] Bazelon thinks he has solved the problem of justice: all that is needed are more "scientific facts" about the defendant. In this New Jerusalem, justice is dispensed not with even-handed impartiality but with tender-hearted psychodynamic insight. "What is usually required of the [psychiatric] experts," explains Bazelon, "is a statement in simple terms of why the accused acted as he did—the psychodynamics of his behavior . . . Where it occurs, under the Durham rule [handed down by Bazelon], the accused may be seen as a sick person and confined to a hospital for treatment, not to a prison for punishment."[86] This is just the point: In the courtroom, the more we talk about the "psychodynamics" of the accused, the more we come to believe that he is a "sick patient" in need of "treatment." The unacknowledged aim, and assuredly the practical effect, of this tactic is that the participation of persons other than the defendant in the creation of social deviance remains obscured. For example, if we consider addicts or homosexuals sick, we do not have to worry about the role of legislators who prohibit taking certain drugs and engaging in certain kinds of sexual conduct; or the role of prosecutors who prefer branding defendants insane to trying their cases in court; or the role of judges, who prefer understanding defendants rather than themselves.*

The upshot of this perspective is that the "psychodynamically oriented" judge trying mentally sick offenders expresses himself in terms wholly analogous to those of the religiously oriented judge trying heretics. The sixteenth-century judge was imbued with the ideology of Christianity and spoke the rhetoric of salvation. His modern counterpart is imbued with the ideology of Medicine and speaks the rhetoric of treatment. "A serious inquiry into the defendant's criminal responsibility . . . can be compared to a post-mortem," says Bazelon. "The post-mortem will not return the dead to life; the trial will not undo a heinous act. But in each case we can learn the causes of failure."[87]

Nothing could be more characteristic of the style of the medical zealot: the court is a morgue, the judge a pathologist, the accused a corpse! But the post-mortem is not supposed to return the dead to life; nor is the trial supposed to undo a heinous act. In the former, the pathologist may or may not be able to determine why the patient died; in the latter, the jury may or may not be able to decide whether the accused is guilty. But even this parallel is misleading, because it conceals the crucial difference between the respective "objects" that are examined: in the post-mortem, *a cadaver;* in the trial, *a living human being.* This is where the unwary may be deceived: to the dead man dissected in the morgue, it makes no difference how honest or crooked, competent or stupid, curious or indifferent, the pathologist is. Not so for the defendant tried in the courtroom: to him it makes a difference, sometimes literally of life and death, how defense attorney, prosecutor, judge, jury, and witnesses conduct themselves. Indeed, the outcome of a

* My analysis here of the mutual authentication of Self and Other owes much to the writings of Jean-Paul Sartre. For a summary of Sartre's rich and complex work, see Robert Denoon Cumming, *The Philosophy of Jean-Paul Sartre.* For an application of some of Sartre's ideas to psychiatry, see Ronald D. Laing, *The Politics of Experience and the Bird of Paradise,* especially Chapter 4.

criminal trial often depends more on these *dramatis personae* than on the accused himself. M'Naghten and Durham were found to be mentally ill not because they were "sick" but because those who tried them wanted them declared mad. It's as simple as that.[88]

In continuing to work out his metaphor, Bazelon becomes only more deeply entangled in it: ". . . in the trial the entire community can learn—and thereby more clearly understand its responsibility for the act and for the redemption [sic] of the actor."[89] Here the analogy between the morgue and the courtroom, the post-mortem and the criminal trial, the pathologist and the public, breaks down completely: the pathologist usually wants to "learn"; but not so the defense attorney, the prosecutor, the jury, or the public: they want to acquit or convict.

Finally, in speaking of the "redemption" of the defendant, Bazelon shows his hand: he considers the accused a kind of heretic who must be "redeemed"—the word signifies, once more, a revealing relapse into the rhetoric of the Crusades and witch trials. One wonders how Bazelon would have "redeemed" such lawbreakers as Gandhi, Nehru, or Thoreau—not to mention Jesus or Socrates. But Bazelon never allows for the possibility that the accused might be more "humane" or more "just" than his accusers and judges. In his refusal to identify with the defendant as a person of equal human worth—upon whom he may, and indeed must, sit in judgment, but whom he cannot, and indeed must not, remake in his own image—Bazelon betrays his commitment to a collectivistic and paternalistic social order in which conformity is synonymous with mental health, and in which the State is the citizen's brother, father, friend, therapist—anything but his adversary. In short, Bazelon treats himself as the Just Man and the accused as the Other, the Stranger.

In this chapter, I have tried to show some of the ways in which Institutional Psychiatry constitutes a social system whose function is to create certain kinds of medical stigmata and to impose them on certain persons. To be sure, contemporary American psychiatry comprises, as we have already noted, more than just Institutional Psychiatry. This has been true, however, only since the early decades of this century. Elsewhere, Institutional Psychiatry is still the only kind of psychiatric practice in existence. And even in the United States, the scope and significance of Institutional Psychiatry greatly overshadows—economically, legally, politically, and socially —that of Private or Contractual Psychiatry.

A recent nationwide survey of 15,200 practicing psychiatrists in the United States revealed that "in contrast to the prevailing belief that the great majority of psychiatrists spend substantially all of their time in private-office practice, in fact more than one third do not see any individual private patients at all."[90] Indeed, only about one half of all American psychiatrists do any private practice at all; and of these 60 percent spend less than 35 hours per week in such work. Of all the psychiatrists, 39 percent spend some time working for state governments, 34 percent for private agencies and organizations, 19 percent for the federal government, and 15 percent for the local government.[91] (Some work for more than one agency.)

These findings demonstrate the immense economic dependence of psychiatrists on institutional employment. In other Western countries, where economic opportunities and social demands for private psychiatric services are much less than in the United States, the proportion of psychiatrists working in mental and other institutions is even greater. In Britain, for example, only 4.5 percent of the psychiatrists spend more than half their working time in private practice; 69 percent are employed on a full-time basis in the National Health Service; and 77 percent spend at least part of their time engaged in the treatment of hospital inpatients (as against 51 percent of American psychiatrists).[92] In communist countries, all psychiatry is, of course, Institutional Psychiatry.

In short, then, the concept of mental illness constitutes the general stigma class of Institutional Psychiatry, with specific psychiatric diagnostic categories or "entities"—such as addiction, psychopathic personality, or schizophrenia serving as members of this class.

Evidence for this thesis derives from three principal sources: the views of leading psychiatrists; the practices of important social institutions, such as colleges or courts; and the empirical studies of sociologists.

I shall next cite the findings of a sociological study showing that people do not recognize "mental illness" as a behavioral condition, but infer it instead from the association of the subject with the stigmatizing officials. This will illustrate that just as the ordinary man in the Middle Ages had no way of knowing who was a witch, and recognized her only from her identification by inquisitors—

so, in our day, the ordinary man has no way of knowing who is a madman, and recognizes him only from his identification by mental health workers.

Derek L. Phillips, a sociologist, undertook to investigate the hypothesis that "Individuals exhibiting identical behavior will be increasingly rejected as they are described as not seeking any help [for mental illness], as utilizing a clergyman, a physician, a psychiatrist, or a mental hospital."[93] To test the hypothesis, Phillips prepared five different case abstracts. "(A) was a description of a paranoid schizophrenic, (B) an individual suffering from simple schizophrenia, (C) an anxious-depressed person, (D) a phobic individual with compulsive features, (E) a 'normal' person."[94] These case abstracts were presented to 300 married white women in a southern New England town of approximately 17,000 population. The abstracts were presented in combination with information about what help-source, if any, an individual was utilizing: "1. Nothing was added to the description of the behavior . . . 2. Affixed to the description was the statement: 'He has been going to see his clergyman regularly about the way he is getting along.' 3. Affixed to the description was the statement: 'He has been going to see his physician regularly about the way he is getting along.' 4. Affixed to the description was the statement: 'He has been going to see his psychiatrist regularly about the way he is getting along.' 5. Affixed to the description was the statement: 'He has been in a mental hospital because of the way he was getting along.' "[95]

Phillips found that "An individual exhibiting a given type of behavior is increasingly rejected as he is described as seeking no help, as seeing a clergyman, as seeing a physician, as seeing a psychiatrist, or as having been in a mental hospital."[96] Indeed, the women interviewed consistently identified the person described in the card as normal but having been in a mental hospital as severely mentally ill; and the schizophrenic who sought no help as normal. Moreover, Phillips found that "Not only are individuals increasingly rejected [as mentally ill] as they are described as seeking no help, as seeing a clergyman, a physician, a psychiatrist, or mental hospital, but they are disproportionately rejected when described as utilizing the latter two help-sources. This supports the suggestion that individuals utilizing psychiatrists and mental hospitals may be rejected not only because they have a health problem, but also because contact with the psychiatrist or a mental hospital defines them as 'mentally ill' or 'insane.' "[97]

This study demonstrates some of the socially pragmatic differences between bodily and mental illness. Though influenced by medical judgment, ordinary people have their own, authentic concepts of bodily illness; but they have no such concepts of mental illness, their opinion being based wholly on the subject's position as an occupant of the sick role. Whenever a "normal" person is presented as seeking "psychiatric" help, he is perceived as seriously mentally ill. "Despite the fact," writes Phillips, "that the 'normal' person is more an 'ideal type' than a normal person, when he is described as having been in a mental hospital he is rejected more than a psychotic individual described as not seeking help or as seeing a clergyman, and more than a depressed-neurotic seeing a clergyman. Even when the normal person is described as seeing a psychiatrist, he is rejected more than a simple schizophrenic who seeks no help, and more than a phobic-compulsive individual seeking no help or seeing a clergyman or a physician."[98]

Actually, it is clear that the subjects are rejected not because they seek out certain sources of "help," but because, by doing so, they become identified as more or less crazy, and are then rejected for this. This interpretation was specifically verified by Phillips. In an investigation of the reactions of a sample population to descriptions of behavior considered typical of mental illness, he found that "those identifying an individual as mentally ill were more rejecting [of him] than those not making such a judgment," and concluded that his findings "do not support the conclusions of [previous authors] that the ability of people to identify mental illness represents a step forward in public attitudes toward the mentally ill."[99] Phillips' findings provide strong support for my contention that the vocabulary of psychiatric diagnoses is in fact a massive pseudomedical justificatory rhetoric of rejection. In short, psychiatrists are the manufacturers of medical stigma, and mental hospitals are their factories for mass-producing this product.

"The term stigma," writes Goffman, "refer[s] to an attribute that is deeply discrediting . . ."[100] Being considered or labeled mentally disordered—abnormal, crazy, mad, psychotic, sick, it matters not what variant is used—is the most profoundly discrediting classification that can be imposed on a person today. Mental illness casts the "patient" out of our social order just as surely as heresy cast the "witch" out of medieval society. That, indeed, is the very purpose of stigma terms. "By definition, of course, we believe," writes Goffman, "that the person with a stigma is not quite human. On this assumption we exercise varieties of discrimination, through which we effectively, if often unthinkingly, reduce his life chances. We construct a stigma-theory, an ideology to explain his inferiority and account for the danger he represents, sometimes rationalizing an animosity based on other differences, such as those of social class."[101] Psychiatry supplies the stigma-theory of mental illness, just as the Inquisition supplied the stigma-theory of witchcraft.

The evidence presented thus far establishes, I believe, the basic similarities between the social situation of witches and involuntary mental patients. At the same time, although, as scapegoats and victims, witches and madmen resemble Jews and Negroes, there are also some important differences between them which deserve some brief remarks.

The main difference between Negroes and Jews on the one hand, and witches and involuntary mental patients on the other, is that membership in the former groups is usually not defined, and in practice need not be determined, by the scapegoating majority or some special agents of it; whereas membership in the latter groups is usually defined, and in practice must be determined, by the scapegoating majority or some special agents of it. Slave traders and slaveholders did not create the category called "Negro"; nor did they have to employ specialists to ascertain who was and who was not a Negro. Those who wanted to enslave the Negro could thus start with a naturally prefabricated category; all they had to do was to impose the role of slave on some or all members of this group.

Whereas the Negro's "stigma signs" are bodily, the Jew's are behavioral.[102] Among Christians, the Jew is as readily identified by his religious and social behavior, as is the Negro among whites by the color of his skin. Hence, those who want to persecute the Jew can also start with a socially prefabricated category; all they have to do is to impose the role of internal enemy ("usurer," "international banker," "Communist," etc.) on some or all members of this group. In short, Negroes living among white men, and Jews among

Christians, are distinguishable as deviants by *overt signs,* or *manifest stigmata.*

This is not true for witches and mental patients. The faithful Christian hunting witches and the devout mental health worker ferreting out cases of undiscovered mental illness must rely on the *covert signs,* or *hidden stigmata,* of witchcraft and mental disease. These supposed signs are not evident to ordinary persons, or even to the person who allegedly exhibits the sign.* This is what justifies, indeed requires, the employment of specialists—witch-finders and psychiatric diagnosticians—to discover heretical and insane members of the community. The result is that in both the Inquisition and in Institutional Psychiatry, the well-doer must first gain social authorization for his "case-finding" before being permitted to practice his "therapy."

The physician in private practice must obtain the subject's consent before he can treat him as a patient. Similarly, the inquisitor and the institutional psychiatrist must obtain the consent of the Church and the State before they can treat their subjects as heretics or madmen. The witch-hunter is the duly authorized agent of the Theological State; his client is the Church and its agency, the Inquisition. This is why he can, and indeed must, accuse persons of witchcraft, prove them witches, and finally save their souls by burning their bodies. The institutional psychiatrist is a duly authorized agent of the Therapeutic State; his client is the State and its agency, Institutional Psychiatry. This is why he can, and indeed must, accuse persons of mental illness, prove them insane, and finally cure their minds by imprisoning their bodies.†

* For an example of the manifest versus the hidden stigma signs of mental illness, consider the following statement by Karl Menninger: "One must distinguish an unconscious tendency in a homosexual direction, which may be quite manifest to other people—at least to psychiatrists—and yet unknown to the possessor, from a conscious desire and preference for homosexual contact." (In *The Vital Balance,* p. 196.) Much of the so-called clinical literature produced by psychiatrists, psychoanalysts, and psychologists deals with the covert signs of depression, schizophrenia, and other mental ills.

† Of course, anyone could, and often did, accuse anyone else of being a witch; but only the experts on witchcraft—the inquisitors—could make the diagnosis stick. Similarly, anyone can, and often does, accuse anyone else of being mentally ill; but only the experts on mental illness—the institutional psychiatrists—can make the diagnosis stick.

In short, the stigma signs that identify Negroes and Jews are not invented by slaveholders and anti-Semites; whereas those that identify witches and mental patients are invented by inquisitors and institutional psychiatrists. But whether the stigma signs are real human characteristics (such as a darkly pigmented skin or the practice of the Jewish religion), or the fabrications of experts (such as witch's marks or the symptoms of masturabatory insanity), their function is the same: to justify the majority in rejecting and persecuting a minority.

These differences—between manifest and hidden stigma signs—account for the nonexistence of a class of specialists charged with ferreting out the victims of Negro slavery and of organized anti-Semitism, and for the enormous significance of such specialists in ferreting out the victims of the witch-hunts and mental health movements. Converted Jews and Negroes who pass the religious and color lines constitute victims of an intermediate type. The presence of such potential scapegoats in situations where they, too, are persecuted calls forth a fresh class of "specialists," like the Nazi experts on "Jewish problems." Society sponsors these "experts" who pretend to possess the competence to distinguish between "pure" Christians and those "tainted by Jewish blood." Psychiatrists who distinguish insane defendants from sane ones perform an identical role. Any criminal trial in which the defense of insanity is raised demonstrates this. The transparent fraudulence of the performance does not impair its social value and is therefore an ineffective argument for its discontinuance. This is also why the fraudulence of the witch-hunter's performance had, as we saw, no deleterious effect on the popularity of the belief in witchcraft and in the dangerousness of witches. In the face of the cosmic danger posed by diabolical enemies like witches and mental patients what does a little deceit matter?* The Just Man of the fifteenth century could always tell himself that most priests were, after all, honest

---

* The "therapeutic" use of fraud—whether by priests, physicians, or politicians—has been satirized by the greatest figures in Western literature. For example, Voltaire puts the following words into the mouth of the fakir Bambabef: "We teach them errors, I confess; but it is for their own good. We make them believe that if they don't buy our blessed nails, if they don't expiate their sins by giving us money, they will turn into post-horses, dogs, or lizards in another life: that intimidates them, and they become decent people." (Voltaire, *Philosophical Dictionary*, p. 280.)

men; and the Just Man of the twentieth century can say the same for most psychiatrists.

Moreover, as the idea of witchcraft was believed to denote the "essence" of the witch's personality, so the idea of mental illness is believed to denote the "essence" of the mental patient's personality. This is a distinguishing feature of all concepts used to define the identity of a scapegoat: a heretic, a Jew, a Negro, or a psychotic is not also a scholar, a physicist, an athlete, or a poet; instead, each is reduced to, and is fully contained in, his role as transcendent malefactor, the Evil One. Today, the so-called mentally ill are society's official and principal scapegoats. Their status as scapegoat is, of course, wholly legal; it is therefore immune to attack from within the accepted rules of the game. Indeed, by accepting the official mythology of mental illness, those who might, on humanitarian grounds, wish to oppose discrimination against mental patients render themselves impotent to do so; in the past, those who might have wished to oppose discrimination against witches rendered themselves similarly impotent by accepting the official mythology of witchcraft.

The implications for social action of this point of view are clear. We can, and indeed must, choose between two mutually exclusive postures. On the one hand, we can define certain persons as helpless, requiring special treatment on the part of the State; those in the "helping professions" will then be able to bask in the glory of their own benevolence, while those being "serviced" will be stigmatized. On the other hand, we can strive toward the creation of a society in which the State, especially in its imposition of social controls through criminal laws, recognizes neither stigma nor status symbols or categories; the manufacture, with State approval, of stigmatized individuals and classes by professional degraders would then cease and, as citizens subject to control by the State, all men would be equal.

This need not be the end of charity and decency. On the contrary, it could be their beginning. For only then would charity be purged of coercion, and decency of domination.

13

THE MODEL PSYCHIATRIC SCAPEGOAT—THE HOMOSEXUAL

It's easier to be accepted by our society as a murderer than as a homosexual.

—Abby Mann[1]

Our secular society dreads homosexuality in the same way and with the same intensity as the theological societies of our ancestors dreaded heresy. The quality and the extent of this aversion is revealed by the fact that homosexuality is considered both a crime *and* a disease.[2]

By legal definition, every homosexual act is a "sex crime." The homosexual is thus subject to the penalties of so-called sexual psychopath laws, and may be sentenced to indeterminate incarceration in a mental institution or in a special facility for "sex criminals." Although this penalty is visited only upon a very small proportion of homosexuals, this negates neither its moral import nor its practical significance.

By medical definition, every homosexual act is the symptom of a "mental disease." The homosexual is thus subject also to the penalties of mental hygiene laws, and may be confined involuntarily in a mental hospital. In Massachusetts, for example, a person is considered a fit subject for involuntary mental hospitalization if he conducts himself "in a manner which clearly violates the established laws, ordinances, conventions or morals of the community."[3] Although homosexuals are rarely committed for their sexual conduct alone, this negates neither the intent of the legislation authorizing such confinement nor its social significance. In short, the homosexual is the subject of repressive legislation as a member not only of the class of criminals but also of the mentally ill. He is, as we shall see, the model psychiatric scapegoat.

The laws of our states prohibit homosexual behavior in much the same way as the laws of fifteenth-century Spain prohibited the practice of the Jewish religion. The results are also analogous. In Spain, the number of persons who admitted to being Jewish decreased precipitously, but vast numbers of individuals, called "Judaizers," practiced their forbidden religion in secret. Similarly, while there are few self-confessed homosexuals in our society, many persons practice their prohibited sexual activities in secret. It is usually estimated that at least 10 percent of American men and women are homosexuals. In addition, there are supposed to be many others who would like to engage in the heretical practice, but refrain because they fear the consequences and prefer conformity.

The reason for the unacknowledged nature of the homosexual's identity lies in the penalties that result from revealing it. Service in the Armed Forces, employment in government or private industry, admission to a school or university—these and other opportunities for economic and social survival are usually denied to the known homosexual.* In an article on the recently formed Student Homophile League at Columbia University, Stephanie Harrington correctly notes that "this minority is trapped . . . in a vicious circle. . . . While the Federal and State governments would find it difficult to ignore demands for civil rights and civil liberties by an organized movement whose members are prepared to stand up and be counted, most homosexuals are not likely to stand up and be counted until their civil rights and civil liberties are firmly established. Under present circumstances the risks to reputations,

---

* For documentation, see Donald Webster Cory, *Homosexuality: A Cross-Cultural Approach*, especially pp. 394–406; and *The Homosexual in America*, especially pp. 267–299.

Document No. 2, Employment of Homosexuals and Other Sex Perverts in Government, issued in 1951 by the U.S. Civil Service Commission, states, in part: "There is no place in the United States Government for persons who violate the laws or the accepted standards of morality . . . those who engage in acts of homosexuality and other perverted sex activities are unsuitable for employment in the Federal Government." (Cory, *The Homosexual in America*, p. 275.)

careers, and families are too great. Even some heterosexual members of homophile organizations are reluctant to be identified for fear of homosexuality by association."[4]

It is misleading, however, to compare the present discrimination against homosexuals with that against Negroes. The Negro, although victimized in the past, is now recognized as a fully human being with an unconditional right to his black skin. The homosexual, in contrast, has neither this status nor the right to his sexual interests and practices. Instead, the homosexual is viewed as a defective object—as a man "afflicted" with a disease to which he has no more right than the heterosexual has to being afflicted with the plague.*

Herein lies another parallel between the situation of the homosexual in contemporary America and that of the Jew in fifteenth-century Spain. As the man with Jewish religion was considered not fully human, because he was not Christian—so the homosexual is considered not fully human because he is not heterosexual. In both cases, the individual is denied recognition as a human being in his authentic identity and selfhood—and for the same reasons: each undermines the beliefs and values of the dominant group. The Jew, by virtue of his Jewishness, refuses to authenticate Jesus as the Son of God, and the Roman Catholic Church as the unquestionable representative of God on Earth. The male homosexual, by virtue of his homosexuality, refuses to authenticate woman as the desirable sex object, and the heterosexual as the unquestionable embodiment of sexual normality. This is why the homosexual is not recognized as having the same rights as the heterosexual—

---

* This comparison requires some qualification. Having darkly pigmented skin is a *biological condition*. Engaging in homosexual conduct is a *personal act*. The latter involves making a choice, whereas the former does not. In other words, white men may or may not recognize the Negro as a human and political equal; but the Negro has no choice about having black skin. Similarly, heterosexuals may or may not recognize the homosexual as a human and political equal; however, the homosexual may choose whether or not to engage in prohibited sexual conduct. In short, the homosexual makes a choice—a deviant one—and society retaliates by declaring that he is "mentally sick" and hence incapable of making a "real" choice! Were he able to choose "freely"—"normally"—he would choose, like everyone else, to be heterosexual. This is the logic behind much of psychiatric rhetoric. The patient's behavior is the product of irresistible compulsions and impulses; the psychiatrist's, of free decisions. The cognitive structure of this explanation conceals the fact that its imagery only serves to degrade the patient as insane, and to exalt the psychiatrist as sane.

just as the Jew was not recognized as a fully human being in many Christian societies, and as the mentally ill are not so recognized in contemporary American society. This injustice is slowly being recognized, as evidenced by a demonstration of the Student Homophile League "to protest the fact that the rights of the Declaration of Independence have yet to be granted to American citizens who are homosexuals."[5]

The homosexual seeking to emigrate to this country finds that he is unwelcome. I shall examine a 1967 decision of the U.S. Supreme Court on the deportability of an alien solely on the basis of homosexuality for the evidence it provides for my thesis that homosexuality is a kind of secular (sexual) heresy.

The case is that of Clive Michael Boutilier, a Canadian national, who was ordered deported by the Immigration and Naturalization Service.[6] The order for deportation having been sustained in the lower courts, Boutilier appealed to the Supreme Court. In a six-to-three decision, the Court upheld the order.

Boutilier was first admitted to the United States on June 22, 1955, at the age of twenty-one. His mother, stepfather, and three of his brothers and sisters live in the United States. "In 1963 he applied for citizenship and submitted to the Naturalization Examiner an affidavit in which he admitted that he was arrested in New York in October, 1959, on a charge of sodomy, which was later reduced to simple assault and thereafter dismissed on default of the complainant."[7]

Thus far, then, Boutilier had not been identified as a homosexual, in accordance with due process of law. However, he was foolish enough—at least from the point of view of gaining permanent admission to this country—to admit that he was a homosexual. "In 1964, petitioner, at the request of the Government, submitted another affidavit which revealed the full history [sic] of his sexual deviate behavior."*[8] In this affidavit, Boutilier admitted that his first homosexual experience occurred when he was fourteen years old, and that between the ages of sixteen and twenty-one he "had homosexual relations on an average of three or four times a year." Boutilier also stated that "prior to his entry he had engaged in heterosexual relations on three or four occasions."

* How the Government knew that this was *really* the full history of Boutilier's homosexuality, we are not told.

Evidently, this was an insufficient frequency of heterosexual activity to satisfy the U.S. Government. Accordingly, in 1964 the Government submitted an affidavit "to the Public Health Service for its opinion as to whether petitioner was excludable for any reason at the time of his entry."[9] The statutory reason for this request was paragraph 212 (a) (4) of the Immigration and Nationality Act of 1952 (66 Stat. 182, 8 U.S.C., paragraph 1182 [a] [4]), which specifies that "Aliens afflicted with psychopathic personality, epilepsy, or a mental defect . . . shall be excludable from admission into the United States." The question put before the Public Health Service was whether homosexuality constitutes "psychopathic personality."

The Public Health Service, after subjecting Boutilier to examination by its physicians, issued a certificate "stating that in the opinion of the subscribing physicians petitioner 'was afflicted with a class A condition, namely, psychopathic personality, sexual deviate,' at the time of his admission."[10] Upholding this judgment of the physicians and of the lower courts, the Supreme Court observed that "The legislative history of the Act indicates beyond a shadow of a doubt that the Congress intended the phrase 'psychopathic personality' to include homosexuals such as petitioner."[11] Since "The Government clearly established that petitioner was a homosexual at entry,"[12] ruled the majority of the Justices, his exclusion comports with the requirements of law and must be upheld.

In his petition to the Supreme Court, Boutilier claimed, among other things, that the section under which he was excluded "is constitutionally defective because it does not adequately warn him that his sexual affliction at the time of entry could lead to his deportation."[13] The Court disallowed this claim. It asserted that "The constitutional requirement of fair warning has no applicability to standards such as are laid down in paragraph 212 (a) (4) for admission of aliens to the United States. It has long been held that the Congress has plenary power to make rules for the admission of aliens and to exclude those who possess those characteristics which Congress has forbidden. See *The Chinese Exclusion Case*, 130 U.S. 581 (1889). Here Congress commanded that homosexuals not be allowed to enter."[14]

The Chinese Exclusion case, which the majority opinion here cites, involved an appeal to the Supreme Court challenging the validity of an Act of Congress prohibiting the entry of Chinese laborers into the United States. In that decision, the Court held that "The power of the legislative department of the government to exclude aliens from the United States is an incident of sovereignty. . . ."[15]

The Justices handing down the opinion in the Chinese Exclusion case cite approvingly the words of Chief Justice Marshall, who asserted that "The jurisdiction of the nation within its territory is necessarily exclusive and absolute";[16] and the words of William Leonard Marcy, Secretary of State under President Pierce, who asserted that "Every society possesses the undoubted right to determine who shall compose its members, and it is exercised by all nations, both in peace and war."[17]

There can be little doubt, then, that the majority opinion of the Supreme Court in the Boutilier case is legally sound. It is impossible to hold that Congress has not the right "to exclude foreigners from the country whenever, in its judgment, the public interest requires such exclusion . . ."[18] In determining *who* should be excluded from entering the United States, however, Congress shows its moral hand. In the past, having excluded Chinese laborers, while favoring the entry of English and Irish immigrants, it expressed its bias against colored peoples. The same considerations hold, of course, for immigration laws excluding anarchists, communists, bigamists—and homosexuals.*

The fact that Boutilier's identification as a homosexual required the expert assistance of physicians merits special comment. Does the physician, in such a situation, have a moral duty to inform the subject of the nature and purpose of the examination and of the

---

* It is, then, precisely the use of a nation's sovereign right to determine who shall compose its members that best reveals that nation's moral and political character. When, for example, the American Republic was formed, the nation withheld citizenship from its black- and red-skinned inhabitants, enfranchising the former in 1865, and the latter only in 1924.

To be sure, there is an important difference between the situation of the American Indian or Negro in 1776 and that of the homosexual alien in 1967. In the one case, the issue is defining criteria for membership in a newly organized group; in the other, formulating rules for admission into an already established group. Specifically, in the Boutilier case, it is a question of granting the privilege of citizenship to an immigrant. My point here is that when a country has a well-defined immigration policy, its regulations will form a sort of moral and political "projective test" of its national character: they will show what kind of persons it wants to add to its body politic, and what kind it wants to exclude from it.

physician's obligations to his employer? In Western societies, the physician occupies an important position of trust. Unlike the policeman, the tax examiner, or the district attorney, the doctor is looked upon as the ally of the sick individual—not the agent of the powerful state.[19]

It follows, then, that whenever the physician represents an interest other than that of the person whom he examines, the subject will be misled unless his tacit assumptions about the situation are corrected. In other words, the physicians who examined Boutilier for the Government had a choice of whether or not to tell him that: (1) they were agents of the Government, charged with ferreting out whether Boutilier was a homosexual; (2) if Boutilier was one, they would so inform their employer; (3) if they reported that Boutilier was a homosexual, he would be barred from entering the United States; and (4) if, in view of these circumstances, Boutilier wished not to incriminate himself, he could do so. Of course, I do not know whether the physicians in question did or did not give Boutilier any of these options. If they did not, they deceived their "patient."

Aside from the immorality of this kind of "medical" procedure, it is important to note that Boutilier's examination by Public Health Service physicians and their report were but gestures in a pseudoscientific ritual.[20] First, the examination could have had no rationally valid aim: Boutilier already admitted that he was a homosexual; how, then, could his "medical examination" reveal anything else? Second, the report only authenticated, with an official, medical signature, what the Court had already known: homosexuality had been *defined* as "sexual deviation" and "psychopathic personality" by the appropriate agencies of the U.S. Government; how, then, could the "medical examiners" report anything else?

Nevertheless, it may be argued that, like typhoid fever, homosexuality is a medical diagnosis, and that the physician's moral responsibility for the use to which this diagnosis is put is the same as that of any other citizen. I cannot agree with this view. It is the physician, not the ordinary citizen, who makes the diagnosis; hence, his responsibility for its use, like the policeman's for the use of his gun, is infinitely greater than that of a bystander.

The argument that homosexuality is a medical diagnosis is faulty on another ground as well. The physicians who examined Boutilier were not called upon to render a diagnosis, but to identify a person as deportable. This is not just my personal opinion; it is the view of the Justices who wrote the majority opinion for the Court. Arguing in opposition to those who would claim that psychopathic personality is too vague a term, the Court held that: "It may be, as some claim, that 'psychopathic personality' is a medically ambiguous term, including several separate and distinct afflictions. . . . But the test here is what Congress intended, not what differing psychiatrists may think. *It was not laying down a clinical test, but an exclusionary standard* which it declared to be inclusive of those having homosexual and perverted characteristics."[21] (Italics added.)

The physicians who examined Boutilier and reported their findings to the Government were thus not expected to diagnose their subject but to decide whether he fitted into "an exclusionary standard" set by Congress. Is this a morally legitimate activity for physicians? If, as it appears, they merely rubber-stamp a decision made by nonmedical personnel, what is their real function? The answer to this question throws further light on the degraded status of the homosexual in American law.

In a legal study of the status of the homosexual alien, Byrne and Mulligan[22] scrutinize the medical examinations of such individuals and note that they are perfunctory. What they fail to grasp, however, is that such examinations are not intended for the purpose of discovering new facts; in short, they are not technical acts, but symbolic rituals.* As a result, they misunderstand the actual, social position of the homosexual alien vis-à-vis his medical examiners. "In deportation proceedings," Byrne and Mulligan explain, "special inquiry officers often request medical personnel from the Public Health Service to give an opinion as to whether an alien was afflicted with a 'psychopathic personality' at the time of entry. This 'opinion' may be based not on a medical examination, however, but solely upon evidence, admitted or discovered, of pre-entry homosexual behavior. *In such cases,* it is tantamount to no medical examination at all."[23] (Italics added.)

Implicit in what Byrne and Mulligan say here is the assumption that homosexuality is a disease. For only if it is a disease is it reasonable to hold that physicians are needed for its diagnosis. By

* The disinction between technical and ritual actions is discussed fully in Chapter 14, especially pp. 266–268.

asserting that in "such cases"—that is, in the examination of immigrants alleged to be homosexuals—psychiatric examination by history alone is "no medical examination at all," Byrne and Mulligan tacitly acknowledge that testing by other psychiatric methods may constitute a bona fide medical examination. I reject both the assumption that homosexuality is a medical illness and the view that accepted methods of psychiatric examination are a species of medical examination. The disease concept of homosexuality was critically examined in an earlier chapter.[24] As to the nature of psychiatric methods, we should remember that in so far as they consist only of listening and talking to a person called "patient," or of giving him psychological tests, they never suffice to establish that the subject has or has not a bodily disease; nor are they suitable for ascertaining, for legal purposes, whether or not the subject engages in a particular kind of conduct.[25] Of course, the subject may admit that, for example, he is a homosexual; but this does not establish that he is one, any more than his denial establishes that he is not. In any examination of an inferior subject by superior authority, we must assume that the former may shape his answers in accordance with the expectations of the latter; in short, that he may lie.

So long as we believe that homosexuality is a disease, we shall require physicians for its official diagnosis. Byrne and Mulligan cite judicial opinion to indicate that this is the guiding assumption in law. A man named LeBlanc, for example, was deported on the basis of "a medical certificate of Public Health Service doctors who had not personally examined the alien but who had relied solely upon a military report and petitioner's admissions."[26] The district court to which LeBlanc appealed his deportation held, ironically I think, "that the deportation statute impliedly demanded a personal [sic] medical examination of petitioners and also that such an examination was necessary to comply with minimum standards of constitutional due process."[27] So LeBlanc was accorded his "constitutional right" to be *personally* examined before being deported! This kind of emphasis on formal due process overlooks completely the ritualistic character of the performance to which it looks for the protection of individual rights and dignities.

Suppose the Congress enacted a statute barring from immigration persons afflicted with the mental disease called "witchcraft."

Would the courts be satisfied that the requirement of due process had been met if the individual were diagnosed as a witch by a physician? Would it make a difference whether this diagnosis was based on the subject's admission or on a "personal examination" of him? Obviously, it is absurd to worry about what constitutes due process for identifying witches without scrutinizing the category of witchcraft. I believe it is similarly absurd to consider what constitutes due process for identifying homosexuals (or any type of "mentally ill" persons) without scrutinizing the category of homosexuality (or mental illness). Failure to scrutinize these categories can only mean that those engaged in their social utilization—as legislators, judges, and psychiatrists—regard them as cognitively valid, approve their strategic uses, or both. The observer must thus choose between accepting the category of "psychopathic homosexual" as valid, as do Byrne, Mulligan, and most contemporary scholars of law and psychiatry, and searching for reliable methods of identifying such persons; or rejecting the category as invalid, as I do, and refusing to so label anyone.

Although the statute under which Boutilier was deported does not apply to post-entry conduct (otherwise heterosexuality in the United States would be an adequate defense against deportation, which it is not), Byrne and Mulligan correctly emphasize that "the Immigration and Naturalization Service does not question all entering aliens as to whether or not they have indulged in pre-entry homosexual conduct."[28] Instead, the Service relies on post-entry activity as a means of identifying homosexuals. "Because post-entry activity plays such an important part in the deportation proceeding," Byrne and Mulligan suggest that "due process should require that the alien be forewarned that homosexual behavior in the United States may lead to subsequent deportation."[29]

This seems like a reasonable proposal. Indeed, it is too obvious: if the U.S. Government wanted to know whether immigrant aliens were homosexuals, it could ask them, rather than spy on them. In offering their common-sense solution, Byrne and Mulligan demonstrate their fundamental misunderstanding of the problem before them: they regard the homosexual, or the individual so incriminated, as a person, whereas the Government regards him as a thing. This is clear from the way the Immigration authorities treat the suspected homosexual. They entrap him—much as the God of the ancient

Hebrews entrapped the homosexuals of Sodom—and, having caught him, deal with him as if he were a menace justifying any method of repression. If Byrne and Mulligan's suggestions were followed, the Government would have to treat the accused homosexual as it does any other human being. But in that case the very ground for deporting him would be undermined.

What would be the effect of warning immigrant aliens that homosexual conduct in the United States may lead to their deportation? First, it might deter some individuals from engaging in such conduct. Evidently our lawmakers do not want to encourage this. Second, it might deter some individuals who engage in homosexual conduct from doing so in public places or otherwise running afoul of laws governing sexual behavior. Evidently our lawmakers do not want to encourage this either. Third, as Byrne and Mulligan note, "If entering aliens are given a fair warning that they may be deported [for homosexual conduct], they may choose to remain in their native lands or emigrate elsewhere."[30] Evidently, this, too, is not something our lawmakers desire. The conclusion is inescapable that what they do want is to persecute the homosexual. First, they fail to discourage him from entry by giving fair warning; then, they harass him by invading his privacy, and degrade him by pinning stigmatizing labels on him; finally, they punish him by expelling him from the country. That the punishment thus imposed is exceedingly severe cannot be doubted.* Boutilier, for example, had resided in the United States for ten years—virtually his entire adult life—before he was deported. Struck by this mistreatment, Byrne and Mulligan remonstrate that: "If, during his residence Boutilier had known that his pre-entry conduct might cause his deportation, he could have avoided deportation by voluntarily leaving the country at an early date and thus have had more time to establish life for himself elsewhere. He could have continued to reside in the United States living a life that would not expose him to official inquiry. Instead, not knowing he was deportable, Boutilier applied for citizenship."[31] It seems improbable that the Congress which enacted the statute under which homosexuals are

---

* In a 1951 decision, Mr. Justice Jackson expressed the opinion that deportation amounted to a criminal proceeding. He characterized it as a "life sentence of exile" and "a savage penalty." (Byrne and Mulligan, "Psychopathic personality" and "sexual deviation": Medical terms or legal catch-alls, *Temple Law Quart.* 40: 328–347 [Spring-Summer], 1967; p. 347.)

deported did not realize all this. Telling American lawmakers that they are hard on homosexuals seems to me like telling inquisitors that they are hard on heretics. Of course they are. They believe it is their medical-patriotic duty.

Byrne and Mulligan's well-intentioned misunderstanding of the real status, and predicament, of the homosexual is reflected in the closing paragraph of their article. "Whether or not the social contract between sovereign and entering aliens is the same one to which ordinary citizens are privy," they write, "must depend on a careful assessment of value priorities, including matters such as fairness, national well-being, reciprocal treatment of American citizens abroad, etc. The least that ought to be required, however, is that entering aliens be given as specific notice as possible of the terms of their contract."[32]

The fact is that the entering alien is given specific notice of the terms of his contract in every significant respect but one: the exact consequences of his violating the American mental health ethic are not specified. Through a "General Information Sheet for Immigrants," he learns that he must not have a contagious disease, or a mental illness or defect; or be a narcotics addict, or a member of the Communist Party; and so forth.* What he does not learn is that he must be a devout heterosexual, lest he be categorized as a psychopathic homosexual; and that he must believe in social reality as verified by psychiatrists, lest he be classified as psychotic. But how many native-born citizens of the United States are fully conversant with this aspect of their relationship to their government? Furthermore, what kind of "specific notice . . . of the terms of their contract" with respect to "homosexuality" and "psychopathic personality" could entering aliens receive? In truth, they would have to be told that American law recognizes only "mentally healthy" persons as human

---

* "The general objective of the Immigration and Nationality Act is to protect the health, welfare and security of the United States. United States law prohibits the issuance of visas to anyone who has a contagious disease, such as tuberculosis; or has had a mental illness or defect; is a narcotics addict or trafficker; or has committed a criminal act, including one involving certain offenses against public morals; is or has been a member or supporter of the Communist Party or any affiliated organization; is an illiterate; or is likely to become a public charge." (Dept. of State, Foreign Service of the United States, Gen. Inf. Sheet for Immigrants [Form DSL–852, Jan., 1964].)

beings, and hence restricts its obligations to be governed by contract—including that great contract called the Constitution—to such persons; and further, that it regards and treats "mentally sick" individuals—including homosexuals, psychopaths, and indeed anyone to whom a psychiatric label may be attached—as semihuman, childlike beings, unfit to function as contracting partners in social relationship.

The opinion of the Supreme Court in the Boutilier case reflects a point of view on the dangers that "psychopathic personalities," and especially "homosexuals," are supposed to present to our society similar to older points of view on the dangers that witches and Jews were supposed to present to earlier societies.[33] Parochial as this majority view is, the dissenting opinion by Justices Douglas and Fortas is even more so. This is not surprising. Both Douglas and Fortas have, in their previous judicial opinions and legal work, expressed views indistinguishable from those of the propagandists of the American Mental Health Movement. Fortas was the court-appointed defense counsel in the celebrated Durham case, which established the precedent for a "liberalized" standard of criminal irresponsibility.[34] Douglas wrote a concurring opinion in the case of *Robinson* v. *California,* where he argued that drug addiction was a disease and advocated the involuntary mental hospitalization of addicts.[35]

Ironically, in the Boutilier case, Douglas and Fortas base their dissent on the proposition that "The term 'psychopathic personality' is a treacherous one, like 'communist' or in an earlier day 'Bolshevik': A label of this kind when freely used may mean only an unpopular person. It is much too vague by constitutional standards for the imposition of penalties or punishment."[36] Thus, Douglas and Fortas recognize and admit that "psychopathic personality" is a label with which the psychiatrist may soil a person's reputation: "Psychopathic personality," they declare, "is so broad and vague as to be hardly more than an epithet."[37]

To be sure, "psychopathic personality" is a "broad" and "treacherous" term. But is it any more treacherous, or uncertain of definition, than terms like "mental illness" or "addiction?" The notion of "mental illness," central to the Durham rule and favored by Fortas, is assuredly *more* treacherous and vague than the concept of homosexuality.[38] Similarly, the notion of "addiction" central to the *Robinson* case and favored by Douglas is also *more* treacherous and vague than the concept of homosexuality.*

Douglas and Fortas are inconsistent in their concept of punishment as well. They regard barring a person from immigration into the United States as a punishment—even though the Supreme Court has held, and Douglas and Fortas do not explicitly disavow, that "The power of the Legislative department of the government to exclude aliens from the United States is an incident of sovereignty."[39] At the same time, they do not regard as punishment the incarceration of an innocent American citizen in a mental hospital, even for life—because such confinement is "intended" to help the alleged patient!

Having refused to come to grips with the social realities of involuntary psychiatric hospitalization and treatment, Justices Douglas and Fortas go on to advance an utterly irrelevant argument against the Boutilier decision. "It is common knowledge," they write, "that in this century homosexuals have risen high in our own public service—both in Congress and in the Executive Branch —and have served with distinction. It is therefore not credible that Congress wanted to deport everyone and anyone who was a sexual deviate, no matter how blameless his social conduct had been nor how creative his work nor how valuable his contribution to society."[40]

But have not Spanish and German Jews risen high in public service as well as in economic and professional pursuits—and been persecuted for their Jewishness nevertheless? Have abbesses and bishops not led virtuous lives—and been burned for heresy nevertheless? And have American Negroes not lived blameless lives, helping to build their country—and been lynched for their Negritude

* The entire *Robinson* decision, but especially Justice Douglas's concurring opinion, may be read as a modern "scientific" counterpart to the opinion of a medieval ecclesiastical court in a witch trial. Addiction is not defined but is nevertheless declared to be an illness whose proper treatment may require, and fully justifies, indeterminate civil commitment. "The addict," asserts Douglas, "is a sick person. He may, of course, be confined for treatment or for the protection of society. Cruel and unusual punishment results not from confinement, but from convicting the addict of a crime . . . a prosecution for addiction, with its resulting stigma and irreparable damage to the good name of the accused, cannot be justified as a means of protecting society where a civil commitment would do as well. . . . If addicts can be punished for their addiction then the insane can also be punished for their insanity. Each has a disease and each must be treated as a sick person." (*Robinson* v. *California*, p. 674.)

nevertheless? In every one of these situations, and in others like them, the victim is not persecuted because he is dangerous or inferior; rather the oppressor declares him dangerous or inferior to justify his aggression as self-defense.*

The history of the Inquisition and of systematic anti-Semitism leaves no doubt that society's official scapegoats are persecuted not because they have committed prohibited acts, or even because they might commit such acts, but because they are considered "enemies within." To destroy such internal enemies is a patriotic duty and a morally meritorious act just as it is to resist and destroy external enemies. It is therefore worse than futile—senseless or even aggravating—to try to prove the moral worth or social usefulness of particular persons, once it is established that they are members of a class of officially designated scapegoats. Heinrich Heine and Albert Einstein did not enhance the position of the Jews in Nazi Germany; if anything, they aggravated it. Persecutors sometimes deal mercifully with an erring and guilt-ridden victim who abases himself before his oppressors; what they cannot forgive is a blameless and virtuous victim, whose very innocence is an intolerable offense to his tormentors and who must, therefore, be destroyed without mercy. In short, men either obey the Rule of Law, or they do not. If they do not, the victim is punished not because of what he did, but because of who he is. Our mental health practices represent a massive re-embracing of this collectivistic and sadistic principle of social control.

This decision of the Supreme Court is significant, not only for the way it symbolically enshrines the homosexual as society's scapegoat, but also for the kind of "scientific" support it relies on for doing so. Many eminent authorities have expressed themselves on the subject of homosexuality; yet out of this spectrum of available opinion, the Court has selected the judgments of the medical and psychiatric employees of the U.S. Government, itself a party to the

* The arguments Douglas and Fortas advance in their misguided effort to protect "good" homosexuals is indistinguishable from the tragic argument of the German Jews who sought exemption from Nazi anti-Semitism on the grounds of proven Jewish patriotism during the First World War or other Jewish contributions to German culture. Such arguments are neither practical nor moral. Actually, they fail to protect the victim, if, indeed, they do not further inflame the passions against him. Ethically, they are ill-conceived, for, by defending "creative" homosexuals, or patriotic Jews, they tacitly affirm that it is proper to persecute "uncreative" homosexuals, or unpatriotic Jews.

action before the Justices. If a case before the Court involved free-dom of religion or the press, the Court might well have looked to authorities of all kinds, both living and dead, American and for-eign. We can only speculate about why it has not done so in this case. Perhaps it was afraid of what it might find; in particular, that it might be unable to conceal, behind a rhetoric of psychiatric diagnosis, that it is not being called upon to evaluate a man medi-cally but to dehumanize him legally.

Had the Court looked for its information on homosexuality to Lindner, instead of to the U.S. Public Health Service, it would have discovered that in our society ". . . nonconformity and mental dis-ease have become synonymous. . . . Hence, the rebellious, the Protestant—in short, the nonconformist—is considered sick and subject to all the arts science can muster or fashion to cure him of his 'sickness.' . . . Declaring the homosexual mentally ill, therefore, brings him within the compass of this regressive view and the range of all the 'therapies' devised to insure his conformity. It may mas-querade as a boon to the invert and a humanitarian modification of historic prejudice and hate; it is, in fact, but another way to obtain the conformance—this time in the area of sex behavior—our dangerously petrifying institutions demand."[41]

Or, had the Court looked to Sartre, it would have found that "Human relations are possible between homosexuals just as between a man and a woman. Homosexuals can love, give, elevate others and elevate themselves. It's surely better to get into bed with a boy friend than to go traveling in Nazi Germany when France has been defeated and strangled."[42]

But views such as Lindner's or Sartre's would not have supported the decision of the majority of the court in its concept of the homo-sexual as a socially dangerous psychopath, nor that of the minority in its concept of the homosexual as a sick man afflicted with a dreaded disease.

The Supreme Court decision in the Boutilier case illustrates Sartre's view that "The homosexual must remain an object, a flower, an insect, an inhabitant of ancient Sodom or the planet Uranus, an automaton that hops about in the limelight, anything you like except my fellow man, except my image, except myself. For a choice must be made: if every man is all of man, this black sheep must be only a pebble or must be *me*."[43] It is nothing less

than obscene to talk about the homosexual as a sick person whom
we are trying to help so long as, by treating him as a defective
thing, we demonstrate through our actions that what we want him
to be is a useful, rather than annoying, *object for us;* and that what
we will not tolerate is his wanting to be an authentic *person for
himself.*

The history of the statute under which Boutilier was deported
provides further support for the view that the homosexual is a
scapegoat. From the dissenting opinion we learn that "The provision for exclusion of persons afflicted with psychological [sic] personality replaced the section of the 1917 Act, 39 Stat. 875, providing
for the exclusion of 'persons of constitutional psychopathic inferiority.' "[44] The purpose of that clause was to keep out "persons
who have medical traits which would harm the people of the
United States if those traits were added to those in this country
who unfortunately are so afflicted."[45] This claim, that our legislators
and judges discriminate against homosexuals in the belief that they
are applying the findings of a modern and liberal psychiatric science
to the making of policy for the national welfare, makes this an
even more monstrous blunder.

I may, however, be using the word "blunder" falsely here. There
is reason to believe that both those who draw up this kind of
legislation, and those who enforce it, know full well what they are
doing. When the immigration law under which Boutilier was excluded from the United States was being considered in Congress,
in response to "the House's request for its opinion on the new
provisions, the Public Health Service noted that: 'The conditions
classified within the group of psychopathic personalities are, *in
effect, disorders of the personality. . . .* individuals with such a
disorder may manifest a disturbance of intrinsic personality trends,
or are persons *ill primarily in terms of society and the prevailing
culture.*' "[46] (Italics added.).

All this, I submit, is an open admission that social nonconformity
is considered an illness; that physicians in the employ of the U.S.
Government are empowered to diagnose such illness; that the Congress may then impose specific penalties on persons suffering from
such illness; and that the Supreme Court will legitimize the con-
stitutionality of such discriminatory legislation, singling out for
repression individuals "afflicted" or incriminated with a specific

disease. In short, this is a kind of medical witch-hunting, doctors persecuting "patients" for their alleged or real medical heresies. Thus has the physician replaced the priest, and the patient the witch, in the drama of society's perpetual struggle to destroy precisely those human characteristics that, by differentiating men from their fellows, identify persons as individuals rather than as members of the herd.

14

THE EXPULSION OF EVIL

Perversions of the sacrificial principle (purgation
by scapegoat, congregation by segregation) are the
constant temptation of human societies, whose orders
are built by a kind of animal exceptionally adept in
the ways of symbolic action.

—*Kenneth Burke*[1]

I have argued that both the medieval witch and the modern mental
patient are the scapegoats of society. By sacrificing some of its
members, the community seeks to "purify" itself and thus maintain
its integrity and survival. Implicit in this thesis is the premise that
communities of men are often in need of venting their frustration
on scapegoats. What is the evidence for this assumption? And what
social and psychological functions does the destruction of scapegoats
fulfill? In this chapter, I shall offer some answers to these questions.

The ritual destruction of men and animals is a prevalent custom
among primitive people. "The notion that we can transfer our
guilt and sufferings to some other being who will bear them for
us is familiar to the savage mind," writes Frazer. "It arises from a
very obvious confusion between the physical and the mental, between the material and the immaterial. Because it is possible to
shift a load of wood, stones, or what not, from our own back to the
back of another, the savage fancies that it is equally possible to
shift the burden of his pains and sorrows to another, who will
suffer them in his stead. Upon this idea he acts, and the result is
an endless number of very unamiable devices for palming off upon

someone else the trouble which a man shrinks from bearing himself."[2]

Anthropological accounts abound in such "unamiable devices." An ancient Hebrew custom is one of the best-known examples of the ritual of transfer of personal guilt to a scapegoat.* I refer to the ceremony of Yom Kippur, the Jewish High Holy Day. When the Temple stood in Jerusalem, the scapegoat was a real goat. His duty was to be the embodiment, the symbol, of all the sins the people of Israel had committed over the past year, and to carry those sins with him out of the community. "And when he has made an end of atoning," we read in Leviticus, ". . . he shall present the live goat; and Aaron shall lay both his hands upon the head of the live goat, and confess over him all the iniquities of the people of Israel, and all their transgressions, all their sins; and he shall put them upon the head of the goat, and send him away into the wilderness by the hand of a man who is in readiness. The goat shall bear all the iniquities upon him to a solitary land; and he shall let the goat go into the wilderness."[3]

The same theme is repeated—but with the significant variation that the scapegoat is a person, not a goat—in Isaiah: "Who has believed what we have heard? And to whom has the arm of the Lord been revealed? For he grew up before him like a young plant, and like a root out of dry ground; he had found no form or comeliness that we should look at him, and no beauty that we should desire him. He was despised and rejected by men; a man of sorrows, and acquainted with grief; and as one from whom men hide their faces, he was despised, and we esteemed him not. Surely he has borne our griefs and carried our sorrows . . . he was wounded for our transgressions, he was bruised for our iniquities; upon him was the chastisement that made us whole, and with his stripes we are healed. All we like sheep have gone astray; and the Lord has laid on him the iniquity of us all."[4]

These passages hint at the Christian ethic, preached but not practiced, that it is better to be wronged than to do wrong, to be a victim than an aggressor. They presage the legend of Jesus,[5] mankind's most illustrious scapegoat, who suffered for and redeemed all

---

* The scapegoat is so named because, by means of it, man escapes from guilt and sin; the term is a contraction of "escape goat." (Wilfred Funk, *Word Origins*, p. 276.)

men for all time.* This imagery of good men suffering for bad, though no doubt lofty in its aim, has probably done mankind little good, and perhaps much harm. It is fruitless to exhort men to be self-sacrificing. Indeed, the more the scapegoat suffers and the more blame he takes upon himself, the more guilt he may engender in those who witness his suffering, and the more onerous is the task he imposes on those who aspire to justify his sacrifice. Christianity thus asks more of man than he can do. In the few, it inspires saintliness; in the many, it often promotes intolerance.† The moral aim of Christianity is to foster identification with Jesus as a model; its effect is often to inspire hatred for those who fail—because of their origins or beliefs—to display the proper reverence toward Him. The Judeo-Christian imagery of the scapegoat—from the ritual of Yom Kippur to the Crucifixion of Jesus as the Redeemer—thus fails to engender compassion and sympathy for the Other. Those who cannot be saints, and who cannot transcend this awesome imagery, are thus often driven, in part by a kind of psychological self-defense, to identifying with the aggressor.‡ If man cannot be good by shouldering blame for others, he can at least be good by blaming others. Through the evil attributed to the Other, the persecutor authenticates himself as virtuous.

The theme of the scapegoat is, of course, not confined to Jewish and Christian religion and folkways. Similar practices are described for other times and places. Frazer tells us that among the Caffres

* This scriptural passage also foreshadows the destiny of the Jews, who both chose the role of scapegoat and were cast into it. Zionism may perhaps be looked upon as, among other things, a collective Jewish rejection of the role of scapegoat—just as conversion may be an individual rejection of it.

† "Of all the religions," observed Voltaire, "Christianity should of course inspire the most toleration, but till now the Christians have been the most intolerant of all men." (Voltaire, *Philosophical Dictionary*, p. 485.)

Mutatis mutandis, the same should be true for psychiatry, but today psychiatrists are as intolerant as priests were formerly. Illustrative is the following statement by one of the leading forensic psychiatrists in the United States and a recipient of the American Psychiatric Association's prestigious Isaac Ray Award: "If it is considered the will of the majority that large numbers of sex offenders . . . be indefinitely deprived of their liberty and supported at the expense of the state, I readily yield to that judgment." (Manfred S. Guttmacher, *Sex Offenses*, p. 132.)

‡ I believe that intelligent self-interest, conscientious self-restraint, and sympathetic identification with others would engender less inclination to hatred than traditional religious teachings based on the promise of redemption through the sacrifice of scapegoats.

of South Africa, for example, "natives sometimes adopt the custom of taking a goat into the presence of a sick man, and confess the sins of the kraal over the animal. Sometimes a few drops of blood from the sick man are allowed to fall on the head of the goat, which is then turned out into an uninhabited part of the veld."[6] In Arabia, "when the plague is raging, the people will sometimes lead a camel through all the quarters of the town in order that the animal may take the pestilence on itself. They then strangle it in a sacred place and imagine that they have rid themselves of the camel and of the plague at one blow."[7] These ceremonies are at once religious and medical; they seek to insure spiritual harmony and protection from illness.

The ceremonial destruction of scapegoats for "therapeutic" purposes was also a common practice in ancient Greece. Together with Jewish customs, these rituals constitute the origin of many later Western medicomoral beliefs and practices. In sixth-century B.C. Greece, the custom of the scapegoat was as follows: "When a city suffered from plague, famine, or other public calamity, an ugly or deformed person was chosen to take upon himself all the evils which afflicted the community. He was brought to a suitable place, where dried figs, a barley loaf, and cheese were put into his hands. These he ate. Then he was beaten seven times upon his genital organs with squills . . . while the flutes played a particular tune. Afterwards he was burned on a pyre . . ."[8]

In first-century A.D. Greece, the custom of the scapegoat was of two kinds. One was recorded by Plutarch (C. 46–120), and is described by Harrison as follows: "The little township of Chaeronea in Boeotia, Plutarch's birthplace, saw enacted year by year a strange and very ancient ceremonial. It was called 'The Driving out of the Famine.' A household slave was driven out of doors with rods of *agnus castus,* a willow-like plant, and over him were pronounced the words, 'Out with Famine, in with Health and Wealth.' "[9] When Plutarch held the office of chief magistrate of his native town, he performed this ceremony, and he has recorded the discussion to which it afterward gave rise.

There was another, darker, form of this practice, which is described by Frazer. Whenever an important locality would be ravaged by the plague, "a man of the poorer classes used to offer himself as a scapegoat. For a whole year he was maintained at public expense, being fed on choice and pure food. At the expiry of the year he was dressed in sacred garments, decked with holy branches, and led through the whole city, while prayers were uttered that all the evils of the people might fall on his head. He was then cast out of the city or stoned to death by the people outside of the walls."[10] In Athens, this practice was institutionalized. The Athenians maintained "a number of degraded and useless beings at public expense; and when any calamity . . . befell the city, they sacrificed two of these outcast scapegoats."[11] One of the victims was sacrificed for the benefit of men, the other for that of women. Sometimes the victim sacrificed for women was a woman.*

Such sacrifices, moreover, were not confined to extraordinary occasions but became regular, religious ceremonials, similar to the Jewish Yom Kippur. Every year, Frazer tells us, "at the festival of the Thargelia in May, two victims, one for the men and one for the women, were led out of Athens and stoned to death. The city of Abdera in Thrace was publicly purified once a year, and one of the burghers, set apart for the purpose, was stoned to death as a scapegoat or vicarious sacrifice for the life of all the others; six days before his execution he was excommunicated, in order that he alone might bear the sins of all the people."[12]

These examples should suffice to illustrate the ancient origins of scapegoat sacrifices and their far-reaching social significance.† They are sobering reminders, too, of the darker underside of classical

* The Athenians maintained a stable of *persons* to be used in such emergencies; we maintain a stable of *words* (and *roles*). Thus when the calamity of an especially horrible crime befalls our society, we reach into our stable of words (and roles) and, instead of coming to grips with the moral problem posed by the crisis, we sacrifice a Symbolic Offender who may be called a "madman," a "schizophrenic," a "homicidal paranoiac," or a "sex-offender." Although these sacrifices are quite ineffective in dealing with the problems that beset our society, they are, because they are fervently believed in, effective in at least temporarily tranquilizing social anxieties.

† Many authors consider it a sign of moral progress when man ceases to sacrifice his fellow man and uses animals as scapegoats. For the victim, this is no doubt true; for the persecutor, however, it may not be. The motives for animal and human sacrifices are the same. The individuals who make use of these practices display the same inability or unwillingness to shoulder moral responsibility for their conduct. The psychological significance of replacing human scapegoats by animal sacrifices has thus been generally overestimated. So long as men engage in the ceremonial destruction of symbolic enemies— whether these be animals, alien peoples, or individuals who formerly belonged to the group—man will not be safe from his fellow predators.

Greece. There was more to ancient Greek democracy, the cradle of Western liberties, than the *polis,* with its great orators, philosophers, and playwrights; there was also Greek slavery, misogyny, and the ceremonial sacrifice of human beings. These beliefs and practices, no less than others of which we are more proud, we have inherited from them and adapted to our own uses.

The ancient Greeks persecuted scapegoats for reasons which, as they saw them, were religious; we do so for reasons which, as we see them, are medical. The differences between these two perspectives, one theological, the other therapeutic, are ideological and semantic, rather than operational or social. Indeed, the similarities between them—which I emphasize throughout this volume by comparing the Inquisition with Institutional Psychiatry, witches with madmen, religious justifications for violence with medical— are demonstrated by Harrison's excellent analysis of the social function of the ritual expulsion of evil. Choosing as paradigm the ceremony of "The Driving out of Famine" as practiced by Plutarch, because "it expresses with singular directness and simplicity . . . the very pith and marrow of primitive religion," Harrison identifies the end goal of the ritual as "the conservation and promotion of life."[13] This end, she notes, "is served in two ways, one negative, one positive, by the riddance of whatever is conceived to be hostile and by the enhancement of whatever is conceived of as favorable to life. Religious rites are primarily of two kinds and two only, of *expulsion* and *impulsion.*"[14]

What is considered good must be included in the body, the person, the community; and what is considered bad, must be excluded from them. When medical values replace religious, the same principle continues to operate: whatever promotes health—good food, good heredity, good habits—must be incorporated or cultivated; whatever promotes illness—poisons, microbes, tainted heredity, bad habits—must be eliminated or rejected. Ancient religious rituals are thus restored in new psychiatric ceremonies of inclusion and exclusion, validation and invalidation, exaltation and degradation. That which is considered good, now defined as mentally healthy, is embraced; that which is considered bad, now defined as mentally sick, is repudiated.

In order that he may live, "Primitive man has before him," says Harrison ". . . the old dual task to get rid of evil, and secure good.

Evil is to him of course mainly hunger and barrenness. Good is food and fertility. The Hebrew word for 'good' meant originally good to eat."[15] With changing cultural conditions, physical and social survival comes to depend on different things: valor in battle, obedience to authority, sexual asceticism; these, then, become dominant moral values, and their antitheses, mortal sins.

From this perspective, the religious, social, and psychiatric functions of the scapegoat ritual merge into a single conceptual framework. To Plutarch, says Harrison, the Chaeronea rite was "religious, yet it contained and implied no god. The kindred rite at Athens, the expulsion of the scapegoat, became associated with the worship of Apollo, but Apollo is no integral part of it."[16] As Harrison here uses it, the concept of religion does not require a godhead. Buddhism, for example, is universally recognized as a religion, yet it is godless. "That the Chaeronea rite is godless and priestless is clear enough. The civil officer, the Archon [or magistrate], expels the slave and pronounces the expulsion of Famine and the incoming of Health and Wealth. . . . The action is what we call 'magical.' "[17] In this usage, "religion" is a collective, and "magic" an individual, activity of a ceremonial or nontechnical type.

It is important that we clearly understand the nature of this kind of ritual action, and not confuse it with technical action. Otherwise, we shall be in grave danger of believing—as indeed we so often believe—that our social behavior, unless explicitly labeled as religious, is always technical. Nothing could be further from the truth.

Until recent decades, much of medical practice was a series of magical acts.* This was even truer of psychiatry. Until the turn of the century, psychiatric practice was a mixture of ceremonial and technical acts, the former predominating over the latter like horsemeat over rabbit in the proverbial Hungarian stew made of equal portions of horse and rabbit: one each. What was medical, was ceremonial; what was punitive, was technical. Freud changed the proportions but not the basic character of the mixture: he enlarged

---

* It was not until "Somewhere between 1910 and 1912," remarked famed Harvard physiologist Lawrence J. Henderson (1878–1942), "[that] in this country, a random patient, with a random disease, consulting a doctor chosen at random had, for the first time in the history of mankind, a better than fifty-fifty chance of profiting from the encounter." (Quoted in Maurice B. Strauss [Ed.], *Familiar Medical Quotations*, p. 302.)

the technical at the expense of the ceremonial. At the same time, he added fresh rituals to those of traditional psychiatric practice—for example, the couch, free association, the voyage through the "depths" of the unconscious, and so forth.*

The point of this discussion is to re-emphasize that Institutional Psychiatry is largely medical ceremony and magic. This explains why the labeling of persons—as mentally healthy or diseased—is so crucial a part of psychiatric practice. It constitutes the initial act of social validation and invalidation, pronounced by the high priest of modern, scientific religion, the psychiatrist; it justifies the expulsion of the sacrificial scapegoat, the mental patient, from the community. Doomed to failure are attempts to understand this performance as a technical act—for example, to analyze in logical and rational terms why aliens labeled as homosexuals should be excluded from citizenship in this country, or what criteria should govern such labeling.[18] Indeed, by confusing ritual acts with technical acts, such efforts distract us from frankly confronting the moral problems which our psychiatric rituals create and pose for us.

Ritual is the product of moral repression. The aim of analyzing ritual is to re-create the moral problem "solved" by it; such analysis is therefore bound to create social anxiety and is likely to be ill-received. When "advanced" societies insist on maintaining the fiction that they engage in no ritual acts; or, more narrowly, that some particular performance of theirs categorized as ritual by their critics is in fact technical—they act like "benevolent" individuals who insist on maintaining the fiction that they engage in no harmful acts; or, more narrowly, that some particular behavior of theirs,

---

* My analysis of the distinction between ritual and technical acts follows closely the standard anthropological view. See especially Bronislaw Malinowski, *Magic, Science, and Religion.*

The English anthropologist Radcliffe-Brown puts it this way: "In any technical activity an adequate statement of the purpose of any particular act or series of acts constitutes by itself a sufficient explanation. But ritual acts differ from technical acts in having in all instances some expressive or symbolic element in them. . . . My own view is that the negative and positive rites of savages exist and persist because they are part of the mechanism by which an orderly society maintains itself in existence, serving as they do to establish certain fundamental social values." (A. R. Radcliffe-Brown, On Taboo, in Talcott Parsons, et al. [Eds.], *Theories of Society,* Vol. II, pp. 951–959; pp. 954, 958.) For a discussion of the distinction between ritual and technical action in psychoanalysis, see Thomas S. Szasz, *The Ethics of Psychoanalysis,* especially pp. 9–77.

categorized as injurious by their victims, is, in fact, beneficial for them. Like individuals, groups prefer to analyze and change others, rather than themselves. It is easier on their self-esteem, and less trouble, too.

The gist of Harrison's interpretation of ritual, then, is that, by expelling evil and incorporating good, it protects and perpetuates life. The scapegoat is necessary as a symbol of evil which it is convenient to cast out of the social order and, which, through its very being, confirms the remaining members of the community as good. It makes sense, too, that man—the animal distinguished by his capacity to make symbols, images, and rules—should employ such a practice. For the animal predator in the jungle, the rule of life is: kill or be killed. For the human predator in society, the rule is: stigmatize or be stigmatized. Because man's survival depends on his status in society, he must maintain himself as an acceptable member of the group. If he fails to do so, if he allows himself to be cast into the role of scapegoat—he will be cast out of the social order, or he will be killed. We have seen the way this rule was enforced in the Middle Ages, in the Age of Faith; and the way it is enforced in the modern world, in the Age of Therapy. Religious classification in the former and psychiatric classification in the latter form the bases for processes of social inclusion (validation) and exclusion (invalidation); for methods of social control (banishment, commitment); and for ideological justifications for the destruction of human differences ("sin," "mental illness").

We have had occasion to see what man has done to man by invalidating him on religious grounds, as bewitched (or unbaptized), and on psychiatric grounds, as mad (or psychologically unfit). In keeping with Frazer's and Harrison's anthropological scheme, which pictures societies (and individuals) as introjecting the good, and expelling the bad, the struggle of (good) Christians against (bad) Jews becomes the essential dynamics of anti-Semitism. This is not merely a hypothesis or a metaphor; it is historical reality. In the Middle Ages, the God of the European was a Christian; his Devil was a Jew.* In the modern world, the source of security for the

---

* Satan was an explicitly Jewish demon, often depicted wearing a Jew's hat or yellow badge. For a fine historical study of Satan as a Jew, and the Jews as the devil's disciples, see Joshua Trachtenberg, *The Devil and the Jews*.

Believing in the reality not only of Christ but also of Antichrist, the medieval mind, Trachtenberg notes, climaxed this parallel by making the latter "the

group has been displaced from God and Pope to nation and leader, from religion to science; its symbols of insecurity have shifted accordingly from witch and Jew to traitor and madman. The Jew remains a scapegoat, not because he is Antichrist, but because he has been rediagnosed as traitor (as in French anti-Semitism during the Dreyfus affair), and as hygienic threat (as in modern German anti-Semitism). As before, by valiantly struggling against the Other as the Symbolic Offender, the Just Man validates himself as good.

Sartre views anti-Semitism as I view the persecution of witches and madmen. His analysis will help to deepen our understanding of oppressor-victim relationships in general, and of the institutional psychiatrist-involuntary patient relationship in particular.

In Sartre's short story, "The Childhood of a Leader,"[19] we encounter Lucien, the only son of a prosperous manufacturer, struggling for direction and meaning in his life. He meets Lemordant, a young man of conviction. Lemordant knows *who he is* and this charms Lucien. Soon Lemordant introduces Lucien to anti-Semitism —its ideology, its literature, its ardent believers—just as an older man might introduce a younger to homosexuality or heroin. The result is a "cure" of Lucien's identity crisis. "Lucien studied himself once more," writes Sartre; "he thought 'I am Lucien! Somebody who can't stand Jews.' He had often pronounced this sentence but today was unlike all other times. . . . Of course, it was apparently a simple statement, as if someone had said 'Lucien doesn't like oysters' or 'Lucien likes to dance.' But there was no mistaking it: love of dancing might be found in some little Jew who counted no more than a fly: all you had to do was look at that damned kike to know that his likes and dislikes clung to him like his odor, like the reflection of his skin, . . . but Lucien's anti-Semitism was of a different sort: unrelenting and pure. . . . 'It's sacred,' he thought."[20]

Lucien's anti-Semitism makes him feel good in the same way that the war on mental illness makes the supporters of the Mental Health Movement feel good. Jurists, legislators, physicians, society matrons—the pillars of society—thus imbue their lives with mean-

---

child of a union between the devil and a Jewish *harlot*—in deliberate contrast to that other son of God and a Jewish *virgin*." (Ibid., p. 35.) Trachtenberg reproduces a number of engravings from the fifteenth, sixteenth, and seventeenth centuries, showing Satanic figures identified with the Jew badge. (Ibid., Frontispiece and pp. 30, 195.)

ing; to be sure, they do so at the expense of unemployed Puerto Ricans addicted to heroin, illiterate Negroes committing petty crimes, and the poor of all kinds who drink too much—whom they declare mentally sick to the last man.

In his book, *Anti-Semite and Jew,* Sartre correctly notes that the role of hatred in anti-Semitism may easily be overestimated: "Anti-Semitism is not merely the joy of hating; it brings positive pleasures too. By treating the Jew as an inferior and pernicious being, I affirm at the same time that I belong to the elite. This elite, in contrast to those of modern times which are based on merit or labor, closely resembles an aristocracy of birth. There is nothing I have to do to merit my superiority, and neither can I lose it. It is given once and for all."[21] We encounter the same superiority in the mentally healthy toward the mentally sick. Once a Presidential assistant is defaced as a homosexual, or an Ezra Pound as mad, even the lowliest of "normal" men can feel superior to him. Indeed, men so defaced through the degradation ceremonies of modern psychiatry are like the dead: the survivors congregate at the cemetery and secretly congratulate themselves for being alive, while their poor luckless "friend" is already finished.

For the true anti-Semite, there can be no good Jew. "The Jew," Sartre acutely observes, "is free *to do evil,* not good; he has only as much free will as is necessary for him to take full responsibility for the crimes of which he is the author; he does not have enough to achieve a reformation."[22] (Italics in the original.) For the conscientious mental health worker there can be no mental illness useful to the patient or society, nor any mental patient capable of achieving his own self-transformation. This justifies the debasement of *all* persons labeled mentally ill, and the imposition of treatment on *any* of them by the authorities (whether such "treatment" exists or not).

Another of the scapegoat's functions is to help the Just Man (as Sartre calls the person we might call the Normal Man) avoid confronting the problem of good and evil. "If all he [the anti-Semite] has to do is to remove Evil," writes Sartre, "that means that the Good is already given. He has no need to seek it in anguish, to invent it, to scrutinize it patiently when he has found it, to prove it in action, to verify it by its consequence, or, finally, to shoulder the moral choice he has made."[23] Just so for the mental health worker:

all he has to do is convert the addict into the ex-addict, the homosexual into the heterosexual, the agitated into the tranquil—and the Good Society will be here.

Because the anti-Semite fights evil, his goodness and the goodness of the society he is fighting for cannot be questioned. This makes it possible for him to use the most ignoble methods, which will be justified by the ends he seeks. The anti-Semite "bathes his hands in ordure,"[24] Sartre writes. The institutional psychiatrist treating involuntary patients is similarly engaged in a task whose goodness is considered so self-evident that it justifies the vilest of means. He deceives, coerces, and imprisons his victims, drugs them into stupor, and shocks them into brain damage. Does this lessen the goodness of his work? Not at all. He is fighting evil.

Combating evil also helps to consolidate the fighters into a well-knit, harmonious group. Thus, all the lonely and incompetent men who lead dull lives may gain admittance, "by repeating with eager emulation the statement that the Jew is harmful to the country . . . to the fireside of social warmth and energy. In this sense, anti-Semitism has kept something of the nature of human sacrifice."[25] Today, in the United States, anti-Semitism will not gain one admittance to such social warmth and energy; but the solemn incantation of slogans like "Mental illness is the nation's number one health problem" or "Mental illness is like any other illness" will.*

Can the problem of anti-Semitism be solved by converting Jews to Christianity? (Or that of mental illness by restoring madmen to mental health?) In the classic tradition of humanism, Sartre argues that this solution does not differ greatly from that proposed by the anti-Semite: both result in the elimination of Jews! Identifying the

---

* It is difficult to pick up a newspaper or medical journal without coming across expressions of this cant. Here is a recent example: "After a quarter of a century in which neurology and psychiatry have been going their separate ways, . . . the boundaries between them are becoming less definable." (Melvin Yahr, Neurology [Annual review], *Med. World News*, Jan. 12, 1968, p. 129.) Dr. Yahr is a professor of neurology and associate dean, Columbia University College of Physicians and Surgeons.

Why this blurring of the boundaries between neurology and psychiatry is a good thing we are not told; it must be self-evident. The ceremonial character of such utterances becomes clear when we stop to think that they are always made by those who most insist that psychiatry is a medical specialty like any other. Of course, none of these men would declare that the boundaries between proctology and ophthalmology, or gynecology and neurosurgery, "are becoming less definable," or be proud that they are.

proponent of Jewish conversion as "the democrat," Sartre writes: ". . . there may not be so much difference between the anti-Semite and the democrat. The former wishes to destroy him as a man and leave nothing in him but the Jew, the pariah, the untouchable; the latter wishes to destroy him as a Jew and leave nothing in him but the man, the abstract and universal subject of the rights of man and the rights of the citizen."[26] In psychiatry we encounter a rivalry between these same two positions, as if none other were conceivable or possible.

As the anti-Semite wants to solve the Jewish problems by destroying the Jew, so the Nazi psychiatrist tries to solve the mental health problem by destroying the mentally sick. In a moral revolt against this, the democrat, as Sartre puts it (or the liberal, as we might put it in our contemporary psychiatric-political jargon), wants to solve the former problem by conversion, and the latter by treatment. Thus, when the liberal defines certain individuals or groups as sick, he does not mean that they have a right to be sick—any more than, in the eye of the anti-Semite, the Jew has a right to be a Jew. Indeed, the diagnosis is but a semantic lever to justify the elimination of the (alleged) "illness."* In both cases, the oppressor is unwilling to recognize and accept a human difference. What the self-righteous person cannot tolerate is inaction toward evil. "To live and let live" is, for him, not a prescription for decent human relations but a pact with the Devil.

* At bottom, we deal here with a deep-seated confusion, or unwillingness to distinguish, between descriptive and prescriptive statements, between what is and what ought to be, between being informed of something and being commanded to do something. I have discussed the importance of this distinction for psychiatry in several works; see, for example, Thomas S. Szasz, *The Myth of Mental Illness,* especially pp. 133–163.

Hannah Arendt has identified the inability or unwillingness to make a distinction between these two categories and linguistic forms as an important characteristic of totalitarian, and especially Nazi, ideologists. "Their superiority," she writes, "consists in their ability immediately to dissolve every statement of fact into a declaration of purpose. In distinction to the mass membership which, for instance, needs some demonstration of the inferiority of the Jewish race before it can safely be asked to kill Jews, the elite formations understand that the statement, all Jews are inferior, means all Jews should be killed . . ." (Hannah Arendt, *The Burden of Our Time,* p. 372.)

What is true for the fascist or communist ideologist, is true as well for the psychiatric. He understands that the statement "John Doe is mentally ill," really means "Commit John Doe to a mental hospital" (or "Take away his driver's license, his job, his right to stand trial, etc."). Nearly all the deprivations of human rights which so-called mental patients suffer are traceable to this source.

Sartre's existentialist interpretation of anti-Semitism closely resembles the sociologic interpretation of deviance:[27] in both, the deviant—scapegoat or victim—is regarded as partly the creation of his persecutors. Although Sartre recognizes that Jews exist in the same way as homosexuals or depressed people exist, he asserts that "The Jew is one whom other men consider a Jew: that is the simple truth from which we must start. . . It is the anti-Semite who makes the Jew."[28] Now, of course, Sartre knows as well as anyone else that Jews may exist without anti-Semites. In saying that the anti-Semite "makes" the Jew, he means the Jew *qua* social object upon whom the anti-Semite proposes to act in his own self-interest. This point cannot be emphasized too strongly about mental illness. It is one thing for an observer to say that someone is sad and thinks of killing himself—and do *nothing* about it; it is quite another to describe such a person as "suicidal" or "dangerous to himself"—and *lock him up in a hospital* (to cure the disease of depression, of which he considers suicidal ideas but a symptom). In the former sense, mental illness may be said to exist without the intervention of the psychiatrist; in the latter, it is created by the psychiatrist. As in the case of anti-Semitism, moreover, the psychiatrist creates mental patients as social objects so that he can act upon them in his own self-interest. That he conceals his self-interest as altruism need not detain us here, as it is but a fresh "therapeutic" justification of interpersonal coercion.

To the extent that people have characteristics that set them apart from others, the truly liberal and humane attitude toward these differences can only be one of acceptance.* Sartre describes this in terms equally applicable to so-called mental patients. "In societies

---

* However, such tolerance of differences, and the conflicts they engender, is contrary to the order of human societies, at least so far as we are familiar with them. Kenneth Burke believes that "the sacrificial principle of victimage (the 'scapegoat') is intrinsic to human congregation." He sums up his argument for this as follows: "If [social] order, then guilt; if guilt, then need for redemption; but any such 'payment' is victimage. Or: If action, then drama; if drama, then conflict; if conflict, then victimage." (Kenneth Burke, Interaction: III. Dramatism, in D. L. Sills [Ed.], *Int. Enc. Soc. Sci.*, Vol. 7, p. 450.)

The deep-seated conviction that victims must somehow be guilty and deserving of their fate—in other words, that, because they have been punished, they must have been guilty of disrupting the social order—is illustrated by Hannah Arendt's observation that "Common sense reacted to the horrors of Buchenwald and Auschwitz with the plausible argument: 'What crime must these people have committed that such things were done to them!'" (Arendt, *The Burden of Our Time*, p. 418.)

where women vote," he writes, "they are not asked to change their sex when they enter the voting booth. . . . When it is a question of the legal rights of the Jew, and of the more obscure but equally indispensable rights that are not inscribed in any code, he must enjoy those rights not as a potential Christian but precisely as a French Jew. It is with his character, his customs, his tastes, his religion if he has one, his name, and his physical traits that we *must* accept him."[29] To apply this attitude to the so-called mentally ill is not an easy task. Present-day American society shows not the slightest interest in even seeing the problem in this light, much less in so resolving it. It prefers the model of conversion and cure: As Benjamin Rush sought the solution of Negritude in vitiligo, we seek the solution of fear and futility, rage and sadness in Community Mental Health Centers.*

Man's basic striving to solve problems is at once the source of his supreme glory and of his ignominious shame. If he cannot solve his problems by instrumental, technical means, he tries institutional, ceremonial performances. As the wheelbarrow is necessary for the former, so the scapegoat is for the latter. Technical artifacts or tools may thus be viewed as the symbols of the problems man has endeavored to solve; and so may animal and human sacrifices. What are these problems? One is disease, which endangers the survival of the body biologic; the other is sin, which endangers the survival of the body politic. In their concrete manifestations, these threats pose vast, well-nigh insoluble, problems. Perhaps because of this, throughout history, men have endeavored to simplify their tasks by drawing nonexistent connections between health and virtue, illness and sin. It is as if men could not accept, and still cannot accept, that good men may be sick and evil men healthy; or that healthy men may be evil, or sick men good. The same intolerance of moral complexity and of human differences has led men to reject the image

---

* Not very long ago, when the critics of psychiatry declared that its aim was social conformity, its practitioners generally denied this charge, defining the aim of their "science" as the promotion of mental health or human well-being. This is no longer true. Institutional psychiatrists now blandly acknowledge that their aim is to adjust the human cog to the social machine. "It is the concern of psychiatry to adjust people to the social environment," is the way John Downing, director of the San Mateo County Mental Health Services, and a prominent figure in the community mental health movement, puts it. (Quoted in Leo Litvak, A trip to Esalen Institute: Joy is the prize, *New York Times Magazine*, Dec. 31, 1967, pp. 8, 21–28; p. 8.)

of a just godhead, who loves all his creations equally: Jews and Christians, whites and blacks, men and women, healthy and sick. Repressing the pluralism inherent in such a world view, men have created, instead, the image of an orderly universe, ruled in a hierarchical fashion by God and his vicars on earth; or, if not by God, by men who govern in the name of the common good. Immersed in this perspective, men naturally come to value unity over diversity, control of the Other over self-control; and they construct appropriate methods for stabilizing this "social reality." Validating themselves by invalidating others, as taught by religious and national mythologies and sanctioned by laws, is one such method. In the past, societies entrusted the implementation of this social mechanism for validation and invalidation to their priests; today, they entrust it to their psychiatrists.

Furthermore, since magical methods are easier to come by than technical, it is not surprising that man has shown remarkable resourcefulness in displacing material problems to the spiritual plane, and spiritual problems to the material plane—treating each institutionally and ceremonially rather than instrumentally and technically. For centuries, man attributed disease to sin, and endeavored to rid himself of illness by attending to his moral conduct. Today, he attributes sin to disease, and endeavors to rid himself of evil by attending to his health.

When it was in power, the Church was worshiped for promising, through its false prophets, the priests, perpetual life in heaven. When it fell out of power, it was reproached for having retarded medical progress. Today, Medicine is worshiped for promising, through its false prophets, the psychiatrists, moral tranquility on earth. When it falls out of power, it will, I think, be similarly reproached for having retarded moral progress. But, since the retardation of moral progress, while it is actually taking place, is invariably hailed as itself moral progress, genuine advancement in our spirituality must depend on the proper resolution of psychological and social problems which we have not even confronted, much less mastered. In the meantime we ought to judge all Great Moral Programs, especially if backed by the power of Churches or States, by the inverse of the Anglo-American decision-rule for judging defendants: immoral until proven otherwise.

15

THE STRUGGLE FOR SELF-ESTEEM

Half of the harm that is done in this world
Is due to people who want to feel important.
They don't mean to do harm—but the harm does
    not interest them.
Or they do not see it, or they justify it
Because they are absorbed in the endless struggle
To think well of themselves.

−T. S. Eliot[1]

In antagonistic relationships there is often no room for neutrals: the participants must be viewed as either foes or friends, aggressors or victims. For example, if we describe homosexuals or mental patients as deviants, or if we call them ill, we imply that they are doing something wrong to somebody, possibly to themselves. Conversely, if we describe them as scapegoats, we imply that other people are doing something wrong to them.

Voltaire understood this dilemma well. He described it, with characteristic irony, in his *Philosophical Dictionary,* under the heading, "Freedom of Thought," cast in the form of a dialogue between Lord Boldmind, an English general, and Count Medroso, a Spanish nobleman. I cite only a fragment of Voltaire's statement:

BOLDMIND: "So you are a sergeant in the Dominicans? That's a sordid trade you are practicing."

MEDROSO: "It's true; but I'd rather be their valet than their victim, and I prefer the unhappiness of burning my neighbor to that of being roasted myself."[2]

Count Medroso's predicament has not vanished with the Inquisition. On the contrary, all too often modern man must face the same painful dilemma. Should he choose domination if only to avoid subjection? No, Camus cries out: "Even those who are fed up with morality ought to realize that it is better to suffer certain injustices than to commit them. . . ."[3]

Traditionally, the madman has been regarded as a dangerous enemy of society, an actual or potential aggressor; correspondingly, society and its policeman-psychiatrist have been viewed as actual or potential victims. This is Count Medroso's solution of the dilemma of "mental illness": destroy the individual identified as the "patient" before he can destroy you. This is as ignoble for a physician as it was for a priest.

If we must choose between roasting and being roasted—a choice that few thoughtful men can escape, and one that arises with special frequency in the psychiatrist's career—then, I believe, we should aspire to Albert Camus's rather than to Count Medroso's solution. However, it is often possible, and indeed desirable, to avoid this choice by rejecting the dimension of domination-submission. The physician who decides to be an institutional psychiatrist puts himself, though he may do so unwittingly at first, into Count Medroso's predicament: He must choose between roasting—that is, being an agent of the State, stigmatizing innocent individuals as malefactors; and being roasted—that is, being an agent of the persecuted mental patient, risking being branded by his colleagues as deviant, uncooperative, irresponsible as a physician, or even mad himself. On the other hand, the psychiatrist who decides to work as a private psychotherapist as, for example, some psychoanalysts do, may transcend this dilemma, by choosing, with Abraham Lincoln, the dimension of equality and noncoercion. "As I would not be a slave, so I would not be a master," said Lincoln. "This expresses my idea of democracy. Whatever differs from this to the extent of the difference, is not democracy."[4]

It is because I try to follow this principle—because I reject, as basically immoral, all forms of "therapeutic" deception and coercion—that I classify the institutional psychiatrist as oppressor, and the involuntary mental patient as victim. This choice can be easily defended, not only on ethical grounds, along the lines already indicated, but also on historical and political grounds.

The history of psychiatry, as I think I have demonstrated in this volume, is largely the account of changing fashions in the theory and practice of psychiatric violence, cast in the self-approbating idiom of medical diagnosis and treatment.* In this respect it resembles traditional religious and nationalistic history, which depicts the violence of ruthless and power-hungry leaders as a series of selfless struggles for God or Nation. (In the Communist idiom, the struggle is waged for the workers or the downtrodden masses.) The feared violence of the madman is thus best understood as largely the projection, onto the victim, of the actual violence of his persecutor. The aggression of society in general, and of its physician-agent in particular, against the so-called insane begins in the seventeenth century, with the dungeon, the chains, physical torture, and starvation; continues in the eighteenth and nineteenth centuries, with the insane asylum, flogging, bleeding, and the physical strait jackets called waistcoats; and luxuriates in the twentieth century, with the vast state mental hospital (housing up to 15,000 inmates), the shock machine, the leucotome (the scalpel for severing the frontal lobe from the rest of the brain), and the chemical strait jackets called tranquilizers. Like all systematic, popularly accepted forms of aggression, psychiatric violence is authorized, and incorporated into, important social institutions, and is sanctioned by law and tradition. The principal social institutions involved in the theory and practice of psychiatric violence are the State, the family, and the medical profession. The State authorizes the involuntary incarceration of "dangerous" mental

---

* As a recent illustration, I offer the document titled "Patients' Rights" prepared by the Committee on the Recodification of the New York Mental Hygiene Law, which begins with the following declaration. "It is axiomatic that the entire Mental Hygiene Law is concerned with patients' rights, especially rights to adequate care and treatment." (Institute of Public Administration, *Patients' Rights: Third Draft of Legislation and Analysis* [Research Memorandum No. 41], December 1967 [Mimeographed; privately circulated].)

In the same way, a Spanish inquisitor might have said that "It is axiomatic that the entire Inquisition is concerned with the rights of the faithful, especially rights to true belief and salvation."

Actually, the Committee's assertion is a brazen falsehood. The primary concern of any mental hygiene law is to empower physicians to imprison innocent citizens and to impose ostensibly medical interventions on them against their will. As one would expect, sitting on the Advisory Committee on the Recodification of the New York Mental Hygiene Law are the Commissioner and two Assistant Commissioners of the New York State Mental Hygiene Department.

patients; the family approves and makes use of the arrangement; and the medical profession, through psychiatry, administers the institution and supplies the necessary justifications for it.[5]

The political grounds for opposing Institutional Psychiatry are those traditionally invoked by libertarians—from John Stuart Mill to Isaiah Berlin—for opposing despotic social practices of all kinds. The argument is briefly this. It is easier for the group to protect itself from the accusation that it victimizes some of its members than for the individual to protect himself from the accusation that he offends the community. In a contest between the citizen and the State, as in any conflict between unequal parties, uncertainties about rule-breaking should be resolved in favor of the weaker party. Why? Because the weaker party is, by definition, less able to defend himself than his adversary. If we want him to survive and stay in the game, we must make it possible for him to do so.

The potential violence of a few clearly does not justify the actual violence of the many. Yet this is the justification we now invoke in the name of mental health, just as we had invoked it formerly in the name of Christianity. The mental patient, we say, *may be* dangerous: he may harm himself or someone else. But we, society, *are* dangerous: we rob him of his good name and of his liberty, and subject him to tortures called "treatments." Of course, the alleged mental patient is considered dangerous *because* he is perceived as "mentally different," an alien and alienated person whose conduct, unlike that of "normals," is unpredictable. In short, he is regarded as a particular kind of deviant—one who violates society's most basic interpersonal and linguistic rules.

It is important to note, however, that deviance is not, as it is often erroneously believed, a defect exhibited by, or contained in the personality of, an individual actor (and hence frequently attributed to bodily or mental illness); it is, instead, an inevitable consequence, and indeed an integral part, of the construction of social compacts or groups. Sociologists of deviance understand this well. For example, Howard S. Becker writes that "*social groups create deviance by making rules whose infraction constitutes deviance,* and by applying those rules to particular people and labeling them as outsiders. From this point of view, deviance is *not* a quality of the act the person commits, but rather a consequence of the application by others of rules and sanctions to an 'offender.' The deviant is one to whom that label has successfully been applied; deviant behavior is behavior that people so label."[6] (Italics in the original.)

Ordinarily, people labeled as deviant have in fact broken some rule (legal, religious, or social)—for example, the "hippies," or homosexuals; frequently, however, they have violated no such rules and are categorized as deviants only because respected authorities cast them in such a role—for example, innocent citizens labeled as Communists by Senator Joseph McCarthy, or prominent persons, like Senator Barry Goldwater, labeled as mentally ill by psychiatrists. Becker correctly emphasizes that "some people may be labeled deviant who in fact have not broken a rule . . . Deviance is not a quality that lies in behavior itself, but in the interaction between the person who commits an act and those who respond to it."[7]

Two important conclusions follow. One is that since deviance is rulebreaking, it is at once a disruptive and a stabilizing factor in society: only by publicly displaying what is not acceptable behavior can the members of the group learn, and remember, what is acceptable. Without rule-following, there cannot be *social life;* but without rulebreaking, there cannot be *personal identity.* Man's distinguishing characteristic is that he both obeys rules and disobeys them!

The other conclusion is that since medical disease (in the sense of deviance from biological, rather than social, norms) does not play the kind of role in social and personal life that social deviance does, the latter cannot be "treated" or eliminated the way the former can. Zealous campaigns to combat deviance, analogized to combating contagious disease—now so popularly waged against alcoholism, addiction, and "mental illness" generally—are therefore not only destined to fail, but contribute to that very dehumanization of man which those who fight for better "mental health" so loudly decry.

Scapegoats, as we have seen, are a species of deviants: they are individuals (or groups) persecuted for their real or imputed deviance. In the preceding chapter, Sartre's ideas on anti-Semitism helped us understand the problem of society's struggle to expel evil; in this one, let us follow some of his thoughts on the scapegoat, to help us understand our attitude toward the mentally ill. For this, we shall look to his book on Genet.[8]

Once more, Sartre's point of departure is the premise that the average man wants to feel that he is good and virtuous. "The evildoer is the Other . . . It is therefore during a war that a Good man has the clearest conscience . . . Unfortunately, one cannot always be fighting. From time to time there must be peace. For peacetime, society has, in its wisdom, created what might be called professional evildoers. These evil men are as necessary to good men as whores are to decent women. They are therefore very carefully recruited. They must be bad by birth and without hope of change."[9]

I have tried to show how "mentally ill" evildoers are recruited in our contemporary society. The massive manpower mobilization in the Mental Health Movement* is best understood as an attempt to increase the number of mental patients "found" in society. Like mine owners hiring more laborers to tear more copper out of the bowels of the earth, the state and federal governments, their subdivisions, and private and philanthropic organizations are hiring more psychiatrists, psychologists, and social workers to tear more madmen out of the bowels of society. And for whose good? The answer can only be: for those who hire them, who define their task, and who, of course, pay them. This is why the transformation of the physician's role from that of healer of the sick individual to that of civil servant or bureaucrat is so important. The implications of this process for psychiatry are especially momentous.†

* The number of psychiatrists in the United States is increasing twice as fast as the population—3 percent versus 1.5 percent annually. (*Psychiat. Progress*, Vol. 4 [Jan.-Feb.], 1966, p. 1.) This rate of increase is especially significant because the number of physicians, from whose ranks psychiatrists are recruited, is barely keeping pace with the increase in the population.

Since physicians cannot meet the new Inquisition's gargantuan appetite for manpower, it is not surprising to find that the total number of "mental health workers" is rising at a much faster rate than the number of psychiatrists. "Between 1960 and 1965, the number of U.S. psychiatrists, psychologists, and other mental-health workers rose 44 percent." (*U.S. News and World Report*, Nov. 6, 1967, p. 48.)

† This perspective is not new to psychiatry. Applied to the family, it was for a while quite fashionable, especially among psychoanalysts and sociologists. One of its consequences was the conception of one or both parents as the "pathogens" in the family, creating mental illness in their children. The expression "schizophrenogenic mother" bears testimony to this point of view. For an example of this viewpoint, applied to the explanation of childhood psychosis, see Jules Henry, *Culture Against Man*, pp. 321–388; for another, applied to the explanation of juvenile delinquency, see Ruth S. Eissler, Scapegoats of Society, in Kurt R. Eissler (Ed.), *Searchlights on Delinquency*, pp. 288–305.

It is absurd to restrict this perspective to examinations of family relationships. The most powerful scapegoaters in modern society are the State and the

And where, asks Sartre, will the Just Man find evil? The same place as the Normal Man finds mental illness. "As Evil is negation, separation, disintegration," writes Sartre, "its natural representatives will be sought among the separated and separatists, among the unassimilable, the undesirable, the repressed, the rejected. The candidates include the oppressed and exploited in every category, the foreign workers, the national and ethnic minorities. But these are still not the best recruits. These people sometimes organize among themselves and become conscious of their race or class. They then discover, through hatred, the meaning of reciprocity, and the oppressor comes to personify Evil for them, just as they personify Evil for the oppressor. Fortunately there exist in our society products of disassimilation, castoffs: abandoned children, 'the poor,' bourgeois who have lost their status, 'lumpenproletariat,' déclassés of all kinds, in short, all the wretched. With these we are tranquil. They cannot unite with any group since nobody wants them. . . . That is why, in general, we give them preference."[10]

Alexander and Zilboorg have led the charge to conquer these cast-off and wretched members of society for psychiatry; Menninger and Bazelon have mopped up the last traces of resistance. It has always been thus. Psychiatry and the jurisprudence it "enlightened" have produced no real innovation in this respect. Were the Just Man to pick someone his own size as the victim of his therapeutically disguised depredations he might encounter resistance, even rebellion. That must be avoided at all cost. For what is at stake here is not just a minor skirmish, or even a major battle; it is the whole war on evil and the insider's privilege to define the rules of the game. "Even choosing scapegoats," Sartre remarks, "the society of the just was careful to remove their means of uniting."[11]

Once the Just has his prey, the rest follows. We saw how it was done to witches. Sartre shows how it was done to Genet: ". . . he [Genet] is not allowed to talk except to confess."[12] Nor is the involuntary mental patient allowed to talk except to incriminate him-

---

psychiatric profession; hence the urgency to direct attention to them, no less than to private individuals. However, scrutiny of professional-client relations in psychiatry creates problems for psychiatrists, while scrutiny of family relations does not. Organized psychiatry's search for the "causes of mental illness" thus reminds one of the drunk who looks for his house key under the street light— not because that's where he dropped it, but because that's where the light is. In this connection, see also Chapter 12.

self as mentally ill. There is no human dialogue between the hospital psychiatrist and his committed patient; instead, the patient's talk is "clinical material." The mental patient is a living corpse, the words he utters the semantic exudates of his disease, to be examined, not heeded. Psychiatrists thus refer to the patient's speech as "productions," as if his words were sputum: they record it on magnetic tape, atomize it into linguistic bits and pieces, and replay his "tape" before students who listen to it as they would view tubercle bacilli under a microscope. These are the essential steps in the processing of man into mental patient; and this is the essential aim, the basic social mandate, of Institutional Psychiatry. The height of obscenity is when society pretends—as we do today, and as our ancestors did during the Inquisition—that in defining the Other as evil, we are helping him become good.

The aim of defining the Other as an alien, or as an alienated person, can only be to cast him out of the order of the normal man who belongs to and constitutes the group. The alienist was correctly named: He was an alienator. To be sure, men have always had their methods of producing deviants, enemies, subhuman humans. But only in the modern world has betrayal of the Other become exalted as the supreme proof of loyalty to the group. As we know, the denunciation of parents, friends, and colleagues as "subversives" has become the hallmark of the totalitarian state. Indeed, the logic of the collectivistic ethic dictates that a willingness to betray others should be regarded as the penultimate proof of one's loyalty to the group. The final torture-scene in Orwell's *Nineteen Eighty-Four*,[13] and Winston Smith's transformation from loving Julia to loving Big Brother, offer a striking illustration of this thesis.

In the confrontation that interests us here, O'Brien is "treating" Smith, whose "illness" is that he loves Julia more than he loves Big Brother. The "treatment" is in the best tradition of the Inquisition and Institutional Psychiatry: It is a threat of violence by a loving authority, communicated to a recalcitrant and misguided individual, aiming at the heretic's return to the fold. O'Brien's threat—so much like Rush's—is a horrible death through torture. "When I press this other lever," explains O'Brien, "the door of the cage will slide up. These starving brutes will shoot out of it like bullets. Have you ever seen a rat leap through the air? They will leap onto your face and bore straight into it. Sometimes they attack the eyes first. Sometimes they burrow through the cheeks and devour the tongue."[14]

Smith is paralyzed with fear. How can he save himself? What can he do? "Everything had gone black [writes Orwell]. For an instant, he was insane, a screaming animal. Yet he came out of the blackness clutching an idea."[15]

It is this idea that interests us here. In presenting it as he does, Orwell reveals his sure grasp of the significance, for collective life as we know it, of man's willingness to sacrifice the Other to save himself: Only through participating in the ritual destruction of the Other, only through committing existential cannibalism, is man admitted to membership in the modern State.

There was one and only one way to save himself [writes Orwell]. He must interpose another human being, the *body* of another human being, between himself and the rats . . .

The mask was closing on his face. The wire brushed his cheek. And then—no, it was not relief, only hope, a tiny fragment of hope. Too late, perhaps too late. But he had suddenly understood [sic] that in the whole world there was just *one* person to whom he could transfer his punishment—*one* body that he could thrust between himself and the rats. And he was shouting frantically, over and over:

"Do it to Julia! Do it to Julia! Not me! Julia! I don't care what you do to her. Tear her face off, strip her to the bones. Not me!"[16]

Smith saves himself. Or what is left of him. Soon he and Julia meet, for the last time.

"I betrayed you," she said baldly.

"I betrayed you," he said . . .

"Sometimes," she said, "they threaten you with something—something you can't stand up to, can't even think about. And then you say, 'Don't do it to me, do it to somebody else, do it to so-and-so.' . . . You think there's no other way of saving yourself, and you're quite ready to save yourself that way. You *want* it to happen to the other person. You don't give a damn what they suffer. All you care about is yourself . . . And after that, you don't feel the same toward the other person any longer."

"No," he said, "you don't feel the same."[17]

Loving the Other as you love yourself is the original sin, the unforgivable crime in a society dominated by the tribal ethic. You must love only the group, the all-embracing collective. Orwell makes this terrifyingly clear in his penultimate paragraph: "He [Smith] gazed up at the enormous face. Forty years it had taken him to learn what kind of smile was hidden beneath the dark moustache. O cruel, needless misunderstanding! . . . But it was all right, everything was all right, the struggle was finished. He had won the victory over himself. He loved Big Brother."*[18]

The tendency (perhaps one ought to call it a "reflex") to sacrifice a scapegoat in order to save the group from disintegration and, hence, the self from dissolution, is clearly basic to man's social nature. It follows that man's *refusal* to sacrifice scapegoats—and his willingness to recognize and bear his own and his group's situation and responsibility in the world—would be a major step in his moral development, comparable, perhaps, to his rejection of cannibalism. I believe, indeed, that in the rejection, or transcending, of the scapegoat principle lies the greatest moral challenge for modern man. On its resolution may hinge the fate of our species. Let me outline briefly what I mean.

The tiger eats his prey; the cannibal his victim. We know, however, that the similarity between these two meals is deceptive. The cannibal incorporates his victim's body, not for its value as *food*, but for its value as *meaning*. He could feed his body in other ways; but not his spirit. The cannibal, by ingesting his victim's flesh, actually feasts on his soul. "The flesh and blood of dead men," says Frazer, "are commonly eaten and drunk to inspire bravery, wisdom, or other qualities for which the men themselves were remarkable, or which are supposed to have their special seat in the particular part eaten."[19]

---

* In an interesting article, Shengold offers a purely psychological interpretation—devoid of moral and political considerations—of Orwell's imagery of the rat torture in *Nineteen Eighty-Four*. His psychological, and my social, analysis of Smith's torture and conversion complement each other. See Leonard Shengold, The effects of over-stimulation: Rat people, *Int. J. Psycho-Anal.*, 48: 403–415, 1967.

There are, of course, important parallels between the child's relations to the parents in the family, and the adult's relations to the State in society. It is by elucidating these similarities, rather than by "analyzing" famous or infamous public figures, that psychoanalysis could, I think, best contribute to the social sciences.

Although relinquishing literal or physical cannibalism was no doubt a vast moral achievement for man, it neither eliminated nor curtailed his symbolic or existential cannibalism. Partaking of the victim's flesh was a ceremonial occasion, constituting the ritual performance through which this double act of cannibalism was carried out. Linton's description of the religious practices of the Aztecs is illustrative. "To the Aztecs," he writes, "the [human] sacrifices were an expression of true religious feeling. The gods required to be strengthened, and nothing was more nutritive than the human heart, which the priest offered the god, still dripping from the body on the stone altars. The victims suffered none of the torture and humilation which the Spanish Inquisition was meting out to heretics at this time. Many of the captives who were dedicated to the gods were treated with honor, given luxurious quarters with handmaidens to attend them, and feasted and regaled. The ceremonial death, executed before crowds of thrilled spectators, frequently brought religious ecstasy to the victim also, for death on the altar insured his entry into the highest heaven. Even the knowledge that his body would be thrown down the steps and carried off to form a ceremonial feast was not a humiliation, for the flesh was consumed in the belief that the eaters were establishing a closer union with the god himself. It was a religious concept not unlike that of the Christian communion, except that the Aztecs were painfully literal about it."[20]

Abolishing this kind of ceremony did not abolish man's greed to rob his neighbor of the meaning he has given his life. On the contrary, freed of the limitations of a method which required the actual sacrifice and eating of human beings, man's rapaciousness for appropriating his fellow man's soul gained in impetus: murder of the soul having been separated from murder of the body, symbolic cannibalism could flourish, henceforth unrestrained by prohibitions against the taking of human life.* In short, our ancestors were, and we remain, existential or spiritual cannibals. As a rule, we live off the meaning others give their lives, validating our humanity

* As we know, the Christian religions strongly foster the belief in and the value of symbolic cannibalism. In this way, they inhibit man's strivings toward spiritual independence and retard the development of social practices and institutions favorable to the free creation, rather than the imitative theft, of life meaning. We touch here on a complex subject whose further treatment must await another occasion.

by invalidating theirs.* If this is true, the most important question for man as a moral being becomes: Can we overcome our existential cannibalism? Can we create meaning for our lives without demeaning the lives of others? Without attempting to answer this question, let me briefly review the problem and offer some remarks about it.

As a carnivorous animal, man learns to live off other animals. He also learns, as do most animals, not to kill members of his own species for food. In eschewing the eating of human flesh, man takes a great leap forward in his moral development.

As a human being, however, man is a particular kind of animal: a social animal. As such, he is always the member of a group, never a solitary individual. The conditions of his membership in the group go far in defining the kind of person he becomes. To remain the member of a group, man must often attack and sacrifice nonmembers. Wars against external enemies have traditionally propelled individuals into playing this role, thus integrating them further into their own groups. In addition, man also converts members of his own group into nonmembers, so that they may then be attacked and sacrificed. These are the wars on internal enemies which members of the group must wage or risk alienation. What purpose does such behavior serve, other than genuine self-defense (whose genuineness can, perhaps, rarely be reliably ascertained by individuals or groups who feel threatened)?

The concept of aggression, innate and acquired, has been long popular as an explanation.[21] But it explains nothing. An instinct of aggression explains war and persecution no better than a drive to power explains economic competition and political leadership. We need more specific, more functional, concepts to explain man's social behavior. The analysis here offered, emphasizing man's self-validation as good through his invalidation of his enemy as bad, points to what is perhaps a fresh clue to man's incredible destructiveness toward his fellow man. The clue may lie in man's double cannibalism, described above.

The evidence for man's rapaciousness as existential cannibal is

* This is no doubt one of the reasons why the creative person—the truly innovative artist or scientist—is admired and valued: transcending symbolic cannibalism, he learns to give his life meaning without robbing others of the meaning they have given theirs. He "produces" more meaning than he "consumes."

incontestable. Typically, we confirm our loyalty to our group by asserting the disloyalty of others (in or outside the group) to it; we thus purchase membership in the community by excluding others from it. This appears to be one of the basic, invariant rules of social behavior. Because of this, the scapegoat is the indispensable victim of noncannibalistic societies.

In "primitive" societies, men not only eat human flesh for its magical-symbolic characteristics, but also endow animals with human and superhuman qualities. In "modern" societies, men do the reverse: they eschew eating human flesh, but endow persons with subhuman and animalistic qualities (for example, witches, Jews, madmen, et cetera).

The cannibal incorporates his victim to give himself virtue; we expel ours to give ourselves innocence. Ours is not only the more sophisticated, but perhaps also the graver, crime. And it is the crime that all of us, as a society, often require each other to commit. To refuse to persecute the socially accredited scapegoat is interpreted as an attack on society itself. This was clear during the Inquisition, in Nazi Germany, and on the West Coast of the United States between Pearl Harbor and the defeat of Japan. It is equally true today for the madman. To defend the rights of alleged mental patients is experienced as an attack on the integrity of society. The tendency is to cast the defender into the role of a thoughtless (or worse) advocate of the "rights" of "sex-fiends" to molest little girls, or of "homicidal maniacs" to assault their neighbors. The fact that far more violence is committed against mental patients than by them does not matter. The action of the tribe, of the collective, of the State, is experienced as right; that of the independent individual, as wrong. Kenneth Burke was right in concluding "that the sacrificial principle of victimage (the 'scapegoat') is intrinsic to human congregation."[22] Hence, we should—as Burke suggested—ask "not how the sacrificial motives revealed in the institutions of magic and religion might be eliminated in a scientific culture, but what new forms they take."[23]

In this book, I have tried to display the forms in which the perennial scapegoat principle manifests itself in the modern world. To this end, I have traced the transformation of medieval ideas about witches and their persecution by priests into our contemporary ideas about madmen and their persecution by physicians.

We have thus seen that, whenever men have wanted to degrade, exploit, oppress, or kill the Other, they have always declared him to be not "really" human. This has been a characteristic feature of human conquests, enslavements, and mass murders throughout history. Indeed, the oppressor is always confronted by the question of whether the victim is or is not a (fully) human being. This was the basic issue in the systematic anti-Semitism of Spain and Germany; in the European witch-hunts; in American Negro slavery; and in the modern, virtually worldwide persecution of the mentally ill. For if the victim is *not* fully human, if he is *not* a person, it follows that he can lay no more claim to the rights enumerated in the Declaration of Independence, the Declaration of the Rights of Man, or the Constitution, than can a cat, a dog, or any other non-human being. The language of the Constitution, said Frederick Douglass in 1895, is " 'We the people'—not we the white people, not even we the citizens, not we the privileged class, not we the high, not we the low, but we the people . . . we the human inhabitants; and if Negroes are people they are included in the benefits for which the Constitution of America was ordained and established."[24]

I suggest that what Douglass said about the Negro, we now extend and apply to the so-called mentally ill: If they are people, they, too, are included in the benefits for which the Constitution of the United States was ordained and established. And if they are not people, what are they?

EPILOGUE

"THE PAINTED BIRD"

To the right-thinking man, to be alone and to be
wrong are one and the same . . .

—Jean-Paul Sartre[1]

The unifying theme of this book—running through and connecting
a number of seemingly diverse topics discussed in it—is the idea
of the scapegoat and his function in the moral metabolism of
society. In particular, I have tried to show that social man fears the
Other and tries to destroy him; but that, paradoxically, he needs
the Other and, if need be, creates him, so that, by invalidating
him as evil, he may confirm himself as good.

These ideas are conveyed with consummate artistic skill by Jerzy
Kosinski in his extraordinary book, *The Painted Bird*. The title
alludes to this theme: "The Painted Bird" is the symbol of the
persecuted Other, of "The Tainted Man."

The story is a harrowing tale of what happens to a six-year-old
boy "from a large city in Eastern Europe [who] in the first weeks
of World War II . . . was sent by his parents, like thousands of other
children, to the shelter of a distant village."[2] To protect their
son from the ravages of war in the capital, his middle-class parents
entrust him to the care of a peasant woman. Within two months of
his arrival, she dies. The parents do not know this, and the child
has no way of making contact with them. He is adrift on a sea of
humanity, sometimes indifferent, often hostile, rarely protective.

During his peregrinations through the countryside of war-torn
Poland, the child lives, for a while, under the protection of Lekh,
a huge, solitary, but decent young man, who makes his living as a

trapper. It is this episode that so movingly portrays the theme that, to the tribe, the Other is a dangerous alien, the member of a hostile species that must be destroyed.

Lekh loves a woman, Ludmila, with whom he has passionate sexual relations. Ludmila had been raped as a young girl and, when we meet her, is crazed with sexual lust. The farmers call her "Stupid Ludmila." The episode that concerns us here occurs after a period of separation between Lekh and Ludmila. I shall quote it in full.

Sometimes days passed and Stupid Ludmila did not appear in the forest. Lekh would become possessed by a silent rage. He would stare solemnly at the birds in the cages, mumbling something to himself. Finally, after prolonged scrutiny, he would choose the strongest bird, tie it to his wrist and prepare stinking paints of different colors which he mixed together from the most varied components. When the colors satisfied him, Lekh would turn the bird over and paint its wings, head, and breast in rainbow hues until it became more dappled and vivid than a bouquet of wildflowers.

Then we would go into the thick of the forest. There Lekh took out the painted bird and ordered me to hold it in my hand and squeeze it lightly. The bird would begin to twitter and attract a flock of the same species which would fly nervously over our heads. Our prisoner, hearing them, strained toward them, warbling more loudly, its little heart, locked in its freshly painted breast, beating violently.

When a sufficient number of birds gathered above our heads, Lekh would give me a sign to release the prisoner. It would soar, happy and free, a spot of rainbow against the backdrop of clouds, and then plunge into the waiting grown flock. For an instant the birds were confounded. The painted bird circled from one end of the flock to the other, vainly trying to convince its kin that it was one of them. But, dazzled by its brilliant colors, they flew around it unconvinced. The painted bird would be forced farther and farther away as it zealously tried to enter the ranks of the flock. We saw soon afterwards how one bird after another would peel off in a fierce attack. Shortly the many-hued shape lost its place in the sky and dropped to the ground. These incidents happened often. When we finally found the painted birds they were usually dead. Lekh keenly examined the number of blows which the birds had received. Blood seeped through their colored wings, diluting the paint and soiling Lekh's hands.[3]

Still, Stupid Ludmila does not return. To vent his frustrated rage, Lekh prepares another bird-sacrifice. This is how Kosinski describes it:

One day he trapped a large raven, whose wings he painted red, the breast green, and the tail blue. When a flock of ravens appeared over our hut, Lekh freed the painted bird. As soon as it joined the flock a desperate battle began. The changeling was attacked from all sides. Black, red, green, blue feathers began to drop at our feet. The ravens ran amuck in the skies, and suddenly the painted raven plummeted to the freshly-plowed soil. It was still alive, opening its beak and vainly trying to move its wings. Its eyes had been pecked out, and fresh blood streamed over its painted feathers. It made yet another attempt to flutter up from the sticky earth, but its strength was gone.[4]

The Painted Bird is the perfect symbol of the Other, the Stranger, the Scapegoat. With inimitable skill, Kosinski shows us both faces of this phenomenon: if the Other is unlike the members of the herd, he is cast out of the group and destroyed; if he is like them, man intervenes and makes him appear different, so that he may be cast out of the group and destroyed. As Lekh paints his raven, so psychiatrists discolor their patients, and society as a whole taints its citizens. This is the grand strategy of discrimination, invalidation, and scapegoating. Man searches for, creates, and imputes differences, the better to alienate the Other. By casting out the Other, Just Man aggrandizes himself and vents his frustrated anger in a manner approved by his fellows. To man, the herd animal, as to his nonhuman ancestors, safety lies in similarity. This is why conformity is good, and deviance evil. Emerson understood this well. "Society everywhere is in conspiracy against the manhood of every one of its members," he warned. "The virtue in most request is conformity. Self-reliance is its aversion."[5]

Anyone who values individual liberty, human diversity, and respect for persons can only be dismayed at this spectacle. To one who believes, as I do, that the physician ought to be a protector of the individual, even when the individual comes in conflict with society, it is especially dismaying that, in our day, the painting of birds has become an accepted medical activity, and that, among the colors used, psychiatric diagnoses are most in fashion.

APPENDIX

A SYNOPTIC HISTORY OF PERSECUTIONS FOR WITCHCRAFT AND MENTAL ILLNESS

> "They question my right to the title of philan-
> thropist," Marat exclaims . . . "Ah, what injustice!
> Who cannot see that I want to cut off a few heads
> to save a great number?" . . . Naturally—all historic
> actions are performed at a price. But Marat, making
> his final calculations, claimed two hundred and
> seventy-three thousand heads. But he compromised
> the therapeutic aspect of the operation by screaming
> during the massacre: "Brand them with hot irons,
> cut off their thumbs, tear out their tongues!"
>
> *—Albert Camus*[1]

The subject matter of psychiatry is human conflict. But conflict must be arbitrated, controlled, resolved. Thus, man has always found it necessary to employ various methods for dealing with interpersonal and social antagonisms. All such methods have one thing in common: the use of force. However, perhaps because men are men and not animals, they cannot simply coerce, oppress, or exterminate their fellows; they must also explain and justify it.

For the past three centuries, Western man found his explanation and justification for oppression in the ideology of science, particularly in medicine, psychiatry, and the social sciences. During the four preceding centuries, religion—through the Scriptures, the churches, and the Inquisition—served this purpose. This dialectic of oppression and liberation constitutes, of course, a subject matter for history.

The themes of witchcraft and mental illness, the Inquisition and Institutional Psychiatry, form two distinct threads which may be pulled from the tapestry of Western man's cultural history and examined separately. This is what I have tried to do in this volume. To place the events and ideas here examined in their historical context, and to provide the reader with a sweeping, though fragmentary, view of the whole fabric from which these threads have been torn, I have assembled, in this Appendix, a synoptic history of the dates, events, men, and opinions that seemed to me illustrative of, and significant in, the unfolding of this aspect of our history.

1204   The last major Crusade ends.

1209   Pope Innocent III orders the Crusade against the Albigenses, a heretical sect in the south of France. By the middle of the fourteenth century, an estimated one million Frenchmen suspected of being Albigensians are killed.

1215   King John grants the Magna Charta.

1215   Pope Innocent III orders the convocation of the Fourth Lateran Council in Rome, to consider the problem of disciplining heretics and Jews. Its resolutions mark the beginning of new Crusades—against heretics and Jews. "By orders of the Lateran Council, Jews could neither hold public office nor employ Christian domestics. They could not charge high rates of interest for loaning money and the crusaders were released from all payments. Severe punishments were hinted at for converts who were lax in their new faith. . . . It was decreed that all Jews were to wear a distinctive garment or a special badge, to set them apart from other men."[2]

1226   Louis VIII establishes the lazar-house law for France. The number of leprosariums in France reaches more than 2,000, with 43 in Paris.

1245   The citadel of Montségur falls to the Inquisition: 200 Cathari are burned in one day.

1298   The Jews of Röttingen, in Franconia, are charged with the desecration of a sacramental wafer. The entire Jewish community is burned alive at the stake.[3]

1348   The confession of the Jew, Agiment, of Geneva, as reported by Jacob von Königshofen (1346–1420), a German historian of Strasbourg: "Agiment took this package full of poison and carried it with him to Venice, and when he came there he threw and scattered a portion of it into a well or cistern of fresh water . . . in order to poison the people . . . He confesses further that he put some of this poison into the public fountain of the city of Toulouse . . ."[4]

C. 1350   The bubonic plague sweeps Europe. One third of the population succumbs to the epidemic. The Jews are accused of causing the plague: in Germany, many are exterminated; the rest flee to Poland and Russia.

C. 1375   The Cathari and the Waldenses are liquidated. The Inquisition turns against witchcraft as heresy.

1377   The Bethlehem Hospital in London is used to house mental patients; thus originates the term "Bedlam."

1400–1492   Large numbers of Spanish Jews are converted to Catholicism.

1400–1500   Leprosy disappears from Europe.

1412   Laws against Jews and Moors become an accepted part of Spanish society. On the advice of a zealous Valencian saint, Vincent Ferrer, and the chancellor of Castile, Bishop Pablo de Santa Maria, himself a converted Jew, it is decreed that Jews and Moors should wear distinguishing badges, be deprived of the right to hold office or possess titles, and should not change their domicile; in addition, they are excluded from various trades, forbidden to bear arms, and not allowed to eat, drink, or even talk with Christians.[5]

1444   The first shipment of Negro slaves from Africa arrives in Portugal.

C. 1450   Johann Gutenberg invents the printing press.

1468   The Church declares witchcraft a *crimen excepta* (exceptional crime); accordingly, in witch trials ordinary legal rules and safeguards are suspended (e.g., all incriminating evidence is admitted; torture to force confession is permitted and even encouraged).

1478   The Spanish Inquisition is established. Its aim is to examine the genuineness of the faith of converted Jews.

1484   The Bull of Pope Innocent VIII: "Desiring with the most heartfelt anxiety . . . that all heretical depravity should be driven far from the frontiers and bournes of the faithful, We very gladly proclaim and even restate those particular means and methods whereby Our pious desire may obtain its wished effect . . ."[6]

1485   At an *auto-da-fé* held by the Spanish Inquisition at Toledo, fifty-two persons are burned at the stake for the heresy of practicing Jewish rites.[7]

1486   Jacob Sprenger and Heinrich Krämer publish the *Malleus*

Malleficarum (The Hammer of Witches); this work goes through at least 16 German editions, 11 French, 2 Italian, and several English; it affirms that "the belief that there are such things as witches is so essential a part of the Catholic faith that obstinately to maintain the opposite opinion manifestly savors of heresy."[8]

1492   Ferdinand and Isabella order the expulsion of Jews from Spain.

1492   Columbus's first voyage to America. "It is memorable that but for *converso* finance Columbus's first voyage in 1492 would not have been carried out; it was the Aragonese who protected and financed the expedition; Jews and *conversos*, including a Jewish interpreter, formed part of the crew; and there is a possibility that Columbus himself was descended from a family of Catalan *conversos*."[9]

1517   Martin Luther nails his ninety-five theses against indulgences on the door of the castle church in Wittenberg.

1518   Heinrich Cornelius Agrippa of Nettesheim, a doctor both of theology and medicine, fights against the belief in witchcraft and the Inquisition. In a letter to a judge on behalf of a young woman accused of witchcraft, and in reference to the *Malleus Maleficarum*, he writes: "Oh, egregious sophism! Is it thus that in these days we theologize? Do figments like these move us to the torturing of harmless women?"[10]

1543   Martin Luther publishes his anti-Semitic pamphlet, *Concerning the Jews and Their Lies.* He accuses the Jews of poisoning wells and murdering Christian children, and urges the princes to destroy Jewish synagogues and to confiscate Jewish property. In one of his last sermons, he denounces Jewish physicians for "understanding the art of poisoning" their patients, and concludes with the admonition: "I say to you lastly, as a countryman, if the Jews refuse to be converted, we ought not to suffer them or bear with them any longer."[11]

1545   Calvin leads a campaign against witchcraft in Geneva; 31 persons are executed as witches.

1553   Michael Servetus, Spanish-born physician and discoverer of the pulmonary circulation, is burned alive as a heretic in Geneva. Servetus's first work, *De Trinitatis Erroribus (On the Erroneousness of the Trinity),* published in 1531, in which he questions the tripersonality of the Godhead and the eternal life of Jesus, makes him a heretic in the eyes of both Catholics and Protestants.

1557 Pope Paul IV causes, through the Inquisition at Rome, the publication of the *Index Librorum Prohibitorum (Index of Prohibited Books)*. The full name of the Index is: *Index Auctorum et Librorum qui Tanquam Haeretici aut Suspecti aut Perversi ab Officio S. R. Inquisitionis Reprobantur et in Universita Christiana Republica Interdictur (Index of Authors and Books Which Were Disapproved as Heretic or Suspected of Heresy or of Being Harmful by the Office of the Holy Roman Inquisition, Sanctae Romanae, and are Prohibited in All Christian Countries.)* "To appear on the Roman Index was almost proof of intellectual distinction, and the complete roster would serve as a sufficient index to the intellectual history of Europe."[12] The Index is abolished in 1966 by Pope Paul VI.

1563 Johann Weyer publishes *De Praestigiis Daemonum (The Deceptions of the Devil)*, in Basel: "But when the great searcher of hearts, from whom nothing is hidden, shall appear, your wicked deeds shall be revealed, you tyrants, sanguinary judges, butchers, torturers, and ferocious robbers, who have thrown out humanity and do not know mercy."[13] The book is placed on the *Index Librorum Prohibitorum*.

1568 The Spanish Inquisition declares the entire population of the Netherlands to be heretics and condemns it to death.[14]

1572 The Massacre of Saint Bartholoméw's Day (August 24): an estimated 30,000 Huguenots (French Protestants, followers of Calvin) are killed in a single day.

1572 Witchcraft is declared a capital crime in Lutheran Saxony.

1580 Jean Bodin publishes *De la démonomanie des sorciers (The Demonomania of Witches)*, a tract to help judges combat witchcraft; he defines a witch as "One who knowing God's law tries to bring about some act through an agreement with the Devil."[15]

1596 Nicholas Rémy, attorney-general of Lorraine, boasts of having had burned 900 persons as witches between 1581 and 1591. He claims that "Everything which is unknown lies . . . in the cursed domain of demonology; for there are no unexplained facts. Whatever is not normal is due to the Devil."[16]

1598 Henry of Navarre proclaims the Edict of Nantes: the Huguenots are promised religious and political freedom.

1600 Giordano Bruno, Italian philosopher and former Dominican monk, is burned at the stake for his advocacy of Copernican theory.

C. 1600 "Slow poisoning" becomes a popular crime. "In the year

1659, it was made known to Pope Alexander VII that great numbers of young women had avowed in the confessional that they had poisoned their husbands with slow poison. The Catholic clergy, who in general hold the secrets of the confessional so sacred, were shocked and alarmed at the extraordinary prevalence of the crime."[17]

1605   Francis Bacon publishes *The Advancement of Learning.*

1610   Last execution for witchcraft in Holland.

1618–1648   The Thirty Years' War, the last of the great religious wars of Europe. National conquest replaces religious conversion as a military aim. The loyalty of the individual is gradually transferred from the Church to the State.

C. 1620   Opening of the House of Correction *(Zuchthaus)* in Hamburg signals the beginning of a vast system of such institutions, for assistance and punishment, similar to the French *hôpitaux généraux.*

1621   Francisco Suarez, S.J., Spanish theologian and philosopher, publishes *On the Means Which May Be Used for the Conversion and Coercion of Unbelievers Who Are Not Apostates:* ". . . the rites of unbelievers ought not to be tolerated; for they are superstitious and injurious to God, Whose true worship the princes of those kingdoms are bound to advance. . . . Familiarity with Jews is placed under a general prohibition. . . . living in the same house with Jews is specifically forbidden. . . . [I]n case of illness, Christians are forbidden to call in Jews; at least they are forbidden to do so for the purpose of treatment. . . . the true reason for this discrimination against the Jews is thought to be the fact that intercourse with the Jews involves more peril on account of their greater pertinacity and their hatred of the Christian religion."[18]

1631   Friedrich von Spee, a Jesuit priest, publishes *Cautio Criminalis (Precautions for Prosecutors)*, a major attempt to stem the tidal wave of witch-hunting. "There is a frequent phrase used by judges, that the accused has confessed without torture and thus is undeniably guilty. I wondered at this and made inquiry and learned that in reality they were tortured . . ."[19] He explained his prematurely gray hair by saying that "Grief has turned my hair white—grief on account of witches whom I have accompanied to the stake."[20]

1632   Galileo publishes *A Dialogue on the Two Principal Systems of the World.* He is tried by the Inquisition. His book remains on the *Index Librorum Prohibitorum* for over 200 years.

1633   Father Urbain Grandier of Loudun is accused of witchcraft. Dr. Claude Quillet, a local physician, detects fraud at the public exorcism wherein Father Grandier was accused and wants to give his testimony before the commission; he is ordered arrested and saves himself only by flight to Italy. Father Grandier is burned at the stake in 1634.[21]

1650 Herman Loher, an official of the law court at Rheinbach, escapes to Amsterdam, becomes a Dutch citizen, and denounces the witch trials. To fall into the hands of a witch judge, he writes, "is just as if a condemned person were forced to fight with lions, bears, and wolves for his life, and were prevented from protecting himself, since he is deprived of weapons of every description."[22]

C. 1650 After the city council of Hall, in Württemberg, gives some privileges to Jewish physicians, the clergy protests that "it were better to die with Christ than to be cured by a Jew doctor aided by the devil."[23]

1656 Louis XIII decrees the founding of the *Hôpital Général* of Paris. "In its functioning, or in its purpose, the *Hôpital Général* had nothing to do with any medical concepts . . . a few years after its foundation, the *Hôpital Général* of Paris alone contained six thousand persons, or around one percent of the population."[24]

1657 The *Academia del Cimento,* with Borelli, Galileo, and Torricelli among the founding members, is established in Florence. It is disbanded in 1667. Several members are prosecuted by the Inquisition.

1662 The Royal Society of London, with Boyle, Hooke, and Newton among the founding members, is established.

1666 The *Académie des Sciences* of Paris is founded.

1676 Louis XIII decrees the establishment of an *hôpital général* in every city of the kingdom. "It confined the debauched, spendthrift fathers, prodigal sons, blasphemers, men who 'seek to undo themselves,' libertines. . . . We leave it to medical archeology to determine whether or not a man was sick, criminal, or insane who was admitted to the hospital for 'derangement of morals,' or because he had 'mistreated his wife,' and tried several times to kill himself."[25]

1684 Last execution for witchcraft in England.

1685 Louis XIV repeals the Edict of Nantes: the Huguenots flee France, many settling in the American colonies.

1687 Newton publishes his *Mathematical Principles of Natural Philosophy*.

1689 Cotton Mather publishes his *Memorable Providences Re-*

lating to Witchcrafts and Possessions, showing that "there is both a God and a Devil and Witchcraft," and setting the stage for the Salem witch-hunts and witch trials.

1692   The witch trials at Salem, Massachusetts.

1693   Cotton Mather publishes his *Wonders of the Invisible World.* Written to justify the witch trials at Salem, it is offered as "an account of the suffering brought upon the country by witchcraft."[26]

1696   Cotton Mather writes in his *Diaries:* "This day, from the dust, where I lay prostrate before the Lord, I lift up my cries: For the Conversion of the Jewish Nation, and for my own having the happiness, at some time or other, to baptize a Jew, that should by my ministry, be brought home unto the Lord."[27]

1700   Robert Calef, a Boston merchant, publishes his *More Wonders of the Invisible World,* a rebuttal to Cotton Mather's *Wonders of the Invisible World.* Because of the censorship exercised by Increase Mather, Cotton's father, then president of Harvard College, Calef's book was published in London; copies of it were publicly burned in Boston.

1711   The General Court of Massachusetts reverses the attainders of 22 of the 31 persons convicted as witches in Salem in 1692.

1716   The theory that masturbation causes insanity is initiated with the publication, in London, of *Onania, or the Heinous Sin of Self-Pollution* (author uncertain). The book is translated into many languages and, by 1764, is in its 80th edition.

1721   Cotton Mather, embittered for having repeatedly been passed over for the presidency of Harvard, persuades Elihu Yale, a London merchant, to found a Calvinist college along his own lines in New Haven, Connecticut.

1728   Daniel Defoe, English journalist and novelist: "This leads me to exclaim against the vile practice now so much in vogue among the better Sort, as they are called, but the worst Sort in fact, namely, the sending their Wives to Mad-Houses at every Whim or Dislike, that they may be more secure and undisturbed in their Debaucheries . . . If they are not mad when they go into these cursed Houses, they are soon made so by the barbarous Usage they there suffer . . . Is it not enough to make anyone mad to be suddenly clap'd up, stripp'd, whipp'd, ill fed, and worse us'd? To have no Reason assigned for such Treatment, no Crime alledg'd, or Accusers to confront?"[28]

1736   Penal laws against witchcraft repealed in England. "To [religious] believers the abolition of the penal laws [against witchcraft] was a dangerous as well as an irreligious act which flouted the Biblical rule that no witch should be suffered to live. Even so wise and gentle a man as John Wesley denounced the Act on the ground that giving up witchcraft was giving up the Bible."[29]

1745　Last execution for witchcraft in France.

1750　Frederick II of Prussia, popularly known as Frederick the Great, issues his *Charter for the Jews of Prussia*: "We herewith establish, regulate, and order earnestly that in the future no Jew shall presume to engage in any manual trade."[30]

1752　The Pennsylvania Hospital in Philadelphia, the first institution in America to receive mental patients, is opened. " 'State care,' in the sense of mental patients as wards of the body politic, has been an accepted principle in the United States since the middle 1700's."[31]

1758　Simon-André D. Tissot publishes his *Onanism, or a Treatise Upon the Diseases Produced by Masturbation* in Lausanne. The book places respectable medical opinion behind the concept of "masturbatory insanity." "The dangers which Tissot sees in masturbation are terrifying. It is hell on earth, but without purgatory."[32]

1764　Voltaire's *Dictionaire philosophique (Philosophical Dictionary)* is published in Geneva.

1765　Chevalier de la Barre, a young admirer of Voltaire's, refuses to uncover and kneel in the presence of a religious procession. He is tortured, his tongue is ripped out, and he is beheaded. His body is burned at the stake unto which the executioners also commit a copy of Voltaire's *Philosophical Dictionary*.[33]

1772　Slavery is abolished in England.

1772　The English theologian, the Reverend Edward Massey, preaches against inoculation for smallpox. He publishes a sermon entitled *The Dangerous and Sinful Practice of Inoculation,* in which he declares that Job's distemper was smallpox; that he had been inoculated by the devil; that diseases are sent by Providence for punishment of sin; and that the proposed attempt to prevent smallpox is "a diabolical operation."[34]

1773　The Williamsburg Asylum, in Williamsburg, Virginia, the first institution in America devoted exclusively to the care of the mentally sick, is opened.

1775　The American Revolutionary War begins.

1776　The Declaration of Independence of the American Colonies.

1784   The *Narrenturm* is built in Vienna. It is the first institution in Europe intended exclusively "for the treatment of the insane." In 1843 it is described as "a wretched, filthy prison, close and ill-ventilated, its smell overpowering, and the sight of the patients, frantic, chained, and many of them naked, disgusting to the visitor."[35]

1787   The U.S. Constitution is drafted.

1789   The French Revolution begins. The Declaration of the Rights of Man.

1791   The Bill of Rights is added to the Constitution.

1792   The guillotine—developed by Dr. Joseph Ignace Guillotin, a physician and member of the Revolutionary Assembly—becomes the official instrument of execution in France. The first machine is assembled at the Bicêtre Hospital, one of the *hôpitaux généraux,* or insane asylums, in Paris. It is tried first on live sheep, then on three cadavers from the Bicêtre. Wrote Guillotin in his will: "It is difficult to do good to men without causing oneself some unpleasantness."[36]

1793   Last execution for witchcraft in Poland.

1793   Louis XVI is guillotined.

1798   A group of clergymen and physicians in Boston form an Anti-Vaccination Society. They denounce vaccination against smallpox as "bidding defiance to Heaven itself, even to the will of God," and declare that "the law of God prohibits its practice."[37]

1801   Philippe Pinel publishes his *Traité médico-philosophique sur l'aliénation mentale, ou la manie* (English translation, 1806). Though opposed to restraining patients by chains, Pinel strongly advocates their coercion and repression, which he calls "moral treatment": "If [the madman] is met, however, by a force evidently and convincingly superior, he submits without opposition or violence. This is a great and invaluable secret in the management of well regulated hospitals."[38] "In the preceding cases of insanity, we trace the happy effects of intimidation, without severity; of oppression, without violence; and of triumph, without outrage."[39] He praises "a system of management . . . in a monastic establishment in the South of France. One of the inspectors visited each chamber, at least, once every day. If he found any of the maniacs behaving extravagantly, stirring up quarrels or tumults, making any objections to his victuals, or refusing to go to bed at night, he was told in a manner, which of itself was calculated to terrify him, that unless he instantly conformed he would have to receive in the morning ten severe lashes, as a punishment for his disobedience."[40] "To apply our principles of moral treatment, with undiscriminating uniformity, to maniacs of every character and condition in society, would be equally ridiculous and unadvisable. A Russian peasant, or a slave of Jamaica, ought evidently to be managed by other maxims than those which would exclusively apply to the case of a well bred irritable Frenchman, unused to coercion and impatient of tyranny."[41]

C. 1803 Johann Christian Reil: "It is a revolting spectacle to see a brash empiric [physician] cavorting with his mental patient . . . Woe unto the image of God who falls into such hands!"[42]

1805 The German mental hospital system is established. Prince Karl August von Hardenberg declares that "The state must concern itself with all institutions for those with damaged minds . . . In this important and difficult field of medicine only unrelenting efforts will enable us to carve out advances for the good of suffering mankind. Perfection can be achieved only in such institutions."[43]

1808 The British Parliament outlaws slave trading.

1811 Theodric Romeyn Beck of New York City publishes his *Inaugural Dissertation on Insanity:* "Moral management . . . consists in removing patients from their residence to some proper asylum; . . . A system of humane vigilance is adopted. . . . The rules most proper to be observed are the following: Convince the lunatics that the power of the physician and keeper is absolute; . . . if unruly, forbid them the company of others, use the strait waistcoast, confine them in a dark and quiet room . . ."[44]

1812 Benjamin Rush publishes his *Medical Inquiries and Observations upon the Diseases of the Mind,* the first American textbook of psychiatry. He declares that "terror acts powerfully on the body through the medium of the mind, and should be employed in the cure of madness"; and that masturbation causes "seminal weakness, impotence, dysury, tabes dorsalis, pulmonary consumption, dyspepsia, dimness of sight, vertigo, epilepsy, hypochondriasis, loss of memory, manalgia, fatuity, and death."[45]

1812 Under the impetus of French Napoleonic laws, the Prussian edict "On the Civil Equality of the Jews" is issued.

1813 The Cortes of Cadiz decrees, by a vote of ninety against sixty, that the Inquisition is "incompatible with the Constitution." Ruiz Padron declares: "Peoples to come, nations who will one day enter the bosom of the Church, future generations—will you in time believe that there once existed in the Catholic Church a tribunal called the Holy Inquisition?"[46] However, this decree does not have legal force to formally abolish the Inquisition.

1814   Ferdinand VII officially restores, by royal decree, the entire machinery of the Spanish Inquisition.

1814   The House of Commons of the British Parliament appoints a committee to investigate the barbarous conditions in madhouses.

1816   John Reid publishes his *Essays on Insanity, Hypochondriasis, and Other Nervous Affections*: "A heavy responsibility presses upon those who preside or officiate in the asylums of lunacy. Little is known how much injustice is committed, and how much useless and wantonly inflicted misery is endured in those infirmaries for disordered, or rather cemeteries for deceased intellect . . . Many of the depots for the captivity of intellectual invalids may be regarded only as nurseries for and manufactories of madness . . ."[47]

1816   Jean Esquirol asserts that masturbation "is recognized in all countries as a common cause of insanity." By 1838 he adds epilepsy, melancholia, and suicide to the conditions caused by masturbation.[48]

1820   Ferdinand VII abolishes the Spanish Inquisition. Despite this, the Inquisition lingers on until terminated by a formal decree, issued by Queen Christina, in 1834.

1826   Last executions in Spain for religious heresy. A Quaker, a *marrano*, and a Deist are put to death.[49]

1828   Samuel William Nicoll, Recorder of Doncaster and York, publishes *An Inquiry into the Present State of Visitation, in Asylums for the Reception of the Insane*: "The keeper must himself be kept. If he be not watched and punished, an asylum is likely to be little beyond an alternation of reciprocal violence between the prisoner and gaoler."[50]

1833   The emancipation of slaves in the British Dominions.

1837   Isaac Ray publishes his *Treatise on the Medical Jurisprudence of Insanity*.

1837   Robert Gardiner Hill, at the Lincoln Asylum in England, abolishes the use of fetters and restraints. John Conolly, at Hanwell in England, does the same by 1839.

1837   Dr. Amariah Brigham, superintendent of the Utica State Asylum in New York, writes: "It is gratifying to be able to state that no fact relating to insanity appears better established than the general certainty of curing it in its early stages."[51]

1840   The sixth census of the United States discloses that free northern Negroes have a much higher incidence of insanity than the white population of the nation or the Negro slaves in the South. Critics of the census claim that the number of Negroes listed as insane in some towns exceeds the total number of Negroes living there.[52]

1840   Dr. Samuel B. Woodward, superintendent of the Worcester State Hospital in Massachusetts, announces that "The cures in recent cases . . . had reached the awe-inspiring point of 90 per cent."[53]

1840–1860   "Huge sums were appropriated for mental hospitals. Unfortunately, the greater part of these outlays was used to line the pockets of politically wise contractors, and to build ostentatious, heavily ornate facades in the Victorian tradition, with little thought given to suitable interiors or to utility in general. Such public hospitals came to be known as 'pauper palaces' and 'lunacy cathedrals.' "[54]

1841   Dom Guéranger: "The spectacle of an entire people placed under a curse for having crucified the Son of God gives Christians food for thought . . . This immense atonement for an infinite crime must continue until the end of the world."[55]

1842   Dr. Thomas S. Kirkbride, superintendent of the Pennsylvania Hospital for the Insane, writes: "The general proposition that truly recent cases of insanity are commonly very curable . . . may be considered as fully established." Comments Albert Deutsch: "The belief . . . that insanity was easily curable if treated early enough rapidly impressed itself on the public and professional mind and soon reached the plane of established, immutable dogma. But what of the psychiatric profession as a whole? Did it raise any objections to the spread of this fallacy? On the contrary: except for a very few instances, it not only subscribed wholeheartedly to the current misconceptions, but stimulated and strengthened them as best it could."[56]

1842   C. F. Lallemand, a French physician, warns in his 3-volume treatise on "involuntary seminal emissions," that if masturbation became any commoner it would "menace the future of modern societies; therefore it is urgently necessary for us to try to extirpate this public calamity."[57]

1843   Daniel M'Naghten, charged with shooting Edward Drummond, Sir Robert Peel's secretary, is acquitted as "not guilty on the grounds of insanity." After being acquitted, M'Naghten is incarcerated, first in the Bethlehem Hospital, and later in the Broadmoor Institution for the Criminally Insane, where he dies in 1865. His case sets precedent as the M'Naghten rule: ". . . to establish a defense on the ground of insanity, it must be clearly proved that, at the time of the committing of the act, the party accused was labouring under such a defect of reason, from disease of the mind, as not to know the nature and quality of the act he was doing; or if he did know it, that he did not know he was doing what was wrong."[58]

1843   Dorothea L. Dix addresses the legislature of Massachusetts, to plead for the building of state mental hospitals: "I come to present the strong claims of suffering humanity. I come to place before the Legislature of Massachusetts the condition of the miserable, the desolate, the outcast. I come as the advocate of the helpless, forgotten, insane, and idiotic men and women; . . . of beings wretched in our prisons, and more wretched in our almshouses. . . . I would speak as kindly as possible of all wardens, keepers, and other responsible officers, believing that most of these have erred not through hardness of heart and wilful cruelty so much as want of skill and knowledge . . ."[59]

1844   Founding of the Association of Medical Superintendents of American Institutions for the Insane. Its first official proposition is: "Resolved, that it is the unanimous sense of this convention that the attempt to abandon entirely the use of all means of personal restraint is not sanctioned by the true interests of the insane."[60] In 1921, this organization becomes the American Psychiatric Association.

1844   James M'Cune Smith, a northern free Negro, rebuts, in three long letters to the *New York Tribune,* the claim that free Negroes are especially prone to insanity: "It is a prevalent opinion that Emancipation has made the Free blacks deaf, dumb, blind, idiots, insane, etc. . . . Freedom has not made us mad; it has strengthened our minds by throwing us upon our own resources, and has bound us to American Institutions with a tenacity which nothing but death can overcome."[61]

1850–1900   The psychiatric doctrine that masturbation causes insanity reaches its crest. "By about 1880 the individual who might wish for unconscious reasons to tie, chain, or infibulate sexually active children or mental patients—the two most readily available captive audiences—to adorn them with grotesque appliances, encase them in plaster of paris, leather or rubber, to beat, frighten, or even castrate them, to cauterize or denervate the genitalia, could find humane and respectable medical authority for doing so in good conscience. Masturbational insanity was now real enough—it was affecting the medical profession."[62]

1851   Illinois commitment statute enacted. "Married women . . . may be entered or detained in the hospital [the state asylum at Jacksonville] at the request of the husband of the woman . . . without evidence of insanity required in other cases."[63]

1854   President Franklin Pierce vetoes a bill, inspired by Dorothea Dix and passed by Congress, which would have appropriated 12,500,000 acres of public land for the "indigent insane."[64]

1854   The Massachusetts Commission on Lunacy releases its *Report on Insanity and Idiocy in Massachusetts:* "Insanity is, then, a part and parcel of poverty; and wherever that involves any considerable number of persons, this disease is manifested."[65]

1855   The New York State legislature authorizes the construction of separate institutions for the criminally insane.[66]

1855   An editorial in the *New Orleans Medical and Surgical Journal* asserts that " . . . neither the plague, nor war, nor smallpox, nor a crowd of similar evils, have resulted more disastrously for humanity, than the habit of masturbation: it is the destroying element of civilized society."[67]

1856   Sigmund Freud is born.

1856   Emil Kraepelin is born.

1858   To rebut abolitionist arguments, the superintendent of the Asylum of the State of Louisiana at Jackson declares that ". . . it is exceedingly seldom that our slaves ever become insane . . . it cannot be got around, that [the slaves'] great exemption from insanity is due to their situation, the protection the law guarantees to them, the restraint of a mild state of servitude, the freedom from all anxiety respecting their present and future wants, the withholding (in a great degree) of all spiritous and drugged liquors, and all other forms of excess into which the free negroes plunge."[68]

1859   Heinrich Neumann, a German psychiatrist who maintains that there are not several kinds of mental diseases but only one, declares: "The time has finally come for us to stop looking for the herb or salt or metal which . . . will cure mania, imbecility, insanity, fury or passion. They will never be found until pills are discovered which will transform a naughty child into a well-mannered child, an ignorant man into a skilled artist, a rude swain into a polished gentleman. We can rub patients with martyr's ointment until . . . [we] turn up more martyrs than the Spanish Inquisition—and still face the fact that we are not one step closer to curing insanity. Man's psychic activities are changed, not by medicines, but by habit, training, and exertion."[69]

1859   John Stuart Mill publishes *On Liberty*: "[T]he only purpose for which power can be rightfully exercised over any member of the community, against his will, is to prevent harm to others. His own good, either physical or moral, is not sufficient warrant. . . . Each person is the proper guardian of his own health, whether bodily, *or* mental and spiritual."[70]

1861   Florence Nightingale observes that "Patients do what they are expected to do."[71]

1863   Lincoln issues the Emancipation Proclamation.

1863   David Skae, a Scottish physician, introduces the term "masturbatory insanity," for insanity believed to be caused by onanism.[72]

1864   The Broadmoor Institution for the Criminally Insane is opened. Among the first inmates is Daniel M'Naghten, transferred there after 21 years at the Bethlehem Hospital.

1865   The Thirteenth Amendment to the Constitution of the United States, abolishing slavery, is enacted.

1865   Ignaz Semmelweis, discoverer of the nature of childbed fever, dies in a private insane asylum.[73]

1865   The *Boston Times Messenger* characterizes the McLean Hospital as the "hobby of the Boston aristocrats," and as a place where sane patients unjustly confined are unable to obtain a hearing. The hospital is described as a "bastille for the incarceration of some persons obnoxious to their relatives."[74]

1867   Henry Maudsley publishes *The Physiology and Pathology of the Mind,* considered, by Aubrey Lewis, "a turning point in English psychiatry."[75]

1868   Henry Maudsley: "A later and still worse stage at which these degenerate beings [i.e., masturbators] arrive is one of moody and morose self-absorption, and of extreme loss of mental powers. They are sullen, silent, etc., . . . Such, then, is the natural history of physical and mental degeneracy produced in men by self-abuse. It is a miserable picture of human degradation . . . I have no faith in the employment of physical means to check what has become a serious mental disease; the sooner he sinks to his degraded rest the better for himself, and the better for the world which is well rid of him. It is a poor and sad conclusion to come to, but it is an unavoidable one."[76]

1869 John Stuart Mill publishes his essay on *The Subjection of Women:* "But was there ever any domination which did not appear natural to those who possessed it? . . . the generality of the male sex cannot yet tolerate the idea of living with an equal . . . In the present day, power holds a smoother language, and whomsoever it oppresses, always pretends to do so for their own good . . ."[77]

1869 Karl Ludwig Kahlbaum, German psychiatrist famous as an early classifier of mental diseases, gives the name "catatonia" to a syndrome which he believes is caused chiefly by prolonged or excessive masturbation.[78]

1872 Emancipation of the Jews throughout the entire territory of the German empire.

1876 T. Pouillet, a French physician, begins his "medicophilosophical" treatise on masturbation with the words: "Of all the vices and of all the misdeeds which may properly be called crimes against nature, which devour humanity, menace its physical vitality, and tend to destroy its intellectual and moral faculties, one of the greatest and most widespread—no one will deny it—is masturbation."[79]

1882 Richard von Krafft-Ebing, professor of psychiatry at the University of Vienna, and one of the foremost psychiatrists of his time, publishes *Psychopathia Sexualis,* establishing himself as the founder of modern psychiatric sexology. He believes that masturbation may lead to homosexuality.[80] Havelock Ellis describes the years of Krafft-Ebing's domination of the field of sex, from 1882 on, "as one vast clinic where no helpful or progressive activities were possible. Sexual science meant for the most part a subdivision of psychiatry; the vague doctrine of 'degeneration' . . . was regarded as the only key to unlock all doors, while the normal psychology of sex was dismissed—when it was mentioned at all—in a few perfunctory lines."[81] In 1896, presiding at the meeting of the Vienna Society of Psychiatry and Neurology, where Freud reads his paper on "The Etiology of Hysteria," Krafft-Ebing dismisses the presentation as a "scientific fairy tale."[82]

1883   Emil Kraepelin publishes his *Psychiatrie, Ein Lehrbuch* (*A Textbook of Psychiatry*). He systematizes psychiatry with a new diagnostic scheme; defines two major psychoses—manic-depressive insanity, which tends to improve and recur spontaneously, and dementia praecox, which tends toward progressive deterioration.

C. 1885   Hysteria is treated by means of the surgical removal of the ovary in Paris; by means of the surgical removal of the clitoris in London and Vienna; and by means of cauterization of the clitoris in Heidelberg.

1886   King Ludwig II of Bavaria is deposed. Dr. Bernard von Gudden, professor of psychiatry at the University of Munich, heads a team of psychiatrists who declare Ludwig to be the victim of a "mental sickness which psychiatrists know well and call paranoia." Ludwig is taken into custody and placed under psychiatric observation; he kills Dr. Gudden and commits suicide.[83]

1890   Jonathan Hutchinson, president of the Royal College of Surgeons, treats masturbation by means of circumcision, and advocates that "measures more radical than circumcision would, if public opinion permitted their adoption, be a true kindness to many patients of both sexes."[84]

1892   Anton Pavlovich Chekhov: "Twelve thousand people are swindled a year; the whole [mental] hospital business is founded, just as it was twenty years ago, on theft, scandal, slander, nepotism, on crude charlatanism, and, as before, the hospital is an immoral institution, exceedingly harmful to the health of the inmates."[85]

1894   Alfred Dreyfus, a Jewish officer of the French General Staff, is accused and convicted of espionage for Germany. Anti-Semitism sweeps France. In 1898, Émile Zola publishes *J'Accuse,* his denunciation of Dreyfus's false conviction; he is tried for calumny of the army, is convicted, and flees to England. In 1906—a year after Church and State are separated in France—Dreyfus's sentence is annulled and he is acquitted of all charges.

1895   Judaism is recognized as a legal religion in Hungary. The rights of full citizenship are bestowed on Hungarian Jews.

1897   Johann Weyer's *De Praestigiis Daemonum* appears on the *Index Librorum Prohibitorum* for the last time.

1900   Sigmund Freud publishes *The Interpretation of Dreams.*

1903   Count Sergey Yulievich Witte, Russian statesman, speaking to Theodor Herzl, founder of Zionism: "I used to say to the late Emperor Alexander III, 'Your Majesty, if it were possible to drown the six or seven million Jews of Russia in the Black Sea, I would be completely in favor of it. If it is not possible, we must let them go on living.' "[86]

1903 *The Protocols of the Elders of Zion* is published in Russia. Commissioned by Czar Nicholas II, it is written by the Greek Orthodox monk Sergei Nilus. It purports to be a document, drafted by a group of conspiratorial Jews, known as the Elders of Zion, about their plan to conquer the world. Its aim is to inflame the passions of the Russian peasants and turn them against the Jews. This forged document becomes an important source in the literature of twentieth-century anti-Semitism.[87]

1904 The Annual Report of the Friends' Asylum, in Philadelphia, records that "It is pleasant to bear witness to the fact that mental medicine has been entering upon a new era during the past few years, and in consequence the purview of asylum practice has largely changed. . . ."[88]

1905 Bernard Sachs, prominent New York psychiatrist and author of *A Treatise on Nervous Diseases of Children,* recommends the treatment of masturbation in children by cautery to the spine and genitals.[89]

1908 Clifford Whittingham Beers sparks the founding of the Connecticut Society for Mental Hygiene, the first state association of its kind and the beginning of the organized mental health movement in the United States. Beers's book, *A Mind that Found Itself: An Autobiography,* is published: "An insane man is an insane man, and while insane, should be placed in an institution for treatment."[90]

1909 The National Committee for Mental Hygiene is founded. The first official business of the Committee, in 1912, is to adopt a resolution "urging Congress to provide for adequate mental examination of immigrants."[91] The Committee also presses "for the principle of complete state care, that is, mental institutions to be owned and operated by state governments."[92]

1910 Charles Binet-Sanglé publishes *La folie de Jésus (The Madness of Jesus):* "In short, the nature of the hallucinations of Jesus, as they are described in the orthodox Gospels, permits us to conclude that the founder of the Christian religion was afflicted with religious paranoia."[93]

1911 Eugen Bleuler coins the term "schizophrenia."

1911 German psychiatry boasts of 225 private mental hospitals, 187 public mental hospitals, 85 institutions for alcoholics, 16 university clinics, 11 mental wards in prisons, and 5 mental wards in military hospitals; 143,410 persons are admitted to these institutions in a single year. The number of "practicing alienists" is 1,376.[94]

1912 William Hirsch, an American psychiatrist, publishes *Conclusions of a Psychiatrist,* in which he claims that Jesus suffered from the mental illness known as paranoia. "Everything that we know about him conforms so perfectly to the clinical picture of paranoia that it is hardly conceivable that people can even question the accuracy of the diagnosis."[95]

1913 Albert Schweitzer publishes his medical dissertation titled *The Sanity of the Eschatological Jesus.* His aim is to refute the contentions of certain psychiatrists that Jesus was insane, and to prove that he was sane. "I have undertaken in the present book to examine thoroughly the conjecture . . . that Jesus . . . is to be adjudged in some fashion as psychopathic. . . . That I command the impartiality necessary for this undertaking I believe I have proved by my former studies in the field of the life of Jesus. . . . The only symptoms [of Jesus] to be accepted as historical and possibly to be discussed from the psychiatric point of view—the high estimate which Jesus has of himself and perhaps also the hallucination at the baptism—fall far short of proving the existence of mental illness."[96]

1917 Emil Kraepelin: "The great war in which we are now engaged has compelled us to recognize the fact that science could forge for us a host of effective weapons for use against a hostile world. Should it be otherwise if we are fighting an internal enemy [i.e., mental illness] seeking to destroy the fabric of our existence? . . . We ought therefore to note with pride and satisfaction that it was possible for us in Germany in the middle of a raging war to take the first step toward establishing a research institute for the purpose of determining the nature of mental diseases and of discovering techniques for effecting their prevention, alleviation, and cure. All those who have contributed to the success of this great undertaking, especially His Majesty our King . . . merit our most cordial thanks . . . Ground has already been broken for new approaches that will enable us to win a victory over the direst afflictions that can beset man."[97]

1918 Ernest Jones, pioneer British psychoanalyst, holds that "true neurasthenia . . . will be found to depend on excessive onanism or involuntary seminal emissions."[98]

1919   The Eighteenth (Prohibition) Amendment is added to the U.S. Constitution. It is repealed in 1933.

1924   The American Orthopsychiatric Association is formed. The organization is initiated by Karl Menninger, who sends a letter to twenty-six leading American psychiatrists urging them to form a new group "of representatives of the neuro-psychiatric or medical view of crime."[99]

1925   Adolf Hitler publishes *Mein Kampf:* "By their very exterior you could tell these [Jews] were no lovers of water, and, to your distress, you often knew it with your eyes closed. . . . I often grew sick to my stomach from the smell of these caftan-wearers. Added to this, there was their unclean dress and their generally unheroic appearance. All this could scarcely be called attractive, but it became positively repulsive when, in addition to their physical uncleanliness, you discovered the moral stains on this 'chosen people.' . . . Was there any form of filth or profligacy, particularly in cultural life, without at least one Jew involved in it? . . . Today I believe that I am acting in accordance with the will of the Almighty Creator: by defending myself against the Jew, I am fighting for the work of the Lord."[100]

1928   Ladislaus Joseph von Meduna of Budapest introduces Metrazol shock treatment into psychiatry.

1929   Franz Alexander and Hugo Staub publish *The Criminal, the Judge, and the Public:* "The neurotic criminal . . . is a sick person. . . . If he is curable, he should be incarcerated for the duration of psychiatric treatment so long as he still represents a menace to society. If he is incurable, he belongs in a hospital for incurables for life."[101]

1930   Karl Menninger publishes *The Human Mind:* ". . . what science or scientist is interested in *justice?* Is pneumonia just? Or cancer?"[102]

1930   The First International Congress on Mental Hygiene is held, in Washington, D.C.

1933   Adolf Hitler becomes Chancellor of Germany.

1933   Louis Thomas McFadden, congressman from Pennsylvania, in a speech in the House of Representatives: "Mr. Speaker, there is no real persecution of Jews in Germany . . . but there has been a pretended persecution of them because there are 200,000 unwanted Communistic Jews in Germany, largely Galician Jews . . . and Germany is very anxious to get rid of those particular Communistic Jews. . . . They are willing to keep the rich Jews like Max Warburg and Franz Mendelssohn."[103]

1933   Manfred Sakel of Vienna introduces insulin shock treatment into psychiatry.

1935   Egas Moniz of Lisbon introduces prefrontal lobotomy into psychiatry.

1935   The Nuremberg Laws are enacted. Sexual intercourse between Germans and Jews is prohibited by law.

1938   U. Cerletti and L. Bini of Rome introduce electric shock treatment into psychiatry.

1938   The Nazis forbid the treatment of Aryans by Jewish physicians on the pain of heavy penalty for both patient and doctor.[104]

1938   Karl Bonhoeffer, professor of psychiatry at the University of Berlin, heads a team of German psychiatrists who, with a group of military men, plan to overthrow Hitler by arresting him, declaring him insane, and confining him in a mental institution. The "psychiatric putsch" is not carried out.[105]

1938   Harry F. Anslinger, U.S. Commissioner of Narcotics: "The Narcotics Section recognizes the great danger of marijuana due to its definite impairment of the mentality and the fact that its continuous use leads directly to the insane asylum."[106]

1939   With the outbreak of the war, Hitler orders, on September 1, the implementation of the National Socialist "euthanasia program": "Incurably sick persons should be granted mercy death." The first gas chambers are built in mental hospitals and the gassing of mental patients (and some other chronically ill persons) begins. During the next two years, approximately 50,000 (non-Jewish) Germans are killed with carbon-monoxide gas in death rooms disguised exactly as they later were in Auschwitz, as shower rooms and bathrooms.[107]

1940   Edward E. Strecker, in his Thomas Salmon Memorial Lecture, declares that "Unquestionably, the world is sick—mentally sick. . . . Political opportunism offers panaceas of communism, fascism, and totalitarianism . . . [which] operate by attempting to produce an intense nationalism. Mental hygiene can scarcely regard them as realities offering much incentive to recovery. Rather they would seem to be mass psychopathologies. . . . Among the extant political ideologies and practices, democracy comes closest to a fulfillment of mental hygiene ideals of mature and independent thinking."[108]

1941   George H. Stevenson, president of the American Psychiatric Association, declares that "This challenge [to prevent the occurrence of wars] comes to us because of the close relationship between the etiological factors as seen in the individual psychosis and in the international psychosis—war. . . . We do know that there are many psychopathological factors constantly determining toward war, which we as psychiatrists are able to evaluate more adequately than other groups who have not had our type of training or experience. . . . When the history of our second century comes to be written, may it be recorded that the American Psychiatric Association was largely responsible for the elimination of the international psychosis—war."[109]

1941   The gassing of mental patients in Germany stops and the systematic gassing of Jews in the East starts. The men in charge of this program come either "from Hitler's Chancellery or from the Reich Health Department . . ." The murder factories at Auschwitz, Chelmno, Majdanek, Belzek, Treblinka, and Sobibor are officially named "Charitable Foundations for Institutional Care."[110]

1943   Jewish leaders deceive their people about the existence of murder factories in some of the concentration camps, because, as for example Dr. Leo Baeck, former chief rabbi of Berlin, claimed, "living in the expectation of death by gassing would only be harder." As a result, "Jews volunteered for deportation from Theresienstadt [where there were no gas chambers] to Auschwitz [where there were], and denounced those who tried to tell them the truth as being 'not sane.'"[111]

1945   Albert Deutsch undertakes ". . . a journalistic survey of state mental hospitals . . . Most of them [the hospitals] were located in or near great centers of culture in our wealthier states, such as New York, Michigan, Ohio, California, and Pennsylvania. In some of the wards there were scenes that rivaled the horrors of the Nazi concentration camps—hundreds of naked mental patients herded into huge, barn-like, filth-infested wards, in all degrees of deterioration, untended and untreated, stripped of every vestige of human decency, many in stages of semistarvation."[112]

1945   Ezra Pound, indicted for treason, is declared mentally unfit to stand trial. He is confined in St. Elizabeths Hospital in Washington, D.C., for thirteen years. In 1958, he released as "incurably insane, but not dangerous." Judge Bolitha J. Laws speaks these words to the jury that declared Pound insane: ". . . in a case of this type, where the Government and the defense representative have united in a clear unequivocal view with regard to the situation, I presume you will have no difficulty in making up your mind." In three minutes the jury brings in a verdict of "unsound mind."[113]

1946 President Harry S. Truman signs the National Mental Health Act into law. The Act authorizes the expansion of the functions of the Mental Hygiene Division of the Public Health Service.

1946 Brock Chisholm, director of General Medical Services in the Canadian army during World War II, and general secretary of the United Nations World Health Organization: "With the other human sciences, psychiatry must now decide what is to be the immediate future of the human race. No one else can. And this is the prime responsibility of psychiatry."[114]

1949 The Mental Hygiene Division of the U.S. Public Health Service is reorganized and becomes the National Institute of Mental Health.

1950 The American mental health movement shifts into high gear: the Psychiatric Foundation, the National Mental Health Foundation, and the National Committee for Mental Hygiene merge to form the National Association for Mental Health.

1952 The tranquilizing drugs are introduced into psychiatric practice; they provide a new chemical method for controlling patients in mental hospitals. These drugs spark the development of a new discipline, called psychopharmacology, the study of drugs useful in the treatment of mental illness and their application in clinical practice. The use of these pharmacologic agents lends support to the belief that psychiatric disorders are medical diseases, curable by specific drugs.

1952 Congress enacts the McCarran Act providing, among other things, that "aliens afflicted with (a) psychopathic personality [are to be] excluded from admission into the United States."[115] Hereafter, homosexual immigrants are automatically categorized as "psychopathic personalities" and, if they have entered the country subsequent to the enactment of this law, are deported.[116]

1954 The New York State Community Mental Health Services Act, the first mental health legislation of its kind in the United States, is enacted.

1954   Monte Durham, a man charged with housebreaking, is acquitted as "not guilty by reason of insanity," and confined in St. Elizabeths Hospital. His case sets legal precedent as the Durham rule: "The rule we now hold . . . is simply that an accused is not criminally responsible if his unlawful act was the product of mental disease or mental defect."[117]

1955   Egas Moniz is awarded the Nobel Prize for Physiology or Medicine for the treatment of schizophrenia by prefrontal lobotomy.

1957   Abe Fortas, court-appointed defense counsel in *Durham* v. *United States* and subsequently Associate Justice of the Supreme Court of the United States: "What, then, is the basic significance of the *Durham* case? It is, I suggest, that the law has recognized modern psychiatry. It has taken notice of and acted upon the discoveries of psychiatry as to the enormous range, complexity, and variety of mental disorders and their profound effect upon behavior. . . . Psychiatry is given a card of admission [into the courtroom] on its own merits, and because of its own competence to aid in classifying those who should be held criminally responsible and those who should be treated as psychologically or emotionally disordered. . . . Durham is a charter, a bill of rights, for psychiatry . . ."[118]

1957   The Commonwealth of Massachusetts reverses the attainders of all those convicted as witches in Salem but not covered by the act of 1711.

1957   The U.S. Court of Appeals for the District of Columbia declares that "If . . . [the defendant] has a mental illness which makes it likely that he will commit other violent acts when his sentence is served, imprisonment is not a remedy. Not only would it be wrong to imprison him, but imprisonment would not secure the community against repetitions of his violence. Hospitalization, on the other hand, would serve the dual purpose of giving him the treatment required for his illness and keeping him confined until it would be safe to release him."[119]

1960   On July 3, George Lincoln Rockwell, commander of the American Nazi Party, is arrested in Washington, D.C., while addressing an open-air gathering. At the request of the prosecution, he is committed for thirty days for psychiatric observation at the District of Columbia General Hospital. In his report to the Court, the chief psychiatrist states, in part: "In my opinion, he [Rockwell] has a Paranoid Personality.

. . . [However, to] bring in psychiatric testimony which may be construed as interference with his right of free speech and his removal from society because of a difference in political ideology will bring discredit to the psychiatric profession and will further Mr. Rockwell's cause." In August, Rockwell is declared mentally fit to stand trial, found guilty of disorderly conduct, and fined one hundred dollars.[120]

1961   George Lincoln Rockwell: "The startling answer to the Jewish enigma is that the Jews are insane. The Jews as a race are paranoid. This sick people must be stopped before they drag the world down with them." In 1965, Rockwell elaborates this thesis as follows: "[The Jews] are a unique people that distinguishes them from the rest of the White Family of People. The Jewish masses are afflicted with the symptoms of paranoia: delusions of grandeur, delusions of persecution. The Jews believe themselves to be 'God's Chosen People,' and they eternally complain about 'persecution' . . ."[121]

1961   Adolf Eichmann, on trial in Jerusalem, is examined by half a dozen psychiatrists and is declared normal.[122] Robert Servatius, a Cologne lawyer defending Eichmann, seeks to exonerate his client by claiming Eichmann innocent of charges bearing on his responsibility for "the collection of skeletons, sterilizations, killings by gas, and similar medical matters. . . ." The presiding judge interrupts: "Dr. Servatius, I assume you made a slip of the tongue when you said that killing by gas was a medical matter." Servatius replies: "It was indeed a medical matter, since it was prepared by physicians; it was a matter of killing, and killing, too, is a medical matter."[123]

1961   The Subcommittee on Constitutional Rights of the Committee of the Judiciary of the U.S. Senate conducts hearings on "The Constitutional Rights of the Mentally Ill." Francis J. Braceland: "It is a feature of some illnesses that people do not have insight into the fact that they are sick. In short, sometimes it is necessary to protect them for a while from themselves . . ."[124] Jack Ewalt: "The basic purpose [of commitment] is to make sure that sick human beings get the care that is appropriate to their needs . . ."[125]

1962   The U.S. Supreme Court declares that narcotic addiction is a disease, not a crime, and that "a State might establish a program of compulsory treatment for those addicted to narcotics. Such a program of treatment might require periods of involuntary confinement."[126]

1963   President John F. Kennedy delivers his "Message to Congress Relative to Mental Illness and Mental Retardation": "I propose a national mental health program to assist in the inauguration of a wholly new emphasis and approach to care for the mentally ill. This approach relies primarily upon the new knowledge and new drugs acquired and developed in recent years which make it possible for most of the mentally ill to be successfully and quickly treated . . . We need a new type of health facility, one which will return mental health care to the mainstream of American medicine . . ."[127]

1963   President John F. Kennedy is assassinated in Dallas, Texas. Lee Harvey Oswald is charged with the murder. He is assassinated in jail by Jack Ruby. Both Oswald and Ruby are widely regarded as insane, and the crimes are dismissed as the senseless violence of two lunatics. "John F. Kennedy was killed by a lunatic, Lee Harvey Oswald, who had momentarily given loyalty to the paranoid Fidel Castro of Cuba. And Oswald was, in turn, within two days, slain by another madman, Jack Ruby."[128] "Had Oswald received psychiatric help when he was young, John Kennedy might be alive today."[129]

1964   1,189 members of the American Psychiatric Association declare Senator Barry Goldwater "psychologically unfit to serve as President of the United States." Many of the psychiatrists holding this opinion diagnose Senator Goldwater as suffering from paranoid schizophrenia or a related condition; sample diagnosis, offered by an anonymous psychiatrist at the Cornell Medical Center: "Senator Goldwater impresses me as being a paranoid personality or a schizophrenic, paranoid type. . . . He is a potentially dangerous man."[130]

1964   Sargent Shriver, director of the U.S. Office of Economic Opportunity: "Give us a healthy world—in the full sense—and Communism will finally disappear from the earth in every sense."[131]

1965   A syndicated columnist reports that the communist press has declared President Johnson ". . . ill, both physically and mentally."[132]

1966   President Lyndon B. Johnson declares that "the alcoholic suffers from a disease."[133] The American Civil Liberties Union urges that individuals accused of public intoxication should be treated as patients, not as criminals.

1967   Suh Tsung-hwa, Communist China's foremost neuropsychiatrist: ". . . Neuroses and psychoses do not exist here, not even paranoia."[134]

1967   An editorial in the *Journal of the American Medical Association* declares that "The contemporary physician sees suicide as a manifestation of emotional illness. Rarely does he view it in a context other than that of psychiatry."[135]

1967   In a "Position Statement on the Question of the Adequacy of Treatment," the American Psychiatric Association declares that "Restraints may be imposed [on the patient] from within by pharmacologic means or by locking the door of a ward. Either imposition may be a legitimate component of a treatment program."[136]

1967   Harvey J. Tompkins, president of the American Psychiatric Association, in his presidential address: "We are approaching a psychiatrist population of nearly 20,000, about four times as many as two decades ago. This gratifying growth could not have occurred without the government subsidies which have been channeled into professional education . . . It behooves us to move with decent haste to the self-acceptance and projection of a different image of ourselves—one that more nearly reflects the intellectual, social, political, and economic currents which, history demonstrates, have as much impact on the character of our practice as does the accumulation of new knowledge."[137]

1967   George Stevenson, former president of the American Psychiatric Association: "For us in the APA, war ought to be a psychiatric public health program. . . . A solution to this problem may still be a long time in the future, but that is no reason why we should continue to ignore it, or leave it only to politicians or to the propagandists of the extreme left or the extreme right . . . war behavior results basically from emotional disturbance."[138]

1967   Dick Gregory, Negro comedian: "This nation [the United States] is the number one racist country in the world, bar none. The country is . . . sick and insane."[139]

1968   Novelist Norman Mailer: "I think American society has become progressively insane . . ."[140]

1968   Herbert Marcuse, professor of philosophy at the University of California: "[In a proper democratic society, there should be] a withdrawal of toleration of speech and assembly from groups and movements which . . . oppose the extension of public services, social security, medical care, etc. . . . Inasmuch as this society [the U.S.] disposes over resources greater than ever before and at the same time distorts and abuses and wastes these resources more than ever before, I call this society insane . . ."[141]

1968 Drew Pearson, syndicated columnist: "For the first time in 192 years of American history, a man with an established mental disability is running for President of the United States. 'The official records,' Sen. [Wayne] Morse told the Senate, 'will show that Gov. Wallace . . . filed claim for compensation in June 1946, and in December 1946 was granted service-connected disability for psychoneurosis, for which an evaluation of 10 per cent was assigned.' . . . Some observers who have watched the mental gymnastics of his current campaign say the doctors were conservative."[142]

1968 The order of 1492, issued by King Ferdinand and Queen Isabella, expelling the Jews from Spain, is declared void by the Spanish government. On the same day (December 16, 1968), the first synagogue built in Spain in 600 years is opened.[143]

1968 Howard P. Rome, senior consultant in psychiatry at the Mayo Clinic and former president of the American Psychiatric Association: "Now, however, . . . we appreciate that in a very meaningful sense society can be sick too . . . Actually, no less than the entire world is a proper catchment area for present-day psychiatry, and psychiatry need not be appalled by the magnitude of this task."[144]

REFERENCES

Page v. Albert Camus, *The Rebel*, pp. 3–4.

PREFACE

1. Albert Camus, *The Rebel*, pp. v–vi.
2. Thomas S. Szasz, *The Myth of Mental Illness*.
3. John Stuart Mill, *The Subjection of Women*, pp. 251–252.
4. Thomas S. Szasz, *The Ethics of Psychoanalysis*.
5. R. G. Collingwood, *The Idea of History*, p. 10.

INTRODUCTION

1. John Stuart Mill, *The Subjection of Women*, p. 229.
2. Thomas S. Szasz, *The Myth of Mental Illness*.
3. Henry Sigerist, Introduction, in Gregory Zilboorg, *The Medical Man and the Witch During the Renaissance*, pp. ix–x.
4. See Thomas S. Szasz, *The Ethics of Psychoanalysis*.
5. See Thomas S. Szasz, *Law, Liberty, and Psychiatry*, and *Psychiatric Justice*.
6. See Thomas S. Szasz: Psychotherapy: A sociocultural perspective, *Comprehensive Psychiat.*, 7: 217–223 (Aug.), 1966.
7. John P. Callahan, Welfare clients called coerced, *New York Times*, July 22, 1967, p. 22.
8. A. Louis McGarry, Competency for trial and due process via the state mental hospital, *Amer. J. Psychiat.*, 122: 623–630 (Dec.), 1965.
9. Edith E. Asbury, Faster mental examinations ordered for defendants here, *New York Times*, July 8, 1967, p. 26.
10. For a sampling, see Anton Pavlovich Chekhov, Ward No. 6, in *Seven Short Stories by Chekhov*, pp. 106–157; Mary Jane Ward, *The Snake Pit*; Frank L. Wright, Jr., *Out of Sight, Out of Mind*; Lois Wille, The mental health clinic, Expressway to asylum, *Chicago Daily News*, Mar. 26, 1962; 11 times 12? Youth flunks mental exam, ibid., Mar. 27, 1962; Misfiled card saves salesman from mental hospital, ibid., Mar. 28, 1962; Why refugee asked for ticket to Russia, ibid., Mar. 29, 1962; S. J. Micciche, Bridgewater holds

colony of lost men, *Boston Globe*, Feb. 20, 1963; Some jailed 40 years for truancy, ibid.; Consultant psychiatrist, The scandal of the British mental hospital, *Manchester Guardian*, Mar. 19, 1965; Norman Shrapnel, Mental hospitals disclosures appall MP, ibid., Mar. 20, 1965; Sylvia Wilson, The Cinderellas (Letters), ibid., Mar. 30, 1965; D. J. Harvey, Typical conditions (Letters), ibid., March 30, 1965.

11. See Chapters 4 and 12–14.
12. Philip Shabecoff, Rightist activity rises in Germany, *New York Times*, Mar. 2, 1966, p. 14; Neo-Nazi activity rises in Germany, ibid., Mar. 6, 1966, p. 14.
13. Study depicts GI who marries in Vietnam as a troubled man, ibid., Feb. 25, 1967, p. 7.
14. John Osmundsen, Doctor discusses "mixed" marriage, ibid., Nov. 7, 1965, p. 73.

PART I THE INQUISITION AND INSTITUTIONAL PSYCHIATRY

1. Ernst Cassirer, *The Myth of the State*, p. 350.
2. Fyodor Dostoyevsky, *The Brothers Karamazov*, p. 301.

1 SOCIETY'S INTERNAL ENEMIES AND PROTECTORS

1. John Emerich Edward Dalberg Acton, Letter to Bishop Mandell Creighton, in *Essays on Freedom and Power*, p. 335.
2. Walter Ullman, *The Individual and Society in the Middle Ages*, p. 37.
3. Ibid.
4. Ibid., p. 25.
5. Ibid., p. 64.
6. Ibid., pp. 66, 69, 127.
7. Abram Leon Sachar, *A History of the Jews*, p. 194.
8. Max I. Dimont, *Jews, God, and History*, p. 224.
9. In this connection, see Norman Cohn, *The Pursuit of the Millennium*, especially pp. 307–319.
10. Dimont, p. 238.
11. Sachar, p. 198.
12. Quoted in Jacob Sprenger and Heinrich Krämer, *Malleus Maleficarum*, pp. xix–xx.
13. Sprenger and Krämer.
14. Ibid., p. 1.
15. Ibid., pp. 2–3.
16. Ibid., p. 41.
17. Ibid., p. 47.
18. Ibid.
19. Ibid., p. 87.
20. Ibid.
21. Ibid.
22. Ibid.

23. For further discussion, see Chapter 6.

24. Charles Mackay, *Extraordinary Popular Delusions and the Madness of Crowds*, p. 582.

25. Quoted in Gregory Zilboorg, *The Medical Man and the Witch During the Renaissance*, p. 140.

26. Quoted in Gregory Zilboorg, *A History of Medical Psychology*, p. 214.

27. Ibid., p. 215.

28. Ibid., p. 237.

29. Zilboorg, *Medical Man and Witch*, pp. 199–200.

30. Sprenger and Krämer, pp. 8–9.

31. Michel Foucault, *Madness and Civilization*, p. 39.

32. Ibid., p. 41.

33. George Rosen, Social attitudes to irrationality and madness in 17th and 18th century Europe, *J. Hist. Med. & All. Sc.*, 18: 220–240, 1963; p. 233.

34. Ibid.

35. Quoted in Rosen, p. 233.

36. Ibid., p. 237.

37. Illinois Statute Book, Sess. Laws 15, Sect. 10, 1851. Quoted in E. P. W. Packard, *The Prisoner's Hidden Life*, p. 37.

38. Foucault, p. 45.

39. Quoted in Emil Kraepelin, *One Hundred Years of Psychiatry*, p. 152.

40. John F. Kennedy, Message from the President of the United States relative to mental illness and mental retardation, Feb. 5, 1963, 88th Cong., 1st sess., H. Rep., Doc. No. 58.

41. Philip Q. Roche, *The Criminal Mind*, p. 241. For additional examples and a more extended criticism of this view, see Thomas S. Szasz, *Law, Liberty, and Psychiatry*, pp. 91–108.

42. Quoted in Jonas B. Robitscher, Tests of criminal responsibility: New rules and old problems, *Land & Water Law Rev.*, 3: 153–176, 1968; p. 157.

43. See, generally, Irving Brant, *The Bill of Rights;* for a critical discussion, see Friedrich A. Hayek, *The Constitution of Liberty*, especially pp. 188–191.

44. Bernard D. Hirsch, Informed consent to treatment: Medicolegal comment, in Albert Averbach and Melvin M. Belli (Eds.), *Tort and Medical Yearbook*, Vol. I, pp. 631–638.

45. Thomas S. Szasz, Science and public policy: The crime of involuntary mental hospitalization, *Med. Opin. & Rev.*, 4: 24–35 (May), 1968.

46. Ibid.

47. Quoted in Zilboorg, *History of Medical Psychology*, p. 557.

48. Jules Michelet, *Satanism and Witchcraft*, p. 145.

49. Christina Hole, *Witchcraft in England*, pp. 94, 101.

2 THE MALEFACTOR IDENTIFIED

1. Eugene Zamiatin, *We*, pp. 76–77.

2. Quoted in Rossell Hope Robbins, *The Encyclopedia of Witchcraft and Demonology*, p. 101.

3. Ibid.

4. For additional documentation, see Thomas S. Szasz, *Law, Liberty, and Psychiatry*, and *Psychiatric Justice*.

5. Quoted in Julien Cornell, *The Trial of Ezra Pound*, p. 37.

6. Ibid., p. 129.

7. Quoted in Robbins, p. 102.

8. Ibid., p. 480.

9. Ibid., pp. 482–483.

10. In this connection, see Erving Goffman, *Asylums*.

11. Ibid., p. 480.

12. Quoted in Frank J. Ayd, Jr., Guest editorial: Ugo Cerletti, M.D., 1877–1963, *Psychosomatics*, 4: A/6-A/7 (Nov.-Dec.), 1963.

13. Robbins, p. 483.

14. Jacob Sprenger and Heinrich Krämer, *Malleus Maleficarum*, p. 231.

15. See George Orwell, *Nineteen Eighty-Four;* and Robert Jay Lifton, *Thought Reform and the Psychology of Totalism*.

16. In this connection, see Thomas S. Szasz, The psychiatrist as double agent, *Trans-action*, 4: 16–24 (Oct.), 1967.

17. Quoted in Robbins, p. 552.

18. Ibid., p. 401.

19. Ibid., p. 492.

20. Ibid., p. 493.

21. See especially Thomas S. Szasz, *The Myth of Mental Illness*, and *Law, Liberty, and Psychiatry*.

22. Sherwin S. Radin, Mental health problems in school children, *J. of Sch. Health*, 32: 390–397 (Dec.), 1962; p. 392.

23. Christina Hole, *Witchcraft in England*, p. 75.

24. Ibid., p. 89.

25. Charles Mackay, *Extraordinary Popular Delusions and the Madness of Crowds*, p. 481.

26. Hole, p. 82.

27. See Thomas S. Szasz, Mental illness is a myth, *New York Times Magazine*, June 12, 1966, pp. 30, 90–92.

28. Mackay, p. 514.

29. Karl Menninger, *The Vital Balance*, pp. 478–482.

30. Ibid., p. 474.

31. Robert H. Felix, *Mental Illness*, pp. 28–29.

32. William C. Menninger, *Psychiatrist to a Troubled World*.

33. For a brilliant literary rendition of this theme, see Joaquin Machado de Assis, The Psychiatrist, in *The Psychiatrist and Other Stories*, pp. 1–45.

34. See, for example Leo Srole, Thomas S. Langer, Stanley T. Michael, Marvin K. Opler, and Thomas A. C. Rennie, *Mental Health in the Metropolis*, p. 138.

35. Karl Menninger, p. 32.

36. Ibid., p. 33.

37. Quoted in Mackay, p. 518.

38. Gregory Zilboorg, *The Medical Man and the Witch During the Renaissance*, p. 67.

39. See On suicide, *Time*, Nov. 25, 1966, p. 48; and Physician suicides cause concern, *Med. World News*, June 9, 1967, pp. 28–29.

3 THE MALEFACTOR AUTHENTICATED

1. Michel Foucault, *Madness and Civilization*, p. 205.
2. Henry Charles Lea, *The Inquisition of the Middle Ages*, p. 17.
3. See Lois Wille, Why refugee asked for ticket to Russia, *Chicago Daily News*, Mar. 29, 1962, p. 1; James E. Beaver, The "mentally ill" and the law: Sisyphus and Zeus, *Utah Law Rev.*, 1968: 1–71 (Mar.), 1968; p. 21.
4. *Duzynski v. Nosal*, 324 F. 2d 924 (7th Cir.), 1963.
5. For numerous case histories of the ways in which the individual accused of mental illness is unprotected by procedural safeguards, see Thomas S. Szasz, *Law, Liberty, and Psychiatry*. For four extensive case records of the denial, on psychiatric grounds, of the right to trial guaranteed by the Sixth Amendment to the Constitution, see Thomas S. Szasz, *Psychiatric Justice*.
6. See Szasz, *Psychiatric Justice*, especially pp. 85–143.
7. Thomas J. Scheff, Social conditions for rationality: How urban and rural courts deal with the mentally ill, *Amer. Behav. Scientist*, 7: 21–27 (Mar.), 1964; p. 21.
8. Lea, p. 37.
9. Ibid., p. 39.
10. Ibid., p. 96.
11. See Thomas S. Szasz, *The Myth of Mental Illness*.
12. Lea, p. 97.
13. Ibid., p. 113.
14. Francis J. Braceland, Testimony, in *Constitutional Rights of the Mentally Ill*, pp. 63–74; pp. 64, 71.
15. Lea, p. 97.
16. Lettres de cachet, in *Encyclopaedia Britannica*, Vol. 13, p. 971.
17. Barrows Dunham, *Heroes and Heretics*, p. 374.
18. Ibid., pp. 374–375.
19. Ibid.
20. Ibid., p. 375.
21. In this connection, see for example Hugh A. Ross: Commitment of the mentally ill: Problems of law and policy, *Mich. Law Rev.*, 57: 945–1–18 (May), 1959; Luis Kutner, The illusion of due process in commitment proceedings, *Northwestern Univer. Law Rev.*, 57: 383–399 (Sept.–Oct.), 1962.
22. See Frank T. Lindman and Donald M. McIntyre, Jr. (Eds.), *The Mentally Disabled and the Law*, pp. 15–106.
23. Testimony presented on behalf of the American Psychiatric Association by Francis J. Braceland, M.D., Psychiatrist in Chief, the Institute of Living, Hartford, Connecticut, and Jack R. Ewalt, M.D., Head of the Department of Psychiatry, Harvard Medical School, Boston, Mass., in *Constitutional Rights of the Mentally Ill*, pp. 79–85; pp. 80–81.
24. Thomas J. Scheff, *Being Mentally Ill*, p. 132.

25. Ibid., p. 133.
26. Ibid.
27. Ibid., p. 144.
28. Ibid., p. 154.
29. Lea, p. 101.
30. Braceland, Testimony, in *Constitutional Rights of the Mentally Ill,* pp. 64–65.
31. Ewalt, Testimony, ibid., p. 75.
32. Testimony presented on behalf of the American Psychiatric Association . . . , ibid., p. 80.
33. See especially Szasz, *Law, Liberty, and Psychiatry.*
34. Lea, p. 231.
35. Ibid., p. 103.
36. Henry Charles Lea, *A History of the Inquistion of Spain,* Vol. 2, p. 585.
37. Lea, *Inquistion of Middle Ages,* p. 103.
38. Lea, *Inquisition of Spain,* Vol. 2, p. 569.
39. Lea, *Inquistion of Middle Ages,* p. 155.
40. Quoted in *Time,* Nov. 20, 1964, p. 76.
41. *Prochaska* v. *Brinegar,* 251 Iowa 834, 102 N.W. 2d, 1960; p. 872.
42. Lea, *Inquisition of Middle Ages,* p. 143.
43. Robert H. Felix, The image of the psychiatrist; Past, present, and future, *Amer. J. Psychiat.,* 121: 318–322 (Oct.), 1964; p. 321.
44. Lea, *Inquisition of Middle Ages,* p. 237.
45. See Chapters 12, 14, and 15.
46. Lea, *Inquisition of Middle Ages,* p. 191.

4 THE DEFENSE OF THE DOMINANT ETHIC

1. Sören Kierkegaard, *The Last Years,* p. 132.
2. Karl Mannheim, *Ideology and Utopia,* pp. 21–22.
3. In this connection, see also Erich Fromm, *Escape from Freedom,* and Karl R. Popper, *The Open Society and Its Enemies.*
4. Rossell Hope Robbins, *The Encyclopedia of Witchcraft and Demonology,* p. 266.
5. Henry Charles Lea, *The Inquisition of the Middle Ages,* p. 87.
6. Ibid., p. 88.
7. Ibid., p. 89.
8. Ibid., p. 88.
9. Ibid.
10. Ibid., p. 89.
11. Johan Huizinga, *The Waning of the Middle Ages,* p. 143.
12. Ibid., p. 237.
13. Henry Kamen, *The Spanish Inquisition,* p. 193.
14. Erving Goffman, The medical model and mental hospitalization: Some notes on the vicissitudes of the tinkering trades, in *Asylums,* pp. 321–386; p. 374.

15. Ibid., pp. 358–359.
16. Andrew Dickson White, *A History of the Warfare of Science with Theology in Christendom*.
17. *The U.S. Book of Facts, Statistics, and Information*, pp. 77, 161.
18. Jonas B. Robitscher, *Pursuit of Agreement*, p. 121.
19. Winfred Overholser, Testimony, in *Constitutional Rights of the Mentally Ill*, p. 36.
20. See Thomas S. Szasz, *Law, Liberty, and Psychiatry*, pp. 182–190.
21. Charles Lam Markmann, *The Noblest Cry*, pp. 400–401.
22. American Civil Liberties Union, *The Policy Guide of the American Civil Liberties Union* (Policy No. 225: The Mentally Ill—Civil Commitment), June, 1966.
23. Ibid.
24. Ibid.
25. See Thomas S. Szasz, Toward the therapeutic state, *New Republic*, Dec. 11, 1965, pp. 26–29.
26. Quoted in Homer W. Smith, *Man and His Gods*, p. vi.

5 THE WITCH AS MENTAL PATIENT

1. Gregory Zilboorg, *The Medical Man and the Witch During the Renaissance*, p. 58.
2. See Chapter 9.
3. Sigmund Freud, Leonardo Da Vinci and a memory of his childhood (1910), in *The Standard Edition of the Complete Psychological Works of Sigmund Freud*, Vol. XI, pp. 57–137; pp. 63, 131.
4. Ibid., p. 63.
5. Ibid., p. 131.
6. Johann Weyer, *De Praestigiis Daemonum* (1563), quoted in Gregory Zilboorg, *A History of Medical Psychology*, p. 215.
7. In this connection see Thomas S. Szasz, Bootlegging humanistic values through psychiatry, *Antioch Rev.*, 22: 341–349 (Fall), 1962.
8. See, for example, M. Ralph Kaufman, Psychiatry: Why "medical" or "social" model? *A.M.A. Arch. Gen. Psychiat.*, 17: 347–360 (Sept.), 1967.
9. M'Naghten's Case, 10 Cl. & F. 200, 8 Eng. Rep. 718 (H.L.), 1843. In this connection, see Thomas S. Szasz, *Law, Liberty, and Psychiatry*, pp. 138–146; and, The insanity defense and the insanity verdict, *Temple Law Quart.*, 40: 271–282 (Spring–Summer), 1967.
10. Henry Charles Lea, *A History of the Inquisition of Spain*, Vol. 3, p. 58.
11. Ibid., p. 59.
12. Philippe Pinel, *A Treatise on Insanity*, p. 238.
13. Ibid., p. 237.
14. Quoted in Zilboorg, *History of Medical Psychology*, pp. 391–392.
15. William E. H. Lecky, *History of European Morals*, Vol. II, p. 54.
16. Ibid., p. 55.
17. Ibid., p. 87.

18. Ibid., p. 55.
19. Sigmund Freud, Charcot (1893), in *The Standard Edition of the Complete Psychological Works of Sigmund Freud*, Vol. III, pp. 7–23; p. 20.
20. Ibid.
21. Sigmund Freud, Letter 56 (to Wilhelm Fliess, January 17, 1897), ibid., Vol. I, p. 242.
22. Sigmund Freud, A seventeenth-century demonological neurosis (1923), ibid., Vol. XIX, pp. 67–105; p. 72.
23. Zilboorg, *History of Medical Psychology*, p. 153.
24. See Chapter 2, p. 41.
25. Zilboorg, *Medical Man and Witch*, pp. 69–70.
26. Ibid., p. 73.
27. Zilboorg, *History of Medical Psychology*, p. 555.
28. Ibid., p. 160.
29. Zilboorg, *Medical Man and Witch*, p. 63.
30. Zilboorg, *History of Medical Psychology*, p. 216.
31. Ibid., p. 231.
32. Ibid., pp. 213–214.
33. Quoted in Robbins, *Encyclopedia of Witchcraft and Demonology*, p. 540.
34. Ibid.
35. Franz G. Alexander and Sheldon T. Selesnick, *The History of Psychiatry*, p. 86.
36. Albert Deutsch, *The Mentally Ill in America*, p. 21.
37. Alexander and Selesnick, p. 68.
38. Lea, *Inquisition of Spain*, Vol. 4, pp. 35–36.
39. Andrew Dickson White, *A History of the Warfare of Science with Theology in Christendom*, pp. 356–357.
40. Zilboorg, *Medical Man and Witch*, p. 45.
41. Karl Menninger, *The Vital Balance*, p. 16.
42. Jules H. Masserman, *The Practice of Dynamic Psychiatry*, p. 370.
43. Robbins, p. 338.
44. Ibid., p. 340.
45. Henry Sigerist, Preface, in Zilboorg, *Medical Man and Witch*, pp. viii–ix.

6 THE WITCH AS HEALER

1. Jules Michelet, *Satanism and Witchcraft*, p. 225.
2. Ibid., p. 77.
3. Ibid., p. 81.
4. Ibid., p. x.
5. Pennethorne Hughes, *Witchcraft*, p. 202.
6. Michelet, p. xiv.
7. Christina Hole, *Witchcraft in England*, pp. 129–130.
8. Thomas Rogers Forbes, *The Midwife and the Witch*, pp. 126–127.
9. Michelet, p. xi.
10. Hole, p. 12.
11. Ibid., p. 13.

12. James George Frazer, *The Golden Bough*, p. 542.

13. Michelet, p. 84.

14. Ibid., pp. 308–309.

15. Hole, p. 191.

16. Ibid., p. 19.

17. Jacob Sprenger and Heinrich Krämer, *Malleus Maleficarum*, p. 8.

18. Andrew Dickson White, *A History of the Warfare of Science with Theology in Christendom*, p. 322.

19. Ibid., pp. 328–329.

20. Ibid., p. 329.

21. Sprenger and Krämer, p. 156.

22. Resolution of the Executive Committee of the American Psychiatric Association, March 7, 1954; quoted in Henry A. Davidson, The semantics of psychotherapy, *Amer. J. Psychiat.*, 115: 410–413 (Nov.), 1958; p. 411.

23. Quoted in Hole, p. 130.

24. Ibid., pp. 159–160.

25. H. R. Trevor-Roper, Witches and witchcraft: An historical essay (II), *Encounter*, 28: 13–34 (June), 1967; p. 13.

26. Ibid.

27. Ibid., p. 14.

28. Michelet, p. xix.

29. Nonmedical hypnotist convicted, *A.M.A. News*, Oct. 2, 1967, p. 9.

30. Thomas S. Szasz, Medical ethics: A historical perspective, *Med, Opin. & Rev.*, 4: 115–121 (Feb.), 1968.

31. In this connection, see Milton Friedman, *Capitalism and Freedom*, pp. 137–160; and Thomas S. Szasz, The right to health, *Georgetown Law J.*, 57: 734–51 (Mar.), 1969.

32. See William J. Sinclair, *Semmelweis: His Life and His Doctrine*, especially pp. 267–270.

33. See Thomas S. Szasz, The concept of transference, *Int. J. Psycho-Anal.*, 44: 432–443, 1963.

34. In this connection, see Kingsley Davis, The application of science to personal relations: A critique of the family clinic idea, *Amer. Sociol. Rev.*, 1: 238–249 (Apr.), 1936; and Mental hygiene and the class structure, *Psychiat.*, 1: 55–65 (Jan.), 1938.

7 THE WITCH AS SCAPEGOAT

1. Jean-Paul Sartre, *Saint Genet*, p. 40.

2. Geoffrey Parrinder, *Witchcraft*, p. 54.

3. Ibid., p. 14.

4. Andrew Dickson White, *A History of the Warfare of Science with Theology in Christendom*, pp. 360–361. In this connection, see also Norman Cohn, *The Pursuit of the Millennium*, and *Warrant for Genocide*.

5. Pennethorne Hughes, *Witchcraft*, p. 64.

6. Adolf Leschnitzer, *The Magic Background of Modern Anti-Semitism*, pp. 144–145.

7. Ibid., pp. 98–99.

8. Ibid., p. 146.

9. Ibid., pp. 164–165.

10. August B. Hollingshead and Frederick C. Redlich, *Social Class and Mental Illness.*

11. Paul M. Roman and Harrison M. Trice, *Schizophrenia and the Poor*, pp. 14 and 37.

12. See Chapter 1.

13. Thomas S. Szasz, The Psychiatric Classification of Behavior: A Strategy of Personal Constraint, in Leonard D. Eron (Ed.), *The Classification of Behavior Disorders*, pp. 123–170.

14. Gregory Zilboorg, *A History of Medical Psychology.*

15. Ibid., pp. 591–606.

16. Franz G. Alexander and Sheldon T. Selesnick, *The History of Psychiatry.*

17. Ibid., p. 66.

18. Ibid., p. 67.

19. See Chapter 11.

20. For a recent account of the persecution of German Jews in the fifteenth century, see Friedrich Heer, *Gottes Erste Liebe* (God's First Love), and its review by Rudolf Augstein, *Die perfiden Juden* (The heretical Jews), *Der Spiegel*, Sept. 4, 1967, pp. 120–126.

21. H. R. Trevor-Roper, Witches and witchcraft: An historical essay (I), *Encounter*, 28: 3–25 (May), 1967; p. 13.

22. Ibid.

23. Ibid., p. 11.

24. Henry Kamen, *The Spanish Inquisition*, p. 15.

25. Walt W. Rostow, *The Dynamics of Soviet Society*, pp. 222–226.

26. Henry Charles Lea, *A History of the Inquisition of Spain*, Vol. 3, pp. 233–234.

27. Ibid., p. 234.

28. Ibid., Vol. 4, pp. 233–234.

29. Charles Williams, *Witchcraft*, p. 249.

30. H. R. Trevor-Roper, Witches and witchcraft, An historical essay (II), *Encounter*, 28: 13–34 (June), 1967; p. 14.

31. Ibid.

32. Herbert J. Muller, *Freedom in the Western World*, p. 173.

33. See Chapters 12 and 13.

34. Herbert Marcuse, quoted in Democracy has/hasn't a future . . . a present, *New York Times Magazine*, May 26, 1968, pp. 30–31, 98–104; p. 102.

35. Anatoly Kuznetsov, *Babi Yar*, p. 236.

36. Lea, *Inquisition of Spain*, Vol. 4, pp. 206–208.

37. Trevor-Roper, (II), p. 15.

38. Jules Isaac, *The Teaching of Contempt.*

39. Michel Foucault, *Madness and Civilization.*

40. See Thomas S. Szasz, The destruction of differences, *New Republic*, June 10, 1967, pp. 21–23.

8 THE MYTHS OF WITCHCRAFT AND MENTAL ILLNESS

1. Herbert J. Muller, *Freedom in the Western World*, pp. 40–41.
2. George Mora, From Demonology to the Narrenturm, in Iago Galdston (Ed.), *Historic Derivations of Modern Psychiatry*, pp. 41–73; p. 50.
3. Albert Camus, *The Plague*, p. 121.
4. John Stuart Mill, *The Subjection of Women*, p. 219.
5. Ibid.
6. H. R. Trevor-Roper, Witches and witchcraft: An historical essay (I), *Encounter*, 28: 3–25 (May), 1967; p. 4.
7. Exodus, 22: 18.
8. Trevor-Roper, p. 4.
9. Ibid., p. 15.
10. Ibid.
11. See Thomas S. Szasz, Criminal insanity: Fact or strategy? *New Republic*, Nov. 21, 1964, pp. 19–22; and The Psychiatric Classification of Behavior: A Strategy of Personal Constraint, in Leonard D. Eron (Ed.), *The Classification of Behavior Disorders*, pp. 125–170.
12. Jacob Sprenger and Heinrich Krämer, *Malleus Maleficarum*, p. 8.
13. See, for example, M. Ralph Kaufman, Psychiatry: Why "medical" or "social" Model? *A.M.A. Arch. Gen. Psychiat.*, 17: 347–360 (Sept.), 1967; pp. 347–348.
14. Sprenger and Krämer, p. 9.
15. Ibid., p. 56.
16. See Chapter 7.
17. Charles Williams, p. 252.
18. Rossell Hope Robbins, *Encyclopedia of Witchcraft and Demonology*, p. 19.
19. Ibid.
20. Geoffrey Parrinder, *Witchcraft*, p. 82.
21. Henry Charles Lea, *A History of the Inquisition of Spain*, Vol. 4, p. 239.
22. Ibid.
23. Ibid., p. 240.
24. Johan Huizinga, *The Waning of the Middle Ages*, p. 68.
25. Ibid., p. 69.
26. Quoted in Maximilian Koessler, Euthanasia in the Hadamar Sanatorium and international law, *J. Crim. Law, Criminol., and Police Sci.*, 43: 735–755 (Mar.–Apr.), 1953; pp. 739–740.
27. In this connection, see Chapter 5; also Thomas S. Szasz, The Mental Health Ethic, in Richard T. De George (Ed.), *Ethics and Society*, pp. 85–110.
28. Bronislaw Malinowski, *Magic, Science, and Religion*, p. 84.
29. Barrows Dunham, *Man Against Myth*, p. 18.
30. Mark, 1: 1. Here and in subsequent chapters, my source for Biblical quotations is the *Revised Standard Version of the Holy Bible*, Self-Pronouncing Edition.
31. Ibid., 1: 9–11.
32. Ibid., 1: 21–24.
33. Ibid., 1: 25–26.

34. Ibid., 3: 10–12.
35. Ibid., 5: 1–7.
36. Lewis Carroll, *Alice's Adventures in Wonderland,* in *The Annotated Alice,* p. 159.
37. Gregory Bateson (Ed.), *Perceval's Narrative,* pp. 186–187.
38. Leo Tolstoy, *The Kreutzer Sonata,* in *The Death of Ivan Ilych and Other Stories,* pp. 157–239; pp. 193–194.
39. Ibid., pp. 200, 201.
40. Samuel Butler, *The Way of All Flesh,* p. 278.
41. Quoted in Albert Deutsch, *The Mentally Ill in America,* p. 10.
42. Michel Foucault, *Madness and Civilization,* p. 40.
43. Andrew Harper, *A Treatise on the Real Cause and Cure of Insanity,* in Richard Hunter and Ida Macalpine (Eds.), *Three Hundred Years of Psychiatry, 1535–1860,* pp. 522–524; p. 524.
44. Thomas Bakewell, A letter to the chairman of the Select Committee of the House of Commons, appointed to enquire into the state of madhouses, in Hunter and Macalpine, pp. 705–709; p. 706.
45. John Reid, *De Insania (On Insanity),* in Hunter and Macalpine, pp. 722–728; pp. 723–725.
46. John Conolly, *An Inquiry Concerning the Indications of Insanity, With Suggestions for the Better Protection and Care of the Insane,* in Hunter and Macalpine, pp. 805–809; pp. 806–807.
47. John Stuart Mill, *On Liberty,* pp. 99–100.
48. Bateson, p. 114.
49. For a moving literary rendition of this theme, see Anton Pavlovich Chekhov, Ward No. 6, in *Seven Short Stories by Chekhov,* pp. 106–157.
50. Bateson, p. 218.
51. Ibid., p. 299.
52. E. P. W. Packard, *Modern Persecution,* Vol. I, p. 95.
53. Deutsch, pp. 424–425.
54. Edmund S. Morgan (Ed.), Mary Easty, Petition of an Accused Witch, 1692, in Daniel Boorstin (Ed.), *An American Primer,* pp. 26–30; p. 28.
55. Ibid., p. 29.
56. H. R. Trevor-Roper, Witches and witchcraft: An historical essay (II), *Encounter,* 28: 13–34 (June), 1967; p. 16.
57. Lea, p. 46.
58. Julien Benda, *The Great Betrayal.*
59. Robbins, p. 17.
60. See especially David Brion Davis, *The Problem of Slavery in Western Culture.*

PART II THE MANUFACTURE OF MADNESS

1. Fyodor Dostoyevsky, *The Brothers Karamazov,* p. 306.
2. John Stuart Mill, *On Liberty,* p. 100.

9 THE NEW MANUFACTURER—BENJAMIN RUSH, THE FATHER OF AMERICAN PSYCHIATRY

1. Daniel J. Boorstin, *The Lost World of Thomas Jefferson*, pp. 148–149.
2. See Chapter 5.
3. Benjamin Rush, *Medical Inquiries and Observations upon the Diseases of the Mind* (1812).
4. Quoted in Carl Binger, *Revolutionary Doctor*, p. 281.
5. Rush, p. 20.
6. Ibid.
7. Ibid., p. 26.
8. Quoted in Boorstin, p. 182.
9. Ibid.
10. Binger, p. 200.
11. Ibid., p. 201.
12. Ibid.
13. Ibid., p. 268.
14. Rush, p. 160.
15. Benjamin Rush, Lecture on the medical jurisprudence of the mind, in *The Autobiography of Benjamin Rush*, pp. 348–351; p. 350.
16. Ibid.
17. Ibid.
18. Ibid.
19. Binger, p. 264.
20. Rush, *Medical Inquiries*, p. 265.
21. Ibid.
22. Ibid., p. 271.
23. Ibid., p. 273.
24. Ibid., pp. 273–274.
25. Binger, p. 296.
26. Rush, *Medical Inquiries*, pp. 265–266.
27. Ibid., p. 267.
28. Binger, p. 269.
29. Ibid., p. 198.
30. Ibid., p. 201.
31. Ibid., p. 173.
32. Ibid., p. 273.
33. Ibid.
34. Rush, *Medical Inquiries*, p. 110.
35. Ibid.
36. Ibid., p. 111.
37. Binger, p. 273.
38. Philippe Pinel, *A Treatise on Insanity*, pp. 27, 63.
39. Rush, *Medical Inquiries*, p. 174.
40. Ibid., p. 175.
41. Ibid.
42. Albert Deutsch, *The Mentally Ill in America*, p. 422.

43. Rush, *Medical Inquiries*, pp. 267–268.
44. Ibid., p. 181.
45. Ibid., p. 183.
46. Ibid., pp. 181–192.
47. Ibid., p. 192.
48. Deutsch, p. 79.
49. Charles Williams, *Witchcraft*, p. 178.
50. Deutsch, p. 79.
51. Ibid.
52. Ibid., p. 81.
53. Ibid., p. 80.
54. Binger, p. 277.
55. Benjamin Rush, *Commonplace Book of Benjamin Rush, 1792–1813*, in *The Autobiography of Benjamin Rush*, pp. 213–360; p. 282.
56. Ibid., p. 288.
57. The story of John Rush is recounted in Appendix 3 of Benjamin Rush's *Autobiography*, pp. 369–371.
58. Quoted in Binger, p. 288.
59. Ibid.
60. Ibid., p. 197.
61. Ibid.
62. William Stanton, *The Leopard's Spots*, p. 6.
63. Benjamin Rush, Observations intended to favour a supposition that the black Color (as it is called) of the Negroes is derived from the LEPROSY, *Trans. Amer. Phil. Soc.*, 4: 289–297, 1799.
64. Boorstin, p. 90.
65. Stanton, p. 7.
66. Ibid., pp. 12–13.
67. Ibid., p. 13.
68. Ibid.
69. See, for example, David Brion Davis, *The Problem of Slavery in Western Culture*, especially Chapters 6 and 7.
70. Stanton, p. 13.
71. Boorstin, p. 91.
72. Ibid.
73. Ibid., p. 92.

10 THE PRODUCT CONVERSION—FROM HERESY TO ILLNESS

1. John Stuart Mill, *Auguste Comte and Positivism*, p. 142.
2. For a classic account of homosexuality in past ages and various cultures, see Edward Westermarck, *The Origin and Development of the Moral Ideas*, Vol. II, Chapter XLIII, pp. 456–489; for a more recent exposition, see, for example, Wainright Churchill, *Homosexual Behavior Among Males*.
3. Genesis, 19: 3–5.

4. Ibid., 19: 6–8.
5. Ibid., 19: 11.
6. Ibid., 19: 24–25.
7. Leviticus, 18: 22.
8. Ibid., 20: 13.
9. Quoted in Simone de Beauvoir, *The Second Sex*, p. xxi.
10. Alfred C. Kinsey, Wardell B. Pomeroy, and Clyde E. Martin, *Sexual Behavior in the Human Male*, pp. 659–666.
11. Gordon Rattray Taylor, Historical and Mythological Aspects of Homosexuality, in Judd Marmor (Ed.), *Sexual Inversion*, pp. 140–164; pp. 145–146.
12. Ibid., p. 145.
13. Westermarck, p. 489.
14. Henry Charles Lea, *A History of the Inquisition of Spain*, Vol. 4, p. 362.
15. Ibid.
16. Ibid.
17. See Chapter 7.
18. Lea, Vol. 4, pp. 365–366.
19. Ibid., p. 367.
20. Ibid., p. 368.
21. Ibid., p. 371.
22. Marmor, p. 15.
23. In this connection, see Thomas S. Szasz, Scientific method and social role in medicine and psychiatry, *A.M.A. Arch. Int. Med.*, 101: 228–238 (Feb.). 1958; and Alcoholism: A socioethical perspective, *Western Med.* 7: 15–21 (Dec.), 1966.
24. René Guyon, *The Ethics of Sexual Acts*, pp. 270–271.
25. André Gide, *Corydon*, pp. 8–10.
26. Ibid., pp. 20–21.
27. See Chapter 10.
28. Karl Menninger, *The Vital Balance*, pp. 195–198.
29. Ibid., p. 198.
30. Ibid., p. 196.
31. Ibid.
32. Ibid., p. 197.
33. Karl Menninger, Introduction, in *The Wolfenden Report*, pp. 5–7; p. 5.
34. Ibid., p. 6.
35. *Crosscurrents of Psychiatric Thought Today*, p. 1.
36. Ibid., p. 13.
37. Ibid., p. 14.
38. William S. Burroughs, *Naked Lunch*, pp. 186–197; p. 186.
39. Ibid., p. 188.
40. Ibid., p. 189.
41. Ibid., p. 196.
42. Ibid., p. 197.
43. See especially Thomas S. Szasz, Scientific method and social role; Alcoholism: A socioethical perspective; and *Law, Liberty, and Psychiatry*.

44. Dick Leitsch, The psychotherapy of homosexuality: Let's forget Jocasta and her little boy, *Psychiat. Opin.*, 4: 28–35 (June), 1967: p. 35.

11 THE NEW PRODUCT—MASTURBATORY INSANITY

1. François Voltaire, *Philosophical Dictionary* (1764), p. 254.
2. See especially Friedrich A. Hayek, *The Counter-Revolution of Science*.
3. Alfred C. Kinsey, Wardell B. Pomeroy, Clyde E. Martin, and Paul Gebhard, *Sexual Behavior in the Human Female*, p. 168.
4. Ibid., p. 473.
5. Alfred C. Kinsey, Wardell B. Pomeroy, and Clyde E. Martin, *Sexual Behavior in the Human Male*, p. 465.
6. E. H. Hare, Masturbatory insanity: The history of an idea, *J. Ment. Sci.*, 108: 1–25 (Jan.), 1962; p. 20.
7. Ibid., p. 2.
8. Ibid., pp. 2–3.
9. Ibid., p. 3.
10. Ibid.
11. Benjamin Rush, *Medical Inquiries and Observations upon the Diseases of the Mind* (1812).
12. Ibid., p. 33.
13. Ibid., p. 347.
14. Ilza Veith, *Hysteria*, p. 179.
15. See Chapter 8.
16. Hare, p. 4.
17. Ibid.
18. Ibid., p. 5.
19. Ibid., p. 6.
20. Ibid.
21. Quoted in John Duffy, Masturbation and clitoridectomy, *J.A.M.A.*, 186: 246–248 (Oct. 19), 1963; p. 246.
22. Quoted in Hare, p. 23.
23. Quoted in Lars Ullerstam, *The Erotic Minorities*, p. 113.
24. Wayland Young, *Eros Denied*, p. 204.
25. Ibid., p. 205.
26. E. C. Spitzka, *Insanity: Its Classification, Diagnosis, and Treatment*, p. 9.
27. Ibid., pp. 378–380.
28. Quoted in Hare, p. 7.
29. Quoted in Alex Comfort, *The Anxiety Makers*, pp. 107–108.
30. Hare, p. 24.
31. Thomas S. Szasz, The Mental Health Ethic, in Richard T. De George (Ed.), *Ethics and Society*, pp. 85–110.
32. René A. Spitz, Authority and masturbation: Some remarks on a bibliographical investigation, *Yearbook of Psychoanalysis*, Vol. 9, pp. 113–145; p. 123.
33. Duffy, p. 248.
34. Comfort, p. 97.

35. Hare, p. 22.
36. Ibid.
37. Comfort, p. 95.
38. Hare, p. 9.
39. Quoted in Karl Menninger, *The Vital Balance*, p. 462.
40. Mary R. Melendy, *Perfect Womanhood*, pp. 32–33.
41. Sigmund Freud. The neuropsychoses of defence (1894), in *The Standard Edition of the Complete Psychological Works of Sigmund Freud*, Vol. III, pp. 41–61; pp. 55–56.
42. Sigmund Freud, Letter 79, December 22, 1897, ibid., Vol. I, p. 272.
43. Sigmund Freud, The Psychopathology of Everyday Life (1901), ibid., Vol. VI, pp. 199–200.
44. Sigmund Freud, Contributions to a discussion on masturbation (1912), ibid., Vol. XII, pp. 239–254; p. 245.
45. Ibid.
46. Ibid., p. 246.
47. Ibid., p. 248.
48. Ibid., pp. 250–251.
49. Ibid., p. 249.
50. Ibid., p. 251.
51. Ibid.
52. Ibid.
53. Quoted in Comfort, p. 111.
54. Ernest Jones, The nature of auto-suggestion, in *Papers on Psychoanalysis*, pp. 273–293; p. 282.
55. Otto Fenichel, *The Psychoanalytic Theory of Neurosis*, pp. 75–76.
56. Ibid., p. 75.
57. Quoted in Spitz, p. 125.
58. Ibid., p. 126.
59. J. P. Crozer Griffith and A. Graeme Mitchell, *The Diseases of Infants and Children*, 2d ed., p. 872.
60. Israel S. Wechsler, The Neuroses or the Psychoneuroses, in Russell L. Cecil and Foster Kennedy (Eds.), *A Textbook of Medicine by American Authors*, 5th ed., pp. 1645–1664; p. 1651.
61. Quoted in Emil A. Gutheil, Sexual Dysfunctions in Men, in Silvano Arieti (Ed.), *American Handbook of Psychiatry*, Vol. I, pp. 708–726; p. 711.
62. Alfred C. Kinsey, Wardell B. Pomeroy, and Clyde E. Martin, *Sexual Behavior in the Human Male*, p. 513.
63. Spitz, p. 125.
64. Karl A. Menninger, *Man Against Himself*, pp. 68–69.
65. Joseph B. Cramer, Common Neuroses of Childhood, in Arieti, pp. 797–815; p. 807.
66. Hare, pp. 9–10.
67. Comfort, p. 111.
68. Ibid., p. 112.

12 THE MANUFACTURE OF MEDICAL STIGMA

1. Jules Romains, *Knock,* pp. 59–60.
2. See Chapters 10 and 13.
3. *The Attack on Narcotics,* p. 1.
4. Ibid.
5. Alexander Dru (Ed.), *The Journals of Kierkegaard* (1835–1854), pp. 123–124.
6. Milton I. Roemer, The future of social medicine in the United States, *The Pharos of Alpha Omega Alpha,* 30: 42–50 (April), 1967; p. 45.
7. Ibid., p. 46.
8. See Thomas S. Szasz, Medical ethics: A historical perspective, *Med. Opin. & Rev.,* 4: 115–121 (Feb.), 1968.
9. Donald Gould, To hell with medical secrecy! *New Statesman,* Mar. 3, 1967.
10. Ibid.
11. Ibid.
12. Ibid.
13. Ibid.
14. Ibid.
15. Donald Gould, The freedom to be unfit, *New Statesman,* Sept. 1, 1967.
16. Ibid.
17. Ibid.
18. Ibid.
19. Ibid.
20. Ibid.
21. See, for example, Floyd W. Matson, *The Broken Image,* and Thomas S. Szasz, Whither psychiatry? *Soc. Res.* 33: 439–462 (Autumn), 1966.
22. See, *Trials of War Criminals Before the Nuernberg Military Tribunals Under Control Council Law No. 10,* Vol. I, pp. 794–896; and Fredric Wertham, *A Sign for Cain,* Chapter 9.
23. Anatoly Kuznetsov, *Babi Yar,* p. 236.
24. Adam Podgorecki, Law and mental illness: Social engineering (Abstract), *Sandoz Psychiat. Spectator,* 4: 15–16 (Sept.), 1967; p. 16.
25. Heinrich Himmler, in a speech in 1937; quoted in Hannah Arendt, *The Burden of Our Time,* p. 373.
26. Quoted in Raul Hilberg, *The Destruction of the European Jews,* in Bernard Rosenberg, Israel Gerver, and F. William Howton (Eds.), *Mass Society in Crisis,* pp. 272–310; p. 295.
27. Ibid., p. 295.
28. Harold Orlans, An American Death Camp, in Rosenberg, Gerver, and Howton (Eds.), pp. 614–628, p. 626.
29. Ibid., p. 627.
30. Ibid., pp. 614–615.
31. Arendt, pp. 395–396.
32. Babs Fenwick, Russians ahead on mental health? *Daily Oklahoman,* Mar. 10, 1967, pp. 1–2.
33. Ibid., p. 2.

34. Ibid.

35. Ibid.

36. Quoted in Soviet MDs find state duties put profession in second place, *A.M.A. News,* May 10, 1965, p. 12.

37. Valeriy Tarsis, *Ward 7.*

38. See Zhenya Belov campaign (Letters), *Economist* (London), Dec. 11, 1965, p. 4; and Peter Grose, Tarsis, anti-Red writer, is denounced in Soviet as he flies to London, *New York Times,* Feb. 9, 1966, p. 16.

39. Lawrence C. Kolb, Soviet psychiatric organization and the community mental health center concept, *Amer. J. Psychiat.,* 123: :433–440 (Oct.), 1966; pp. 437–438.

40. Isadore Ziferstein, The Soviet psychiatrist: His relationship to his patients and to his society, *Amer. J. Psychiat.,* 123: 440–446 (Oct.), 1966; p. 445.

41. Ibid.

42. Vincent J. Burke, Soviet atheist's life happier than believer's, sociologist reports, Syracuse (N.Y.) *Herald-Journal,* Dec. 2, 1966, p. 28.

43. In this connection, see Thomas S. Szasz, The moral dilemma of psychiatry: Autonomy or heteronomy? *Amer. J. Psychiat.,* 12: 521–528 (Dec.), 1964; and Medical ethics: A historical perspective, *Med. Opin. & Rev.,* 4: 115–121 (Feb.), 1968.

44. Quoted in Alexander Mitscherlich and Fred Mielke, *Doctors of Infamy,* p. xxxviii.

45. Quoted in Jeanne Brand, *Doctors and the State,* p. 240.

46. Michel Foucault, *Madness and Civilization,* especially Chap. IX.

47. Oliver Garceau, The morals of medicine, *Ann. Acad. Pol. & Soc. Sci.,* 363: 60–69 (Jan.), 1966; p. 68.

48. G. Brock Chisholm, The re-establishment of peacetime society, *Psychiat.,* 9: 3–11 (Jan.), 1946; p. 7.

49. Ibid., p. 9.

50. Ibid.

51. Ibid., p. 11.

52. Quoted in Martin Gansberg, Peace Corps sets world health aid, *New York Times,* Nov. 16, 1964, p. 1.

53. Goffredo Parise, No neurotics in China, *Atlas,* 13: 46–47 (Feb.), 1967; p. 46.

54. Thomas S. Szasz, The Mental Health Ethic, in Richard T. De George (Ed.), *Ethics and Society,* pp. 85–110.

55. Parise, p. 47.

56. Quoted in Gansberg, p. 1.

57. In this connection, see Friedrich A. Hayek, *The Counter-Revolution of Science.*

58. See Szasz, The Mental Health Ethic, in De George (Ed.), *Ethics and Society.*

59. Harold Visotsky, Social psychiatry rationale: Administrative and planning approaches, *Amer. J. Psychiat.,* 121: 433–441 (Nov.), 1964; p. 434.

60. Gerald Caplan, Community Psychiatry: Introduction and Overview, in S. Goldston (Ed.), *Concepts of Community Psychiatry,* pp. 3–18; p. 4.

61. Quoted in MD's role in mental health stressed, *A.M.A. News,* Mar. 13, 1967, p. 3.

62. Leopold Bellak, Epilogue, in Leopold Bellak (Ed.), *Handbook of Community Psychiatry and Community Mental Health*, pp. 458–460; p. 458.

63. Ibid., p. 459.

64. Ibid.

65. Ibid.

66. Ibid., p. 460.

67. Fyodor Dostoyevsky, *The Brothers Karamazov*, p. 298.

68. Leopold Bellak, Introduction, in Bellak, pp. 1–11; p. 11.

69. Dostoyevsky, p. 305.

70. Bellak, p. xi.

71. Gerald Caplan, *Principles of Preventive Psychiatry*, p. 79.

72. Ibid., p. 56.

73. Stanley Yolles, Community mental health: Issues and policies, *Amer. J. Psychiat.*, 122: 979–985 (Mar.), 1966; p. 980.

74. *Brown* v. *Board of Education*, 347, U.S. 483, 1954; reprinted in Robert B. McKay, *An American Constitutional Law Reader*, pp. 204–210.

75. Ibid., p. 208.

76. *Boutilier* v. *Immigration and Naturalization Service*, 387, U.S. 118, 1967; see Chapter 14.

77. Gunnar Myrdal, *An American Dilemma*.

78. Burke, Soviet atheist's life happier than believer's, sociologist reports, Syracuse (N.Y.) *Herald-Journal*, Dec. 2, 1966, p. 28.

79. See especially Thomas S. Szasz, *Law, Liberty, and Psychiatry*, and *Psychiatric Justice*.

80. David L. Bazelon, Justice stumbles over science, *Trans-action*, 4: 8–17 (July-Aug.), 1967.

81. Ibid., p. 8.

82. Thomas S. Szasz, *The Ethics of Psychoanalysis*.

83. See, for example, Seymour L. Halleck, *Psychiatry and the Dilemmas of Crime*.

84. Bazelon, p. 9.

85. Ibid., p. 13.

86. Ibid., p. 14.

87. Ibid., p. 17.

88. See Szasz, *Law, Liberty, and Psychiatry*, pp. 127–137.

89. Bazelon, p. 17.

90. See Robert F. Lockman, Nationwide study yields profile of psychiatrists, *Psychiat. News*, 1: 2 (Jan.), 1966.

91. Ibid.

92. See Brian Cooper and Alexander C. Brown, Psychiatric practice in Great Britain and America: A comparative study, *Brit. J. Psychiat.*, 113: 625–636, 1967.

93. Derek L. Phillips, Rejection: A possible consequence of seeking help for mental disorders, *Amer. Sociol. Rev.*, 28: 963–972 (Dec.), 1963; p. 965.

94. Ibid., p. 966.

95. Ibid.

96. Ibid., p. 968.

97. Ibid., pp. 968–969.
98. Ibid., p. 969.
99. Derek L. Phillips, Identification of mental illness: Its consequences for rejection, *Community Ment. Health J.* 3: 262–266 (Fall), 1967; pp. 265–266.
100. Erving Goffman, *Stigma*, p. 3.
101. Ibid., p. 5.
102. Ibid., pp. 43–62.

13 THE MODEL PSYCHIATRIC SCAPEGOAT— THE HOMOSEXUAL

1. Abby Mann, quoted in Vincent Canby, On the set here, a man and his entourage: Sinatra starts work in city on filming of "Detective," *New York Times*, Oct. 18, 1967, p. 37.
2. See Thomas S. Szasz, Legal and Moral Aspects of Homosexuality, in Judd Marmor (Ed.), *Sexual Inversion*, pp. 124–139.
3. Mass. Ann. Laws, chapter 123, par. 1, 1957; quoted in Frank T. Lindman and Donald M. McIntyre, Jr. (Eds.), *The Mentally Disabled and the Law*, p. 18.
4. Stephanie Harrington, Homosexual sortie: An anonymous crusade, *Village Voice*, May 25, 1967, pp. 9–10; p. 9.
5. Ibid., p. 10.
6. *Boutilier* v. *Immigration and Naturalization Service*, 387 U.S. 118, 1967.
7. Ibid., p. 19.
8. Ibid.
9. Ibid., p. 120.
10. Ibid.
11. Ibid.
12. Ibid., p. 122.
13. Ibid., p. 123.
14. Ibid., p. 124.
15. Chinese Exclusion case, 130 U.S. 581, 1889; p. 581.
16. Ibid., p. 604.
17. Ibid., p. 607.
18. Ibid., p. 606.
19. See Thomas S. Szasz, *Psychiatric Justice*, especially pp. 56–82 and 264–272.
20. See this chapter, p. 246, and Chapter 14, especially pp. 266–268.
21. *Boutilier* v. *Immigration and Naturalization Service*, p. 124.
22. Thomas R. Byrne, Jr. and Francis M. Mulligan, "Psychopathic personality" and "sexual deviation": Medical terms or legal catch-alls. Analysis of the status of the homosexual alien, *Temple Law Quart.*, 40: 328–347 (Spring–Summer), 1967.
23. Ibid., p. 335.
24. See Chapter 10.
25. In this connection, see Thomas S. Szasz. *The Ethics of Psychoanalysis*, especially pp. 11–45.
26. Byrne and Mulligan, p. 336.

27. Ibid.
28. Ibid., p. 342.
29. Ibid.
30. Ibid., p. 343.
31. Ibid., p. 344.
32. Ibid., p. 347.
33. See Chapters 2 and 4; also Jack C. Landau, GI justice: A 2d class system, Syracuse (N.Y.) *Herald-American*, Sept. 10, 1967, p. 69, and 30,000 GI's "branded" by "less than honorable" discharges, Syracuse (N.Y.) *Herald-Journal*, Sept. 14, 1967, p. 39.
34. Abe Fortas, Implications of Durham's case, *Amer. J. Psychiat.* 113: 577–582 (Jan.), 1957.
35. William O. Douglas, Concurring opinion, in *Robinson* v. *California*, 370 U.S. 660, 1961; pp. 668–678.
36. *Boutilier* v. *Immigration and Naturalization Service*, p. 125.
37. Ibid., p. 132.
38. See, for example, Thomas S. Szasz, *The Myth of Mental Illness*, or Chapter 8 in this volume.
39. Chinese Exclusion case, p. 581.
40. *Boutilier* v. *Immigration and Naturalization Service*, p. 129.
41. Robert Lindner, *Must You Conform?*, p. 65.
42. Jean-Paul Sartre, *Saint Genêt: Actor and Martyr*, p. 225.
43. Sartre, p. 587.
44. *Boutilier* v. *Immigration and Naturalization Service*, p. 133.
45. Ibid.
46. Ibid., pp. 134–135.

14 THE EXPULSION OF EVIL

1. Kenneth Burke, Interaction: III. Dramatism, in David L. Sills (Ed.), *International Encyclopedia of the Social Sciences*, Vol. 7, pp. 445–452; p. 451.
2. James George Frazer, *The Golden Bough*, p. 539.
3. Leviticus, 16: 20–22.
4. Isaiah, 53: 1–6.
5. See also Isaiah, 53: 7–12.
6. Frazer, p. 540.
7. Ibid.
8. Ibid., p. 579.
9. Jane Ellen Harrison, *Epilegomena to the Study of Greek Religion and Themis*, p. xvii.
10. Frazer, pp. 578–579.
11. Ibid., p. 579.
12. Ibid.
13. Harrison, p. xvii.
14. Ibid.
15. Ibid.

16. Ibid., p. xxi.
17. Ibid.
18. See Chapter 13.
19. Jean-Paul Sartre, The Childhood of a Leader, in *Intimacy and Other Stories*, pp. 81–159.
20. Ibid., p. 156.
21. Jean-Paul Sartre, *Anti-Semite and Jew*, pp. 26–27.
22. Ibid., p. 39.
23. Ibid., p. 44.
24. Ibid., p. 45.
25. Ibid., p. 51.
26. Ibid., p. 57.
27. See Chapter 15.
28. Sartre, *Anti-Semite and Jew*, p. 69.
29. Ibid., pp. 146–147.

15 THE STRUGGLE FOR SELF-ESTEEM

1. T. S. Eliot, *The Cocktail Party*, p. 111.
2. Voltaire, *Philosophical Dictionary* (1764), p. 353.
3. Albert Camus, Preface to Algerian Reports, in *Resistance, Rebellion, and Death*, p. 114.
4. Abraham Lincoln, From a letter (1858); quoted in Christopher Morley and Louella D. Everett (Eds.), [*Bartlett's*] *Familiar Quotations*, p. 455.
5. In this connection, see Thomas S. Szasz, *Law, Liberty, and Psychiatry*, especially pp. 149–158.
6 Howard S. Becker, *Outsiders*, p. 9.
7. Ibid., pp. 9, 14.
8. Jean-Paul Sartre, *Saint Genet*.
9. Ibid., p. 30.
10. Ibid, pp. 30–31.
11. Ibid., p. 118.
12. Ibid., p. 278.
13. George Orwell, *Nineteen Eighty-Four*.
14. Ibid., p. 288.
15. Ibid., p. 289.
16. Ibid.
17. Ibid., pp. 294–295.
18. Ibid., p. 300.
19. James George Frazer, *The Golden Bough*, p. 497.
20. Ralph Linton, *The Tree of Culture*, pp. 644–645.
21. See, for example, Konrad Lorenz, *On Aggression*.
22. Kenneth Burke, Interaction: III. Dramatism, in David L. Sills (Ed.), *International Encyclopedia of the Social Sciences*, Vol. 7, pp. 445–452; p. 450.
23. Ibid., p. 451.

24. Frederick Douglass, The anti-slavery movement (A lecture delivered in Rochester, New York, 1885); quoted in *Civil Liberties*, No. 214, Mar., 1964, p. 1.

EPILOGUE
"THE PAINTED BIRD"

1. Jean-Pauil Sartre, *Saint Genêt: Actor and Martyr*, p. 24.
2. Jerzy Kosinski, *The Painted Bird*, p. 1.
3. Ibid., pp. 43–44.
4. Ibid., pp. 44–45.
5. Ralph Waldo Emerson, Self-reliance (1841), in Eduard C. Lindeman (Ed.), *Basic Selections from Emerson*, pp. 53–73; p. 55.

APPENDIX
A SYNOPTIC HISTORY OF PERSECUTIONS
FOR WITCHCRAFT AND MENTAL ILLNESS

1. Albert Camus, *The Rebel*, p. 126.
2. Abram Leon Sachar, *A History of the Jews*, p. 194.
3. Ibid., p. 198.
4. Quoted in Arnold A. Rogow (Ed.), *The Jew in a Gentile World*, pp. 93–94.
5. Henry Kamen, *The Spanish Inquisition*, p. 19.
6. Quoted in Jacob Sprenger and Heinrich Krämer, *Malleus Maleficarum*, p. xix.
7. Kamen, p. 122.
8. Sprenger and Krämer, p. 1.
9. Kamen, p. 28.
10. Quoted in Gregory Zilboorg, *History of Medical Psychology*, p. 205.
11. Quoted in Sachar, p. 229.
12. Herbert J. Muller, *Freedom in the Western World*, p. 274.
13. Quoted in Rossell Hope Robbins, *The Encyclopedia of Witchcraft and Demonology*, p. 540.
14. Herbert J. Muller, p. 173.
15. Quoted in Robbins, p. 54.
16. Ibid., p. 408.
17. Charles Mackay, *Extraordinary Popular Delusions and the Madness of Crowds*, p. 578.
18. Quoted in Rogow, pp. 116, 119–121, 123.
19. Quoted in Robbins, p. 484.
20. Ibid., p. 479.
21. Ibid., p. 314.
22. Ibid., p. 308.
23. Quoted in Andrew Dickson White, *A History of the Warfare of Science with Theology in Christendom*, p. 329.
24. Michel Foucault, *Madness and Civilization*, pp. 40, 45.
25. Ibid., pp. 65–66.

26. Quoted in Robbins, p. 341.
27. Quoted in Rogow, p. 228.
28. Quoted in Richard Hunter and Ida Macalpine, *Three Hundred Years of Psychiatry, 1535–1860,* pp. 266–267.
29. Christina Hole, *Witchcraft in England,* p. 197.
30. Quoted in Rogow, p. 136.
31. Nina Ridenour, *Mental Health in the United States,* p. 77.
32. René A. Spitz, Authority and masturbation: Some remarks on a bibliographical investigation, *The Yearbook of Psychoanalysis,* Vol. 9, pp. 113–145; p. 117.
33. Wade Baskin, Foreword, in *Voltaire's Philosophical Dictionary,* p. 3.
34. White, p. 339.
35. Quoted in Zilboorg, *History of Medical Psychology,* p. 575.
36. André Soubiran, *The Good Doctor Guillotin and His Strange Device,* pp. 141, 214.
37. White, p. 342.
38. Philippe Pinel, *A Treatise on Insanity* (1801), pp. 27–28.
39. Ibid., p. 63.
40. Ibid., p. 65.
41. Ibid., p. 66.
42. Quoted in Emil Kraepelin, *One Hundred Years of Psychiatry,* p. 69.
43. Ibid., p. 152.
44. Theodric Romeyn Beck, *An Inaugural Dissertation on Insanity,* pp. 27–28; quoted in Norman Dain, *Concepts of Insanity,* pp. 12–13.
45. Benjamin Rush, *Medical Inquiries and Observations upon The Diseases of the Mind* (1812), pp. 211, 347.
46. Quoted in Kamen, p. 271.
47. Quoted in Hunter and Macalpine, pp. 724–725.
48. Quoted in Alex Comfort, *The Anxiety Makers,* p. 76.
49. Sachar, p. 287; Kamen, p. 282.
50. Quoted in Hunter and Macalpine, p. 792.
51. Quoted in Albert Deutsch, *The Mentally Ill in America,* p. 151.
52. Dain, pp. 104, 239.
53. Quoted in Deutsch, p. 150.
54. Ibid., p. 142.
55. Quoted in Jules Isaac, *The Teaching of Contempt,* p. 112.
56. Deutsch, pp. 150–151.
57. Quoted in E. H. Hare, Masturbatory insanity: The history of an idea, *J. Ment. Sci.,* 108: 1–25 (Jan.), 1962; p. 23.
58. Quoted in Abraham S. Goldstein, *The Insanity Defense,* p. 45.
59. Dorothea L. Dix, *Memorial to the Legislature of Massachusetts,* 1843, p. 2.
60. Quoted in Ridenour, p. 76.
61. Quoted in Dain, p. 107.
62. Comfort, p. 95.
63. Quoted in Deutsch, p. 424.
64. National Association for Mental Health, *Calendar for 1968* (May); and Dain, p. 176.

65. Massachusetts, Commission on Lunacy, 1854, *Report on Insanity and Idiocy in Massachusetts,* p. 55; quoted in Dain, p. 68.
66. National Association for Mental Health, *Calendar for 1968* (Apr.).
67. Quoted in John Duffy, Masturbation and clitoridectomy, *J.A.M.A.* 186: 246–248 (Oct. 19), 1963; p. 246.
68. Quoted in Dain, p. 106.
69. Quoted in Kraepelin, pp. 69–70.
70. John Stuart Mill, *On Liberty* (1859), pp. 13, 18.
71. Quoted in Hare, p. 18.
72. Ibid., p. 6.
73. William J. Sinclair, *Semmelweis, His Life and His Doctrine,* especially pp. 267–270.
74. Quoted in Dain, p. 197.
75. Quoted in Franz G. Alexander and Sheldon T. Selesnick, *The History of Psychiatry,* p. 154.
76. Quoted in Comfort, pp. 107–108.
77. John Stuart Mill, *The Subjection of Women,* pp. 229, 266.
78. Hare, p. 21.
79. Quoted in Hare, p. 23.
80. Ibid., p. 9.
81. Quoted in Aron Krich, Introduction: The Humanization of Sex, in Aron Krich (Ed.), *The Sexual Revolution,* Vol. 1, *Pioneer Writings on Sex,* p. 10.
82. Ibid., p. 14.
83. Werner Richter, *The Mad Monarch,* p. 250; see also Thomas S. Szasz, *Law, Liberty, and Psychiatry,* pp. 48–53.
84. Quoted in Comfort, p. 108.
85. Anton Pavlovich Chekhov, Ward No. 6 (1892), in *Seven Short Stories by Chekhov,* pp. 106–157; p. 126.
86. Adolf Leschnitzer, *The Magic Background of Modern Anti-Semitism,* p. 193.
87. Max I. Dimont, *Jews, God, and History,* p. 321.
88. Quoted in Dain, p. 137.
89. Spitz, p. 123.
90. Clifford Whittingham Beers, *A Mind That Found Itself,* p. 218.
91. Ridenour, p. 77.
92. Ibid.
93. Quoted in Albert Schweitzer, *The Psychiatric Study of Jesus,* p. 44.
94. Kraepelin, pp. 106–107.
95. Quoted in Schweitzer, p. 40.
96. Ibid., pp. 27–28, 72.
97. Kraepelin, pp. 152–154.
98. Quoted in Hare, p. 9.
99. Ridenour, p. 39.
100. Quoted in Rogow, pp. 195, 202.
101. Franz Alexander and Hugo Staub, *The Criminal, the Judge, and the Public,* p. xiii.
102. Karl A. Menninger, *The Human Mind,* p. 428.
103. Quoted in Rogow, p. 321.

104. Leschnitzer, p. 49.
105. Terence Prittie, *Germans Against Hitler*, pp. 61–63.
106. Quoted in Antoni Gollan, The great marijuana problem, *Nat. Rev.*, Jan. 30, 1968, pp. 74–80; p. 74.
107. Hannah Arendt, *Eichmann in Jerusalem*, p. 95.
108. Edward A. Strecker, *Beyond the Clinical Frontiers*, p. 180.
109. George H. Stevenson, Presidential address: The psychiatric public health aspects of war, *Amer. J. Psychiat.*, 98: 1–8 (July), 1941, pp. 3, 8.
110. Arendt, p. 96.
111. Ibid., p. 105.
112. Deutsch, pp. 448–449.
113. Quoted in Thomas S. Szasz, *Law, Liberty, and Psychiatry*, pp. 202–203.
114. G. Brock Chisholm, The psychiatry of enduring peace and social progress, *Psychiat.* 9: 3–11 (Jan.), 1946; p. 11.
115. *Immigration and Nationality Act of 1952*, par. 212 (a) (4), 8 U.S.C., par. 1182 (a) (4), 1964; popularly known as the McCarran Act.
116. Thomas R. Byrne, Jr. and Francis M. Mulligan, "Psychopathic personality" and "sexual deviation": Medical terms or legal catch-alls—Analysis of the status of the homosexual alien, *Temple Law Quart.*, 40: 328–347 (Spring–Summer), 1967.
117. *Durham v. United States*, 214 F. 2d, 862 (D.C. Circ.), 1954; pp. 874–875.
118. Abe Fortas, Implications of Durham's case, *Amer. J. Psychiat.*, 113: 577–582 (Jan.), 1957; pp. 581, 579.
119. *Williams v. United States*, 250 F. 2d, 19 (1957); p. 26.
120. A. M. Rosenthal and Arthur Gelb, *One More Victim*, pp. 119–120.
121. Quoted in ibid., p. 235.
122. Arendt, p. 22.
123. Ibid., p. 64.
124. *Constitutional Rights of the Mentally Ill*, p. 64.
125. Ibid., p. 75.
126. *Robinson v. California*, 370 U.S. 660, 1962; p. 665.
127. John F. Kennedy, Message from the President of the United States relative to mental illness and mental retardation (U.S. 88th Cong., 1st sess., 1963 H. Rep., Doc. No. 58), p. 2.
128. Theodore H. White, *The Making of the President*, p. 29.
129. Abraham Ribicoff, Why I proposed a commission to study the problem of childhood mental illness, *Psychiat. News*, Jan., 1966, p. 6.
130. The unconscious of a conservative: A special issue on the mind of Barry Goldwater, *Fact*, Vol. 1, No. 5 (Sept.–Oct.), 1964; p. 55.
131. Quoted in Martin Gansberg, Peace Corps sets world health aid, *New York Times*, November 16, 1964, p. 1.
132. Quoted in William F. Buckley, Jr., LBJ is "getting it in the neck" unfairly, *Syracuse (N.Y.) Herald-American*, July 18, 1965, p. 17.
133. Quoted in Ruth Fox, Alcoholism in 1966 (Editor's Notebook), *Amer. J. Psychiat.*, 123: 337–338 (Sept.), 1966; p. 337.
134. Quoted in Goffredo Parise, No neurotics in China, *Atlas*, 13: 46–47 (Feb.), 1967; p. 47.

135. Editorial: Changing concepts of suicide, *J.A.M.A.*, 199: 162 (Mar. 6), 1967.
136. Council of the American Psychiatric Association, Position statement on the question of adequacy of treatment, *Amer. J. Psychiat.*, 123: 1458–1460 (May), 1967; p. 1459.
137. Harvey J. Tompkins, The presidential address: The physician in contemporary society, *Amer. J. Psychiat.*, 124: 1–6 (July), 1967; p. 3.
138. George Stevenson, Psychopathology of international behavior (Letter to the Editor), *Amer. J. Psychiat.*, 124: 166–167 (Nov.), 1967.
139. Quoted in William F. Buckley, Jr., Reagan and Yale, Syracuse (N.Y.) *Post-Standard*, Dec. 26, 1967, p. 5.
140. Quoted in Democracy has/hasn't a future . . . a present, *New York Times Magazine*, May 26, 1968, pp. 30–31, 98–104; p. 101.
141. Quoted in ibid., pp. 98, 102.
142. Drew Pearson, Wallace's mental record, Syracuse (N.Y.) *Post-Standard*, Oct. 16, 1968, p. 11.
143. Richard Eder, 1492 ban on Jews is voided by Spain, *New York Times*, Dec. 17, 1968, pp. 1, 14.
144. Howard P. Rome, Psychiatry and foreign affairs: The expanding competence of psychiatry, *Amer. J. Psychiat.*, 125: 725–730 (Dec.), 1968; pp. 727, 729.

BIBLIOGRAPHY

Acton, J. E. E. D. Acton-Creighton Correspondence. In Acton, J. E. E. D., *Essays on Freedom and Power*. Selected and with a new Introduction by Gertrude Himmelfarb. Pp. 328–345. New York: Meridian, 1955.

Alexander, F., and Staub, H. *The Criminal, the Judge, and the Public: A Psychological Analysis*. Rev. Ed. With new Chapters by Franz Alexander. Original Ed. translated by Gregory Zilboorg. Glencoe, Ill.: Free Press and Falcon's Wing Press, 1956.

Alexander, F. G., and Selesnick, S. T. *The History of Psychiatry: An Evaluation of Psychiatric Thought and Practice from Prehistoric Times to the Present*. New York: Harper & Row, 1966.

American Civil Liberties Union. *The Policy Guide of the American Civil Liberties Union*. Policy No. 225. The Mentally Ill—Civil Commitment. June, 1966.

American Civil Liberties Union. *New Dimensions . . . New Challenges: 46th Annual Report* (July 1, 1965–Jan. 1, 1967), p. 35.

American Medical Association. Changing concepts of suicide (Editorial). *J.A.M.A.*, 199: 162 (Mar. 6), 1967.

American Psychiatric Association. Position statement on the question of adequacy of treatment. *Amer. J. Psychiat.*, 123: 1458–1460 (May), 1967.

Arendt, H. *The Burden of Our Time*. London: Secker & Warburg, 1951.

Arendt, H. *Eichmann in Jerusalem: A Report on the Banality of Evil*. New York: Viking, 1963.

Asbury, E. E. Faster mental examinations ordered for defendants here. *New York Times*, July 8, 1967, p. 26.

Attack on Narcotics: New York State's Bold New Program for the Prevention, Treatment, and Control of Narcotic Addiction. Albany: New York State Narcotic Addiction Control Commission, 1967.

Attorneys-at-psychiatry. *Smith, Kline & French Psychiatric Rep.* July–Aug., 1965, pp. 23–25.

Augstein, R. Die perfiden Juden (The heretical Jews). *Der Spiegel,* Sept. 4, 1967, pp. 120–126.

Ayd, F. J., Jr. Ugo Cerletti, M.D., 1877–1963 (Guest Editorial). *Psychosomatics,* 4: A/6–A/7 (Nov.–Dec.), 1963.

Bakewell, T. A letter to the chairman of the Select Committee of the House of Commons, appointed to enquire into the state of madhouses (1815). In Hunter and Macalpine, pp. 705–709.

Baskin, W. Foreword. In *Voltaire's Philosophical Dictionary: A Compendium.* Translated and edited by Wade Baskin, pp. 3–5. New York: Philosophical Library, 1961.

Bateson, G., (Ed.). *Perceval's Narrative: A Patient's Account of His Psychosis, 1830–1832.* Stanford, Calif.: Stanford Univer. Press, 1961.

Bazelon, D. Justice stumbles over science. *Trans-action,* 4: 8–17 (July–Aug.), 1967.

Bean, W. B. Bring out your dead (Editorial). *Arch. Intern. Med.,* 117: 1–3 (Jan.), 1966.

Beauvoir, S. de. *The Second Sex* (1949). Translated by H. M. Parshley. New York: Bantam, 1961.

Beaver, J. E. The "mentally ill" and the law: Sisyphus and Zeus. *Utah Law Rev.,* 1968: 1–71 (Mar.), 1968.

Becker, H. S. *Outsiders: Studies in the Sociology of Deviance.* New York: Free Press, 1963.

Beers, C. W. *A Mind That Found Itself: An Autobiography* (1908). 7th Ed. Garden City, N.Y.: Doubleday, 1956.

Bellak, L., (Ed.). *Handbook of Community Psychiatry and Community Mental Health.* New York: Grune & Stratton, 1964.

Benda, J. *The Great Betrayal* (1927). Translated by Richard Aldington. London: George Routledge & Sons, 1928.

Binger, C. *Revolutionary Doctor: Benjamin Rush, 1746–1813.* New York: Norton, 1966.

Boorstin, D. J. *The Lost World of Thomas Jefferson.* Boston: Beacon, 1948.

Boorstin, D., (Ed.). *An American Primer.* Chicago: Univer. of Chicago Press, 1966.

Boutilier v. *Immigration and Naturalization Service.* 387 U.S. 118, 1967.

Braceland, F. J. Testimony. In *Constitutional Rights of the Mentally Ill,* pp. 63–74, 183–199.

Braceland, F. J., and Ewalt, J. R. Excerpts from testimony presented on behalf of the American Psychiatric Association. In *Constitutional Rights of the Mentally Ill,* pp. 79–85.

Brand, J. *Doctors and the State: The British Medical Profession and Government Action in Public Health, 1870–1912.* Baltimore: Johns Hopkins Press, 1965.

Brant, I. *The Bill of Rights: Its Origins and Meaning.* Indianapolis: Bobbs-Merrill, 1965.

Brown v. *Board of Education.* 347 U.S. 483, 1954.

Buckley, W. F., Jr. LBJ is "getting it in the neck" unfairly . . . Innuendoes resented. Syracuse (N.Y.) *Herald-American,* July 18, 1965, p. 17.

Buckley, W. F., Jr. Reagan and Yale. Syracuse (N.Y.) *Post-Standard,* Dec. 26, 1967, p. 5.

Burke, K. Interaction: III. Dramatism. In Sills, D. L., (Ed.), *International Encyclopedia of the Social Sciences,* Vol. 7, pp. 445–452. New York: Macmillan and Free Press, 1968.

Burke, V. Soviet atheist's life happier than believer's, sociologist reports. Syracuse (N.Y.) *Herald-Journal,* Dec. 2, 1966, p. 28.

Burroughs, W. S. *Naked Lunch* (1959). New York: Grove, 1966.

Butler, S. *The Way of All Flesh* (1903). Baltimore: Penguin, 1953.

Byrne, T. R., Jr., and Mulligan, F. M. "Psychopathic personality" and "sexual deviation": Medical terms or legal catch-alls—Analysis of the status of the homosexual alien. *Temple Law Quart.,* 40: 328–347 (Spring–Summer), 1967.

Callahan, J. P. Welfare clients called coerced. *New York Times,* July 22, 1967, p. 22.

Camus, A. *The Plague* (1947). Translated by Stuart Gilbert. New York: Modern Library, 1948.

Camus, A. *The Rebel: An Essay on Man in Revolt* (1951). With a Foreword by Sir Herbert Read. Translated by Anthony Bower. New York: Vintage Books, 1956.

Camus, A. Preface to Algerian Reports (1958). In *Resistance, Rebellion, and Death,* pp. 111–125. Translated by Justin O'Brien. New York: Knopf, 1961.

Caplan, G. Community Psychiatry: Introduction and Overview. In Goldston, S. E., (Ed.), *Concepts of Community Psychiatry: A Framework for Training,* pp. 3–18. Washington: U.S. Government Printing Office, 1965.

Caplan, G. *Principles of Preventive Psychiatry.* New York: Basic Books, 1964.

Carroll, L. *Alice's Adventures in Wonderland* (1865). In *The Annotated Alice.* With an Introduction and Notes by Martin Gardner. Harmondsworth: Penguin, 1965.

Cassirer, E. *The Myth of the State* (1946). Garden City, N.Y.: Doubleday-Anchor, 1955.

Cervantes, S. M. de. *The Adventures of Don Quixote* (1604, 1614). Translated by J. M. Cohen. Baltimore: Penguin, 1954.

Chekhov, A. P. Ward No. 6 (1892). In *Seven Short Stories by Chekhov,* pp. 106–157. Translated by Barbara Makanowitzky. New York: Bantam Books, 1963.

Chinese Exclusion case, The. 130 U.S. 581, 1889.

Chisholm, G. B. The psychiatry of enduring peace and social progress. *Psychiat.*, 9: 3–11 (Jan.), 1946.

Churchill, W. *Homosexual Behavior Among Males: A Cross-Cultural and Cross-Species Investigation.* New York: Hawthorn, 1967.

Cobb, S. Discussion of "Is the term 'mysterious leap' warranted?" In Deutsch, F., (Ed.), *On the Mysterious Leap from the Mind to the Body: A Workshop Study on the Theory of Conversion*, p. 11. New York: International Universities Press, 1959.

Cohn, N. *The Pursuit of the Millennium: Revolutionary Messianism in Medieval and Reformation Europe and Its Bearing on Modern Totalitarian Movements.* 2d Ed. New York: Harper Torchbooks, 1961.

Cohn, N. *Warrant for Genocide: The Myth of the Jewish World-Conspiracy and the Protocols of the Elders of Zion.* New York: Harper & Row, 1966.

Collingwood, R. G. *The Idea of History.* New York: Oxford Univer. Press, 1946.

Comfort, A. *The Anxiety Makers: Some Curious Preoccupations of the Medical Profession.* London: Nelson, 1967.

Conolly, J. An inquiry concerning the indications of insanity, with suggestions for better protection and care of the insane (1830). In Hunter and Macalpine, pp. 805–809.

Constitutional Rights of the Mentally Ill: Part I, Civil Aspects. Washington: U.S. Government Printing Office, 1961.

Consultant psychiatrist. The scandal of the British mental hospital. *Manchester Guardian*, Mar. 25, 1965.

Cooper, B., and Brown, A. C. Psychiatric practice in Great Britain and America: A comparative study. *Brit. J. Psychiat.*, 113: 625–636, 1967.

Cornell, J. *The Trial of Ezra Pound: A Documented Account of the Treason Case by the Defendant's Lawyer.* New York: John Day, 1966.

Cory, D. W. *Homosexuality: A Cross-Cultural Approach.* New York: Julian, 1956.

Cory, D. W. *The Homosexual in America.* 2d Ed. New York: Castle Books, 1960.

Cramer, J. B. Common Neuroses of Childhood. In Arieti, S., (Ed.), *American Handbook of Psychiatry*, Vol. I, pp. 797–815. New York: Basic Books, 1959.

Crosscurrents of Psychiatric Thought Today: On Homosexuality. Nutley, N.J.: Roche Laboratories, 1967.

Cumming, R. D. *The Philosophy of Jean-Paul Sartre.* New York: Random House, 1965.

Dain, N. *Concepts of Insanity in the United States, 1789–1865.* New Brunswick: Rutgers Univer. Press, 1964.

Davidson, H. The semantics of psychotherapy. *Amer. J. Psychiat.,* 115: 410–413 (Nov.), 1958.

Davidson, H. The image of the psychiatrist. *Amer. J. Psychiat.,* 121: 329–333 (Oct.), 1964.

Davis, D. B. *The Problem of Slavery in Western Culture.* Ithaca, N.Y.: Cornell Univer. Press, 1966.

Davis, K. The application of science to personal relations: A critique of the family clinic idea. *Amer. Sociol. Rev.,* 1: 238–249 (Apr.), 1936.

Davis, K. Mental hygiene and the class structure. *Psychiat.* 1: 55–65 (Jan.), 1938.

De George, R. T., (Ed.). *Ethics and Society: Original Essays on Contemporary Moral Problems.* Garden City, N.Y.: Doubleday Anchor, 1966.

Democracy has/hasn't a future . . . a present. *New York Times Magazine,* May 26, 1968, pp. 30–31, 98–104.

Deutsch, A. *The Mentally Ill in America: A History of Their Care and Treatment from Colonial Times.* 2d Ed. New York: Columbia Univer. Press, 1952.

Dimont, M. I. *Jews, God, and History.* New York: Simon & Schuster, 1962.

Dix, D. L. *Memorial to the Legislature of Massachusetts, 1843.* Pamphlet published by the Directors of the Old South Works, Boston, Mass., 1843. Reprinted in Facsimile by Roche Laboratories, Nutley, N.J., 1968.

Dostoyevsky, F. *The Brothers Karamazov* (1880). Translated by Constance Garnett. New York: Random House, 1950.

Douglass, F. The anti-slavery movement (A lecture delivered in Rochester, New York, 1885). Quoted in *Civil Liberties,* No. 214, Mar., 1964, p. 1.

Dru, A., (Ed.). *The Journals of Kierkegaard* (1853–1854). New York: Harper Torchbooks, 1959.

Duffy, J. Masturbation and clitoridectomy. *J.A.M.A.,* 186: 246–248 (Oct. 19), 1963.

Dunham, B. *Man Against Myth* (1947). New York: Hill & Wang, 1962.

Dunham B. *Heroes and Heretics: A Political History of Western Thought.* New York: Knopf, 1964.

Durham v. *United States.* 214 F. 2d, 862 (D.C. Circ.), 1954.

Duzynski v. *Nosal.* 324 F. 2d, 924 (7th Cir.), 1963.

Eder, R. 1492 Ban on Jews is voided by Spain. *New York Times,* Dec. 17, 1968, pp. 1, 14.

Eissler, R. S. Scapegoats of Society. In Eissler, K. R., (Ed.), *Searchlights on*

Delinquency, pp. 288–305. New York: International Universities Press, 1949.

Elinson, J., Padilla, E., and Perkins, M. E. *Public Image of Mental Health Services.* New York: Ment. Health Materials Center, 1967.

Eliot, T. S. *The Cocktail Party.* New York: Harcourt, Brace & World, 1950.

Ellenberger, H. F. The Evolution of Depth Psychology. In Galdston, I. (Ed.), *Historic Derivations of Modern Psychiatry,* pp. 159–184. New York: McGraw-Hill, 1967.

Emerson, R. W. Self-reliance (1841). In Lindeman, E., (Ed.), *Basic Selections from Emerson: Essays, Poems, and Apothegms,* pp. 53–73. New York: Mentor, 1954.

Ewalt, J. Statement. In *Constitutional Rights of the Mentally Ill,* pp. 74–79.

Fanon, F. *The Wretched of the Earth* (1961). Translated by Constance Farrington. New York: Grove, 1966.

Feinstein, H. M. Hamlet's Horatio and the therapeutic mode. *Amer. J. Psychiat.,* 123: 803–809 (Jan.), 1967.

Felix, R. H. The image of the psychiatrist: Past, present and future. *Amer. J. Psychiat.,* 21: 318–322 (Oct.), 1964.

Felix, R. H. *Mental Illness: Progress and Prospects.* New York: Columbia Univer. Press, 1967.

Fenichel, O. *The Psychoanalytic Theory of Neurosis.* New York: Norton, 1945.

Fenwick, B. Russians ahead on mental health? *Daily Oklahoman,* Mar. 10, 1967, pp. 1–2.

Flexner, J. T. He sought to do good. *New York Times Book Review,* Nov. 13, 1966, p. 60.

Forbes, T. R. *The Midwife and the Witch.* New Haven: Yale Univer. Press, 1966.

Fortas, A. Implications of Durham's case. *Amer. J. Psychiat.* 113: 577–582 (Jan.), 1967.

Foucault, M. *Madness and Civilization: A History of Insanity in the Age of Reason* (1961). Translated by Richard Howard. New York: Pantheon, 1965.

Fox, R. Alcoholism in 1966 (Editor's Notebook). *Amer. J. Psychiat.,* 123: 337–338 (Sept.), 1966.

Frazer, J. G. *The Golden Bough: A Study in Magic and Religion* (1922), 1-vol., Abridged Edition. New York: Macmillan, 1942.

Freud, S. Charcot (1893). In *The Standard Edition of the Complete Psychological Works of Sigmund Freud,* Vol. III, pp. 7–23. London: Hogarth, 1962.

Freud, S. The neuro-psychoses of defence (1894). In *The Standard*

Edition of the Complete Psychological Works of Sigmund Freud, Vol. III, pp. 41–61. London: Hogarth, 1962.

Freud, S. Letter 21, Aug. 29, 1894. In *The Standard Edition of the Complete Psychological Works of Sigmund Freud*, Vol. I, p. 199. London: Hogarth, 1966.

Freud, S. Letter 56, Jan. 17, 1897. In *The Standard Edition of the Complete Psychological Works of Sigmund Freud*, Vol. I, p. 242. London: Hogarth, 1966.

Freud, S. Letter 79, Dec. 22, 1897. In *The Standard Edition of the Complete Psychological Works of Sigmund Freud*, Vol. I, pp. 272–273. London: Hogarth, 1966.

Freud, S. The Psychopathology of Everyday Life (1901). In *The Standard Edition of the Complete Psychological Works of Sigmund Freud*, Vol. VI. London: Hogarth, 1960.

Freud, S. Leonardo da Vinci and a memory of his childhood (1910). In *The Standard Edition of the Complete Psychological Works of Sigmund Freud*. Vol. XI, pp. 57–137. London: Hogarth, 1957.

Freud S. Psycho-analytic notes on an autobiographical account of a case of paranoia (Dementia paranoides) (1911.). In *The Standard Edition of the Complete Psychological Works of Sigmund Freud*. Vol. XII, pp. 1–82. London: Hogarth, 1958.

Freud, S. Contribution to a discussion on masturbation (1912). In *The Standard Edition of the Complete Psychological Works of Sigmund Freud*, Vol. XII, pp. 239–254. London: Hogarth, 1958.

Freud, S. A seventeenth-century demonological neurosis (1923). In *The Standard Edition of the Complete Psychological Works of Sigmund Freud*, Vol. XIX, pp. 67–105. London, Hogarth, 1961.

Freud, S., and Bullitt, W. C. *Thomas Woodrow Wilson, Twenty-eighth President of the United States: A Psychological Study*. Boston: Houghton Mifflin, 1967.

Friedman, M. *Capitalism and Freedom*. Chicago: Univer. of Chicago Press, 1962.

Fromm, E. *Escape from Freedom*. New York: Rinehart, 1941.

Funk, W. *Word Origins*. New York: Grosset & Dunlap, 1950.

Gansberg, M. Peace Corps sets world health aid. *New York Times*, Nov. 16, 1964, p. 1.

Garceau, O. The morals of medicine. *Ann. Pol. & Soc. Sci.*, 363: 60–69 (Jan.), 1966.

Gay, P. *The Enlightenment: An Interpretation*. New York: Knopf, 1967.

Gide, A. *Corydon* (1911). New York: Noonday, 1961.

Glaser, F. G. The dichotomy game: A further consideration of the writings of Dr. Thomas Szasz. *Amer. J. Psychiat.*, 121: 1069–1074 (May), 1965.

Glasser, W. *Reality Therapy: A New Approach to Psychiatry.* New York: Harper & Row, 1965.

Goffman, E. *Asylums: Essays on the Social Situation of Mental Patients and Other Inmates.* Garden City, N.Y.: Doubleday Anchor, 1961.

Goffman, E. *Stigma: Notes on the Management of Spoiled Identity.* Englewood Cliffs, N.J.: Prentice-Hall, 1963.

Goldstein, A. S. *The Insanity Defense.* New Haven: Yale Univer. Press, 1967.

Goldston, S. E., (Ed.). *Concepts of Community Psychiatry: A Framework for Training.* U.S. Public Health Service Publication No. 1319. Washington: U.S. Government Printing Office, 1965.

Gollan, A. The great marijuana problem. *Nat. Rev.,* Jan. 30, 1968, pp. 74–80.

Gould, D. To hell with medical secrecy! *New Statesman,* Mar. 3, 1967, p. 4.

Gould, D. The freedom to be unfit. *New Statesman,* Sept. 1, 1967, p. 4.

Griffith, J. P. C., and Mitchell, A. G. *The Diseases of Infants and Children.* 2d Ed. Philadelphia: Saunders, 1938.

Grose, P. Tarsis, anti-Red writer, is denounced in Soviet as he flies to London. *New York Times,* Feb. 9, 1966, p. 16.

Guillain, G. *J.-M. Charcot, 1825–1893: His Life, His Work.* Translated by Pearce Bailey. New York: Hoeber, 1959.

Gutheil, E. A. Sexual Dysfunctions in Men. In Arieti, S., (Ed.), *American Handbook of Psychiatry,* Vol. I, pp. 708–726. New York: Basic Books, 1959.

Guttmacher, M. S. *Sex Offenses.* New York: Norton, 1951.

Guttmacher, M. S. Critique of views of Thomas Szasz on legal psychiatry. *A.M.A. Arch. Gen. Psychiat.,* 10: 238–245 (Mar.), 1964.

Guyon, R. *The Ethics of Sexual Acts* (1930). Translated by J. C. and Ingeborg Flugel. Garden City, N.Y.: Blue Ribbon Books, 1941.

Haggard, H. W. *Devils, Drugs, and Doctors: The Story of the Science of Healing from Medicine-Man to Doctor* (1929). New York: Pocket Books, 1946.

Halleck, S. L. *Psychiatry and the Dilemmas of Crime: A Study of Causes, Punishment, and Treatment.* New York: Harper & Hoeber, 1967.

Hare, E. H. Masturbatory insanity: The history of an idea. *J. Ment. Sci.,* 108: 1–25 (Jan.), 1962.

Harper, A. *A Treatise on the Real Cause and Cure of Insanity* (1789). In Hunter and Macalpine, pp. 522–524.

Harrington, S. Homosexual sortie: An anonymous crusade. *Village Voice,* May 25, 1967, pp. 9–10.

Harrison, J. E. *Epilegomena to the Study of Greek Religion and*

Themis: A Study of the Social Origins of Greek Religion (1912, 1921). New Hyde Park, N.Y.: Univer. Books, 1962.

Harvey, D. J. Typical conditions (Letters). *Manchester Guardian*, March 30, 1965, p. 6.

Hayek, F. A. *The Counter-Revolution of Science: Studies on the Abuse of Reason* (1955). New York: Free Press, 1964.

Hayek, F. A. *The Constitution of Liberty*. Chicago: Univer. of Chicago Press, 1960.

Heer, F. *Gottes Erste Liebe (God's First Love)*. München: Bechtle Verlag, 1967.

Henry, J. *Culture Against Man*. New York: Random House, 1963.

High rate of suicide among physicians. *Med. World News*, July 3, 1964, p. 87.

Hilberg, R. *The Destruction of the European Jews*. Chicago: Quadrangle Books, 1961.

Hirsch, B. D. Informed consent to treatment: Medicolegal comment. In Averbach, A., and Belli, M. M., (Eds.), *Tort and Medical Yearbook*, Vol. I, pp. 631–638. Indianapolis: Bobbs-Merrill, 1961.

Hole, C. *Witchcraft in England* (1947). New York: Collier Books, 1966.

Hollingshead, A. B., and Redlich, F. C. *Social Class and Mental Illness: A Community Study*. New York: Wiley, 1958.

Holy Bible. RSV. Cleveland: Meridian, 1965.

Hughes, P. *Witchcraft* (1952). Harmondsworth: Penguin, 1965.

Huizinga, J. *The Waning of the Middle Ages* (1924). Garden City, N.Y.: Doubleday Anchor, 1954.

Hunter, R., and Macalpine, I. *Three Hundred Years of Psychiatry, 1535–1860: A History Presented in Selected English Texts*. New York: Oxford Univer. Press, 1963.

Isaac, J. *The Teaching of Contempt: Christian Roots of Anti-Semitism* (1962). Translated by Helen Weaver. New York: McGraw-Hill, 1965.

Jones, E. The nature of autosuggestion (1923). In *Papers on Psycho-Analysis*, pp. 273–293. Baltimore: Williams & Wilkins, 1948.

Kamen, H. *The Spanish Inquisition*. New York: New American Library, 1965.

Kaplan, J., and Waltz, J. R. *The Trial of Jack Ruby*. New York: Macmillan, 1965.

Kaufman, M. R. Psychiatry: Why "medical" or "social" model? *A.M.A. Arch. Gen. Psychiat.*, 17: 347–360 (Sept.), 1967.

Kennedy, J. F. Message from the President of the United States relative to mental illness and mental retardation, Feb. 5, 1963, 88th Cong., 1st sess., H. Rep., Doc. No. 58.

Kierkegaard, S. All-nothing (1854). In *The Journals of Kierkegaard*

(1835–1854), pp. 245–246. Edited and with an Introduction by Alexander Dru. New York: Harper Torchbooks, 1959.

Kierkegaard, S. *The Last Years: Journals, 1853–1855*. Translated and edited by Ronald Gregor Smith. London: Collins, 1965.

Kinsey, A. C., Pomeroy, W. B., and Martin, C. E. *Sexual Behavior in the Human Male*. Philadelphia: Saunders, 1948.

Kinsey, A. C., Pomeroy, W. B., Martin, C. E., and Gebhard, P. *Sexual Behavior in the Human Female*. Philadelphia: Saunders, 1953.

Koessler, M. Euthanasia in the Hadamar Sanatorium and international law. *J. Crim. Law, Criminol., and Police Sci.*, 43: 735–755 (Mar.–Apr.), 1953.

Kolb, L. Soviet psychiatric organization and the community mental health center concept. *Amer. J. Psychiat.*, 123: 433–440 (Oct.), 1966.

Kosinski, J. *The Painted Bird*. Boston: Houghton Mifflin Co., 1965.

Kraepelin, E. *One Hundred Years of Psychiatry* (1917). Translated by Wade Baskin. New York: Philosophical Library, 1962.

Krich, A. Introduction: The Humanization of Sex. In Krich, A., (Ed.), *The Sexual Revolution, Vol. I, Pioneer Writings on Sex: Krafft-Ebing, Ellis, Freud*, pp. 7–39. New York: Delta, 1964.

Kutner, L. The illusion of due process in commitment proceedings. *Northwestern Univer. Law Rev.*, 57: 383–399 (Sept.–Oct.), 1962.

Kuznetsov, A. *Babi Yar: A Documentary Novel*. Translated by Jacob Guralsky. New York: Dial Press, 1966.

Laing, R. D. *The Politics of Experience and the Bird of Paradise*. Harmondsworth: Penguin, 1967.

Landau, J. C. GI justice: A 2d class system. Syracuse (N.Y.) *Herald-American*, Sept. 10, 1967, p. 69.

Landau, J. C. 30,000 GI's "branded" by "less than honorable" discharges. Syracuse (N.Y.) *Herald-Journal*, Sept. 14, 1967, p. 39.

Lawson, J. D. *Modern Greek Folklore and Ancient Greek Religion* (1909). New Hyde Park, N.Y.: Univer. Books, 1964.

Lea, H. C. *The Inquisition of the Middle Ages: Its Organization and Operation* (1887). New York: Citadel, 1961.

Lea, H. C. *A History of the Inquisition of Spain*. 4 vols. New York: Macmillan, 1906–1907.

Lecky, W. E. H. *History of European Morals* (1869). 2 vols. New York: Braziller, 1955.

Leitsch, D. The psychotherapy of homosexuality: Let's forget Jocasta and her little boy. *Psychiat. Opin.*, 4: 28–35 (June), 1967.

Leschnitzer, A. *The Magic Background of Modern Anti-Semitism: An Analysis of the German-Jewish Relationship*. New York: International Universities Press, 1956.

Lettres de cachet. In *Encyclopaedia Britannica*, Vol. 13, p. 971. Chicago: Encyclopaedia Britannica, Inc., 1949.

Lhermitte, J. *True and False Possession* (1955). Translated by P. J. Hepburne-Scot. New York: Hawthorn Books, 1963.

Lifton, R. J. *Thought Reform and the Psychology of Totalism: A Study of "Brainwashing" in China.* New York: Norton, 1961.

Lincoln, A. From a letter (1858). In Morley, C., and Everett, Louella D., (Eds.), *[Bartlett's] Familiar Quotations*, p. 455. Boston: Little, Brown & Co., 1951.

Lindman, F. T., and McIntyre, D. M., Jr., (Eds.). *The Mentally Disabled and the Law: The Report of the American Bar Foundation on the Rights of the Mentally Ill.* Chicago: Univer. of Chicago Press, 1961.

Lindner, R. *Must You Conform?* (1956). New York: Grove Press, 1961.

Linton, R. *The Tree of Culture.* New York: Knopf, 1957.

Litvak, L. A trip to Esalen Institute: Joy is the prize. *New York Times Magazine*, Dec. 31, 1967, pp. 8, 28–31.

Lockman, R. F. Nationwide study yields profile of psychiatrists. *Psychiat. News:* 1:2 (Jan.), 1966.

Lofty career cut short at its peak. *Med. World News*, Jan. 19, 1968, p. 30.

Lorenz, K. *On Aggression* (1963). Translated by Marjorie Kerr Wilson. New York: Harcourt, Brace & World, 1966.

McGarry, A. L. Competency for trial and due process via the state mental hospital. *Amer. J. Psychiat.*, 122: 623–630 (Dec.), 1965.

Machado De Assis, J. The Psychiatrist (1881–1882). In *The Psychiatrist and Other Stories.* Translated by William L. Grossman, pp. 1–45. Berkeley and Los Angeles: Univer. of Calif. Press, 1963.

Mackay, C. *Extraordinary Popular Delusions and the Madness of Crowds* (1841, 1852). New York: Noonday Press, 1962.

McKay, R. B., (Ed.). *An American Constitutional Law Reader.* New York: Oceana, 1958.

M'Naghten's Case. 10 Cl. & F. 200, 8 Eng. Rep. 718 (H.L.), 1843.

Malinowski, B. *Magic, Science, and Religion* (1948). Garden City, N.Y.: Doubleday Anchor, 1954.

Mann, A. Quoted in Vincent Canby, On the set here, a man and his entourage: Sinatra starts work in city on filming of "Detective." *New York Times*, Oct. 18, 1967, p. 37.

Mannheim, K. *Ideology and Utopia: An Introduction to the Sociology of Knowledge* (1929). Translated by Louis Wirth and Edward Shils. New York: Harcourt, Brace, 1936.

Markmann, C. L. *The Noblest Cry: A History of the American Civil Liberties Union.* New York: St. Martin's Press, 1965.

Masserman, J. H. *The Practice of Dynamic Psychiatry.* Philadelphia: Saunders, 1955.

Matson, F. *The Broken Image: Man, Science, and Society.* New York: Braziller, 1964.

Maymandi, A. Community psychiatry. *Hospital Tribune,* Jan. 1, 1968, p. 8.

MD's role in mental health stressed. *A.M.A. News,* Mar. 13, 1967, p. 3.

MD suicides: "Role strain" seen as a cause of high rate. *Med. World News,* May 29, 1967, pp. 1, 20.

Melendy, M. R. *Perfect Womanhood: A Complete Medical Guide for Women.* Copyright 1903, K. T. Boland; publisher not otherwise identified.

Menninger, K. *The Human Mind.* New York: Literary Guild of America, 1930.

Menninger, K. *Man Against Himself.* New York: Harcourt, Brace, 1938.

Menninger, K. *The Vital Balance: The Life Process in Mental Health and Illness.* New York: Viking, 1963.

Menninger, K. Introduction. In *The Wolfenden Report: Report of the Committee on Homosexual Offenses and Prostitution,* pp. 5–7. New York: Stein & Day, 1964.

Menninger, W. C. *Psychiatrist to a Troubled World.* New York: Viking, 1967.

Micciche, S. J. Bridgewater holds colony of lost men. Boston *Globe,* Feb. 20, 1963, p. 1.

Michelet, J. *Satanism and Witchcraft: A Study in Medieval Superstition* (1862). Translated by A. R. Allinson. New York: Citadel, 1965.

Mill, J. S. *On Liberty* (1859). Chicago: Regnery, 1955.

Mill, J. S. *Auguste Comte and Positivism* (1865). Ann Arbor: Univer. of Michigan—Ann Arbor Paperbacks, 1965.

Mill, J. S. *The Subjection of Women* (1869). London: Dent-Everyman's Library, 1965.

Mitscherlich, A., and Mielke, F. *Doctors of Infamy: The Story of Nazi Medical Crimes.* Translated by Heinz Norden. New York: Henry Schuman, 1949.

Mora, G. From Demonology to the Narrenturm. In Galdston, I., (Ed.), *Historic Derivations of Modern Psychiatry,* pp. 41–73. New York: Blakiston-McGraw-Hill, 1967.

Morgan, E. S., (Ed.). Mary Easty, Petition of an Accused Witch, 1692. In Boorstin, D., (Ed.), *An American Primer,* pp. 26–30. Chicago: Univer. of Chicago Press, 1966.

Morley, C., and Everett, Louella D., (Eds.). [*Bartlett's*] *Familiar Quotations.* Boston: Little, Brown & Co., 1951.

Muller, H. J. *Freedom in the Western World: From the Dark Ages to the Rise of Democracy.* New York: Harper & Row, 1963.

Myrdal, G. *An American Dilemma: The Negro Problem and Modern Democracy.* New York: Harper, 1944.

National Association for Mental Health. *Calendar for 1968.*

New Catholic Encylopedia. New York: McGraw-Hill, 1967.

New York Mental Hygiene Law, Patients' Rights: Third Draft of Legislation and Analysis. Institute of Public Administration, Research Memorandum No. 41, Dec., 1967, mimeographed.

Nisbet, R. A. *The Sociological Tradition.* New York: Basic Books, 1966.

Nonmedical hypnotist convicted. *A.M.A. News,* Oct. 2, 1967, p. 9.

Nouwen, H. J. M. Homosexuality: Prejudice or mental illness? *Natl. Catholic Rep.,* Nov. 29, 1967, p. 8.

Orlans, H. An American death camp (1948). In Rosenberg, B., Gerver, I., and Howton, F. W., (Eds.), *Mass Society in Crisis: Social Problems and Social Pathology,* pp. 614–628. New York: Macmillan, 1964.

Orwell, G. *Nineteen Eighty-Four.* New York: Harcourt, Brace, 1949.

Osmundsen, J. Doctor discusses "mixed" marriage: Sees interracial unions as outlets for revenge. *New York Times,* Nov. 7, 1965, p. 73.

Overholser, W. Statement. In *Constitutional Rights of the Mentally Ill,* pp. 19–39.

Packard, E. P. W. *The Prisoner's Hidden Life.* Chicago: Published by author, 1868.

Packard, E. P. W. *Modern Persecution: Or Insane Asylums Unveiled,* Vol. I. Hartford: Case, Lockwood, & Brainard, 1873.

Parise, G. No neurotics in China. *Atlas,* 13:46–47 (Feb.), 1967.

Parrinder, G. *Witchcraft.* Harmondsworth: Penguin, 1958.

Pearson, D. Wallace's mental record. Syracuse (N.Y.) *Post-Standard,* Oct. 16, 1968, p. 11.

Phillips, D. L. Rejection: A possible consequence of seeking help for mental disorders. *Amer. Sociol. Rev.,* 28:963–972 (Dec.), 1963.

Phillips, D L. Identification of mental illness: Its consequences for rejection. *Community Ment. Health J.,* 3:262–266 (Fall), 1967.

Physician suicides cause concern. *Med. World News,* June 9, 1967, pp. 28–29.

Pinel, P. *A Treatise on Insanity* (1801). Translated by D. D. Davis. Facsimile of the London 1806 Edition. New York: Hafner, 1962.

Podgorecki, A. Law and mental illness: Social engineering (Abstract). *Sandoz Psychiat. Spectator,* 4:15–16 (Sept.), 1967.

Popper, K. R. *The Open Society and Its Enemies* (1945). Princeton: Princeton Univer. Press, 1950.

Prittie, T. *Germans Against Hitler.* Boston: Little, Brown, 1964.

Prochaska v. *Brinegar.* 251 Iowa 834, 102 N.W. 2d, 1960.

"Psychopathic homosexuals?" *Playboy,* Dec., 1967, p. 86.

Radcliffe-Brown, A. R. On Taboo (1952). In Parsons, T. et. al., (Eds.),

Theories of Society: Foundations of Modern Sociological Theory, Vol. II, pp. 951–959. New York: Free Press, 1961.

Radin, S. S. Mental health problems in school children. *J. Sch. Health,* 32: 390–397 (Dec.), 1962.

Redlich, F. C., and Freedman, D. X. *The Theory and Practice of Psychiatry.* New York: Basic Books, 1966.

Reid, J. *Essays on Insanity, Hypochondriasis, and Other Nervous Affections* (1816). In Hunter and Macalpine, pp. 722–725.

Ribicoff, A. The dangerous ones: Help for children with twisted minds. *Harper's,* Feb., 1965, pp. 88–90.

Ribicoff, A. Why I proposed a commission to study the problem of childhood mental illness. *Psychiat. News,* 1:6 (Jan.), 1966.

Richter, W. *The Mad Monarch: The Life and Times of Ludwig II of Bavaria.* Translated by William S. Schlamm. Chicago: Regnery, 1954.

Ridenour, Nina. *Mental Health in the United States: A Fifty Year History.* Cambridge: Harvard Univer. Press, 1961.

Riedman, Sarah R., and Green, C. C. *Benjamin Rush: Physician, Patriot, Founding Father.* New York: Abelard-Schuman, 1964.

Robbins, R. H. *The Encyclopedia of Witchcraft and Demonology.* New York: Crown, 1959.

Robinson v. *California.* 370 U.S. 660, 1962.

Robitscher, J. B. *Pursuit of Agreement: Psychiatry and the Law.* Philadelphia: Lippincott, 1966.

Roche, P. Q. *The Criminal Mind: A Study of Communication Between Criminal Law and Psychiatry.* New York: Farrar, Strauss, & Cudahy, 1958.

Roemer, M. I. The future of social medicine in the United States. *Pharos of Alpha Omega Alpha,* 30: 42–50 (Apr.), 1967.

Rogow, A. A., (Ed.). *The Jew in a Gentile World: An Anthology of Writings About Jews by Non-Jews.* New York: Macmillan, 1961.

Romains, J. *Knock (Knock, ou le triomphe de la médecine, 1923).* Translated by James B. Gidney. Great Neck, N.Y.: Barron Educational Series, Inc., 1962.

Roman, P. M., and Trice, H. M. *Schizophrenia and the Poor.* New York State School of Industrial and Labor Relations Paperback No. 3. Ithaca, N.Y.: Cayuga Press, 1967.

Rome, H. P. Psychiatry and foreign affairs: The expanding competence of psychiatry. *Amer. J. Psychiat.,* 125: 725–730 (Dec.), 1968.

Rosen, G. Social attitudes to irrationality and madness in 17th and 18th Century Europe. *J. Hist. Med. & All. Sc.,* 18: 220–240 (July), 1963.

Rosenberg, B., Gerver, I., and Howton, F. W., (Eds.). *Mass Society in Crisis: Social Problems and Social Pathology.* New York: Macmillan, 1964.

Rosenthal, A. M., and Gelb, A. *One More Victim.* New York: New American Library, 1967.

Ross, H. A. Commitment of the mentally ill: Problems of law and policy. *Mich. Law Rev.,* 57: 945–1018 (May), 1959.

Ross, H. A. Testimony. In *Constitutional Rights of the Mentally Ill,* pp. 183–199.

Rostow, W. R. *The Dynamics of Soviet Society.* New York: Mentor Books, 1954.

Rush, B. Observations intended to favour a supposition that the black Color (as it is called) of the Negroes is derived from the LEPROSY. *Trans. Amer. Phil. Soc.,* 4: 289–297, 1799.

Rush, B. *Medical Inquiries and Observations upon the Diseases of the Mind* (1812). Facsimile of the Philadelphia 1812 Edition. Introduction by S. Bernard Wortis. New York: Hafner Publishing Co., 1962.

Rush, B. *The Autobiography of Benjamin Rush: His "Travels Through Life" together with his "Commonplace Book for 1789–1813."* Edited with Introduction and Notes by George W. Corner. Princeton: Princeton Univer. Press, 1948.

Russell, B. *Unpopular Essays.* New York: Simon & Schuster, 1950.

Sachar, A. L. *A History of the Jews.* 5th ed. New York: Knopf, 1966.

Salomon, A. *The Tyranny of Progress: Reflections on the Origins of Sociology.* New York: Noonday Press, 1955.

Sartre, J.-P. *Anti-Semite and Jew* (1946). Translated by George J. Becker. New York: Schocken, 1965.

Sartre, J.-P. The Childhood of a Leader. In *Intimacy and Other Stories* (1948). Translated by Lloyd Alexander. New York: Berkeley Publ. Co., 1960.

Sartre, J.-P. *Saint Genêt: Actor and Martyr* (1952). Translated by Bernard Frechtman. New York: Braziller, 1963.

Sartre, J.-P. Preface. In Frantz Fanon, *The Wretched of the Earth* (1961), pp. 7–26. Translated by Constance Farrington. New York: Grove, 1966.

Schachner, N. S. *Thomas Jefferson: A Biography.* New York: Thomas Yoseloff, 1951.

Scheff, T. J. Social conditions for rationality: How urban and rural courts deal with the mentally ill. *Amer. Behav. Scientist,* 7: 21–27 (March), 1964; p. 21.

Scheff, T. J. *Being Mentally Ill: A Sociological Theory.* Chicago: Aldine, 1966.

Scheff, T. J., (Ed.). *Mental Illness and Social Processes.* New York: Harper & Row, 1967.

Schneck, J. *A History of Psychiatry*. Springfield, Ill.: Charles C. Thomas, 1960.

Schweitzer, A. *The Psychiatric Study of Jesus: Exposition and Criticism* (1913). Translated by Charles R. Joy. Boston: Beacon Press, 1948.

Shabecoff, P. Rightist activity rises in Germany: Neo-Nazi and anti-Semitic action up sharply in '65. *New York Times,* Mar. 2, 1966, p. 14.

Shabecoff, P. Neo-Nazi activity rises in Germany: Government's report meets indifference from public. *New York Times,* Mar. 6, 1966, p. 14.

Shengold, L. The effects of over-stimulation: Rat people. *Int. J. Psycho-Anal.,* 48: 403–415, 1967.

Shrapnel, N. Mental hospitals disclosures appall MP. *Manchester Guardian,* Mar. 20, 1965, p. 2.

Sigerist, H. Introduction. In Gregory Zilboorg, *The Medical Man and the Witch During the Renaissance,* pp. i–x. Baltimore: Johns Hopkins Press, 1935.

Sinclair, W. J. *Semmelweis, His Life and His Doctrine: A Chapter in the History of Medicine.* Manchester, England: Univer. Press, 1909.

Smith, H. W. *Man and His Gods.* Boston: Little, Brown, 1953.

Solomon, P. The burden of responsibility in suicide. *J.A.M.A.,* 199: 321–324 (Jan. 30), 1967.

Some jailed 40 years for truancy. Boston *Globe,* Feb. 20, 1963, p. 4.

Soubiran, A. *The Good Doctor Guillotin and His Strange Device.* Translated by Malcolm MacCraw. London: Souvenir Press, 1963.

Soviet MDs find state duties put profession in second place. *A.M.A. News,* May 10, 1965, p. 12.

Spitz, R. A. Authority and masturbation: Some remarks on a bibliographical investigation. *Yearbook of Psychoanalysis,* Vol. 9, pp. 113–145. New York: International Universities Press, 1953.

Spitzka, E. C. *Insanity: Its Classification, Diagnosis, and Treatment.* New York: Bermingham & Co., 1883.

Sprenger, J., and Krämer, H. *Malleus Maleficarum* (1486). Translated with an Introduction, Bibliography, and Notes by Montague Summers. London: Pushkin Press, 1948.

Srole, L., Langer, T. S., Michael, S. T., Opler, M. K., and Rennie, T. A. C. *Mental Health in the Metropolis: The Midtown Manhattan Study.* New York: McGraw-Hill, 1962.

Stanton, W. *The Leopard's Spots: Scientific Attitudes Toward Race in America, 1815–59.* Chicago: Univer. of Chicago Press, 1960.

Stevenson, G. Presidential address: The psychiatric public health aspects of war. *Amer. J. Psychiat.,* 98: 1–8 (July), 1941.

Stevenson, G. Psychopathology of international behavior (Letter to the Editor). *Amer. J. Psychiat.,* 124: 166–167 (Nov.), 1967.

Strauss, M. B., (Ed.). *Familiar Medical Quotations.* Boston: Little, Brown & Co., 1968.

Strecker, E. A. *Beyond the Clinical Frontiers: A Psychiatrist Views Crowd Behavior.* New York: Norton, 1940.

Study depicts GI who marries in Vietnam as a troubled man. *New York Times,* Feb. 25, 1967, p. 7.

Suicide, On. *Time,* Nov. 25, 1966, p. 48.

Summers, M. Introduction. In Sprenger and Krämer, *Malleus Maleficarum,* pp. xi–xvi.

Szasz, T. S. *Pain and Pleasure: A Study of Bodily Feelings.* New York: Basic Books, 1957.

Szasz, T. S. Scientific method and social role in medicine and psychiatry. *A.M.A. Arch. Int. Med.,* 101: 228–238 (Feb.), 1958.

Szasz, T. S. Psychiatry, psychotherapy, and psychology. *A.M.A. Arch. Gen. Psychiat.,* 1: 455–463 (Nov.), 1959.

Szasz, T. S. The myth of mental illness. *Amer. Psychologist,* 15: 113–118 (Feb.), 1960.

Szasz, T. S. Moral conflict and psychiatry. *Yale Rev.,* 49: 555–566 (June), 1960.

Szasz, T. S. Three problems in contemporary psychoanalytic training. *A.M.A. Arch. Gen. Psychiat.,* 3: 82–94 (July), 1960.

Szasz, T. S. Civil liberties and mental illness. *J. Nerv. & Ment. Dis.,* 131: 58–63 (July), 1960.

Szasz, T. S. The ethics of birth control: Or, who owns your body? *Humanist,* 20: 332–336 (Nov.-Dec.), 1960.

Szasz, T. S. *The Myth of Mental Illness: Foundations of a Theory of Personal Conduct.* New York: Hoeber-Harper, 1961.

Szasz, T. S. Mind tapping: Psychiatric subversion of constitutional rights. *Amer. J. Psychiat.,* 119: 323–327 (Oct.), 1962.

Szasz, T. S. Bootlegging humanistic values through psychiatry. *Antioch Rev.,* 22: 341–349 (Fall), 1962.

Szasz, T. S. The concept of transference. *Int. J. Psycho-Anal.,* 44: 432–443, 1963.

Szasz, T. S. *Law, Liberty, and Psychiatry: An Inquiry into the Social Uses of Mental Health Practices.* New York: Macmillan, 1963.

Szasz, T. S. Criminal insanity: Fact or strategy? *New Republic,* Nov. 21, 1964, pp. 19–22.

Szasz, T. S. The moral dilemma of psychiatry: Autonomy or heteronomy? *Amer. J. Psychiat.,* 121: 521–528 (Dec.), 1964.

Szasz, T. S. *The Ethics of Psychoanalysis: The Theory and Method of Autonomous Psychotherapy.* New York: Basic Books, 1965.

Szasz, T. S. *Psychiatric Justice.* New York: Macmillan, 1965.

Ssasz, T. S. Legal and Moral Aspects of Homosexuality. In Marmor, J.,

(Ed.), *Sexual Inversion: The Multiple Roots of Homosexuality*, pp. 124–139. New York: Basic Books, 1965.

Szasz, T. S. Toward the therapeutic state. *New Republic*, Dec. 11, 1965, pp. 26–29.

Szasz, T. S. Mental illness is a myth. *New York Times Magazine*, June 12, 1966, pp. 30, 90–92.

Szasz, T. S. The Mental Health Ethic. In De George, R. T., (Ed.), *Ethics and Society: Original Essays on Contemporary Moral Problems*, pp. 85–110. Garden City. N.Y.: Doubleday Anchor, 1966.

Szasz, T. S. Psychotherapy: A sociocultural perspective. *Comprehensive Psychiat.*, 7: 217–223 (Aug.), 1966.

Szasz, T. S. Whither psychiatry? *Soc. Res.*, 33: 439–462 (Autumn), 1966.

Szasz, T. S. The Psychiatric Classification of Behavior: A Strategy of Personal Constraint. In Eron., L. D., (Ed.), *The Classification of Behavior Disorders*, pp. 123–170. Chicago: Aldine, 1966.

Szasz, T. S. Alcoholism: A socioethical perspective. *Western* Med., 7: 15–21 (Dec.), 1966.

Szasz, T. S. The destruction of differences. *New Republic*, June 10, 1967, pp. 21–23.

Szasz, T. S. The insanity defense and the insanity verdict. *Temple Law Quart.*, 40: 271–282 (Spring–Summer), 1967.

Szasz, T. S. The psychiatrist as double agent. *Trans-action* 4: 16–24 (Oct.), 1967.

Szasz, T. S. Medical ethics: A historical perspective. *Med. Opin. & Rev.*, 4: 115–121 (Feb.), 1968.

Szasz, T. S. The Psychology of Persistent Pain: A Portrait of L'Homme Douloureux. In Soulairac, A., Cahn, J., and Charpentier, J., (Eds.), *Pain*, pp. 93–113. London: Academic Press, 1968.

Szasz, T. S. Science and public policy: The crime of involuntary mental hospitalization. *Med. Opin. & Rev.*, 4: 24–35 (May), 1968.

Szasz, T. S. The right to health. *Georgetown Law J.*, 57: 734–751 (Mar.), 1969.

Tarsis, V. *Ward 7: An Autobiographical Novel*. Translated by Katya Brown. London and Glasgow: Collins & Harvill, 1965.

Taylor, G. R. Historical and Mythological Aspects of Homosexuality. In Marmor, J., (Ed.), *Sexual Inversion: The Multiple Roots of Homosexuality*, pp. 140–164. New York: Basic Books, 1965.

Thurber, J. A Unicorn in the Garden. In Thurber, J., *The Thurber Carnival*. 2d Ed., pp. 268–269. New York: Harper & Brothers, 1945.

Tocqueville, A. de. *Democracy in America* (1835–1840). 2 vols. New York: Vintage, 1945.

Tolstoy, L. The Kreutzer Sonata (1889). Translated by Aylmer Maude.

In *The Death of Ivan Ilych and Other Stories*, pp. 157–239. New York: Signet, 1960.

Tompkins, H. J. The presidential address: The physician in contemporary society. *Amer. J. Psychiat.*, 124: 1–6 (July), 1967.

Trachtenberg, J. *The Devil and the Jews: The Medieval Conception of the Jew and Its Relation to Modern Anti-Semitism*. New Haven: Yale Univer. Press, 1943.

Trevor-Roper, H. R. Witches and witchcraft: An historical essay (I). *Encounter*, 28: 3–25 (May), 1967.

Trevor-Roper, H. R. Witches and witchcraft: An historical essay (II). *Encounter*, 28: 13–34 (June), 1967.

Trials of War Criminals Before the Neurnberg Military Tribunals, Under Control Council Law No. 10, Nuremberg, October 1946–April 1949, Vol. I. Washington: U.S. Government Printing Office, n.d.

Ullerstam, L. *The Erotic Minorities* (1964). Translated by Anselm Hollo. New York: Grove, 1966.

Ullman, W. *The Individual and Society in the Middle Ages*. Baltimore: Johns Hopkins Press, 1966.

Unconscious of a conservative: A special issue on the mind of Barry Goldwater. *Fact*, Vol. 1, No. 5, Sept.–Oct., 1964.

U.S. Book of Facts, Statistics, and Information, The. New York: Washington Square Press, 1966.

U.S. Department of State, The Foreign Service of the United States. General Information Sheet for Immigrants (Form DSL-852), Jan., 1964.

Veith, I. *Hysteria: The History of a Disease*. Chicago: Univer. of Chicago Press, 1965.

Villinger, W. Erwiderung auf vorstehende Arbeit "Über Onanie im Kindesalter," von J. K. Friedjung. *Zeitschrift für Kinderforschung*, 31: 293–295, 1926.

Visotsky, H. Social psychiatry rationale: Administrative and planning approaches. *Amer. J. Psychiat.*, 121: 433–441 (Nov.), 1964.

Voltaire, F. *Philosophical Dictionary* (1764). Translated by Peter Gay. New York: Basic Books, 1962.

Ward, Mary Jane. *The Snake Pit*. New York: Random House, 1946.

Warshofsky, F. When does a child need a psychiatrist? *Parade*, Jan. 10, 1965, pp. 4–5.

Wechsler, I. S. The Neuroses or the Psychoneuroses. In Cecil, R. L., and Kennedy, F., (Eds.), *A Textbook of Medicine by American Authors*. 5th Ed., pp. 1645-1664. Philadelphia: Saunders, 1942.

Wertham, F. *A Sign for Cain: An Exploration of Human Violence*. New York: Macmillan, 1966.

Westermarck, E. *The Origin and Development of the Moral Ideas.* London: Macmillan, 1908.

White, A. D. *A History of the Warfare of Science with Theology in Christendom* (1896). Abridged with a Preface and Epilogue by Bruce Mazlish. New York: Free Press, 1965.

White, T. H. *The Making of the President, 1964.* New York: Atheneum, 1965.

Wille, L. The mental health clinic: Expressway to asylum. Chicago *Daily News*, Mar. 26, 1962, p. 1.

Wille, L. 11 times 12? Youth flunks mental exam. Chicago *Daily News*, Mar. 27, 1962, p. 1.

Wille, L. Misfiled card saves salesman from mental hospital. Chicago *Daily News*, Mar. 28, 1962, p. 1.

Wille, L. Why refugee asked for ticket to Russia. Chicago *Daily News*, Mar. 29, 1962, p. 1.

Williams, C. *Witchcraft* (1941). Cleveland: Meridian, 1959.

Williams v. *United States.* 250 F. 2d 19, 1957.

Wilson, Sylvia. The Cinderellas (Letters). *Manchester Guardian*, Mar. 30, 1965, p. 8.

Wright, F. L., Jr. *Out of Sight, Out of Mind.* Philadelphia: National Ment. Health Foundation, 1947.

Yahr, M. Neurology (Annual review). *Med. World News*, Jan. 12, 1968, p. 129.

Yolles, S. Community mental health: Issues and policies. *Amer. J. Psychiat.*, 122: 979–985 (Mar.), 1966.

Young, W. *Eros Denied: Sex in Western Society* (1964). New York: Grove, 1966.

Zamiatin, E. *We* (1924). Translated by Gregory Zilboorg. New York: Dutton, 1952.

Zeligs, M. A. *Friendship and Fratricide: An Analysis of Whittaker Chambers and Alger Hiss.* New York: Viking, 1967.

Zhenya Belov campaign (Letters). *Economist*, Dec. 11, 1965, p. 4.

Ziferstein, I. The Soviet psychiatrist: His relationship to his patient and to his society. *Amer. J. Psychiat.*, 123: 440–446 (Oct.), 1966.

Zilboorg, G. *The Medical Man and the Witch During the Renaissance.* Baltimore: Johns Hopkins Press, 1935.

Zilboorg, G., and Henry, G. *A History of Medical Psychology.* New York: Norton, 1941.

INDEX

ABOUT THE AUTHOR

Thomas S. Szasz was born in Budapest in 1920. He took his A.B. and M.D. degrees at the University of Cincinnati, his psychiatric training at the University of Chicago, and his psychoanalytic training at the Chicago Institute for Psychoanalysis.

From 1950 to 1954, he was a staff member at the Chicago Institute for Psychoanalysis and was in private practice in Chicago. After two years of active duty in the Medical Corps of the Naval Reserve, Dr. Szasz in 1956 joined the faculty of the Upstate Medical Center of the State University of New York at Syracuse as Professor of Psychiatry. He has also been a Visiting Professor of Psychiatry at the University of Wisconsin and at Marquette University and has lectured widely in colleges, law schools, medical schools, and to lay groups.

He is the author of seven books and more than two hundred articles and reviews.